GOVERNMENT CONTRACTS

IN A NUTSHELL

Fourth Edition

By

W. NOEL KEYES
Pepperdine University School of Law

Mat #40251093

COPYRIGHT © 1990 WEST PUBLISHING CO.
COPYRIGHT © 2000 WEST GROUP
© 2004 West, a Thomson business
       610 Opperman Drive
       P.O. Box 64526
       St. Paul, MN 55164–0526
       1–800–328–9352
Printed in the United States of America

ISBN 0–314–15316–0

TEXT IS PRINTED ON 10% POST CONSUMER RECYCLED PAPER

To my wife Jeannine R. Keyes for her patience and
understanding and to those others too numerous to
mention who reviewed portions of the text or discussed
many of the ideas and opinions expressed therein.

*

PREFACE TO THE FOURTH EDITION

My continued attempt is to remain neutral between the parties (the government, representing the taxpayer) and the contractor, (who usually is representing corporate shareholders). I have tried to stand for the contract itself and the uniquely high value it has for our society when not overly tampered with after the fact by courts and boards.

Further, many of the subjects treated herein could or should perhaps be treated at greater length and some interesting areas are discussed little, or not at all. On occasion I remain critical of courts and boards which do not follow the law, but seek to bend it significantly in order to reach a given result or simply ignore the law or the analysis needed for its correct interpretation or application.

In this field some reportedly critical works favor the interests of the industries which employ attorneys and they often have some difficulty in appreciating the plight of the taxpayer. On the other hand, occasions have arisen when government representatives act with a measure of arbitrariness.

This book is intended to assist those with the problems most often met by the business world in its dealings with the government and/or with its contractors (and vice versa). The emphasis is on the law of contracts and subcontracts with the federal government; contracts with state or local bodies are not included, nor is the law of grants, or other subjects noted below.

The areas covered by the book are of equal interest to contract administrators as well as to lawyers, and certainly the lawyer must be aware of some administrative matters in order to counsel effectively. However, the aim of this book is to limit discussion of administration to those occasions where it is necessary to delineate the legal background, and to show how a government contract currently exists as a business proposition.

Significant changes in the Federal Acquisition Regulation (FAR) were made during the last four years of the 20th Century and into the first three of the new millennium. This first uniform procurement regulation in the United States has been undergoing continuous review and modification for almost 20 years.

When first promulgated, the FAR was marked by the major landmark of the legislation known as the Competition in Contracting Act of 1984. A decade later, the most dominant legislative change was the Federal Acquisition Streamlining Act (FASA) of 1994, which emphasized improvement in the acquisition of commercial items, created a new exception from the submission of cost or pricing data under the Truth in Negotiations Act (TINA) and increased the Simplified Acquisition Threshold (SAT) from $25,000 to $100,000 for certain procurements expected to include commercial items not exceeding $5,000,000. Emphasis has been placed on the use of "past performance" in the source selection process and the use of "performance-based service contracting." Courts and boards have sometimes pushed the law controlling the validity of government contracts away from the standard of the "general law of contracts" that was set by the Supreme Court at mid-century in the absence of statutory mandates. However, the law controlling the validity and interpretation of government contracts is done by the lower courts claiming they use the "best" of the decisions of other jurisdictions regarding the law of contracts—meaning, of course, that their decisions deviate from the "general law of contracts" whenever it suits their convenience. This often results in a widening of the gap between contract law applicable to the Federal government and that applicable to private contracts and those with state or municipal governments.

Fraud and whistleblower litigation significantly increased against the DoD, DOE, and healthcare organizations (Chapter 3). The newer procedures on acquisition of commercial items (Chapter 12) and simplified acquisitions (Chapter 13) appear to be thriving. The procedures on contracting by negotiation (Chapter 15) has been largely a rewrite of existing provisions.

The Administrative Disputes Resolution Act of 1996 expanded the protest jurisdiction of the U.S. Court of Federal Claims and extended it to include post-award protests; on January 1, 2001, eliminated the protest jurisdiction of the United States District Courts. The Rehabilitation Act Amendments of 1998 imposed new accessibility requirements for electronic and information technology. The National Defense Authorization Act for Fiscal Year 2000 limited the scope of the Cost Accounting Standards (CAS), doubling the threshold for full CAS-coverage and reinstituting the trigger contract concept. The enactment of the Electronic Signatures in Global and National Commerce Act 2000 has facilitated the use of electronic contracting.

The FAR became modified with these changes. Procedures were added for the acquisition of commercial items and acquisitions below the "simplified acquisition threshold." Government employees who are not contracting officers are permitted to make purchases up to the "micro-purchase threshold" using the "Governmentwide commercial purchase card." The applicability of the Truth in Negotiations Act was curtailed, and contracting officers were prohibited from asking for cost or pricing data in certain situations. Federal and military specifications and standards gave way to voluntary consensus standards and performance-based contracting. Quality and past performance became mandatory evaluation factors in every acquisition over the simplified acquisition threshold. The venerable Commerce Business Daily was largely replaced by an Internet site known as the "Governmentwide point of entry." Many practitioners stopped using paper copies of the FAR, and turned to online versions.

It is interesting to note that other countries are now looking at the FAR for guidance with respect to their laws governing public procurements. For example, in 2002 the National Congress of China enacted its "Law of Public Procurement in China." A professor at a Beijing Law School (legal advisor for preparing the regulations) requested the right to translate my Government Contracts under the Federal Acquisition Regulation 3rd Edition West (2003).

Although the procurement system itself has changed very little since the Wars on Terrorism began, Section 836 of the National Defense Authorization Act for Fiscal Year 2002 gave the department of Defense increased flexibility for using existing streamlined procedures by temporarily increasing the micro-purchase and simplified acquisition thresholds for certain types of procurements. It also allowed DoD to treat as commercial items any biotechnology goods and services that are purchased to facilitate a defense against terrorism or biological or chemical attack.

Into the 3rd Millennium, the United States has continued as the largest buyer in the world; government contract expenditures constitute a total of more than $250 billion by both the military and all U.S. executive agencies every year. However, another field greatly exceeds this amount; government expenditures in the field of healthcare for grants have amounted to more than one trillion dollars per year since the beginning of the 3rd Millennium. Because healthcare organizations involve the making of contracts with Federal funds and have undergone billions of dollars in fines owing to various fraudulent actions within the past few years, I recommended in the 2003, 3rd Edition on government contracts (and the one I am writing, "Bioethics on Medicine and the Law for the 21st Century") that the FAR be assigned as a guideline for all healthcare organizations receiving hundreds of billions of dollars in grants such, such as Medicare and Medicaid and many others including research. Government contract law and regulation (FAR) is currently inapplicable to grants.

The Federal Acquisition Regulation is cited as "FAR" throughout this volume. However, severe limitations on its length (without modification of its quality) have necessitated some choices. These have been made in a manner so as to give extensive coverage to those subjects treated herein. Accordingly, chapters normally given more specialized treatment have been eliminated. These include; 7.3, Equipment Lease on Purchase; 17, Special Contracting Methods; 19, Small Business and Small Disadvantaged Business Concerns; 22, Application of Labor Laws to Government Acquisitions; 23, Environment, Conservation and Occupational Safety; 24, Protection of Privacy and Freedom of Information; 25, Foreign Acquisition; 26, Other Socioeconomic Programs; 27, Patents, Data, and Copyright; 29, Taxes; 30, Cost Accounting Standards; 31, Contract Cost Principles; 32, Contract Financing; 34, Major System Acquisition; 37, Service Contracting; 38, Federal Supply Schedule Contracting; 39, Management, Acquisition, and Use of Information Resources; 41, Management of Utility Services; 45, Government Property; 46, Quality Assurance; 47, Transportation; 48, Value Engineering; 50, Extraordinary Contractual Actions and 51, Use of Government Sources by Contractors. Of course, all of these are covered in my Treatise "Government Contracts Under the Federal Acquisitions Regulation," 3rd Ed. West (2003). Fuller treatment and citations to cases and other material will require examination of the full treatise.

W. NOEL KEYES

Corona del Mar
May 2004

TABLE OF ABBREVIATIONS

ABA   American Bar Association

ACO   Administrative Contracting Officer

ALJ   Administrative Law Judge

A–E   Architect Engineer

APA   Administrative Procedures Act

ADR   Alternate Dispute Resolution

ADRA   Administrative Dispute Resolution Act

ATO   Agency Tender Official

B&P   Bid and Proposal

BPAS   Blanket Purchase Agreements

CAFC   Court of Appeals for the Federal Circuit

CAO   Contract Administration Office

CBD   Commerce Business Daily

CDA   Contract Disputes Act

CERCLA   Comprehensive Environmental Response, Compensation, and Liability Act

CICA   Competition in Contracting Act

CLIN   Contract Line Item Number

COC   Certificate of Competency

CODP   Capital Ownership Development Program

TABLE OF ABBREVIATIONS

OGE	Office of Governmental Ethics
OMB	Office of Management and Budget
PALT	Procurement Administrative Leave Time
POGO	Project on Government Oversight
QBL	Qualified Bidders List
QML	Qualified Manufacturers List
R&D	Research and Development
REA	Request for Equitable Adjustment
RFP	Request for Proposal
RFQ	Request for Quotation
SEC	Security and Exchange Commission
TCO	Termination Contracting Officer
T&M	Time & Material [Contract]
UCC	Uniform Commercial Code
U.S.C.A.	United States Code Annotated

OUTLINE

PART II. ACQUISITION PLANNING

PART V. GENERAL CONTRACTING RE-QUIREMENTS

*

TABLE OF CASES

References are to Pages

INTRODUCTION

GOVERNMENT CONTRACTS UNDER THE
FEDERAL ACQUISITION REGULATION

INTRODUCTION TO CONTRACTS WITH THE FEDERAL GOVERNMENT

I. The FAR Vision and the Reasons for Government Contracting

The "vision" for the Federal Acquisition System established in the mid–1980's (just prior to the publication of the first edition of this volume) is to "deliver on a timely basis the best value product or service to the customer, while maintaining the public's trust and fulfilling public policy objectives." The Federal Acquisition Regulation (FAR) was the first in U.S. history to establish, codify, and publish uniform policies and procedures for acquisition by all executive agencies. As such, it has carried out its vision significantly better than any of its predecessor approaches. However, following a decade of operation it became evident that a number of improvements were needed. Although the implementation of the Federal Acquisition Streamlining Act of 1994 has been completed (and was also contained in the second edition of this volume where all chapters correspond to FAR Parts), regulatory revisions occur frequently.

The revised "visions" of the system state:

All participants in the System are responsible for making acquisition decisions that deliver the best value product or service to the customer. Best value must be viewed from a broad perspective and is achieved by balancing the many competing interests in the System.

Whether "the many competing interests" are indeed balanced and whether they "result is a system which works better and costs less" with these changes will become more evident as time progresses.

This volume concerns binding agreements made with the federal government or what are sometimes called "government contracts." What are they? How do they differ from other contracts? How do such agreements serve our society? What needs are met among the parties to such agreements— one of whom is a private organization and the other a public body? The answers lie, at least initially, in the concept and use of contracts as they are institutionalized in all developing and advanced countries, as well as in the purposes for which contracts are made with the government.

First, it is important to distinguish contracts from grants and cooperative agreements. Procurement contracts are used when the agency's principal purpose is to acquire construction, products, or services for the direct benefit or use of the Federal government. Grants and cooperative agreements, on the other hand, are used when the principal purpose is to transfer a thing of value to a State or local government or other recipient in order to promote a broad national interest. The principal difference between a grant and a cooperative agreement is that there is a greater degree of Federal participation during performance of the former than the latter. So-called "other transactions agreements" (OTAs) have been used by the Department of Defense for research and prototyping projects.

The Federal Grant and Cooperative Agreement Act of 1977 encourages competition in the award of grants and cooperative agreements, and statutes for some grants, such as those awarded by the United States Department of Agriculture, specifically require competition. However, grants, co-operative agreements and OTAs are not subject to the Competition in Contracting Act or other procurement statutes and regulations. Accordingly, there is typically neither any bidding (as described in Chapter 14) nor any source selection evaluation (in the manner described in Chapter 15). Moreover, the recipient of a grant need not even be "responsible" (as described in Chapter 9).

Because (1) government grants into healthcare industries have exceeded $1 trillion per year (four times the annual expenditure on government contracts) (2) qui tam (False Claims Act) recoveries from healthcare grantees have exceeded those from defense contractors by almost $5.3 billion ($3.9 billion from healthcare and $1.4 billion from Defense [See Chapter 3]), and (3) other needs of healthcare grantees, it is recommended that the Federal Acquisition Regulation (FAR) be made a required guideline for all healthcare organizations to the full extent that prime contractors are controlled in connection with subcontracting (See Chapter 44).

A. The Need for Defense Contracting

During the 45 years of the Cold War (following World War II), the great impetus toward defense spending came from a fear of the aims, capabilities and intention of international communism. For the United States, costs of increased weapons and social programs produced a national debt of trillions of dollars putting a huge burden on our children into the 21st Century; the Soviet Union could no longer "keep up" and it dissolved. In the U.S., almost all of the buildup of weapons, economic and political power, and scientific and technological development was carried on through government contracts. When the Cold War ended in 1989, we could not stop quickly enough.

In 1991, Yeltsin emerged with a promise for Soviet democracy for a nation without the necessary history to know what this meant. Nevertheless, communist government of the Soviet Union "had died." But, the United States, having "won" the Cold War, began to perceive the economic costs of that victory. A year following the turn of the 21st century, the president initiated the costly conquest and occupation of Iraq. Today we must learn to modify our approach, while staying prepared through government defense and guarding against dominance of Congressional free spending complexes.

> The worth of a state, in the long run, is the worth of the individuals composing it.
>
> John Stuart Mill

B. The Value of Risking the Union in Defense Contracting

In the centuries following Martin Luther, there was much bloody actualizing and verbalizing over deviations from a religion. Beginning with the second half of the Twentieth Century, we have experienced such actualization and verbalization over religion and science.

Perhaps an approach to a solution can be found in some version of the golden rules that are found in the Old and New Testaments, and other religions and philosophies as well. Lawyers may recognize the possible injustice of doing unto others as we would that others do unto us for, as G. B. Shaw noted, "they" are not "us" and their views may and do differ greatly. In fact, we often feel more strongly about defending their right to differ from us. Hence, one reasonable defense of the Union lies here. It is when "they" are seeking actively to prevent "us" from differing, that we consider utilizing huge sums in order to gather a potential to combat them.

After the terrorist attacks on the World Trade Center and Pentagon, Congress approved $40 billion in emergency supplemental appropriations, and authorized the President "to use all necessary and appropriate force against those nations, organizations, or persons he determines planned, authorized, committed, or aided the terrorist attacks that occurred on September 11, 2001, or harbored such organizations or persons, in order to prevent any future acts of international terrorism against the United States by such nations, organizations or persons." The President issued Executive Order 13223, authorizing the Secretaries of the Military Departments to order members of the Ready Reserve to active duty and delegating certain authorities to the Secretary of Defense and Secretary of Transportation. The Undersecretary for Acquisition, Technology, and Logistics subsequently announced that these actions met the statutory definition of a "contingency operation" under 10 U.S.C.A. § 101(a)(13)(B), thus authorizing certain exigent contracting procedures.

On October 8, 2001, the President issued Executive Order 13228, establishing a new Office of Homeland Security within the Executive Office of the President and the Homeland Security Council. On October 24, 2001, the President amended Executive Order 10789, originally issued on November 14, 1958, to include the Department of Health and Human Services in the list of agencies permitted to exercise certain contracting authority in connection with national defense functions. On June 18, 2002, the President proposed legislation to establish a Department of Homeland Security (DHS), which became the most significant and extensive reorganization of the Federal government since World War II, and brought together 22 entities with homeland security missions. DHS's "normal procurement operations" would be subject to the existing procurement statutes and regulations, but it would be authorized "to avoid the application of any procurement statute or regulation that would impair the accomplishment of the Department's mission." The legislation would also grant DHS considerable flexibility in obtaining consultant services by authorizing DHS to contract for private sector services, including consultants and experts, using a form of contracting that allows for the creation of an employer-employee relationship. In addition, the bill contains provisions that would limit the liability of manufacturers of antiterrorism technologies and establish a presumption that the government contractor defense (as described in Chapter 28) applies to covered products.

II. The Cost of Current Procurements

In 2002, President Bush cited the Vietnam-era War Powers Act and notified Congress he had concluded that "only the use of armed force" could disarm Iraq and protect U.S. security. In October 2002 he signed into law the biggest military spending since that of President Reagan; namely, $355.5 billion, the biggest increase in 20 years. His $2.23 trillion budget for 2004 was sent to Congress in February 2003.

A. Economics and Contracting

Like commercial contracts, government contracts have an economic base; in one sense a taxpayer is always worse off economically by government expenditures for defense; however, ignoring the insistence of some analysts of the "dismal science" that economics can and does explain everything, we observe that the taxpayer's involuntarily extracted funds have been used for a hopefully equal value of protection without which his other material values may become utterly lost. Thus, the outcome of a contract may be just if the parties to the outcome agree, prior to the event in question, to the rules that would determine the outcome. In such event, it is not essential that both parties be better off because all contracts involve future work that entails a degree of risk. It is not the function of tribunals to reduce risks undertaken by consent within the parameters of these rules; contractor bailouts by tribunals are outside the system and operate against the taxpayer and government. Optimality, whereby both parties become better off after the transaction than before, is the goal of the parties and should not be confused with risks actually incurred during performance. Unfortunately, some courts attempt to exceed their prescribed functions.

B. Future of Government Contracting as a Result of Changes in Resources and Other Conditions

Because much of the work of government is done by contracting out, i.e., privatizing of government functions, consideration must be given to the changes taking place in order to enter into long-term planning. Contracts are for the needs of a government agency and they can only be made if the resources are available.

In 1980, a report was made to the President on the "probable changes in the world's population, natural resources, and environment through the end of the century." The conclusions were called "disturbing." They indicated "the potential for global problems of alarming proportions by the year 2000." The trends suggested "a progressive degradation and impoverishment of the earth's natural resource base" and the necessity for changes which go beyond the capability of any single nation. But "our nation can itself take important and exemplary steps ... [including] sustainable economic development, coupled with environmental protection, resource management, and family planning is essential and effective responses to such global problems as the buildup of carbon dioxide in the atmosphere and the threat of species loss on a massive scale." Particularly disturbing was the projection concerning more people who are among the governed civilians seeking help. "For every two persons on the earth in 1975 there will be three in 2000. The number of poor will have increased." Further, prices will be higher and the price of many of the most vital resources is projected to rise "in real terms—that is, over and above inflation."

These increased aggravations can only augment the government's role in contracting out for goods and services as well as construction because most of the work to be done cannot be accomplished directly by the hiring of more government employees.

A large number of accounting failures at big companies in the two years preceding 2004 cost U.S. households nearly $60,000 on average as some $5 trillion in market value was lost. The Office of Management and Budget has found agencies that cannot account "for tens of billions of dollars." As noted in Chapter 3, a number of large government contractors have paid fines under the False Claims Act and other statutes. As a result, Congress enacted the Sarbanes–Oxley Act in 2002 calling for a change to a cost accounting practice requiring review for effectiveness of and certification of a system of internal controls and reports thereon. (See Chapter 42)

III. What is Procurement—Purposes and Processes, Training, and Improvements

Just as it is not possible for a new car dealer to avoid being in the used car business, so must government agencies that buy also dispose. Hence, and for good reason, it has been traditional for procurement statutes to authorize both functions. Perhaps with less than good reason, there has been an attempt to substitute the term "acquisition" for procurement and deal virtually with the purchasing side alone.

The Comptroller General has held that agencies have discretion for determining both their needs and whether certain supplies, services, or construction of facilities will satisfy them. This determination can rarely be successfully challenged through bid protest procedures. (See Chapter 33) That determination may result in any agency ordering goods, services, or even the construction of a building well beyond the true needs of the agency. Nevertheless, in 1995 for the first time, one part (see Chapter 11) of the regulation was devoted to describing agency needs using market research. (See Chapter 10) Further, requirements with respect to acquisition of supplies and services "to the maximum extent practicable" must be stated in terms of (A) "functions to be performed, (B) performances required, or (C) essential physical characteristics," and "encourage offerors to supply commercial items," or "nondevelopmental" ones. (As pointed out in Chapter 11, the concept of increasing the government's procurement of commercial products is not new. The Commission on Government Procurement so concluded in 1972, as did the Congress in 1984, 1986, and 1988 with only limited effect at those particular times.) Most importantly, if it is actually followed, avoiding conflicting interest (Chapter 9) is the direction to give potential offerors "an opportunity to comment on agency requirements or to recommend application and tailoring of requirements documents and alternative approaches." All steps concerning the definition of that need through purchase, delivery and much of the economic life thereafter and disposal will involve procurement and procurement laws. As noted above, certain procurement standards must be extended to include procurement by recipients of Federal grants as well.

Perhaps the point which might slip by unnoticed is that the actual solicitation, evaluation and award of a contract represents only a portion of the work involved in a procurement; normally most of this work precedes these particular actions. It is the unfortunate perception by many legislators and members of the public that these particular actions appear to be essentially of a "clerical" nature; as a result they fail to appreciate what a procurement really amounts to. The 1979 Amendments to the Federal Procurement Policy Act contained a new definition of procurement as including "*all stages* of the acquisition process, *beginning with the process for determining a need* for property and services through to the Federal Government's disposition of such property and services." But some portion of the need describes a legislative function preceding the more detailed needs which fall into the area and which can properly be called procurement. Perhaps all that can be said is that true procurement follows that basic legislative determination of a more general need.

The Federal government procurements are made for purposes of acquiring supplies and services by such means as purchasing, renting, leasing, contracting, or bartering, but not by seizure, condemnation, donation, or requisition. Procurement also includes the functions necessary to obtain supplies and services, such as description of requirements, selection and solicitation of sources, preparation and award of contracts and all phases of contract administration.

A. Unfortunate Directions of "The Restatements of the Law"

Although Federal law does not follow the law of any particular state, it has been referred to as "the general law of contracts" which in turn refers back to state law. A serious problem results when one attempts to find this law. Great hopes were placed upon the use of the Restatements published by the American Law Institute (ALI) that was formed in 1923. The ALI completed the Restatement of Contracts in 1932. As originally conceived, the Restatements themselves turned out to be just that, " 'restatements' of law found in other sources." The first Restatement was on contracts and it generally "restated" the law as of 1932, thus carrying out its mandate. Thirty years later, in 1962, the Institute initiated the preparation of the Restatement, Second, of Contracts. However, here as in other Restatements Second, the exceptions became much more predominant. At times the Reporters candidly report that "the law is in flux and offer a formula *preferred on policy grounds*." (Emphasis added.) That is, the Reporters issued a so-called "restatement" which in fact does *not* restate the law, but rather reflects whatever "policy" the Reporter thinks to be desirable for society and which he can persuade the other members of the A.L.I. is a "better policy." Thus, it often misleads those who for some reason actually believe that these newer works do in fact restate the law. Obviously the new, even radical, ideas of the professors of law who drafted Second Restatements and their colleagues in the Institute ought to be published and considered; but their promulgation should not be mislabeled as a "Restatement of the Law" when their goals differ so much from those of their predecessors who drafted the original Restatements.

B. The Need for a Uniform Public Procurement Law for State and Local Governments

Attention has been given to public procurement by state and local governments. However, lack of uniformity between Federal and state procurement laws and regulations continues. In the 1970's, the American Bar Association's Public Contract Law Section sponsored a Model Procurement Code (MPC) for state and local governments. A decade later, with the enactment of the "Competition in Contracting Act," some of the basic approaches to the Federal law have become closer to those of the MPC, and a study ought to be made for possible further revision of the MPC. Consideration should be given to working with the Commissioners on Uniform State Laws for this purpose in order to develop a Uniform Procurement Code. Just as we have a Uniform Commercial Code (UCC) for private transactions, there should be a Uniform Code for procurements by states and the larger municipalities.

We are now at the point in public procurement law where the states were when Professor Llewellyn decided to rally them behind a uniform approach to our state commercial law; as the UCC was eventually successful throughout the Union, so could be a uniform state law on public procurement.

C. The Requisite Training or Experience of Attorneys in the Field of Government Contracting

The 2003 American Bar Association (ABA) Rules of Professional Conduct commence with the requirement that a lawyer possess "the legal knowledge, skill, thoroughness, and preparation reasonably necessary for the representation." The comment lists: "the lawyer's general experience, the lawyer's training and experience in the field in question." Not all fields of law have the significant facilities for doing so that is presently available in the area of government contracts—particularly at the Federal level. Although few courses in government contracting have been available in ABA accredited law schools today, the number of schools offering such training is increasing. The principal training sessions now available are those offered by nonprofit organizations such as the Public Law Section of the American Bar Association; The Federal Bar (FBA), Government Contracts Section; the National Contract Management Association (NCMA) and a number of other private organizations such as The Bureau of National Affairs (BNA) and West Group, which hold a "Government Contracts Year In Review Conference" in Washington, D.C. near the beginning of each year.

D. Some Differences With Private Contracting—Limitations in Government Contracts

The cost-plus-percentage-of-cost (CPPC) prohibition, originally found in various appropriation acts as a restriction on the use of funds, indicates the extreme antipathy of Congress toward agreements that might give incentive toward increasing costs in order to gain increased profits.

A government agency cannot contract for the furnishing of supplies and services needed for a period beyond the current fiscal year, unless specifically so authorized by statute, or regulation even though the government's liability is specifically made contingent upon the availability of appropriations for future fiscal years. The Comptroller General has held that a contract for the delivery of materials in future fiscal years, containing a cancellation clause obligating the government to pay, in one fiscal year, a charge in excess of its needs for that year, was improper because the contract did not fulfill the requirement of a bona fide need in the current year.

E. Dangers and Improvements on the Horizons of Contract Law

With the rules in the Federal Acquisition Regulation (many of which are in the imperative) it has been argued that a faceless bureaucracy must prevail in their administration. There are two sides of the table when contracts are negotiated. A business enterprise is always a party and it is continually testing the other party, its people and its regulations. Having been at different times and careers in my life on each side of the table, I recall feelings of dynamism as well as of frustration; but only on few occasions was the latter feeling due to "functionally subordinated specialized cogs" who were sitting either on my side of the table or across from me. Most situations permitted a mutually beneficial result although this would take some time and a party may never specifically admit this to be the case. Because government employees who uncover waste, fraud, or corruption may be hesitant to promulgate this fact for fear of loss of job, demotion, or transfer, the Civil Service Reform Act was enacted in order to partially protect them and on occasion to remove incompetents.

(1) *Extension of Remedies—Non-consensual "Agreements"*

For the philosopher David Hume, security of the person, stability of property, and the obligation of contract were the bases of a civilized society. The question may be asked how far have we substantially turned away from the language used by Associate Justice Oliver Wendell Holmes, Jr. when he said: "Men must turn square corners when they deal with the government." Yet, some of the newer courts, with members who generally have little business experience, would move contract law toward the tort law.

Pacta Sunt Servanda was an ancient and is a modern rule that agreements are to be observed. In law we limit this to agreements entered into as binding deals, as, for example, agreements made with consideration. But such agreements, called contracts, are obligatory philosophically as a matter of "social fairness" as well as at law. Judges have no philosophical grounds for inserting any other view of "fairness" into binding agreements where for some reason they feel that one party ought not to be held accountable for his nonperformance. The Federal law of contracts has a standard which normally avoids permitting the courts to decide cases on the basis of their own subjective views of what that law should be.

As noted in Chapter 33, where not specifically governed by statute or regulation, Federal law is "the general law of contracts"—that is, the law as generally applied in the states of our union. Although this standard was originally set by the Supreme Court, the former Court of Claims and its successor courts have succeeded in their approach to Federal law because only rarely has the Supreme Court reviewed their decisions and they have thus generally rendered their law "supreme." This has caused a significant split between the law of contracts applicable to contracts with the Federal government and that applied in the state courts that normally constitutes "the general law of contracts." Accordingly, from time to time throughout various chapters, particular opinions of these courts have been criticized in areas where they have taken the law unto themselves in lieu of applying "the general of contracts" as they should. In the majority of the decided cases, they reach a correct result. But it would appear that Congress should ascertain whether legislation with respect to use of the proper standard for interpretation of government contracts may be needed in order to avoid further separation of that law from the law applied in the rest of the United States.

F. The Federal Acquisition Streamlining Act of 1994

On October 13, 1994, President Clinton signed into law the Federal Acquisition Streamlining Act (FASA), the most significant acquisition legislation since the creation of the FAR. The law included some 225 changes. A principal segment of this legislation dealt with the acquisition of commercial items. The legislation did not adopt the Uniform Commercial Code (UCC) for procurement of commercial items. The UCC is state law and neither covers pre-award matters nor includes contract clauses. However, numerous changes would be made to increase use of commercial items at commercial prices. Advantages include exemptions from the provisions from certain statutes, and amendment of several clauses. Other changes include (1) the so-called "simplified purchase procedures" (See Chapter 13) which essentially raised the threshold (of the former "small purchase procedures") from \$25,000 to \$100,000. This chapter also listed 10 laws which became inapplicable "to all contracts and subcontracts (if otherwise applicable to subcontracts) at or below the simplified acquisition threshold" and the FAR Council must also add any laws enacted after the Federal Acquisition Streamlining Act of 1994 which pertain to those on that list, (2) the incorporation of "past performance" as a source selection factor (See Chapters 9, 15 and 42), (3) the requirements for agencies to employ life cycle cost analysis whenever feasible in making product and service selections and in connection with product descriptions and specifications, and many others. The emphasis is on having "the authority to make decisions ... accountability for the decision made [and] delegation to the lowest level with the System consistent with law," as well as on the "absence of direction" so as to permit the use of "sound business judgment that is otherwise consistent with law" when "acting on behalf of the American taxpayer." They are standards that almost totally depend upon both the technical and business quality of the employee and on his integrity (not the same), which are essentially beyond the bounds of the regulation. It has been said that "far too many high-ranking officers and civilians evidently still see themselves as salesmen—rather than managers—for the programs they are running."

At the time FASA was adopted, the critics of this approach commented in different manners. One of them, Philip Howard, a lawyer and author of a book called "The Death of Common Sense," has argued that what is needed is a system that discards most of the assumptions of the Federal Acquisition Regulation. Howard asserted that the system should be replaced by focus on oversight and accountability, not rigid instructions.

However, Marshall Doke, a Dallas lawyer specializing in contracts, has replied that "[s]imilar arguments are often made by 'reformers' who are not familiar with the Federal procurement system. [The] FAR—a product of years of work to bring uniformity to the previous hodgepodge of regulations among many different agencies—provides needed guidance and protection for procurement officials. Government studies consistently have shown that competition reduces cost."

In 1996, the Federal Acquisition Reform Act (FARA) was signed into law as part of the Defense Department Authorization Act for fiscal year 1996. Among other things (1) it eliminated the use of the General Services Administration Board of Contract Appeals to conduct bid protest adjudications in procurements involving computers, software and telecommunications technology products and services, (2) the procurement integrity law was rewritten on post-employment restrictions for government procurement officials, and (3) it eliminated several certification requirements.

Many of the changes incorporated into the Federal Acquisition Regulation have been criticized; they are among the parts that are commented upon in the text that follows.

GOVERNMENT CONTRACTS

IN A NUTSHELL

Fourth Edition

*

PART I

GENERAL

CHAPTER 1

FEDERAL ACQUISITION REGULATIONS SYSTEM

A. REGULATIONS ISSUED UNDER THE BASIC STATUTES

§ 1.1 In General

The Federal procurement system as of the early 1940's was largely formulated from the Civil War era. After World War II, the Armed Services Procurement Act of 1947 and the Federal Property and Administrative Services Act of 1949 were enacted. These Acts, as amended, together with voluminous regulations issued under them comprise most of the procedures governing the Federal procurement system for many years. They remained applicable for a number of years following the initial publication of the Federal Acquisition Regulation [FAR] in 1984.

As a result of the World War II experience, in 1947 the War Department was renamed the Department of the Army, a Department of the Air Force was created; together with the Navy Department, these became the National Military Establishment. In 1949, this name was changed to the Department of Defense (DoD). Immediately afterwards, these departments experienced the highest expenditures in government procurement. Only more recently were they exceeded by healthcare institutions.

In light of constant developments in the field of government contracts, the quantity of regulations appeared to reach a zenith. In 1981 virtually for the first time in this century there commenced some serious endeavor toward a uniformity in the regulatory growth in all government contracting. In 1988, Public Law 100–679 established a Federal Acquisition Regulatory Council. The Council comprised four members, the Administrator of the OFPP, and the official assigned by statute with the responsibility for acquisition policy in the GSA, DoD, and NASA. The new layer of management of the FAR members of the Council became responsible for (1) approving or disapproving procurement regulations in each of their own agencies: (2) carrying out procurement-related paperwork reduction responsibilities for their agencies; and (3) reducing levels of regulatory review in their agencies' procurement systems. It was not always effective in curbing the seemingly endless proliferation of agency implementations and supplements to the FAR. In 1989, the Office of Federal Procurement Policy estimated that the government's procurement-related information requirements cost government contractors more than 289 million hours a year. Only tax reporting and record keeping posed a greater burden on the public.

On August 21, 1990, a new guide was issued to all Federal agencies on writing regulations. It constitutes advice for agencies from the Office of Management and Budget, called "Regulatory Impact Analysis Guidance." It is contained in an appendix to a 705 page book known as the *Regulatory Program of the United States*. The foreword by the first President Bush states that Federal regulations impose costs on taxpayers that may amount to $1,700 per taxpayer. Also, in 1990, the length of procurement administrative lead time (PALTs) were estimated to have doubled in some agencies over a five-year period.

On October 26, 1993, President Clinton issued a memorandum directing the heads of departments and agencies to streamline procurement through electronic commerce by January 1997; and on July 3, 1995, the FAR was modified for the purpose of maximizing the use of commercial products and services, and using contractors who have a track record of successful past performance or who demonstrate a current superior ability to perform.

§ 1.2   The Federal Acquisition Regulation

Effective April 1, 1984, the Federal Acquisition Regulation (FAR) was established for the codification and publication of uniform policies and procedures for acquisition by all executive agencies. The System consists of the FAR (which is called "the primary document") and agency acquisition regulations that implement or supplement the FAR.

The FAR was originally drafted by personnel of both the Department of Defense and the General Services Administration under the direction of the Office of Federal Procurement Policy. Revisions were circulated among government agencies without public release and the final text reflecting changes from that review was published in September 1983. It is now codified as Chapter 1 of Title 48 of the Code of Federal Regulations and contains 52 parts (with some parts being reserved) categorized in eight Subchapters: (A) General; (B) Competition and Acquisition Planning; (C) Contracting Methods and Contract Types; (D) Socioeconomic Programs; (E) General Contracting Requirements; (F) Special Categories of Contracting; (G) Contract Management; and (H) Clauses and Forms. This treatise shall follow its sequence in treating the subject matter of government contract law herein.

The two councils—namely, the Defense Acquisition Regulations Council and the Civilian Agency Acquisition Council—prepare, issue and maintain the FAR upon agreeing with each other and are subject to its being "in accordance with the requirements of the Office of Federal Procurement Policy Act."

The FAR System was, and continues to be, developed in accordance with the requirements of the Office of Federal Procurement Policy Act Amendments of 1979. It is prepared, issued, maintained, and "prescribed," jointly by the Secretary of Defense, the Administrators of General Services, and the National Aeronautics and Space Administration, under their several statutory authorities. Except where expressly excluded, the FAR applies to all "acquisitions." This means "the acquiring by contract with appropriated funds of supplies or services (including construction) by and for the use of the Federal Government through purchase or lease." Thus, the FAR by its terms applies to both personal property and construction but does not apply to procurement with non-appropriated funds. Furthermore, it applies to the purchase of new and old property, i.e., to the supplies or services "already in existence" or which "must be created, developed, demonstrated, and evaluated."

The "statement of guiding principles for the Federal Acquisition System" tells participants in the acquisition process "to work together as a team" and not only (a) to "exercise personal initiative and sound business judgment;" but also (b) that they "may assume" if a "specific strategy is not addressed in the FAR, nor prohibited by law (statute or case law), Executive order or other regulation" that the strategy is a permissible exercise of authority. This regulation demonstrates a new lead in a single direction. Although one "performance standard" actually states that it is "the policy of the system to promote competition in the acquisition process," one commentator has pointed out that the possible limits on competition have actually been emphasized.

Another uncertainty created by the above guiding principle is that it creates significant inconsistency with the rules on FAR deviations. In contrast to the wide discretion granted to the acquisition team to innovate, strict controls on deviations are broadly defined. One variety of a deviation is any policy, practice, or procedure "inconsistent with the FAR." Another variety is the issuance of any policy or procedure that has not been properly incorporated into agency acquisition regulations.

A newer law added a section to reflect a 1996 statute which prohibits the inclusion of a new certification requirement in the FAR for contractors or offerors unless the certification is specifically imposed by statute. A newer rule also adds "conventions" to enhance a common understanding of the regulation among all members of the acquisition team and other users, including all contracting officers who use the FAR. For example, a statement that "words and terms" listed in the FARs' dictionary (Part 2) "applies to the entire regulation unless specifically defined in another part, subpart, section, provision, or clause." (Chapter 2 sets forth the Parts in which the listed words and terms mostly appear). It states that any authority is delegable, "unless specifically stated otherwise." It also describes the normal meanings of "dollar thresholds" and the "application of FAR changes to solicitations and contracts."

§ 1.3 Revisions to the FAR

A possible threat to the efficient promulgation of future regulations exists as a result of the separation between military and civilian councils. Revisions to the FAR are prepared and issued through the coordinated action of two councils, the Defense Acquisition Regulations Council (DAR Council) and the Civilian Agency Acquisition Council (CAA Council). The chairperson of the CAA Council is the representative of the Administrator of General Services. The other members of this council are "one each representative from the (1) Departments of Agriculture, Commerce, Energy, Health and Human Services, Housing and Urban Development, Interior, Labor, and Transportation, and (2) Environmental Protection Agency, Small Business Administration, and Department of Veterans Affairs and the Social Security Administration."

The Director of the DAR Council is the representative of the Secretary of Defense. The operation of the DAR Council is as prescribed by the Secretary of Defense. Membership includes representatives of the military Departments, the Defense Logistics Agency, and the National Aeronautics and Space Administration. Each Council has cognizance over specified parts or subparts of FAR and is responsible for agreeing on all revisions with the other Council; submitting to the FAR Secretariat information; and publication in the Federal Register of a notice soliciting comments on a proposed revision to the FAR. All comments received in response to a notice of proposed revisions must be considered. Each Council must arrange for public meetings; prepare any final revision in the appropriate FAR format and language; and submit any final revision to the FAR Secretariat for publication in the Federal Register and printing for distribution. Notice of a proposed regulation and a comment period must be published in the Federal Register.

Unsolicited recommendations for revisions for meeting certain criteria may also be considered and public meetings may be held.

Federal Acquisition Circulars (FACs) updating portions of the Federal Acquisition Regulation (FAR) are made quickly available from GSA's website. Both suggested and actual revisions in portions of the FAR have normally come from several sources. Discussion of the recent revisions will be made in this volume. They were mostly derived from the Office of Federal Procurement Policy (OFPP). Yet, we ought to first view the next section (1.4) in order to discuss the force of procurement regulations concerning mandatory clauses that have been omitted from contracts.

§ 1.4   The Force of Procurement Regulations—The *Christian* Doctrine

Regulations published in the Federal Register have the force and effect of law, i.e., they are binding on Federal agencies and the general public. Publication in the Federal Register gives legal notice of their contents to all who may be affected thereby.

The *Christian* doctrine affects contracts in those instances where the government has failed to follow a regulation. The case of *G.L. Christian & Associates v. United States* concerned a contract that did not include a clause required by a regulation, i.e., the standard termination for convenience clause. In holding that the particular clause must be read into the contract, the Court of Claims ruled that the validity of the contract was dependent upon inclusion of the clause; that is, the contracting officer had no authority to contract except in accordance with the regulation which had the force and effect of law. Furthermore, the only regulations governing the legality of a contract are those that were in existence at the time the contract was awarded. A court must "reasonably be able to conclude that the grant of authority contemplates the regulations issued." The *Christian* Doctrine does *not* result in the automatic incorporation of non-mandatory clauses. However, continuous use of the word "shall" throughout virtually all segments of the Federal Acquisition regulation indicates that its drafters were cognizant of the *Christian* Doctrine and anticipated its being applied to errors of inadvertent omission on the part of a contracting officer. However, in 1996 a board of contract appeals refused to hold that an omitted mandatory NASA FAR Supplement property clause must be incorporated into a contract. This was done on the board's subjective conclusion that the clause rose only to the level of a fundamental procurement policy and the fact that it was not in the FAR itself.

§ 1.5   The Federal Acquisition Regulation as a "Code"

In both common law and code countries today, we are in an age when the amount of unwritten law is becoming small as compared to written law. The Justinian System used by Trebonius in the codification of Roman Law influenced the French Code of March 21, 1804 (or the "Code Napoleon" as it was later called) and German code of January 1, 1900, that in turn often served as models for codes in many other countries.

The codes constitute attempts to bring all laws together in one place so that Maitland's "seamless web" would actually be woven. Of course, there would be separate codes—civil, criminal, and commercial—but they would be very few in number and none of them was more than one volume. Further, the codes would be "civilizing" because they would result from comparative legal studies of Roman law and the law of modern foreign countries. Yet, it should be noted that the Roman law (which some have termed the greatest of the ancient civilizations with a 1000–year duration) avoided over-codification. Codes contained enough simplicity of expression that they could be generally read by ordinary men and not only by lawyers. However, civil law codes are not statutes that are traditionally in derogation of the common law; those countries have no common law.

To a great extent the Civil code more resembles a constitution than a statute in a "common law" country. No "Codes" in a common law country are "Codes" in the sense of the word in a civil law country. In this country, we often use the word "code" to express an ethical position; for example, a "code of ethics" (which has been so expressed for business ethicists). However, although California adopted a "code" in the mid-nineteenth century, it officially rejected its use as if it were like a "civil law country." Today that code remains a primary law update, with the codification of laws and annotated with court decisions. That code also contains some regulations, but not all of them are updated. Federal "public law" is also later "codified," using different numbers that are often cited in Federal regulations.

The FAR starts with a code focus by stating that the system "is established for the codification and publication of uniform policies and procedures for acquisition by all executive agencies." Thus, it was not to be merely a guidance system in the manner requested by the former Vice President's National Performance Report (NPR). See Section 1.6.

§ 1.6 Office of Federal Procurement Policy and the Prescription of Procurement Regulations

The Office of Federal Procurement Policy (OFPP) is part of the Executive Office of the President and answers to the

Director of OMB, the President, and Congress. It consists of a small office of about 40 persons often staffed by DoD officials. A June 1983 report of the General Accounting Office concluded that without strong OFPP leadership for resolving conflicts, the FAR system would likely crumble under a proliferation of supplemental agency procurement regulations. In November 1983, the Office of Federal Procurement Policy was continued by Congress for a period of four years but it was authorized to issue binding regulations only when the OFPP administrator found that GSA, NASA, and DoD were unable to agree upon, or failed to issue, government-wide rules "in a timely manner." In such event, OFPP became empowered to "prescribe government-wide regulations, procedures and forms which shall be followed by the executive agencies." Serious concern with the new system was expressed by the Congress.

The Office of Federal Procurement Policy Reauthorization Act that permanently established the Federal Acquisition Regulatory Council empowered the OFPP Administrator, at the request of any party, to review a procurement regulation to determine whether it is inconsistent with the government-wide FAR.

In July 1990, the OFPP established an inter-agency group to develop a detailed Procurement Professionalism Plan for agencies to identify a comprehensive program of workforce improvement. Four subgroups devised recommended actions on the recruitment, training, retention, and evaluation of performance of the procurement workforce, along with the Federal Acquisition Institute (FAI). In 1992, the FAI published these "Units of Instruction" under the title *Contract Specialist Workbook* that covers almost 80 duties and more than 800 related tasks. Agencies may modify this standard by assigning levels of learning commensurate with agency needs. In 1995, FAR 1.6 was revised by adding a requirement that agencies establish a "procurement career management program and a system for the selection, appointment and termination of appointment of contracting officers."

§ 1.7   The National Performance Report (NPRT) and Changes Based Thereon

In the mid–1990s, Vice President Al Gore announced his desire to "reinvent the government" in a National Performance Review (NPR). His approach was toward a simpler and an allegedly more efficient procurement guidance system than a largely mandatory one.

The newer NPR approach, which appeared to follow Gore's approach toward simplification, was published in the *Federal Register*. For example, a statement was added that the "Guiding Principles for the System" are part of its "framework." One of these principles states that the FAR will be "using contractors who have a record of successful past performance." (This matter will be discussed in later chapters). It also states that the FAR system will "minimize administrative operating costs"—a policy which actually resulted in a significant reduction of government procurement personnel. This was done in spite of the passage of a law by Congress specifically limiting such action.

A new section states that the government members of a Federal acquisition team "must be empowered to make acquisition decisions within their areas of responsibility, including election, negotiation, and administration of contracts consistent with the Guiding Principles." It thereafter adds that "If a policy or procedure, or a particular strategy or practice, is in the best interests of the government, and is not specifically addressed in the FAR, nor prohibited by law (statute or case law), executive order, or other regulation, government members of the Team should not assume it is prohibited."

§ 1.8   Implementation and Supplementation of FAR by Government Agencies

The Federal Acquisition Regulation is subject to modification by agencies having statutory authority to do some things differently. The FAR itself specifically provides that "an agency head may issue or authorize the issuance of agency acquisition regulations that implement or supplement the FAR." ("Supplementary material" means that there is no counterpart in the FAR.) These regulations are for the military departments and defense agencies, NASA, and the civilian agencies other than NASA. The latter civilian agency regulations are "issued by the heads of those agencies subject to the overall authority of the Administrator of General Services or any independent authority the agency may have." Such implementing or supplementing regulations incorporate, together with the FAR, agency-wide policies, procedures, contract clauses, and solicitation provisions that govern the contracting process. In addition, they control the relationship between the agencies, including any of its suborganizations, and contractors or prospective contractors and must be published in the Federal Register (as required by the Federal Register Act) and codified (under an assigned chapter in Title 48, Code of Federal Regulations). They are parallel to the FAR in format, arrangement, and numbering system. An agency's acquisition regulations "shall not unnecessarily repeat, paraphrase, or otherwise restate material contained in the FAR or higher-level agency acquisition regulations; or (except as required by law or as provided in Subpart 1.4) conflict or be inconsistent with FAR content" unless an agency's statutes specifically require such an inconsistency. Yet, they are very detailed.

Another threat to the FAR system is the apparent lack of control of implementations, supplementations, and other issuances exhibited by many agencies following several years of operations "under" the FAR. Its goal, which was essentially to establish a single, government-wide system of regulations to reduce individual agency acquisition policies, regulations, and clauses, may be undermined by lower level agency issuances which are not being published in the Federal Register even though they may have a significant effect upon cost or have other impacts upon contractors or potential contractors. They may be circumventing the FAR if no advance comments are obtained and they are used and/or reused without any finding of "urgent and compelling circumstances".

The U.S. Supreme Court had held that the Office of Management and Budget might not invoke the Paperwork Reduction Act to annul rules of Federal agencies requiring disclosure of information to third parties. The court held the "collection of information" that the act regulates refers to information gathered for agencies' own use, not to rules requiring disclosures to employees, consumers, or others. The FAR requires all agencies to "ensure that they comply" with that statute.

§ 1.9   Deviations

The making of "Deviations" from the FAR is a practice of conducting procurement actions of any kind and at any stage of the acquisition process that is "inconsistent with the FAR." The term also includes "the omission of any prescribed solicitation provision or contract clause," as well as the use of any such provision or clause with modified or alternate language that is not authorized by the FAR. The

FAR states that deviations from the FAR may be granted when necessary to meet the specific needs and requirements of each agency. Part of the justification for this authority to deviate is to permit "the development and testing of new techniques and methods of acquisition."

If the deviation is to affect more than one contract action and is to be used on a permanent basis, it is called a "class deviation" and the agency then "should propose an appropriate FAR revision to cover the matter." The use of the word "should" raises the questions of (a) how long an agency may wait before submitting the proposal, and (b) how long an agency may continue to use a "class deviation" after submission to the FAR Secretariat while awaiting a possible revision of the FAR. Although the term "may" is defined in the definition section as "permissive," no definition is contained with respect to the precatory word "should."

A deviation from the FAR is authorized when it is required to comply with a treaty (a government to government agreement). However, this cannot be authorized if it has become inconsistent with FAR coverage based on a law enacted after the execution of the treaty.

B. CONTRACTING AUTHORITY AND RESPONSIBILITIES

§ 1.21 Who Is Authorized to Represent the United States—The Contracting Officer

The person executing or terminating a contract on behalf of the government is called a "contracting officer." The term includes authorized representatives of the contracting officer acting within the limits of their authority delegated by the contracting officer. Thus, several individuals may represent the public body in the capacity of contracting officers. For example, a "termination contracting officer" (TCO) is only authorized to settle terminated contracts while a single contracting officer may be responsible for duties in this area as well as many others.

Today, agency heads are authorized to delegate micro-purchase authority ($2,500 or below, except for construction, where the threshold is $2,000). Agency heads may also "assign contracting functions and responsibilities from one agency to another;" as well as create "joint or combined offices" to exercise acquisition functions and responsibilities.

Contracting officers have unique authority to bind the government to purchase above the micro-purchase threshold after ensuring that all requirements of law, executive orders, regulations and all other applicable procedures, including clearances and approvals, have been met. Such officials receive instructions regarding the limits of their authority. If they are without authority, payment under a contract will generally be refused because their power is limited to binding the government "only to the extent of the authority delegated to them." As stated above, contracting officers receive from the appointing authority instructions in writing regarding the limits of their authority. For his part a claimant must show that the constitutional rights were clearly established at the time they were violated.

Only a limited number of agency officials are designated contracting officers solely by virtue of their position. Contracting officers are allowed wide latitude to exercise business judgment and are responsible for ensuring "compliance with the terms of the contract, and safeguarding the interests of the United States in its contractual relationships" and they must ensure that "contractors receive impartial, fair, and equitable treatment."

A statute makes the Administrator of General Services (GSA) responsible for a detailed list of items which may be beyond the power of the manager on a government project who generally needs such authority in order to direct the work most efficiently. Some government departments possess no authority to make certain procurements. For example, the Treasury Department lacks specific statutory authorization (or a delegation of authority from the GSA), to procure building services by entering into a service contract with an independent third party contractor. Hence, it has been held that any building services the Treasury Department desires would have to be provided or otherwise arranged by the GSA that has the statutory authority and responsibility to make repairs, etc., to public buildings. On the other hand, courts have sometimes appeared to favor delegation. Thus, although a regulation existed limiting the authority for procurements in excess of $50 million to the Secretary of the Department of Energy, a delegation of authority to make award of a $70 million contract for telecommunications services was upheld. There a DOE regulation vested exclusive authority for procurements in excess of $50 million in the DOE Secretary; the regulation also stated that lesser authorities could be delegated. However, a statute provided that the Secretary's authority could be delegated unless "expressly prohibited." Since the regulation did not expressly prohibit delegation, the delegation was held to be permissible. However, it has been held that a procurement and award failed not because GSA did not make an appropriate delegation above $2.5 million of procurement authority to the agency, but rather because this authority was not redelegated to the procurement level within the agency. The FAR states that "Contracting Officers may bind the government only to the extent of the authority delegated to them" and that these limits shall be readily available to the public and agency personnel.

Sometimes, the government will seek to escape a bargain on the theory that the contracting officer exceeded his authority by making a poor business judgment. Some cases state that the contracting officer's obligation to protect the government's business interests does not immunize the agency from improvident agreements. But the contracting officer is prohibited from exceeding statutory or regulatory restrictions.

In an attempt to safeguard against a contracting officer's tendency to over enhance his reputation as one who can "get along with" a contractor and because a contracting officer in many instances cannot make many decisions alone, he is required to "request and consider the advice of specialists in audit, law, engineering, transportation, and other fields, as appropriate." However, these persons are advisors only and are without contractual authority to bind the government. Hence, a contracting officer who may not find it appropriate to seek such advice may find his reputation within a government agency to suffer; and, if he acts against such advice, he may find that a government file exists which so indicates.

As a result of the acquisition streamlining reforms of the 1990's, Government agencies may delegate micro-purchase authority to employees and members of the Armed Forces who are not contracting officers. The micro-purchase threshold is currently $2,500, except for construction, for which the threshold is $2,000. Micro-purchases do not require any provisions or clauses, with certain exceptions. The Governmentwide commercial purchase card is the preferred method to purchase and pay for micro-purchases.

The Governmentwide commercial purchase card may be used to make micro-purchases, place task or delivery orders, or make payments when the contractor has agreed to accept payment by that means. Although the micro-purchase threshold and use of government purchase cards revolutionized government contracting, some have expressed concern about the lack of effective oversight.

§ 1.22 Authority of Government Agents and the Inadequacy of Apparent Authority

In a government of delegated powers, no activity may be undertaken by the government employee except pursuant to such power. Authority to act is the first question generally considered by a government attorney. Whenever this question arises, it receives a lot of attention and often is referred to an agency's headquarters that are usually located in Washington, D.C. If a government attorney has approved the agreement, the contracting officer will probably be found to have acted within the scope of his authority; but in some instances he may have acted beyond his authority. Accordingly, the private practitioner should have knowledge of the limitations of his authority, in negotiating a government contract, in order to meet or, if necessary, to counter proposals or actions of the government.

Unlike in the making of a private contract, a major concern in the negotiation of a government contract is the principle that lack of knowledge of actual authority is normally not reason enough to hold the government liable if such authority is absent. Unlike in dealings with private parties, one is charged with knowledge of the extent of the actual authority of the government's contracting agent since no agent of the government can hold himself out to have any authority not sanctioned by law. It is presumed that one can always ascertain the extent of his authority.

The requirement of actual authority is illustrated by the decision of the United States Supreme Court in Federal Crop Insurance Corp. v. Merrill. However, this does not restrict the use of electronic commerce. A government corporation created under the Crop Insurance Act was vested with the authority to insure crops against loss. In spite of regulations issued by the corporation prohibiting reseeding, the plaintiff, who had applied for crop insurance, reseeded after his crop was destroyed by drought; further, this was apparently done with the knowledge and consent of an agent of the government corporation. When the government refused to pay for his loss, the plaintiff sued in an Idaho Court and recovered. The Idaho Court held that the knowledge and consent of an agent of a private insurance company, under circumstances identical or similar to this case, would bind a private insurance company in addition to binding the government corporation.

The government appealed and the Supreme Court reversed the decision of the Idaho Court and granted judgment for the government on the grounds that the regulations specifically prohibited insurance of the wheat that was reseeded and such regulations are binding, regardless of plaintiff's lack of knowledge thereof. The Court noted that:

> Whatever the form in which the government functions, anyone entering into an arrangement with the government takes the risk of having accurately ascertained that he who purports to act for the government stays within the bounds of his authority.

Although the dissent argued that it was absurd to require farmers to take cognizance of such regulations, the majority held that "not even the temptations of a hard case can elude the clear meaning of the regulations." This is because the concept that this is a government of delegated powers goes to the Federal constitution and the authority of all contracting officers is limited.

Although a contractor may be able to recover costs based on implied-in-fact contract to pay for such costs, there can be no recovery if the contracting officer lacked the requisite authority to bind the government. Further, lack of proper delegation of authority may void a contract. Thus, the United States Court of Appeals for the Federal Circuit has held that the Army's failure to obtain a delegation of procurement authority (under a now-superseded statute) for the purchase of information technology resources resulted in a contract being declared void.

Except as provided by statute, the doctrine of apparent authority is not applicable against the Federal government. As a practical matter, in contracting with the Federal government one should ask the government agent to show evidence of his authority. For example, it may be advisable to ask for a copy of the government agent's delegation of authority to contract for the government. The regulations provide that "information on the limits of the contracting officers' authority shall be readily available to the public and agency personnel." The problem is illustrated in Gordon Woodroffe Corp. v. United States where a government agent representing the State Department contracted to buy a generator for $906,000 for the American Mission for aid to Greece. Later, the generator was purchased by the Greek government for $524,400. The issue was whether the government agent had the authority to make the contract. The government agent had wired plaintiff accepting the unit "for and on behalf of the American Mission for Aid to Greece." The Court of Claims found that the authority had been placed by President Truman in the Chief of the American Mission for Aid to Greece and that neither he nor any of his assistants had had any dealings with plaintiff;

the government agent was an assistant in the "Office of the Coordinator for Aid to Greece and Turkey," and that such office had no right to commit the funds which Congress had appropriated. Hence, the Court found that the government agent had no authority to bind the United States. Two judges dissented, pointing out that by statute and executive order subdelegation was expressly permitted and that the problem arose because the state department and mission were acting at cross-purposes.

The seriousness of the problem is also shown in connection with the award of a research and development contract to the General Electric Company on a cost-plus-fixed-fee (CPFF) basis as a result of an unsolicited proposal. A cost-plus-fixed-fee (CPFF) contract is a contract that essentially places no financial responsibility on the contractor to continue work when he reaches the ceiling on funds committed to the contract. The proposal was to design and manufacture two "20 MM Automatic Weapons Systems." A Board of Contract Appeals found General Electric failed to stop work, under the "Limitation of Cost" clause of the contract, when it became aware of the overrun. The "board considered it likely that General Electric was motivated primarily by a desire to obtain the production contract which would naturally flow from the successful completion of the research and development performance."

Later, a contracting officer's signature was found at the bottom of a legal opinion and recommendation that funding of the overrun was within his discretion indicating that he "concurred" therewith. However, his successor did not agree and no notice of funding was sent to the contractor, who then sued to recover on the overrun. A majority of the court somehow held that this act bound the United States government to fund the overrun in spite of the lack of notice to the contractor. The court stated, "we believe that, when an authorized contracting officer expresses a definite opinion concerning the merits of a claim with knowledge of the relevant facts, a 'decision' has been made." The dissent remarked that it is questionable "whether any purely intra-government document, not communicated to the contractor, can be a notification to the contractor as the contract contemplated." The dissent stated that:

> The writing here relied on purports simply to be advice to other government officials. The commitment of the government to reimburse for cost overruns is a serious matter and involves the control of expenditures by Congress and by fiscal officials. I would not knowingly do anything to weaken that control. The amount here involved is small, as government contract expenditures go, but the principle is large.

§ 1.23 Apparent Authority, vs. Actual Authority, Estoppel and Ratification

(a) Generally

Although government and private contracts are similar, when a contract is executed by a government official or employee without authority to do so, or if funds have not been appropriated by the Congress for a contract so executed, it has generally been held that the agreement does not bind the government. A leading case is The Floyd Acceptances, in which the court held that the United States was not bound by bills of exchange accepted by government agents where the bills constituted advance payments that were prohibited by statute. The Court stated:

> We have no officers in this government, from the President down to the most subordinate agent, who does not hold office under the law, with prescribed duties and limited authority.

In a government contract, the contracting officer differs from the agent of a private corporation in that the doctrine of apparent authority is normally inapplicable.

(b) Estoppel

Where a contract is made on an unauthorized basis, it has been held that payment thereon cannot be made on the grounds of an estoppel against the United States. In United States v. Zenith–Godley Co., the government sought the return of sums paid to the defendant by the Department of Agriculture through the Commodity Credit Corp. (CCC) because the payments were made without authority. The Agriculture Act directed the Secretary of Agriculture to make available price supports to milk producers but the Department issued regulations which exceeded the Secretary's authority as determined by the Comptroller General. The defendant argued that the government's error led him to change his position and therefore the United States was estopped. The Court held otherwise. Estoppel in this circumstance was not a remedy available against the U.S. because "no one may rely upon the apparent authority of an agent of the government" and "the government may not be estopped by the action or representation of an agent *not within* the *scope* of his *actual authority* .... The burden is on him who deals with the government accurately to discover the scope of statute and regulations."

The Supreme Court in 1981 confirmed the doctrines pertaining to the necessity of authority (in the *Merrill* Case) and the general inapplicability of estoppel in Schweiker v. Hansen. There the Respondent was erroneously told by a Social Security representative that she was not eligible for certain benefits. In reliance thereon she failed to file an application as required by statute and regulation. Later she did file and then sought and received a district court ruling for retroactive benefits on the ground of estoppel against the United States. The Court of Appeals affirmed and stated "misinformation provided by a government official combined with a showing of misconduct (even if it does not rise to the level of a violation of a legally binding rule) should be sufficient to require estoppel." The Supreme Court reversed, claiming it "has never decided what type of conduct by a government employee will estop the government from insisting upon compliance with valid regulations." The Court suggested that approval might occur where "estoppel [does] not threaten the public fisc as estoppel does here."

Nevertheless, the Court of Claims continued applying an estoppel in the similar case of Broad Avenue Laundry and Tailoring v. United States. There, after a contract was awarded to operate a government-owned laundry facility, the contractor was about to negotiate a new union contract at higher wages and was erroneously told by the contracting officer that if the Department of Labor issued a new prevailing wage determination, it would be applicable to the contract, and a price adjustment could be requested. The contractor thereafter agreed with the union on the new rates and affirmed a modification from the contracting officer to increase the price. But, when it was discovered that the new prevailing wage did not apply to any contracts then in effect, the government disallowed his claim. The contractor appealed to the ASBCA, which upheld the disallowance because it appeared to have lacked consideration and, if so, it would have been in effect a gift of taxpayer funds. The Court of Claims reversed by ignoring the holding of the Supreme Court in Schweiker v. Hansen. It applied estoppel against the government in a case and made a statement that such a contracting officer "has actual authority to embody mistakes of law in her decisions and the government is estopped, having endowed her with the powers it has, to assert otherwise." Some lower courts are still attempting to narrow these rulings to their precise facts in order to continue granting an estoppel knowing that the likelihood of review of any particular case by the Supreme Court is minimal.

In many cases, the former Court of Claims appears to have normally applied estoppel against a government agent who had general authority to contract almost as if he were a private citizen. Yet, the U.S. Supreme Court has stated, "it is well-settled that the government may not be estopped on the same terms as any other litigant." While this Court did not lay down a rule that estoppel may not in any circumstances run against the government, the cases were diverging between the Court of Claims (and its successors) and the Supreme Court. Justice Rehnquist and Chief Justice Berger went further, noting that the Court's treatment of that question gives an impression of hospitality towards claims of estoppel against the government which decided cases do not warrant, perhaps, because of an awareness that so few cases reach the Supreme Court on the issue. For example, in 1990, the Supreme Court held that equitable estoppel cannot form the basis for a monetary claim against the United States contrary to statute; this was because of a constitutional rule requiring disbursements from the treasury only by congressional authorization. Notwithstanding this decision, the United States Court of Appeals for the Federal Circuit held in 1993 that equitable estoppel has not been foreclosed as a possible theory for recovery on a contract claim. One court indicated that the doctrine is "disfavored," mandates proof of "serious injustice," and requires courts to exhibit the utmost caution and restraint. Another stated the view in the circuit courts is that a party seeking to estop the Government must prove the agency's "affirmative misconduct." Boards continue to apply estoppel against the government in cases in which representations were *within* the scope of the agent's authority.

Accordingly, although older decisions absolved the government of liability when its agents lacked authority, there can be no estoppel against the government for actions taken in reliance on regulations that exceed the authority of a government agency; such estoppels were distinguished from the application of estoppel against an officer who may be found to have the requisite authority.

(c) Ratification

Courts and boards have often taken on the responsibility of determining whether ratification has occurred. If it has not occurred (that is, if the government agent has not ratified unauthorized acts), then courts held that they "are powerless to do it for him." In the past, some law principles of ratification have been applied to contracting officers with respect to actions by government employees who did not have authority to bind the government. Of course, the ratifying officials themselves must have the authority to take the questionable action. For example, the case of Fox Valley Engineering Inc. v. United States concerned an agreement to prepare maps for the Army. The Army representative went to the contractor's plant and made suggestions and sketches were approved. Later, the government found the work unsatisfactory. The contracting officer admitted his lack of technical knowledge and his reliance on the field representative. The claim of the contractor was upheld because the field representative approved the sketches, made suggestions, gave directions that were followed and told the contractor not to make changes. The court said that under these circumstances it would be unfair to order changes at a later time at greatly increased expense to the contractor. The court said this would be the same as a deliberate "trap." The government contended that the field representative was not authorized to accept work in the field, but the court said that he was sent to the contractor's plant to give necessary guidance and directions; powers which were confirmed in writing by the contracting officer.

In 1988, the regulation finally provided for ratification of "unauthorized commitments"—namely, "an agreement that is not binding solely because the Government representative who made it lacked the authority to enter into that agreement on behalf of the Government." The regulation even permits delegation of ratification authority to the chief of a contracting office. They also may be under progressively lower monetary ceilings the further down the delegation, but this authority may only be exercised in limited circumstances. An example is where supplies or services have been provided to and accepted by the government, or the government otherwise has obtained or will obtain a benefit resulting from performance of the unauthorized commitment. The price must have been determined as "fair and reasonable." The funds must have been available at the time the authorized commitment was made. The regulation requires legal advice to be obtained in cases that are not ratifiable and states that agencies should process unauthorized commitments instead of referring such actions to the General Accounting Office for resolution. The regulation further advises that unauthorized commitments that would involve claims subject to resolution under the Contract Disputes Act of 1978 "should be processed" in accordance with Disputes and Appeals. See Chapter 33.

The Anti–Assignment Act and the Assignment of Claims Act generally prohibit the transfer of government contracts and the assignment of claims against the government. Nevertheless, the Claims Court permitted a company that took over contract performance under a name change agreement and fully performed the contract to recover in quantum meruit. The court stated that these statutes should be "applied pragmatically." Secondly, it held that the transfer should be "upheld when the government recognizes it either expressly as by novation or implicitly as by ratification or waiver." A board of contract appeals held that it might not authorize an agency to ratify a contract where the agency had no authority to make the contract.

§ 1.24   Illegal Contracts

(a) Generally

Contracting officers have discretionary authority to void and rescind a contract where there has been a final conviction for certain improper activity. Thus, heads of agencies (or a designee) may apply such an administrative remedy for a final "conviction for bribery, conflict of interest, disclosure or receipt of contractor bid or proposal information in exchange for a thing of value or to give anyone a competitive advantage in the award" of a Federal contract.

Where the contract voiding is not based on final conviction, such action must be based upon a "preponderance of the evidence" that the contractor has "engaged in conduct constituting such an offense." Further, the initiation of suspension or debarment proceedings may justify the conclusion that the contractor is not responsible. The "minimum" process pertaining to voiding of the contract includes notice of a proposed action, and holding a hearing upon the contractor's request (without further inquiry regarding the validity of a conviction). The final decision must be sent by certified mail, return receipt requested, and accompanied by a demand for recovery of amounts expended and property transferred. This is not a claim under the Contract Disputes Act (see Chapter 33).

Bargains to obtain appropriations in settlement of a claim against a public body on a contingent fee basis have traditionally tempted many to gain payment by improper means. Public employees may be unwilling to search out the facts. For example, where the law provides that there should be a formal advertisement and it was ignored by the procuring agency, the resulting contract has been held to be illegal. In one such case, the Comptroller General held that:

> Since the subject contract was entered into ... and it is reported that the contractor has accomplished a substantial amount of work thereunder, it does not appear to be practicable to take any action to terminate it, and no further objection will be raised.

The reasons given for permitting payments to be made out of public funds for an illegal contract with the Federal Government may be inadequate. State courts, which have considered the matter, do not appear to follow either the Comptroller General or the Court of Claims with respect to the granting of quantum meruit recovery.

In 1999, Judge Newman of the United States Court of Appeals for the Federal Circuit (CAFC) did not correctly state the law when she declared for the majority of the divided court:

> Where a contract or a provision thereof is in violation of law, but has been fully performed, the courts have variously sustained the contract, reformed it to correct the illegal term, or allowed recovery under an implied contract theory; the courts have not, however, simply declared the contract void ab initio.

As pointed out by the dissenter, the CAFC ignored the positive command of the law being violated in the case. He stated that the majority of the court "recognizes the language of the [Appropriation] Act expressly prohibits the use of Government funds for such a contract ... the court reaches exactly the opposite conclusion, and finds the contract valid, and presumably enforceable."

In certain instances, a subsequent appropriation could authorize the agency to pay for those received and accepted goods in a different manner; namely, based on their value under an implied contract, as is the case with private organizations.

(b) *Cost Plus Percentage of Cost (CPPC) Prohibitions*

Illegal contracts are generally void from their conception. An example of an illegal contract that the Federal system prohibits is a cost-plus-percentage-of-cost (CPPC) contract. This is any agreement whereby the profit to be received by a contractor is based upon the cost he incurs in performing the contract. The Supreme Court stated that the purpose of Congress behind the CPPC contract prohibition "was to protect the government against the sort of exploitation so easily accomplished under cost-plus-a-percentage-of-cost contracts under which the government contracts and is bound to pay costs, undetermined at the time the contract is made and to be incurred in the future, plus a commission based on a percentage of these future costs." The evil of such contracts is that the contractor's profit increases in proportion to the costs he expends in the performance. "The danger guarded against by the Congressional prohibition was the incentive to a government contractor who already had a binding contract with the government for payment of undetermined future costs to pay liberally for reimbursable items because higher costs meant a higher fee to him, his profit being determined by a percentage of cost."

CPPC subcontracts also give the subcontractor an incentive to increase costs since he makes more profit by doing so. During an audit of cost-type contracts with the Chrysler Corporation, the Army Audit Agency disallowed reimbursement claims for payments made to many subcontractors, because they were performed on a CPPC basis that was expressly prohibited by the First War Powers Act. Chrysler argued that even though the contracts may be void, the United States was obligated to pay the reasonable value of goods and services furnished upon an implied contract for a quantum meruit. The Comptroller General, however, was unable to state that the costs to the United States represented a reasonable value because the function of their audit was to determine the existence and accuracy of recorded costs, and not the fairness or reasonableness of the price paid. Also, the determination required a comparison of the subcontractor's rates with commercial rates, as well as business and engineering analyses. Accordingly, the matter was returned to the contracting officer to make these determinations and a review thereof by appropriate "Boards of Review." The reason given for this consideration was that failure to make payments would "strain Army contractor relationships."

A decision that permits payment for goods and services received and accepted by a contractor, regardless of the fact that the contractor used illegal methods in subcontracting, is not free from doubt; this is done through the rationale whereby the subcontract itself is disregarded and the payment is made through the implied contract. The alternative would be the disapproval of any reimbursement of the prime contractor by the government for these subcontractors, thus leaving the subcontractor to his remedy against the prime contractor—a solution consistent with the fact that there is no privity of contract between the government and subcontractor. But the fact that the government benefited from the deliveries by the subcontractors is only to the extent that there may be quasi-contractual recovery by the prime contractor. Any benefit to the prime contractor that does not concurrently result in benefit to the government, to that extent, would not result in reimbursement to the prime contractor. Nevertheless, in many states, no payments can be made on illegal contracts, regardless of the possible benefit to the public body for work performed. The procedures approved by the Comptroller General for establishing the fair and reasonable price in order to permit quantum meruit recovery demand considerable talent on the part of government personnel in making determinations, independent of the contractor, regarding a comparison of rates charged for commercial work, engineering evaluation and price evaluation, a capability not available to some agencies of the Federal government. This may partially account for those decisions of state courts which do not even consider the possible benefits received by the public agency representing the taxpayers in these states to the extent these benefits cannot be measured or paid for. The sole answer to this problem appears to be to continue to refuse payment unless and until appropriate methods can be found to measure these benefits.

On occasion an agreement that would seem prohibited as a CPPC agreement may in fact be free from the defect. For example, assume that a cost-type contractor intends to subcontract to various experts or firms in accordance with a program developed by the contractor, who will also recommend to the government those specialists it believes would be most effective.

On the other hand, bonus payments to a contractor's employees that are based on a percentage of costs increased are illegal payments and hence will be disallowed. In one case a bonus paid at the rate of 2.5% of the company's billing under the contract was held to be a direct violation of the statutory prohibition against the CPPC system of contracting and reimbursement therefore was disallowed. Guidelines applied by the General Accounting Office in determining whether a contract constitutes a CPPC system of contracting include whether payment is at a predetermined rate, this rate is applied to actual performance costs, the contractor's entitlement is uncertain at the time of contracting, and it increases commensurately with increased performance costs. The presence of a ceiling on costs does not save it from violating the statute.

The Comptroller General has ruled that after-the-fact pricing violates the CPPC prohibition when a contractor or subcontractor then knows his actual costs and he will be basing his profit factor thereon. Thus, he was indicating that Federal agencies must not only avoid violation of the law but also violation of the spirit behind this law. In the case of subcontracts, one must consider privity of contract, which is essential in order for one party to maintain an action on the contract against the other. It has been argued that the portion of the contract containing the illegal provisions is void and the remaining portions are valid, provided that the contract is divisible into a legal portion, supported by valid consideration, and an illegal portion, invalid because the method of payment specified is contrary to statute.

Even though the government insisted on including a cost plus percentage of cost (CPPC) pricing clause in a Small Business contract, (unenforceable because its agents lack authority to do so), the contractor was held entitled to compensation, quantum valebat under Federal law (unlike the law in many states).

(c) Time and Materials (T & M) Contracts

T & M contracts have aspects of cost-plus-percentage-of-cost contracts. Because an hourly rate payable under a contract includes both profit and overhead, the longer the contract remains in force the more profit accrues to the contractor. Where the contract, however, is terminable at any time by the government, the contractor has no control over the amount of profit he may be entitled to beyond the notice period for termination.

Of course, in any given case, the evils of the system may or may not still be present, but this may be an administrative matter. As the U.S. Supreme Court observed in *Muschany* when presented with a set of facts involving aspects of the problem: "The fact that the procurement system is improvident obviously does not make it illegal." In the Federal system, at least, it is apparent that quantum meruit payment is possible under a CPPC contract, although the contract is invalid.

(d) The Doctrine of "Palpable" Illegality v. "Improper" Action

An improper award may conceivably either be terminated for convenience, or canceled. If terminated for convenience, the contractor may recover his reasonably incurred costs prior to the termination plus a reasonable profit (for work done up to the time of termination) unless he was in a loss situation. (See Chapter 49)

When the making of an award violates statutes or regulations, it would appear that an illegal contract has resulted and an illegal award should not permit action under the contract terms. However, Federal practice has developed permitting a termination for convenience in many cases and the contractor is still paid out of taxpayer funds, including an allocated portion for his profit. For example, where the records, including a pre-award survey, clearly show no basis for concluding that a low bidder can meet all requirements of the invitation for bids, the award is improper. Yet, unlike the law in most states, any resulting contracts with the Federal government are required to contain a clause permitting the agency to be terminated for convenience that, if used, will permit the contractor to recover his reasonable costs and a profit. (The clause will be implied as a matter of law. See Section 1.4). The Comptroller General has recommended that the clause be so implied. In other cases, he does not even recommend that the contract be canceled. The Comptroller General has summarized the doctrine of the Court of Claims as follows:

> Our finding that the contract was improperly negotiated does not lead us to the further conclusion, … that the contract must be canceled. Cancellation is reserved for contracts illegally awarded. An illegal award, under the rationale of several Court of Claims decisions, results only if it was made contrary to statutory or regulatory requirements because of some action or statement by the contractor or if the contractor was on direct notice that the procedures being followed were violative of the requirements.

The so-called doctrine of "palpable illegality" determines whether no contract exists and that an award be cancelled, or whether the error was not "palpably illegal" and an existing contract should be terminated for convenience.

The Yosemite Park and Curry Co. (YPC) entered into a concession contract with the National Park Service whereby the Service agreed to reimburse YPC's costs, including Federal income taxes, and pay a profit calculated at twelve and one-half percent of YPC's average gross investment in the transportation equipment. A Department of Interior certifying officer informed YPC that the terms providing for reimbursement of Federal income taxes and allowing more than ten percent profit on a cost-plus contract violated Federal procurement statutes and regulations, the contract was illegal and invalid, and payments could not be made. YPC brought suit in the Court of Claims seeking the contract price for services provided. In spite of the fact that the Court agreed with the government that the contract was illegal and invalid, it nevertheless allowed a recovery in quantum meruit not to exceed YPC's cost plus ten percent. The decision has been criticized. Only in rare circumstances do such cases reach the Supreme Court that then takes corrective action where the decision below departs from the correct standard. Thus in Acme Process Equipment Co. v. United States the government canceled a contract for the production of rifles, after the contractor had prepared for production at considerable expense, because the contractor violated the Anti–Kickback Act. The court granted recovery on the grounds that cancellation of contracts was not one of the sanctions provided in the Anti–Kickback Act. The Supreme Court reversed because a contract should not be enforced when enforcement would vitiate the purpose of a statute.

The former Court of Claims approach may be contrasted with state courts where it is generally held that a municipality is not estopped to deny the invalidity of a contract let without complying with competitive bidding requirements. Most state courts do not appear to permit recovery in such circumstances because it results in the payment of taxpayer funds for a procurement that was not made in the manner prescribed by the legislature. In S.T. Grand, Inc. v. New York, the Court of Appeals of New York stated:

> Turning to the question of remedy, the rule is that where work is done pursuant to an illegal municipal contract, no recovery may be had by the vendor, either on the contract or in quantum meruit. We have also declared that the municipality can recover from the vendor all amounts paid under the illegal contract. The reason for this harsh rule, which works a complete forfeiture of the vendor's interest, is to deter violation of the bidding statutes.

It might well be asked, since the general law of contracts would deny recovery, what is the legal basis for recovery in contracts with the Federal government that violate its statutes regarding competition.

Federal courts no longer look to the Restatement (Second) of the Law for this purpose because, unlike the original Restatements, the Restatement (Second) does not attempt to set forth the general law of contracts in the United States, but, in general, it sets forth as "Black Letter Law" the opinion of what the Reporter of the particular Restatements and the American Law Institute believe that law ought to be. Examples might be given where no recovery may be had when a contract is declared to be invalid for illegality. Other examples would indicate an objective evaluation of the benefits received by the government, and provide that in no event would there be recovery as an illegal contract (palpable or otherwise), of amounts in excess of the reasonable value of the benefits received by the government.

C. NECESSITY OF DETERMINATIONS
AND FINDINGS

§ 1.31 In General

The regulations state that for certain contract actions, a Determination and Findings (called "D & F") is required. These consist of written approval by an authorized official that is required by statute or regulation. The "determination" is a conclusion or decision supported by the "findings." The findings are statements of fact or rationale essential to support the determination and it covers each requirement of the statute or regulation. These approvals may also be granted for classes of contract actions for the same or related supplies or services. Both individual and class D & F's may provide for a flexibility in their application, such as reasonable variations in estimated quantities or prices. If a D & F is superseded by another D & F, that action shall not render invalid any action already taken under the original D & F. Further, a modification of the D & F does not require cancellation of a solicitation where the D & F, as modified, supports the contract action.

CHAPTER 2

DEFINITIONS OF WORDS AND TERMS

§ 2.1 In General

The definition section of the Federal Acquisition Regulation (FAR) sets forth the meanings of terms that are used throughout the regulation; this meaning prevails unless a different definition appears elsewhere or the context "clearly requires a different meaning." Two of these definitions ("Head of Agency," and "Contracting Office") are included in a "Definitions Clause" to be included in all significant solicitations in contracts. More definitions are being found to be commonly used in the regulation. Hence, in July 1996 definitions pertaining to micro-purchases (Part 13), and simplified acquisition procedures (Part 13) were transferred to Part 2.

This approach by the drafters of the FAR is similar to that taken by the American Law Institute when drafting the Uniform Commercial Code (UCC), Article 1 of which contains 46 definitions generally used throughout the other eight articles in that Code. Further, just as the UCC contains many additional definitions in each of those eight articles, the FAR in its prescriptive parts as well as in its forms and clauses contains over 600 additional definitions peculiar to a part, subpart or clause.

Definitions in FAR Part 2 apply to the entire regulation unless specifically defined in another part, subpart, section, provision, or clause. Words or terms defined in a specific part, when used in one of those places have that meaning when used in that part, subpart, section, provision, or clause. Throughout the FAR, the word "shall" is repeated more than any other word. Although its definition normally has a "mandatory" meaning, a state court has held that it may, in proper cases, be construed as permissive only.

The overwhelming majority of terms appear in the particular parts of the Federal Acquisition Regulation (FAR); each one is set forth in Part 2, "Definitions," without indicating another Part. Some terms found elsewhere become among those set forth in Part 2. For example, the definitions of "bid sample" and "descriptive literature" were moved from FAR Part 14 to FAR 2.101 because the definitions apply to more than one FAR part (i.e., Parts 14 and 25).

"A 'definition,'" according to Aristotle, "is a phrase signifying a thing's essence." This essence is constituted of fundamental attributes that will depend upon the purpose for which a term is used. Thus, almost all the terms included in the FAR are limited to the purpose(s) for which the particular definition applies. Nevertheless, there are certain rules or tests which apply to definitions and it is of particular importance they be met in regulations issued by public bodies. Of course, the FAR is not all-inclusive and many of the terms utilized in several aspects of government procurement and by the courts and boards are not to be found in that regulation. "Keyes Encyclopedic Dictionary of Contract and Procurement Law" contains many contract terms and explains them with citations to decisions of the Courts and Boards. The Supreme Court has referred to dictionaries in more than 600 cases and in recent years, has come to rely on dictionaries to an unprecedented degree. However, the definitions appear to be generally internally consistent with both the prescriptive parts of the regulation as well as with the standard contract clauses. Nevertheless, care should be taken that a definition prescribed for one particular purpose is not inadvertently used for a different purpose without first conducting an appropriate functional analysis. This is particularly important in view of the fact that the FAR terms and concepts have become quite a significant standard of worldwide "legal English."

Significant changes in these initial definitions occur from time to time. For example, some occurred in 1995 when "signature" was modified to include electronic symbols, and where the regulators provided comprehensive definitions of a "commercial item" and "electronic commerce."

CHAPTER 3

IMPROPER BUSINESS PRACTICES AND PERSONAL CONFLICTS OF INTEREST

§ 3.1 Ethics In Contracting

(a) Standards of Conduct

In an attempt to assure that government business be conducted in a manner above reproach and with impartiality, certain statutes have been enacted and regulations promulgated thereunder. The current regulations state that "as a rule, no government employee may solicit or accept, directly or indirectly, any gratuity, gift, favor, entertainment, loan, or anything of monetary value from anyone who has or is seeking to obtain government business with the employee's agency ... ". The words "as a rule" themselves appear to denote that the words which follow are not necessarily to be taken literally, and the paragraph ends by specifying that "certain limited exceptions are authorized in agency regulations." This could be either an unfortunate loophole in the regulation or a method intentionally designed to emphasize the use of other parts of the regulation.

In 1995 the Supreme Court held unconstitutional Section 501(b) of the Ethics in Government Act, which prohibited Members of Congress and Federal employees from accepting honoraria. The portion of the FAR dealing with the acceptance of gratuities by government personnel ends by stating, "certain limited exceptions are authorized in agency regulations."

(b) Agency Regulations

A statute prohibits officers and employees from participating "personally and substantially" in particular matters in which they or organizations in which they serve or with which they are negotiating for prospective employment have a financial interest. Agencies are required to prescribe "Standards of Conduct." These agency standards contain agency-authorized exceptions and disciplinary measures for persons violating the standards of conduct.

The debarment of a contractor is action taken by an official to exclude a contractor from government contracting (see Chapter 9). Executive Order 12549 provides that Executive departments and agencies must also participate in a governmentwide system for non-procurement debarment and suspension; a person who is debarred or suspended shall be excluded from Federal financial and nonfinancial assistance and benefits under Federal programs and activities.

In 1998, the Supreme Court unanimously held that Federal agencies might sanction Federal employees for making false statements in investigations or misconduct. An agency is not barred by the Fifth Amendment's Due Process Clause or by the Civil Service Reform Act from taking action against an employee because he made false statements in response to an underlying charge of misconduct. Chief Justice Rehnquist wrote that Federal workers " 'cannot with impunity knowingly and willfully answer with a falsehood.' " Further, the Court held that there is no exception to liability under a statute 18 U.S.C.A. § 1001, which prohibits making any "false, fictitious, or fraudulent statement or representation."

(c) Ethical Considerations

The Office of Government Ethics was established by the same statute to provide, in consultation with the Office of Personnel Management, direction for executive branch policies relating to the prevention of conflict of interests on the part of the officers and employees of any executive agency.

Ethics has been defined as "the branch of philosophy that investigates morality and, in particular, the varieties of thinking by which human conduct is guided and may be appraised." Its special concern is with "the meaning and justification of utterances about the rightness and wrongness of actions, the virtue or vice of the motives which prompt them, the praiseworthiness or blameworthiness of the agents who perform them, and the goodness or badness of the consequences to which they give rise." Traditionally there has existed the problem of distinguishing values of various kinds. In law we are chiefly concerned with those types of responsibility that sanctions can influence. There is no statute of limitations on professional responsibility.

Significant strides were made in connection with lawyer ethics in the American Bar Association's Model Rules of Professional Conduct, adopted by the House of Delegates of the American Bar Association on August 2, 1983 (and amended in 2002). A number of these rules were cast in terms of imperatives using "shall" or "shall not" for lawyers in a manner similar to the FAR with respect to a contracting officer or his representative. Model Rule 1.11 states that a lawyer who has formerly served as a public officer or employee of the government:

> Shall not otherwise represent a client in connection with a matter in which the lawyer participated personally and substantially as a public officer or employee, unless the

appropriate government agency gives its informed consent, confirmed in writing, to the representation.

This Rule is designed to prevent lawyers from "exploiting public office for the advantage of a private client" and it specifically applies to lawyers who represent government agencies. Statutes and regulations may circumscribe the extent to which the government agency may give consent under this Rule. Hence, consent may not be given in violation of one statute that makes certain restrictions on a government officer or employee who is prohibited from representing a party on a particular matter in which he participated "personally and substantially". Such a matter typically involves a "proceeding affecting legal rights" or transactions "between identifiable parties" as distinguished from the formulation of general policy. The former employee is prohibited for two years from representing a party when the particular matter in question had been merely pending under his official responsibility.

Although a "communication solely for the purpose of furnishing scientific or technological information" to an agency is allowed, this statute prohibits a former senior level employee from representing any party before the department or agency in which he served for one year regardless of his prior involvement in the matter. There is no other overall Federal prohibition against contracts between the government and a former employee.

Until 1983, the Code of Professional Responsibility held that " ... [i]n the event that the client in a non-adjudicatory matter insists upon a course of conduct that is contrary to the judgment and advice of the lawyer but not prohibited by Disciplinary Rules, the lawyer may withdraw from the employment." In 1992 the American Bar Association modified the Model Rules to provide that in representing corporations, lawyers may not withdraw, even when the client is pursuing a course "clearly" in violation of the law, unless the action is "likely to result in substantial injury to the organization." ABA Model Rule 1.6 Comment states that "A lawyer ordinarily must decline or withdraw from representation if the client demands that the lawyer engage in conduct that is illegal or violates the Rules of Professional conduct or other law." Rule 1.6 specifies that his services "will be used by the client in materially furthering a course of criminal or fraudulent conduct, the lawyer must withdraw." Rule 8.3(a) directs attorneys "who know that another lawyer has committed a violation of the Rules of Professional Conduct that raises a substantial question as to that lawyer's honesty, trustworthiness, or fitness as a lawyer in other respects, shall inform the appropriate professional authority." Rule 8.4 lists "professional misconduct for a lawyer," including paragraph (e) which is to "state or imply an ability to influence improperly a government agency or official or to achieve results by means that violate the Rules of Professional Conduct or other law."

A similar unfortunate incident had occurred in 1974 when in voting that the lawyer's duty of confidentiality to the client was paramount, the ABA added "except when the information is protected as a confidence or secret." However, the privilege does not apply to government attorneys who ascertain criminal activity through contact with clients.

A law firm may not represent an adversary of a former client in litigation "substantially related" to prior representation, irrespective of conflict-of-interest safeguards established by the law firm. Similarly, a district court concluded that under Rule 1.11(a) of ABA Model Rules of Professional Conduct, former government lawyers were disqualified from representing a private client in a matter in which both of them participated while employed for the government.

During their employment by the government, certain personnel are required to disclose financial information under the Ethics in Government Act of 1978. Such disclosures are required to be made by all political appointees and all civil service employees of GS–16 and above (called the "supergrades"). Further, it has been held that merely receiving wrong advice from a government standards of conduct officer regarding such disclosures may form the basis of an entrapment by estoppel defense for that employee, even though the statute creates a strict liability offense. The Federal government is by far the largest single employer of attorneys in the world, and in certain instances must comply with state ethics rules.

(d) Procurement Integrity

Effective January 1, 1997, all of the procurement integrity certifications required by a previous statute are eliminated by a statute and implementing regulations.

The current regulations state "a former official of a Federal agency may not accept compensation from a contractor as an employee, officer, director, or consultant of the contractor within a period of one year after such official" so served in a procurement in which that contractor was selected for award of a contract in excess of $10,000,000. However, it adds that this shall not be construed to prohibit the former official from accepting compensation from any division or affiliate of a contractor that does not produce the same or similar products or services as the entity of the contractor that is responsible for the contract. With stated exceptions, source selection information may not be disclosed "to any person other than a person authorized, in accordance with applicable agency regulations or procedures, by the head of the agency or designee, or the contracting officer, to receive such information." Thus, contractor bid or proposal information and source selection information shall be protected from unauthorized disclosure. Individuals responsible for preparing material that may be source selection information "shall mark the cover page and each page that the individual believes contains source selection information with the legend Source Selection Information—See FAR 2.101 and 3.104."

However, nothing prohibits "the disclosure or receipt of information, not otherwise protected, relating to a Federal agency procurement after it has been canceled by the Federal agency, before contract award, unless the Federal agency plans to resume the procurement." Further, the regulation does not authorize the withholding of any information pursuant to a proper request "from the Congress, any committee or subcommittee thereof, a Federal agency, the Comptroller General, or an Inspector General of a Federal agency, except as otherwise authorized by law or regulation."

An agency official who must disqualify himself is required to promptly submit to the head of the contracting activity (HCA), a written notice of disqualification from further participation in the procurement. He remains disqualified until such time as the agency has authorized him to resume participation in the procurement. But such employee may not be reinstated to participate in a procurement matter affecting the financial interest of someone with whom he or she is seeking employment unless he or she receives a waiver. An official or former official of a Federal agency who does not know whether he or she is or would be precluded by subsection 27(d) of the Act from accepting compensation from a particular contractor may request advice from the appropriate agency ethics official prior to accepting such compensation.

Where the HCA has concluded that the prohibitions of section 27 of the Act have been violated, then he may direct the contracting office to cancel the procurement; disqualify an offeror; or take any other appropriate actions in the interests of the government. If a contract has been awarded, he may affect contractual remedies including referral of the matter to the agency suspension and debarment official.

§ 3.2   Contractor Gratuities to Government Personnel

Virtually all contracts must contain a clause providing for termination, by written notice, following a hearing where it is determined that a contractor or his representative made a gratuity to a government employee with the intent "to obtain a contract or favorable treatment under a contract." As a result, a contract obtained through bribery is void. Further, the government need not pay for work performed—even work ordered after the government learned of the bribery, since the contract cannot be ratified. However, under one Federal statute, the Supreme Court has held that:

> The government must prove a link between a thing of value conferred upon a Federal official and a specific "official act" for or because of which it was given. The government's contention that Section 201(c)(10)(A) is satisfied merely by a showing that respondent gave Secretary Espy a gratuity because of his official position does not fit comfortably with the statutory text.

The exceptions are solicitations and contracts for "personal services and those between military departments or defense agencies and foreign governments that do not obligate any funds appropriated to the Department of Defense." Each agency has its own published reporting and hearing procedures.

With respect to the requirement that the contractor intended by the gratuity to obtain a contract or favorable treatment under a contract, the regulation states parenthetically that "intent generally must be inferred." In addition to termination of a contractor's right to proceed following a determination that a violation has occurred, the government may also initiate debarment or suspension measures and "assess exemplary damages, if the contract uses money appropriated to the Department of Defense." There appears to be no logic for authorizing the assessment of exemplary damages where contracts use money appropriated to defense, without allowing the same for contracts using money appropriated to civilian agencies of the government.

In a case of first impression, an appellate court held that a contractor employee who monitored a contract for the government is a "public official" under a gratuity statute. The contractor was advised that this employee was to be the Air Force's "eyes and ears" on the contract. He suggested savings by changes in materials and in boxes provided that he received part of the savings. Thereafter, he was convicted of soliciting a gratuity as a public official. That conviction was affirmed, even though he had no authority to approve changes on the contract.

§ 3.3   Reports of Suspected Antitrust Violations

Prohibitions against officials benefiting by having an interest in a government contract or receiving gratuities, and clauses setting forth requirements for independent pricing, do not suffice to remedy the potential problems because other practices can also eliminate competition or restrain trade and lead to excessive prices. Such practices, which may warrant criminal, civil, or administrative action against the participants, include "follow-the-leader" pricing, where all vendors participating in the scheme submit bids but by agreement take turns being the low bidder. This may be coupled with a scheme for awarding subcontracts to losing bidders who take turns according to the size of the contract. Division of a market for this purpose may be based on the customer or geographic area involved. The result of such a division is that competing firms will not bid or will submit only complementary bids when a solicitation for bids is made by a customer or in an area not assigned to them. These are called "antitrust violations" which include "collusive price estimating systems," an agreement whereby "certain competitors bid low only for contracts let by certain agencies."

Government contracting personnel are an important potential source of investigative leads for antitrust enforcement. The regulation requires agencies to report to the Attorney General that "evidence of suspected antitrust law violations" of either sealed bids or competitively negotiated acquisitions. Agencies are also responsible for contractor debarment and suspension. Bidding information is available for possible use in the prosecution of anti-trust litigation, and bidding documents are often used in litigation regarding predatory pricing and restraint of trade. Under certain circumstances, the bid of a highway repair contractor above its total average cost was held not to violate Section 2 of the Sherman Act following a claim of predatory pricing. The U.S. Court of Appeals for the Sixth Circuit held that predatory pricing not only must be based on the seller's intent, but also must "accommodate the economic policies of the antitrust laws to promote efficiency, encourage vigorous competition and maximize consumer welfare." The bids were "above the total average costs," and the court found "as a matter of law, Sherman Act liability cannot be premised on alleged predatory pricing without some evidence that a defendant has charged prices below its total cost for the product sold." The dissent interpreted the majority decision to say, "in effect, that irrespective of any direct evidence of intent to predatorily price, if a defendant can prove objectively that his prices were above his average total costs, his conduct is per se legal." In another case, the U.S. District Court for the Northern District of Illinois held that, although a bidder on a construction project may be able to demonstrate that a competitor engaged in an unreasonable restraint of trade, based on award to a rival whose project specifications required use of its materials giving it an unfair advantage, state action immunity shielded the city from the bidder's argument based upon the Illinois Antitrust Act.

The Supreme Court has held that a parent company and its wholly owned subsidiary are incapable, as a matter of law, of conspiring to restrain trade in violation of the Sherman Act. The Court noted "a business enterprise should be free to structure itself in ways that serve efficiency of control, economy of operations, and other factors dictated by business judgment without increasing its exposure to antitrust liability."

§ 3.4 Contingent Fees for Soliciting

Procurement regulations prescribe procedures restricting contingent fee arrangements for soliciting or obtaining government contracts to those permitted by statutes. Under these statutes, a contractor's arrangements to pay contingent fees for soliciting, or obtaining government contracts are contrary to public policy because such arrangements may lead to attempted or actual exercise of improper influence. They require a warranty by the contractor against contingent fees in every negotiated contract. They also provide that, for breach or violation of the warranty by the contractor, the government may annul the contract without liability or deduct from the contract price, or otherwise recover, the full amount of the contingent fee. However, as an exception to the warranty, contingent fee arrangements are permitted between contractors and bona fide employees customary in the trade or bona fide agencies. The statutory requirements for negotiated contracts, as a matter of regulation, were extended to contracting by sealed bidding in excess of $100,000. The evaluation criteria of improper influence is intended to help contracting officers determine whether to "reject a bid or proposal" or, after award, to annul the contract or take on a debarment action.

§ 3.5   Other Improper Business Practices

(a) Buying–In

Buying-in is accomplished by submitting an offer below anticipated costs, expecting to either increase the contract amount after award (e.g., through unnecessary or excessively priced change orders), or to receive follow-on contracts or change orders on the original contract at artificially high prices to recover losses incurred on the buy-in contract. Contractors may legally bid or prepare to perform at less than cost because this may result from competitive bidding requirements. Hence, such a bid or proposal is neither per se illegal nor even unacceptable for award. However, the procuring agency must consider this fact when making a sometimes difficult determination of responsibility. Thus, the General Accounting Office (GAO) held that the Navy reasonably rejected an extremely low quote due to a suspected mistake even though the protester had not claimed to have made any mistake. The decision was based on responsibility of the quoter, as opposed to the acceptability of the quote. In that case, a quote was 300 percent lower than the government estimate and at least 300 percent lower than the other quotes received.

Further, if award is made, the contracting officer must preclude the contractor from making up his losses through requests for change orders or follow-on contracts. The practice may decrease competition or result in poor contract performance. The government can minimize the opportunity for buying-in by seeking a price commitment covering as much of the entire program concerned as is practical. This may be done by using multiyear contracting, (with a requirement in solicitation that a price be submitted only for the total multiyear quantity) or by using priced options for additional quantities that, together with the firm contract quantity, equal the program requirements. Further, if a successful offer has indicated an intent to absorb nonrecurring costs (such as preproduction engineering, special tooling, special plant rearrangement, training programs, initial rework or pilot runs), the contract should expressly provide that these costs will not be charged to the government in any future procurement.

(b) Subcontractor Kickbacks

The Anti–Kickback Act of 1986 was enacted to deter subcontractors from making payments to influence the award of subcontracts. The statute prohibits payments, by or on behalf of a subcontractor in any tier under any government negotiated contract, as an inducement to or acknowledgment of the award of a subcontract or order. Payment includes a fee, commission, compensation, gift, or gratuity to the prime contractor or any higher tier subcontractor or to any officer, partner, employee, or agent of the prime contractor or any higher tier subcontractor. It also prohibits the subcontractor from charging these payments to the prime contractor or higher tier subcontractor.

The government may recover these payments from the subcontractor by court action or by setoff of moneys otherwise due the subcontractor. This may be accomplished either by the government directly or by the prime contractor. Criminal penalties are imposed on any person who knowingly makes or receives these payments. Further, a prime contractor can be held civilly liable under the Racketeer Influenced and Corrupt Organizations Act (RICO) for an employee's fraudulent actions in extorting kickbacks and rebates from subcontractors. However, a whistleblower who claimed he was fired for refusing to participate in allegedly fraudulent company practices has been held to lack standing to sue his employer under the RICO.

A district court has held that a law firm playing a management role in concealing a client's kickback scheme of mail fraud may be held liable for participating in the enterprise's affairs through patterns of racketeering activity. The firm was held liable under Section 1962(c) of RICO. One circuit court of appeals has held that two related predicate acts were sufficient to constitute a "pattern" of racketeering activity under RICO. One appellate court has ruled that to the extent a subcontractor kickback did not violate a law, then the subcontractor could deduct first payments to the prime contractor from its income as an "ordinary" business expense because, for some reason, a Treasury regulation stated that a deduction for business expenses cannot be disallowed on public policy grounds. The Supreme Court has ruled that state courts have concurrent jurisdiction over civil RICO claims.

Several circuit courts of appeals have held that RICO, 18 U.S.C.A. § 1963, does not authorize the post-indictment, pre-trial restraint of substitute assets. However, the Fourth Circuit has held that Congress intended Section 1963 to be "liberally construed" and that "[l]iberal construction of Section 1963 requires reading its several subsections together, rather than in isolation, to achieve the congressional purpose of pretrial restraint." See also Section 3.11.

§ 3.6 Conflicts of Interest of Government Employees or Companies They Control

The government may contract with its employees or organizations owned or controlled by them. However, it can do so only if there is a most compelling reason to do so, "such as when the government's needs cannot reasonably be otherwise met." Because this is likely to be a rare case, the general policy prohibits a contracting officer from "knowingly making an award of a contract to a government employee or to a business concern or other organization owned, substantially owned, or controlled by one or more government employees." The purpose of this prohibition is not only to avoid any conflict of interest that might arise between the employees' interests and their governmental duties, but also "to avoid the appearance of favoritism or preferential treatment by the government toward its employees." However, it has been held that this regulation does not prohibit the award of a contract to a company whose owner left government employment between bid opening and award.

As regards government employees, they are covered by a statute that imposes a penalty upon them for participating, on behalf of the government, in matters in which they have a personal financial interest. The statute was enacted in 1962 in order to broaden the disqualification to embrace any participation on behalf of the government in a matter in which the employee has an outside financial interest, even though his participation does not involve the transaction of business.

The suggestion by a budget employee that a company furnish audio-visual equipment for two HEW educational programs (which resulted in contracts being awarded to the company) was held to be a violation where he actually participated in the purchase. Where an employee of the government who participated in the letting of a contract also arranged to receive a percentage of the profit under the contracts which he assisted in obtaining for the contractor, this was held to be a violation. The fact that members of an Advisory Board or their respective institutions were recipients of funded grants, in itself, was held not to have created a conflict of interest within the statute. The rationale was that in no way would the individuals involved have benefited financially by denying grant money to the plaintiff, unless it had been shown that their denial would have left more money for future grant proposals made by them. This latter possibility was deemed to have been too remote. However, the court noted that conflicts of interest in the grant review process could have arisen if a study section, or an Advisory Board member, had contributed to a decision as to whether to award himself or his institution a funding grant.

In one case, the contractor challenged the government's decision to disqualify it. The former Claims Court enjoined making an award to the second bidder. In an appeal to the Federal Circuit Court of Appeals, the court noted the duty of an agency not to reject a bid in an arbitrary and capricious manner. After his disqualification, he had the opportunity to be heard thereon. The court stated that the Ethics in Government Act is not "the exclusive means for dealing with all ethical problems." Further, the notification by the agency after its decision was held "sufficient to satisfy any due process requirements." Hence, the agency's "decision to disqualify because of an impropriety was not irrational, arbitrary or capricious" and the Claims Court's order was vacated. The court also held that the Small Business Administration (SBA) did "not require that the contracting officer should have to receive input from the SBA before disqualification." Thereafter, the regulation was changed to require agencies to both "cooperate" with and refer to the SBA for a certificate of competency before rejecting such a concern on the basis of nonresponsibility.

Because the contracting officer's decision to disqualify the low bidder was based upon reasonable grounds and satisfied due process requirements inherent in the disqualification, it properly focused on integrity of the bidding system.

Where performance has commenced, a government employee's violation of a conflict of interest statute will preclude a contractor from recovering for the contract's termination and permit the government to recover contract payments even though the employee has not been charged with its violation. The former Claims Court found a conflict of interest arising from a procurement official's return to private business to be too slight under certain factual situations; but, the General Accounting Office reported that the laws requiring former employees who pass through "the revolving door: to work for defense contractors to report such employment, are not being enforced."

§ 3.7 Conflicts With Former Government Employees

The subject of employment activities of a government employee after retirement or separation is beyond the scope of this treatise. Mention is made of some of the laws and regulations thereon because if these activities are found to be illegal, they may not only jeopardize retirement pay of such former employees and result in criminal sanctions, but they may also affect the validity of contracts that have been made.

The General Accounting Office concluded that a majority of former military officers and upper-level civilian employees of the Department of Defense (DoD) did not comply with the law that requires former DoD personnel to disclose their subsequent employment with defense contractors. The law requiring former DoD personnel to disclose their employment was repealed on February 10, 1996.

The Ethics in Government Act of 1978 ("the Act") established the Office of Government Ethics (OGE) to provide overall direction of executive branch policies related to preventing conflicts of interest on the part of officers and employees of any executive agency. Although originally a part of the Office of Personnel Management (OPM), OGE became a separate agency under the Office of Government Ethics Reauthorization Act of 1988. Sections 402 (a) and (b) of the Act, as amended, require the Director of OGE to provide and propose, in consultation with OPM and the Attorney General, rules and regulations to be promulgated by the President or OGE pertaining to conflicts of interest and ethics in the executive branch. In 1993, OGE promulgated the Standards of Ethical Conduct for Employees of the Executive Branch ("the Standards"). The Standards are applicable to all executive branch officers and employees, except that certain sections do not apply to enlisted members of the armed forces. Agencies are permitted to supplement the Standards only with the prior approval of OGE.

The Standards and Regulations Concerning Post Employment Conflicts of Interest promulgated by OGE bar certain acts by former government employees that may reasonably give the appearance of making unfair use of prior government employment and affiliations. However, neither the statute nor regulations are intended to "bar any former Government employee, regardless of rank, from employment with any private or public employer after Government service;" nor are they "intended to discourage the movement of skilled professionals in Government, to and from positions in industry, research institutions, law and accounting firms, universities and other major sources of expertise." Although criminal enforcement of statutory conflict of interest restrictions remains the exclusive responsibility of the Attorney General, statutory or regulatory violations may also lead to disciplinary or other administrative action, either initiated by the employing agency or recommended by the Director of the Office of Government Ethics.

There is a prohibition against a former government employee who, after terminating government employment, knowingly acts as an agent or attorney for, any other person with the intent to influence the United States, in connection with any particular government matter in which such employee participated personally and substantially as a government employee. However, communications that do not include an "intent to influence" are not prohibited. Thus, a question by an attorney as to the status of a particular matter, a request for publicly available documents, or a communication by a former employee, not in connection with an adversary proceeding, imparting purely factual information is not prohibited.

Once a conflict exists, the government is entitled to cancel a contract as tainted. The government may also recover payments made to former contractor employees as "severance" payments where it is concluded that the payments were intended to be compensation for Federal employment.

The former Claims Court held that the possibility that the source selection board chairman on a $1 billion Department of Energy procurement had a conflict of interest warranted a preliminary injunction against the award. A company need not make an actual offer of employment for the conflict of interest law to apply. A violation was held to have occurred where a reserve officer participated in a foreign sales project for the Air Force by negotiating future employment with a prospective contractor for that project, and by attending a program status conference on behalf of the contractor after leaving government service.

A conflict was found where a subcontractor employed a former government employee during the early development of the work statement but such employment ended before the Request for Proposals (RFP) was issued. The employment of a former government employee who was familiar with the type of work required on a contract for which proposals were being submitted was upheld where he was not privy to the contents of proposals or any other inside information and the procurement was initiated seven months after his retirement from Federal service.

§ 3.8 Contractor Responsibility to Avoid Improper Business Practices

A subpart to the DoD FAR Supplement establishes a policy of promoting contractor programs to improve compliance with laws, regulations, and contracts. It provides that contractors should have a system of management controls that includes: (1) a written code of business ethics and conduct and an ethics training program for all employees; (2) periodic reviews of company business practices, procedures, policies, and internal controls for compliance with standards of conduct and the special requirements of Government contracting; (3) a mechanism, such as a hotline, by which employees may report suspected instances of improper conduct, and instructions that encourage employees to make such reports; (4) internal and/or external audits, as appropriate; (5) disciplinary action for improper conduct; (6) timely reporting to appropriate Government officials of any suspected or possible violation of law in connection with Government contracts or any other irregularities in connection with such contracts; and (7) full cooperation with any Government agencies responsible for either investigation or corrective actions. In addition, contractors awarded a DoD contract of $5 million or more are generally required to display a DoD Hotline Poster prepared by the DoD Office of the Inspector General. In 2003, after ethical lapses were made by the Boeing Company (which cost at least $1 billion worth of Air Force rocket business) more than 70,000 Boeing Co. employees stopped working and began to file into auditoriums and conference rooms for four hours of training on corporate ethics.

§ 3.9 Voiding and Rescinding Contracts

A subpart was added to the regulation in order to implement a statute and Executive Order which prescribes procedures for exercising discretionary authority to declare void and rescind contracts in relation to which there has been "a final conviction for bribery, conflict of interest, disclosure or receipt of contractor bid or proposal information or source selection information in exchange for a thing of value or to give anyone a competitive advantage in the award of a Federal agency procurement contract, or similar misconduct." Administrative remedies may apply, authorizing the voiding or rescission of such contracts and recommending the initiation of suspension or debarment proceedings. See Chapter 9.

"Final conviction" includes a plea of nolo contendere, for which sentence has been imposed. Such final convictions must be reported to the agency head or his designee, who may issue a notice of the proposed action to declare void and rescind the contract by certified mail. The contractor then has 30 days to submit pertinent information and an opportunity to be heard if "no inquiry shall be made regarding the validity of the conviction." If a decision is made to declare void and rescind the contract, it must reflect consideration of the fair value of any tangible benefits received and retained by the agency and state the amount due and the property to be returned to the agency. This decision is not a claim within the meaning of the Contract Disputes Act of 1978 (CDA).

It is a crime for a government employee to accept anything of value from anyone outside the government who has, or could have, business with the government. The statute may be violated even where the official act has long ago been completed or such action was not possible to take, if the official act requested or connected with it would have been done with or without the offer.

The Supreme Court has held that to establish a violation of the Federal gratuity statute, the United States must prove a link between the gratuity and a specific "official act" for or because of which it was given. The Court reasoned, the gratuity statute's "insistence upon an 'official act,' carefully defined, seems pregnant with the requirement that some particular official act be identified and proved."

§ 3.10 Limits on Payment to Influence Federal Transactions

A Federal statute prohibits a recipient of a Federal contract, grant, loan, or cooperative agreement from using appropriated funds to pay any person for attempting to influence an employee of an agency or Congress in connection with the award or notification of any such agreement. Offerors are required to make a certification and disclosure thereon where the contract exceeds $100,000. However, the Secretary of Defense may determine that a transaction is exempt in the national interest. Agencies must impose and collect penalties.

§ 3.11   Fraud, Whistleblowers, and the False Claims Act

The Federal Acquisition Streamlining Act of 1994 has been implemented by regulations in a FAR Subpart. Effective September 19, 1995, FAR prohibits government contractors from discharging, demoting, or otherwise discriminating against an employee as "a reprisal for disclosing information to a Member of Congress, or an authorized official of an agency or of the Department of Justice, relating to a substantial violation of law related to a contract (including the competition for or negotiation of a contract)." Upon receipt of a complaint, the Inspector General must conduct an inquiry. The complainant and contractor shall be afforded the opportunity to submit a written response to the report of findings within 30 days to the head of the agency or designee. If the head of the agency or designee determines that a contractor has subjected one of its employees to a reprisal, he may order the contractor to reinstate the person to the position that the person held before the reprisal, together with compensation (including back pay). In addition, he may order the contractor to pay the complainant an amount equal to the aggregate amount of all costs and expenses (including attorneys' fees and expert witnesses' fees) that were reasonably incurred by the complainant in connection with bringing the complaint regarding the reprisal.

Upon a contractor's failure to comply with an order, he must request the Department of Justice to file an action for enforcement of such order in the United States district court. The court may grant appropriate relief, including injunctive relief and compensatory and exemplary damages. However, any person adversely affected by an order may obtain review of the order's conformance with the law in the United States Court of Appeals.

If the contractor is unable to support any part of the claim and there is evidence that the inability is attributable to misrepresentation of fact or to fraud on the part of the contractor, the matter must be referred to the agency official responsible for investigating fraud. In the Defense Department, it might result in a subpoena issued by that department's Inspector General (IG) for the contractor's internal audit records. Unlike the Comptroller General, the IG's authority to subpoena information is not subject to a requirement that the records be "directly pertinent" to a contract. An order to comply with such a subpoena has been upheld even when it was issued at the request of the Defense Contract Audit Agency (DCAA), which is subject to the supervision and control of the IG. The doctoring of records has a long history; it did not begin with, but was exemplified by, man's first trip around the world in the early 16th Century:

> Only Magellan's iron courage against the elements and his deft mastery of men kept him going. He had suffered another unpleasant surprise, in addition to the mutiny. At Port San Julian, the last stop on the Patagonian coast before Cape Virgins, when they unloaded the ships to prepare for careening, he received a shock. The suppliers

back in Seville had cheated him by actually loading provisions not for the fully specified year and a half but for only six months, and then had falsified the records.

Fraud has not abated in government contracts since the 16th century. The principal difference has been in the size of the deceptions that have been expended and the monetary penalties to be paid by some of the largest contractors in the 1990's as well as the rewards payable to the whistleblowers. Procurement involves taxpayer funds and public trust. The Transparency International's 2003 Corruptions Perceptions Index (CPI) ranked the U.S. 18th out of the 133 nations (four of the much smaller four Nordic countries were among the top ten).

Contractor employees who report contract fraud are protected from retaliation. This is true even if neither the employee nor the government has filed formal charges under the False Claims Act (FCA). However, to state a viable claim, the whistleblower must have engaged in some act in furtherance of a FCA action filed or to be filed, and his or her employer must have retaliated against the whistleblower because he or she engaged in that protected activity. Where a contractor is making a claim under the Contract Disputes Act, he becomes liable to the government for an amount equal to the unsupported parts of the claim and all costs to the government attributable to the cost of reviewing such parts of his claim.

While claims of fraud fall under the Contract Disputes Act's "fraud exception," the fact of an indictment of a subcontractor for false claims regarding the handling of government overpayments does not bring claims against the primes within the fraud exception. This may also be separate from any rights possessed by the government under the False Claims Act, and the Forfeiture Statute. Boards of contract appeal have no jurisdiction over appeals from fraud penalty assessments under the Contract Disputes Act. Fraud as a defense to payment must be raised by the government prior to a decision by a board of contract appeals unless it can be shown that the board's findings of fact were erroneous.

A contractor that is a corporation may be held criminally liable for actions of employees at various levels where they were acting within the scope of their actual or apparent authority for the benefit of the corporation. Furthermore, such liability exists even where the acts were against corporate instructions. A contractor may also be held liable under the False Claims Act for its employee's conduct, even if senior executives of the company had no knowledge of the wrongdoing. Prosecution for fraud is typically based upon one or more criminal statutes, such as the one governing false statements, false claims, conspiracy, mail fraud, and anti-kickback statutes.

A False Claims Act was originally enacted in 1863 as a reaction to the corruption occurring in connection with the procurement of war material by the Union (In 2003, the Supreme Court ruled that local government entities (unlike states) are "persons" subject to liability under the federal civil False Claims Act relying upon the historical interpretation of the term "persons" at the time the FCA was passed in 1863). The current Act provides for qui tam actions granting citizens the power to sue in the name of the United States. Hence, it is sometimes called the "Whistle-blower statute."

Effective October 17, 1986, substantial amendments to the False Claims Act provide that an action may be brought against members of the Armed Forces as well as civilian employees. It also invigorated its qui tam provisions.

Among other things, the 1986 amendments: (1) replaced the "government knowledge" jurisdictional bar with a more relaxed "public disclosure" bar; (2) reduced the *scienter* requirement; (3) extended the statute of limitations; (4) lowered the burden of proof; (5) increased the statutory penalties; (6) increased the bounty available to qui tam Realtors; and (7) permitted actions to be brought against members of the Armed Forces as well as civilian employees.

In 1997, the United States Supreme Court unanimously held that the 1986 amendments to the False Claims Act do not apply retroactively to conduct occurring before their effective date. On May 22, 2000, the Supreme Court held that states and state agencies are not "persons" subject to qui tam liability under the False Claims Act. Having concluded that Congress did not intend to subject States and State agencies to qui tam liability, the Supreme Court expressly left open whether qui tam actions against a state violate the Eleventh Amendment. In that case, the Supreme Court also concluded that qui tam Realtors have standing under Article III—reasoning that they meet the " 'irreducible constitutional minimum' " of standing because they "su[e] as *partial* assignee[s] of the United States" and, therefore, sue to "remedy an injury in fact suffered by the United States"—but expressly left open "the question whether qui tam suits violate Article II, in particular the Appointments Clause of § 2 and the 'Take Care' Clause of § 3." On May 25, 2001, the U.S. Court of Appeals for the Fifth Circuit, sitting en banc, reversed a district court opinion—originally affirmed by a Fifth Circuit panel—which held the qui tam provisions of the False Claims Act were unconstitutional, holding that the qui tam provisions do not violate either the Appointments or Take Care clauses of the Constitution.

The penalties for civil false claims of "not less than $5,000 and not more than $10,000" may be trebled. However, consequential damages cannot be recovered. In 1998, the U.S. Court of Appeals for the Federal Circuit held that the reasonable cost of remedying the defects is an acceptable measure of the government's damages, provided that cost is not "clearly disproportionate" to the probable loss to the government. However, the government's own expert found no damage to the structural integrity of the channel as a result of the deficiency. Hence, the court held that the contractor was only liable for a $10,000 statutory penalty for falsely certifying that it had done the required testing and not liable for damages with regard to the deficient testing. Although the statute of limitations on false claims suits is six years, the government may bring an action within 6 years of when the false claim is submitted, or within 3 years of when the government reasonably should have known of the violation, whichever occurs last, provided that suit is brought within 10 years after the date of the violation. However, in 1998 the U.S. Court of Federal Claims held that where the government sues for damages after paying a false claim, the statute of limitations begins to run on the date of final payment, not on the date the contractor submitted the claim.

The law provides that a defendant can be found liable if conduct includes "deliberate ignorance of the truth" and "no proof of specific intent to defraud is required." The First Circuit Court of Appeals has held that "a corporation could be held liable under the False Claims Act for the fraud of an agent who acts with apparent authority even if the corporation received no benefit from the agent's fraud."

The False Claims Act precludes a qui tam Realtor from bringing an action based on "publicly disclosed" allegations or transactions, unless the Realtor qualifies as the "original source" of the information on which the allegations are based. An "original source" is defined by the False Claims Act to mean "an individual who has direct and independent knowledge of the information on which the allegations are based and has voluntarily provided the information to the Government before filing an action under this section which is based on the information." It suffices the whistle-blower to have direct and independent knowledge of the information underlying or supporting the fraud allegations in order to qualify as an "original source." Nevertheless, it has been held that a government employee who is partici-pating in an ongoing government fraud investigation is not a "person" under the False Claims Act. As the Chief Judge of a Circuit Court stated:

At least with respect to an ongoing government investiga-tion, a Federal employee who is involved in the investiga-tion pursuant to employment duties is the government.

The National Whistleblower Center, a non-profit, tax exempt organization in Washington D.C., was created in 1988 "to support precedent setting litigation on behalf of employee whistleblowers, provide legal advice and referrals for counsel to whistleblowers nationwide, and educate the public about the rights of employees to make disclosures regarding nuclear safety, corporate or government miscon-duct, environmental protection or health and safety viola-tions." Pursuant to the False Claims Act's "first-to-file" limitation, a whistleblower's lawsuit under the FCA will be dismissed when the court finds other lawsuits involving substantially the same claims had been filed earlier by other whistleblowers.

A Realtor's qui tam suit is not barred by a concurrent government action under the Service Contract Act. Howev-er, it should be recalled that the government might veto a voluntary settlement in a qui tam suit even if it declined to intervene. Nevertheless, a Federal district court ruled that the government lacks an "absolute right" to block a settlement and force the parties to continue litigating.

(a) Some Defenses

There are a number of defenses against a qui tam action. For example, a court could direct a verdict in favor of the contractor, as it did in a qui tam case charging Hughes Helicopter Co.—now part of McDonnell Douglas—with manufacturing defective helicopter avionics and communications systems and conducting inadequate testing of these systems. Further, where the lawsuit can be shown to be "clearly frivolous," a qui tam plaintiff can be ordered to reimburse the defendant contractor for attorney fees.

While the 1986 amendments unquestionably invigorated qui tam actions, they also provided fertile ground for pretrial motions to dismiss. In addition, these amendments provided that qui tam complaints must be filed *in camera* and remain under seal for at least 60 days. The complaint, and substantially material evidence possessed by the plaintiffs, must be disclosed to the government. This gives the government an adequate opportunity to evaluate the lawsuit, as well as to prevent defendants from having to answer complaints without knowing whether the government or only the Realtors would pursue the litigation. In one case a former General Electric Co. employee named Pilon alleged that GE had submitted false claims in connection with the production and delivery of radar systems and services that were supplied to the Egyptian government. However, he failed to both file his complaint under seal and provide the government with a copy of all relevant documentation. The court held that the claim must be dismissed with prejudice because, as the court stated, "[t]he Pilons' failure to comply with the service and filing requirements incurably frustrated all of these interests." Nevertheless, contrary arguments have been made by another circuit court.

Where the government has not intervened in a qui tam case, the Realtor cannot prevent the government from communicating with the defendant contractor. Further, the release by a former employee of a qui tam claim prior to the filing of an action is not enforceable where it was entered into without the knowledge and consent of the United States. However, where the Federal government had investigated the allegations prior to the settlement, a qui tam plaintiff's settlement and release in a state court wrongful termination case precludes a subsequent qui tam suit based on the same allegations. When the Justice Department has already intervened and settled a qui tam suit with a contractor, the qui tam Realtor is barred from pursuing any further claims. The court stated that after the government recovers the money it paid on a false invoice, "there is no more to be recovered by anyone." Further, even after interviewing, the government may request the court to dismiss a qui tam case over the whistleblower's objections. The government recovered $1.39 billion in actions filed by qui tam plaintiffs following the 1996 amendments to the False Claims Act. Of that amount, all but $26 million was recovered in cases where the government chose to intervene.

A qui tam plaintiff must both have direct and independent knowledge of alleged fraud, and also have "had a hand" in disclosing allegations of fraud in order to be considered an original source who can bring the action. Where Federal investigators' disclosure of fraud allegations to "innocent employees" of a suspect company during a search of company premises constituted a "public disclosure" sufficient to bar a qui tam action filed under the False Claims Act. However, an appellate court has held that a qui tam suit based in part on disclosed information, such as discovery material filed with court, that by itself exposes neither the existence of fraud nor the nature of a fraudulent transaction, does not fall within False Claims Act's jurisdictional bar for suits "based upon public disclosure of allegations or transactions." The court stated:

> [T]he courthouse doors do not swing shut merely because innocuous information necessary though not sufficient to plaintiff's suit has already been made public.

Another court has held that a Realtor's status as auditor in a Federal agency's inspector general office when he obtained information suggesting fraud against Federal government does not bar the Realtor's qui tam suit under the False Claims Act based on such information. However, the majority of a panel of the Tenth Circuit Court of Appeals upheld the dismissal of a qui tam suit brought by a former Department of Energy Office of the Inspector General audit supervisor. The panel ruled that the sending of a DOE audit report to Oregon state officials constituted a public disclosure under the False Claims Act because the state was not a party to the contract and the auditor's suit was based upon the work of others. An action is barred where the alleged fraud has been publicly disclosed even though the qui tam plaintiff was unaware of the disclosure.

Federal auditors cannot participate in a whistleblower suit where there has been a public disclosure of information because their duty obligates them to reveal the fraud and, therefore, they cannot meet the "voluntarily" provided criteria necessary to qualify as an original source. Further, the bar to any FCA action after public disclosure applies even though the qui tam plaintiff was unaware of the disclosure. A circuit court of appeals has held that "public disclosure" prohibits only those suits where there has been public disclosure by the *Federal government.*

A qui tam plaintiff's failure to allege that a contractor's false representation was made "knowingly" will result in a failure to state a claim under the FCA. It has also been held that a contractor who allegedly intentionally withheld certain documents and exercised an option of submitting subpoenaed documents to the Justice Department instead of the grand jury cannot be indicted under the False Statements Act. Where a contractor substantially performed and was entitled to termination costs, this was held to collaterally estop the government from maintaining an FCA action against the contractor.

An attorney who learned of alleged fraud against the government from a client who was being investigated is barred by statute from bringing a qui tam action based upon "public disclosure" of alleged wrongdoing. Further, a contractor that is the target of a qui tam action may not assert counterclaims against the qui tam plaintiffs. The court stated that "to permit a defendant to pursue a counterclaim for breach of contract and breach of loyalty for the failure to first raise its concerns with the alleged wrongdoer, would allow wrongdoers to retaliate against whistleblowers, and is contrary to legislative intent." Further, it has been held that the tolling provision of the False Claims Act applies to qui tam plaintiffs as well as to the government.

New qui tam provisions were added in order to authorize any "person" to bring a civil action under the False Claims Act "for the person and for the United States. The action is brought in the name of the United States." The qui tam plaintiff (or "Realtor") files under seal a civil complaint and serves on the government a "written disclosure of substantially all material evidence and information the person possesses." The government has 60 days in which to review the complaint and the written disclosure and decide whether to intervene in the action. An appellate court has held that a qui tam plaintiff has 60 days to file an appeal in a False Claims Act suit even if the government has not intervened. The defendant is not served until the Department of Justice completes its review and the complaint is unsealed. Upon intervention by the Department of Justice, it bears "primary responsibility" for prosecuting the action. But the Realtor remains a full participant in the litigation unless the court finds this would interfere with the government's participation or would be "repetitious, irrelevant, or for the purpose of harassment." Nevertheless, the Justice Department is authorized to dismiss or settle the suit, provided that the court finds the disposition is "fair, adequate, and reasonable under all the circumstances." For his part, the employee (or "whistleblower") is protected against adverse personnel action, being entitled to "all relief necessary to make the employee whole." A qui tam lawsuit survives the Realtor's death.

There is no need for a qui tam plaintiff to establish that the government suffered monetary damages for a false claim to be actionable. Further, depending on its determination as to the extent of the Realtor's contribution to the case, the court may award a Realtor from 15 to 30 percent of the proceeds, plus reasonable attorney's fees and costs. Very large payments have been made. The statute requires the government to notify the Realtor in advance of its decision to intervene. Where the government fails to do so and settles the case, the Realtor has no opportunity to object to the settlement agreement. Accordingly, the qui tam Realtor is entitled to share in the proceeds from the government's undisclosed negotiation of the settlement. In 2002, a circuit court of appeals stated:

> While we acknowledge that the treble damage provision of the civil FCA produces a harsher result than mere recovery of the expended funds, we note that these damages and other remedies are authorized by Congress.

The burden of proof is "a preponderance of the evidence" applicable to civil lawsuits. A *nolo contendere* plea in a criminal fraud case has a collateral estoppel effect in a subsequent civil fraud action. Jurisdiction and venue in false claims suits are proper in any Federal district in which any defendant resides, transacts business, is doing business, or can be found; or where false claims are made. Hence, prosecutors can generally file one action against all defendants in the district court within the venue of any single defendant. The Attorney General may issue a Civil Investigative Demand (CID) before any judicial proceeding begins or a complaint filed requiring production of documents, answers to interrogatories, or oral testimony.

A "Whistleblower" provision protects both Realtors and any other employee who assists in furthering an action under the section against job retaliation by the employer. It gives the employee the right to relief in order to make the employee whole, including reinstatement, double any back pay, special damages, and reasonable attorneys' fees. The employee is given a cause of action in a U.S. District Court as well as a share in the amount recovered.

In 1992 a Federal court awarded $13.5 million to the man who blew the whistle on an Israeli bribery scheme involving General Electric Co. It was the largest such award ever. General Electric pleaded guilty to criminal and civil charges in connection with the scheme to bilk the U.S. government out of nearly $42 million from the F–110 and maintenance contracts with Israel. GE paid the government $59.5 million to settle civil charges and $9.5 million to settle criminal charges. Under the False Claims Act, Walsh, a former GE manager, was entitled to up 25 percent of the total amount collected by the government through the civil charges. The government however, tried to reduce the amount Walsh was to get, charging that he knew of the bribery scheme for years before he filed suit. In rebuking the Justice Department, the court stated:

> This is not the first case where this court has noted the antagonism of the Justice Department to a whistleblower. The reason continues to be unknown but the attitude is clear. Mr. Walsh performed a service to the United States.

A whistleblower alleged that a Department of Energy management and operating contractor misrepresented the need for and costs of subcontracting a portion of the work in order to obtain approval for the subcontract. In 1999, the U.S. Court of Appeals for the Fourth Circuit upheld his suit holding that the false statements led the government to pay a higher price for the work than had the contractor performed it.

The government was held entitled to a $1.75 million share of a $2.5 million negotiated settlement agreement with defense contractor TRW Inc., even though it failed to intervene. The plaintiff and his attorneys received $750,-000—30 percent of the total recovery, because that share was the statutory maximum available under the 1986 False Claims Act Amendments when the Department of Justice does not intervene and control a qui tam case.

(b) Duties of Attorneys—Fees

It is interesting to note that discharged lawyers who were employees of the company on which they blow the whistle may not have a right based upon retaliatory discharge because they are obligated to act in the public interest by the rules of professional conduct. The dissent argued that, regardless of their professional responsibilities, lawyers need the same encouragement as anyone else to come forward, stating:

> As reluctant as I am to concede it, the fact is that this court must take whatever steps it can, within the bounds of the law, to give lawyers incentives to abide by their ethical obligations, beyond the satisfaction inherent in their doing so.

> We cannot continue to delude ourselves and the people of the state of Illinois that attorneys' ethical duties, alone, are always sufficient to guarantee that lawyers will "do the right thing."

In 1993, the New York Court of Appeals held that lawyers who follow the requirements of the professional disciplinary rules and report dishonest colleagues cannot be fired in retaliation. It stated that the right of employers to fire employees at will for nondiscriminatory reasons did not apply to lawyers who had a duty to report wrongdoing. "Associates are, to be sure, employees of the firm but they remain independent officers of the court, responsible in a broader public sense for their professional obligations." The American Bar Association (ABA) registers the names of lawyers who have been censured. It is sad to note that not all state courts and state bar associations (which are responsible for fining or suspending or disbarring lawyers) notify the American Bar Association. If the government intervenes, where the Realtor is dismissed, the defendant is not liable to pay the Realtor's attorney fees.

The 1993 report of The American Law Institute's restatement of the law governing lawyers contains the following provisions:

§ 132.   The attorney-client privilege does not apply to a communication occurring when a client consults a lawyer for the purpose of obtaining assistance in engaging in conduct or aiding a third person in engaging in conduct if the client, at the time of the communication, knows or reasonably should know that the conduct is a crime or fraud.

§ 34.   As between client and lawyer, a lawyer retains the authority, which may not be overridden by an agreement or an instruction from the client:

(1) to refuse to perform, counsel or assist future or ongoing acts that the lawyer reasonably believes to be unlawful;

No further details are given. In fact, excerpts from § 192, Comment b, states: that *"The definition and precise applicability of such substantive liability standards are beyond the scope of this Restatement."* The law is restated *if* and *as it exists* in most court opinions. The Institute often claims it is "restating the general law" when in fact it is setting forth the views of the restaters themselves, something that the originators of the Restatement of the Law promised that they would not do. A comment on Rule 1.6, Confidentiality of Information, ABA Model Rules of Professional Conduct (2003 Edition), states:

If the lawyer's services will be used by the client in materially furthering a course of criminal or fraudulent conduct, the lawyer <u>must withdraw</u>. (emphasis added)

Should the defendant corporation prevail in a fraud-tort action due to negligence in the investigation, attorneys' fees for defending such action are barred by the Federal Tort Claims Act's discretionary exception. It has also been held that government attorneys investigating a whistleblower's claims are barred from talking to the contractor's employees.

(c) Retaliation, Bankruptcy Stays, Primary Jurisdiction and Counterclaims

A portion of the False Claims Act provides a right to sue for employees who are discharged or otherwise discriminated against for actions taken "in furtherance of an action under this section." This has been held to refer to a qui tam action brought under another section of the Act. That is, "it does not dispense with the requirement that the wrongful termination action must be in furtherance of or with reference to an action actually filed under § 3730(b)." Hence, a whistleblower cannot rely upon the False Claims Act in connection with his claim against a contractor for wrongful termination (for allegedly retaliating against him for disclosing evidence of potential fraud) unless he first files a qui tam lawsuit under the Act.

These provisions, designed to protect whistleblowers against retaliation, apply only to employees. Hence, they do not extend to independent contractors. Further, a whistleblower who was the victim of retaliation by a Department of Energy contractor could not seek court relief to enforce a judgment under the department's Contractor Employee Protection Program.

The entitlement of the plaintiff in a qui tam action is not barred by the Bankruptcy Code's automatic stay provision. This is because "civil actions by the government to enforce the FCA serve to inflict the 'sting of punishment' on wrongdoers and, more importantly, deter fraud against the government, which Congress has recognized as a severe, pervasive, and expanding national problem." Another court stated that when a governmental proceeding will not conflict with the bankruptcy court's control of the property of the debtor and will not otherwise create a pecuniary advantage for the government, the proceeding will be excepted from the automatic stay provision of the Bankruptcy Code. It has been held that where the government suffered no economic loss, it may not recover from a law firm that submitted inflated bills for research expenses to a bankruptcy court under the False Claims Act.

However, the involuntary dismissal of the qui tam Realtors' adversary proceeding challenging the dischargeability of the qui tam award in bankruptcy is res judicata against the government, who is in privity with the Realtor. Another district court held that, even though the government has not yet decided whether to intervene, a whistleblower action against a defendant in bankruptcy can proceed.

The doctrine of primary jurisdiction is a court set of rules concerning judicial and administrative tribunals and preventing judicial interference with the administrative process. It is subject to possible application when these tribunals have concurrent jurisdiction over portions of a case or involving the same or similar matters. A court of appeals in a split decision refused to apply one aspect of the doctrine of primary jurisdiction. There the Defense Contract Audit Agency (DCAA) found that certain costs on one contract (the DIVAD contract also called Sergeant York) had been mischarged to accounts on other government contracts. After a grand jury returned an indictment against one of its divisions, General Dynamics filed a notice of appeal with the ASBCA. The Board held that it did not have jurisdiction over cases involving fraud but later issued an order directing the contracting officer to issue decisions on related claims. General Dynamics then requested, and a Federal district court granted, a motion staying the criminal proceedings and referring ten questions concerning contract issues in the case to the Board. He did this because the complex nature of the DIVAD contract produced issues requiring specialized expertise outside the conventional experience of judges. This ruling was appealed even though the Board rejected the referral. In reviewing the district court, the Ninth Circuit Court of Appeals distinguished boards of contract appeals from regulatory bodies as follows:

The Board [ASBCA] is not involved in the creation of regulations or in the drafting of military contracts and nothing in the CDA implies congressional intent to delegate policy-making or policy-implementing power to the Board. Thus, it has little in common with such bodies as the Interstate Commerce Commission and the Securities and Exchange Commission, which have quasi-legislative powers and are actively involved in the administration of regulatory statutes.

Where a contracting officer has some evidence of possible fraud on the part of the contractor, he must refer the matter to the agency official responsible for investigating fraud. He may withhold payment, initiate suspension or debarment proceedings, cancel the contract, and refer the matter to the Department of Justice. The government's knowledge of the facts underlying an alleged false claim together with lack of any injury to the government precludes an action under the False Claims Act. But, matters that are clearly severable from those claims or portions of claims incurred with the fraud may be considered by a contracting officer or board of contract appeal. Furthermore, a most important aspect of the doctrine of primary jurisdiction may continue to be applied. That is, in lieu of dismissing a case for want of jurisdiction, a board in its discretion may suspend the proceedings pending resolution of the fraud issues.

It has been held that qui tam defendants may bring counterclaims for "independent damages" against whistleblowers who file qui tam lawsuits because unlike counterclaims seeking indemnification or contribution, the counterclaims are not dependent on the qui tam defendant's liability. If the defendant is found liable, the counterclaims can be dismissed. On the other hand, if the defendant is found not liable, the counterclaims can be addressed on their merits.

As regards government counterclaims filed more than three years after the government learned of the contractor's misleading vouchers, but less than six years after the government made final payment under the vouchers, the U.S. Court of Federal Claims stated:

Six years ... is the minimum statute of limitations period under the statute.... The three-year period is designed to enlarge the time in which to bring a claim if a party does not learn of the fraud until years after the fraud is committed. It is not meant to curtail the period in which claims can be filed.

In 1999, the government paid a Texas joint venture $15 million in a settlement of a False Claims Act whistleblower lawsuit of a contract counterclaim against the government.

A government's so-called "reverse False Claims Act" lawsuit against contractor Pemco Aeroplex Inc. alleged that it knowingly misled the Air Force by listing aircraft wings as surplus scrap. The majority of the court dismissed the case, stating, "[w]e agree that Congress intended that the government must premise a reverse false claim upon a specific, legal obligation at the time a defendant used or caused to be used an alleged false claim." However, Pemco simply "initiated the plant clearance procedure." The dissent stated Pemco had a written contract which obligated it to be "responsible and accountable for the Government property in its possession," and to return that property or dispose of it in accordance with the government's instructions.

(d) Other Whistleblower Statutes

The Whistleblower Protection Act of 1989 prohibits Federal agencies from taking adverse personnel actions against civil servants for disclosures of legal violations or "gross mismanagement, a gross waste of funds, an abuse of authority, or a substantial and specific danger to public health or safety." Certain institutions receiving grants for research must undertake diligent efforts to "protect the positions and reputations of those persons who, in good faith, make allegations [of scientific misconduct]." The National Institutes of Health Revitalization Act of 1993 requires whistleblower standards, procedures, and remedies. These people are protected from retaliation both in employment and in connection with civil defamation suits. The Energy Policy Act of 1992 provides employees with 180 days, after the alleged discriminatory action, to file a complaint with the Department of Labor raising safety issues with their employers. In 1993, the NRC established the Special Review Team for Reassessment of the NRC Program for Protecting Allegers Against Retaliation.

§ 3.12   The Major Fraud Act

The Major Fraud Act constitutes another weapon for procurement fraud prosecutions. It applies to the execution or attempted execution of a major fraud scheme "in any procurement of property or services as a prime contractor with the United States or as a subcontractor or supplier on a contract in which there is a prime contract with the United States, if the value of the contract, subcontract, or any constituent part thereof, for such property or services is $1,000,000 or more."

A question has arisen whether a subcontractor would face liability if he perpetrated a fraud in connection with a subcontract valued less than $1,000,000 where the prime contract is valued $1,000,000 or more. If the subcontract was less than $1,000,000 but the fraud were committed by the prime contractor and its agent, does the statute apply? A Circuit Court of Appeals has ruled on such a matter. A contract for $1,074,000 was awarded to Robbins Sales Co. ("Robbins"), a broker with no production capacity of its own. My Brands, a Bronx based condiment packager, was to perform the contracts as the only subcontractor. In the event of termination, My Brands had the right to claim reimbursement for actual "out of pocket" expenses. In order to expand its production capability, Nadi of My Brands reached a purchase order agreement with Suffolk Mechanical, Inc. ("SMI") for machines at $50,000 each. SMI billed at this price. After Operation Desert Storm ended, the government terminated the contract. Nadi then billed the government $575,000 for five condiment packaging machines at $115,000 each. Later, the government received from Nadi "false" invoices he had obtained from SMI as support for his claims. He was convicted of violation of the Act. In affirming the conviction, the court quoted the statute and stated:

> We interpret this tracking language to mean that where the prime contractor is accused of fraud, we look to the value of the prime contract, but where the subcontractor is accused of fraud we look to the value of the subcontract, and where the supplier is accused of fraud we look to the value of the related constituent part of the contract.

Similarly, it has been held that contract modifications valued at less than $1 million are not separate contracts for purposes of determining liability under the statute.

Another question arose concerning an indictment that charged a defense contractor's senior executive with a count of major fraud for each allegedly inflated bill submitted under a single contract. A district court held that the charges were multiplicitous and violated the Double Jeopardy clause that prohibits multiple punishments for the same offense.

CHAPTER 4

ADMINISTRATIVE MATTERS

§ 4.1 In General

Administration of contracts in a general sense covers all matters treated in this volume. The regulation however, has limited one part solely to prescribing policies and procedures relating to the administrative aspects of contract execution, distribution, reporting, retention, and files. These minimum administrative guidelines were for files made uniform among all agencies of the government, which constituted an advancement in and of itself.

§ 4.2 Signatures of Contracting Officer and Contractor, Duplicates

Only a contracting officer can sign contracts on behalf of the United States. Further, his name and official title must be "typed, stamped, or printed on the contract."

In addition he has the duty to ensure that the "signer(s) have authority to bind the contractor." In this connection, a contract with an individual must be signed by that individual. A contract with an individual doing business as a firm must be signed by that individual, and the signature must be followed by the individual's typed, stamped, or printed name and the words, "an individual doing business as _____."

In the case of partnerships, a contract must be signed in the partnership name. Before signing for the government, the contracting officer must obtain a list of all partners and ensure that the individual(s) signing for the partnership "have authority to bind the partnership." A contract with a corporation is signed in the corporate name, followed by the word "by" and the signature and title of the person authorized to sign. The regulations prescribe that a contracting officer ensures that the person signing for the corporation "has authority to bind the corporation." Normally this is done by having the corporate secretary certify that the corporate officer who signed in fact held that office at the time he signed; the secretary will also stamp the corporate seal on top of (or after) his certification. Each signed or reproduced copy of the signed contract or modification that is intended to have the same force and effect as the signed original was formerly required to be marked "DUPLICATE ORIGINAL." Once signed by both parties, contracting officers must distribute copies of contracts or modifications within ten working days. However, where approval of a contract is not binding until written approval at a level higher than that of the contracting officer, the contract must so provide, and presumably final distribution will await written approval by the higher level.

The government must ascertain the authority of the signor, and requires his often-illegible script be followed by the typed or printed name that can be read. In the case of a corporation, where the contract involves a significant amount, it is commonplace for the signature of the corporate officer to be certified by corporate secretary after execution. This is because the board of directors could have modified or eliminated that officer's authority on the eve of the date the contract was executed. Since 1995 the contracting officer normally signs the contract after it has been signed by the contractor.

By contrast, the California Corporations Code requires *two* corporate officer signatures on a document binding the corporation. A question might arise regarding whether this will replace the usual corporate certificate of the authority of a single signor of a government contract where the officer lacks the requisite authority. Could a company that later wanted to back out of a deal do so? Federal law would govern prime contracts (see § 33.22). Because FAR 4.102(c) states a contracting officer must ensure that the signer "has authority to bind the contractor," and such authority may be that conferred by state law, it could be argued that the regulation requires the contracting officer to seek two signatures under the California statute. It seems that this argument would be even stronger with respect to subcontracts (see Chapter 44).

In addition, in 1995, it became the policy that a contractor submitting paper documents to the Government relating to an acquisition should, if possible, submit those documents printed/copied double-sided on recycled paper. The change that year pertained to the Federal Acquisition Computer Network (FACNET) and the Governmentwide Electronic Commerce/Electronic Data Interchange (EC/EDI) systems that provide for electronic data interchange of acquisition information between the Government and the private sector.

In 1999 the GAO promulgated a "first malfunction is free" rule for a vendor's quote submitted electronically under the Federal Acquisition Computer Network (FACNET), which became lost by the agency due to "isolated" computer system malfunctions. The Year 2000 Information and Readiness Disclosure Act was intended "[t]o encourage the disclosure and exchange of information about computer processing problems, solutions, test practices and test results, and related matters in connection with the transition to the year 2000."

On June 30, 2000, the president digitally signed into law the Electronic Signatures in Global and National Commerce Act. "E-sign," as the Act is known, provides for acceptance of digital signatures in commercial contracts, and allows the public and private sectors to maintain and supply most business records in electronic form. A digital signature uses secured codes and identifying markers, rather than handwriting, to ascertain the identity of the signer. It is interesting to note that the U.S. Comptroller General has recognized the validity of other-than-handwritten signatures (such as rubber stamps and machine-generated signatures) since at least 1951. In 1996, the Comptroller General held that digital signatures meeting the Digital Signature Standard promulgated by the National Institute of Standards and Technology can constitute evidence of a binding agreement.

§ 4.3 Safeguarding Classified Information

Information may be classified by agencies pursuant to Executive Order. For example, the Department of Defense (DoD) has incorporated the requirements of these Executive Orders into the Defense Industrial Security Program (DISP). During review of proposed solicitations, access to classified information may be needed by offerors or by a contractor during contract performance; the prescribed procedures must be followed and a special contract clause inserted. A huge number of people have access to classified data, and it has not always been well protected.

§ 4.4 Contract Reporting, Record Retention and Closeout

The Federal Procurement Data System (FPDS) collects data on contracts from government agencies. It then disseminates statistical data to provide a basis for recurring a special report to the President, the Congress, the General Accounting Office, executive agencies, and the general public. This provides a means of measuring and assessing the impact of contracting on the economy and the extent to which small business concerns and small disadvantaged business concerns are sharing in contracts. It also provides data for other policy and management control purposes. A clause entitled "Data Universal Numbering System (DUNS) Number" must be placed in solicitations that are expected to result in a requirement for the generation of a Federal Procurement Data System (FPDS)—Individual Contract. All contract actions over $2,500 must be reported to FPDS–NG as individual contract actions after September 30, 2004.

In general, contractors must retain records in order to make them available for administration, audit requirements of the contracting agencies, and inspection by the Comptroller General for a period of 3 years after final payment. Certain clauses may require record retention for a longer or shorter period of time. The Audit Clauses used in sealed bid or negotiated procurements require retention of records "until 3 years after any resulting final payment termination settlement," and those pertaining to disputes or litigation must be kept until "such appeals, litigation, or claims are disposed of." These clauses are required to be inserted in all subcontracts over $100,000. Financial and cost accounting records, including pay administration records, must be retained for 4 years. Labor cost distribution cards and petty cash records need be held for only two years. The regulation sets forth many examples of the contents of contract files, including purchase requests, acquisition planning information, solicitation documents, request for authority to negotiate, determination and findings, evidence of availability of funds, synopsis of proposed acquisition as published in the Commerce Business Daily, and the list of sources solicited. Procedures are given for the close-out of files, which, of course, will not take place if a contract is in litigation or under appeal, or in the case of a termination; all termination actions have not been completed. A schedule is set forth for the disposal of contract files which varies according to the documents from six months (for expediting records) until six years and three months after final payment (for signed originals of Determination and Findings and for other documents). Except in the case of litigation or termination, files for contracts using simplified acquisition procedures should be considered closed when the contracting officer receives evidence of receipt of property and final payment. Other files for firm-fixed-price contracts should be closed within 6 months after the date on which the contracting officer receives evidence of physical completion. Files for all other contracts should be closed within 20 months of the month in which the contracting officer receives such evidence, but for files requiring settlement of indirect cost rates should be closed within 36 months of the month in which the contracting officer receives that evidence.

The regulation permits contractors to satisfy the record retention requirements by duplicating or storing records in electronic form "unless they contain significant information not shown on the record copy." Original paper records need not be retained or submitted for audit purposes, so long as the contractor is able, with respect to the electronic record, to: (1) establish procedures ensuring the integrity of the record, (2) provide timely and convenient access through indexing, and (3) retain the original document for one year after imaging to permit validation of the imaging system. Information maintained on a computer must be retained "on a reliable medium" that must not be overwritten for the time periods prescribed for the retention of paper records.

§ 4.5   Electronic Commerce in Contracting

The regulation requires agencies to use electronic commerce "whenever practicable or cost-effective." It further provides that the "use of terms commonly associated with paper transactions (*e.g.*, 'copy,' 'document,' 'page,' 'printed,' 'sealed envelope,' and 'stamped') shall not be interpreted to restrict the use of electronic commerce." Agencies are given broad discretion to select the hardware and software they will use for conducting e-commerce, provided the selected systems, technologies and procedures: (1) are uniform throughout each agency to the maximum extent practical; (2) are implemented only after considering the use of existing infrastructures (including FACNET); (3) facilitate access by small, small disadvantaged and women-owned small business concerns; (4) provide widespread public notice of acquisition opportunities through a "single, Government-wide point of entry" and a means of responding to notices or solicitations electronically; and (5) comply with nationally and internationally recognized standards that broaden interoperability and ease the electronic interchange of information. Additionally, before using e-commerce methods, agencies must ensure their systems are capable of providing appropriate authenticity and confidentiality measures "commensurate with the risk and magnitude of the harm" that may arise from the loss, misuse or modification of electronic information.

CHAPTER 5

PUBLICIZING CONTRACT ACTIONS

§ 5.1   Dissemination of Information

With few exceptions (such as emergency procurements or those involving classified matter or perishable goods), information on proposed contracts in amounts over $25,000 must be disseminated to affected industries. This dissemination of opportunities to contract is accomplished by transmitting a brief synopsis to the Governmentwide Point of Entry ("GPE"). The Federal Business Opportunities website (*http://www.FedBizOpps.gov*) has been designated the GPE for federal procurement opportunities, replacing the *Commerce Business Daily* ("CBD") as the primary source for information on competitive opportunities. All proposed contract actions expected to exceed $25,000 in value must be disseminated by synopsizing in the GPE, rather than in the CBD.

Notice of proposed contract actions expected to exceed $10,000 but not to exceed $25,000 must be publicly displayed by the contracting officer or electronically posted for at least ten days or until after quotations have been opened, whichever is later. The notice must include a statement that all responsible sources may submit a response, which, if timely received, will be considered by the agency. However, the contracting officer need not comply with these display requirements when oral or Federal Acquisition Computer Network (FACNET) solicitations are used, or when access to a notice of proposed contract action and solicitation are provided through the GPE and the notice permits the public to respond to the solicitation electronically.

Other methods may also be used, including preparing and displaying periodic handouts listing proposed contracts, assisting local trade associations in disseminating information to their members, making brief announcements of proposed contracts to newspapers, trade journals, magazines, or other mass communication media for publication without cost to the government, and placing paid advertisements in newspapers or other communications media, subject to certain limitations. The GPE, however, generally, substitutes for what statutes in many states require; namely, publication of official notices and advertisements, be made in newspapers of "general circulation." It is difficult, if not impossible, to determine where the lines should be drawn between a newspaper, in a legal and common usage of the term, and publications devoted to some special purpose, which circulate only among a certain class of people, and which are not within the purview of statutes requiring publication of legal notices in a newspaper of general circulation.

§ 5.2   Synopses of Proposed Contract Actions

(a) In General

Contracting officers are required to make available though the GPE solicitations (including specifications and other pertinent information) that were synopsized through the GPE, unless (1) disclosure of the solicitation would compromise the national security or create other security risks, (2) the nature of the file makes providing access through the GPE impracticable or not cost-effective, (3) the agency's senior procurement executive has determined in writing that access through the GPE is not in the government's interest, or (4) the contracting office is unable to access the GPE and the synopsis was issued before October 1, 2001. If the solicitation is not made available through the GPE, the contracting officer should make it available through other electronic means whenever practicable and cost-effective. If the solicitation is provided electronically on physical media (such as CD–ROM or by electronic mail) or in paper form, the contracting officer is required to maintain a reasonable number of copies, provide copies on a "first-come-first-served" basis, and retain a copy for review and duplication after the initial supply of copies is exhausted. "Notices" (synopses) of proposed contract actions other than the acquisition of commercial items must be published at least fifteen days before issuance of a solicitation. For acquisitions of commercial items, the contracting officer may establish a shorter period for issuance of the solicitation or use a combined solicitation/synopsis.

The contracting officer is required to transmit a synopsis for each proposed effort to locate private commercial sources to the GPE, and he is forbidden from concluding that there are no such sources until publicizing the requirement in the GPE at least three times in a 90–day period. Prime contractors awarded a contract in excess of $100,000, and subcontractors and suppliers under a contract exceeding $100,000, may use the GPE to publicize subcontracting opportunities. On occasion, the GPE is given inaccurate or incomplete information and concerns who rely on this may be misinformed. Even if it is correct, one board has held that it may be inadequate notice. On the other hand, before the advent of the GPE, the GAO had held that the government's electronic "CBDNet" synopsis provided reasonable notice of a solicitation, even though the solicitation number had changed, because all of the necessary information was available on the agency's website. It has been held that a response to a synopsis must precede a protest against a sole-source award.

The regulation requires that synopses be published of modifications to existing contracts "for additional supplies or services" that exceed the $25,000 threshold. Accordingly, when an agency has failed to synopsize that action a protest may lay against the issuance of the modification. Thus, the failure by an agency to synopsize in the Commerce Business Daily (now GPE) a proposed acquisition of more than $50,000 of a product for a witness protection program was held not justified. The Regulation provides additional guidance to contracting officers on how to proceed with a contract action when the contracting officer learns that a synopsis has not been published within prescribed time frames. However, no notice of proposed contract actions is now required for non-competitive procurements under section 8(a) of the Small Business Act, for many defense agency actions "performed outside the United States," nor in many cases when the proposed contract action is not expected to exceed $100,000 (the "simplified acquisition threshold"), nor for services to the government of an expert in litigation or disputes.

(b) Special Situations

Although some exceptions exist to the requirement of synopsizing proposed procurements noted above (such as emergency purchases) seem obvious, other exceptions require significant inquiry. For example, consider the exception referring to international agreements and other special legislation pertaining to foreign purchases. (However, North American Trade Agreement contract actions above the threshold must be synopsized) Where an agency has an interest in "Research and Development" (R & D), it publishes a synopsis in the GPE in order to enable sources to submit information for evaluation of their R & D capabilities. (See Chapter 25)

Frequently an agency can do in-house work where it is less costly than if it were contracted out. In this connection it is important to be cognizant of restrictions in the regulations requiring cost comparisons between contractor and government performance. However, as noted above the contracting officer cannot arrive at a conclusion that there are no commercial sources capable of providing the required supplies or services until publicizing the requirement.

(c) *Publicizing Subcontract Opportunities*

In instances where significant subcontracting opportunities exist, the names and addresses of prospective offerors are published in the Governmentwide Point of Entry (GPE) with the suggestion that small business firms or others interested in subcontracting opportunities in connection with the acquisition make direct contract with firm(s) listed. Prime contractors and subcontractors are to be encouraged to use the GPE to publicize subcontracting opportunities stemming from their government business. Accordingly, where a contract or subcontract exceeding $100,000 is likely to result in award of subcontracts, a notice may be used to seek competition for small, disadvantaged, and women-owned small business concerns.

The exception to the requirement that a notice be published in the Commerce Business Daily (now the GPE) underwent an apparent major change in August 1988. Then it was changed so that there is no exception for a contract action which "results from an unsolicited research proposal and acceptance is based solely upon the unique capability of the source to perform the particular research services proposed."

§ 5.3 Synopses of Contract Awards

Unless specifically excepted, agencies are required to synopsize through the GPE awards exceeding $25,000 that are subject to the Trade Agreements Act (see subpart 25.4) or likely to result in the award of any subcontracts. Publicizing of contract actions for smaller amounts is authorized when it would be advantageous to industry or to the government. Agencies are required to make information available on awards over $3 million in sufficient time for the agency concerned to announce it by 5:00 p.m. Washington, D.C. time on the day of award. Contracts excluded from this reporting requirement include those placed with (1) the Small Business Administration under Section 8(a) of the Small Business Act and (2) foreign firms when the place of delivery or performance is outside the United States or its possessions. Agencies may also release information on contract awards to the local press or other media.

CHAPTER 6

COMPETITION REQUIREMENTS

§ 6.1 In General; Merger Guidelines

The Competition in Contracting Act (CICA) requires, with certain limited exceptions, that full and open competition be obtained in soliciting offers and awarding government contracts. Like the former regulation, the current FAR requires use of "competitive procedures" which are "best suited to the circumstances of the contract action." Two of the procedures available for use in fulfilling the requirement are use of sealed bids and competitive proposals. If sealed bids are not appropriate, then the use of competitive proposals may be appropriate. Alternatively, any combination of competitive procedures (e.g., two-step sealed bidding) or other competitive procedures can be used such as the selection of sources under statutory or regulatory procedures (without the solicitation of prices for architect-engineer contracts).

An example of a violation of the Competition in Contracting Act (CICA) was the use of a requotes arrangements clause used by GSA in multiple award Federal Supply Service (FSS) contracts. Under the clause, GSA limited the competition to FSS vendors who had already received contracts for certain sales. The method was held to violate CICA's requirement for full and open competition. Similarly, a $99 million "modification" of AT & T's FTS 2000 telecommunication contract with the GSA was held to represent a new service, called T3, which was beyond the scope

100

of the original FTS 2000 contract and required new competition under CICA requirement for use of "full and open competition. However, this decision was reversed by the U.S. Court of Appeals for the Federal Circuit, which noted that the new T3 technology conveys the same voice and data information as other forms of dedicated transmission service, but at a higher rate of speed and is the next generation of dedicated transmission service. In light of the contractor's obligations to propose improvements to keep the Government's telecommunications technology in step with technology advances, T3 falls within the scope of the FTS 2000 contract."

The courts, boards and Comptroller General do not evaluate first hand an agency's needs. Their concern is with an agency's use of some restrictions that were held not reasonably necessary to meet those needs. There are exceptions to the requirement for full and open competition that are discussed later in this chapter. During the first year following the term of the third millennium, Professor Steven Schooner, a major critic of the changes, pointed out that:

> In the last decade, Congress appears to have toiled mightily to ensure that procurement officials were understaffed and overworked ... Compared to the private sector, some suggest that government buyers are not as well informed about what they are buying.

Both the downsizing of the Defense base and other reasons have contributed to the recent "merger mania." In 1992, Horizontal Merger Guidelines were issued jointly by the Department of Justice and the Federal Trade Commission. Relevant markets are defined as a product type and a geographic area. Market participants include firms that are currently producing or selling in the relevant geographic area and "uncommitted entrants," or those firms that "in response to a 'small but significant and non-transitory' price increase ... likely would enter rapidly into production or sale of a market product in the market's area, without incurring significant sunk costs of entry and exit." The Guidelines state "in some situations, market share and market concentration data may either understate or overstate the likely future competitive significance of a firm or firms in the market or the impact of a merger." Antitrust analysis requires an examination of the "recent or ongoing changes in the market" that may reflect a change in a firm's future competitive impact. The Guidelines set forth tests to determine if entry into the relevant market "is so easy that market participants, after the merger, either collectively or unilaterally could not profitably maintain a price increase above premerger levels." The entry is easy if it "would be timely, likely and sufficient in its magnitude, character and scope to deter or counteract the competitive effects of concern." The government is a monopsonist (the only purchaser) for many products; yet, such a "power buyer" may not effectively constrain anticompetitive prices. Cognizable efficiencies may "achieve economies of scale, better integration of production facilities, plant specialization, lower transportation costs," and "reduction in general selling, administrative, and overhead expenses." However, "if equivalent or comparable savings can reasonably be achieved by the parties through other means," claimed efficiencies will be rejected.

The FAR recognizes that contractor team arrangements may be desirable from both a government and industry perspective, particularly in complex research and development acquisitions (see Subpart 9.6). Collaborations among contractors enable the companies to complement each other's capabilities and may offer the government the best combination of performance, cost, and delivery. However, there is a concern that federal antitrust authorities may take a dim view of agreements among actual or potential competitors. In April 2000, the Federal Trade Commission and Department of Justice jointly issued Antitrust Guidelines for Collaborations Among Competitors. They provide guidance on horizontal agreements between competitors, including joint ventures, strategic alliances, and other competitor collaborations. In issuing the guidelines, FTC Chairman Robert Pitofsky observed that they "will help businesses assess the antitrust implications of collaborations with rivals, thereby encouraging pro-competitive collaborations and deterring collaborations likely to harm competition and consumers."

As a result of a lawsuit by the Department of Justice, the attempt by General Dynamics to acquire Newport News Shipbuilding, Inc. was terminated. The Defense Department had notified Justice that the acquisition "would eliminate competition for a nuclear submarine resulting in a monopoly." General Dynamics and Newport News remain the sole manufacturers of nuclear submarines.

§ 6.2   Full and Open Competition After Exclusion of Sources

"Full and open competition" was formerly defined as a method whereby "all responsible sources are permitted to compete." The regulation now promotes procedure for either (1) "full and open competition," (2) "full and open competition after exclusion of sources," or (3) other than full and open competition. The second one could be called "closed competition," the third falls outside of a competitive category.

The right of an agency to exclude a particular source from a contract action in order to establish or maintain an alternative source for the supplies or services exists because an agency is often "locked in" on one source and it becomes very difficult for other sources to attempt to compete by incurring significant start up costs and necessary experience. Under current procedures, an agency head may establish or maintain an alternate source where it would be "likely to result in reduced overall costs," or be in the interest of national defense in having a supplier available for furnishing the supplies or services in case of a national emergency or industrial mobilization. Nevertheless, in 2003, the General Accounting Office upheld a protest against proposals calling for a specific type of aircraft to fulfill a requirement was found unduly restrictive of competition where the agency's own marketing reports revealed that other aircrafts could also adequately meet its needs.

Similarly, the FAR allows an exception for an educational or other nonprofit institution or a federally-funded research and development center that may be needed in order to maintain an essential engineering, research, or development capacity.

Another category of procurements with closed competition is represented by solicitations which are set aside to fulfill the statutory requirements relating to small business concerns, in order to allow only such business concerns to compete. No separate justification or determination and findings is required for these set asides.

The decision by the Department of Labor to standardize its office software to the Microsoft Office suite was held not subject to the Competition in Contracting Act (CICA) because it was not a "procurement" decision. The courts have held that CICA's competitive bidding rules apply only to the "procurement" of goods and services by the federal government and did not apply to a decision to adopt the Microsoft standard. On the other hand, the fact that companies' desire to extinguish their rivals was held "consistent with" competition; statements such as "we will not be underbid" and "we'll do whatever it takes," are often legitimately used by business people in the heat of competition.

§ 6.3 Other Statutes Providing for Contracting Without Full and Open Competition

(a) In General

There are two other statutes that together authorize, under certain conditions, contracting without providing for full and open competition. In cases where the contract action is pursued without providing for full and open competition, the agency must "solicit offers from as many potential sources as is practicable under the circumstances." The regulation implementing these two statutes sets forth circumstances permitting other than full and open competition.

(b) Only One Responsible Source

All civilian agencies must follow the portion of the regulation which states that when the supplies or services required are "available from only one responsible source, . . . full and open competition need not be provided for." However, for DoD, NASA and the Coast Guard, this applies where "only one or a limited number of responsible sources" are available. (Former criterion used the expression that it was "impracticable to obtain competition.") Examples include follow-on contracts for the continued development or production of a major system or highly specialized equipment, including major components thereof. These may be deemed to be available only from the original source when it is likely that award to any other source would result in (A) "substantial duplication of cost to the government (that is not expected to be recovered through competition), or (B) unacceptable delays in fulfilling the agency's" requirements. Follow-on procurements "for the continued development or production of a major system or highly specialized equipment" are further limited to where

> it is likely that award to a source other than the original source would result in (i) substantial duplication of cost to the government which is not expected to be recovered through competition, or (ii) unacceptable delays in fulfilling the agency's requirements.

The statute regulation also provides that an agency may exclude a particular source in order to "maintain facility, producer, manufacturer, or other supplier available for furnishing supplies or services in case of a national emergency or to achieve industrial mobilization."

The GAO has upheld the award of a sole-source contract for litigation support to an incumbent contractor in order to meet a tight, court-imposed discovery schedule in a "complex, high-dollar claim." The regulation also states that competition need not be provided "to acquire the services of an expert or neutral person for any current or anticipated litigation or dispute."

Most sole source procurements require notice of the proposed action in a synopsis in the GPE. The agency will search the marketplace and confirm that the proposed action remains a justifiable sole source. Indeed, publication of contract actions is most important. The agency need not submit the required notice in a large number of types of action. Some of these exceptions appear to be significantly more important than others. These become applicable when such disclosure would "compromise the national security" and (a) for purchases "using simplified acquisition procedures," if unusual and compelling urgency [which alone somehow] precludes competition, or (b) because a foreign government or (c) international organization actually requires use of "specified sources." A contract for a "neutral person," e.g., mediators or arbitrators, to resolve issues of alternate dispute processes is also exempt.

An unsolicited research proposal must be considered to be available from only one source if the source has submitted an unsolicited research proposal that demonstrates a unique and innovative concept. In the past, the award of unsolicited proposals had been made after agency technical personnel concluded that they were unaware of any other source to justify a sole source procurement. This authority cannot be used unless notices have been published in the GPE and any bids or proposals received have been considered. It has been held that the Small Business Administration erred in making a sole source award for a budget and accounting software package based on criteria not identified in the procurement synopsis. This may be a limitation on seeking competition for an allegedly "unique and innovative" concept to do a job that may be done more cheaply by a different firm using an equally unique and innovative approach that is unknown to the procuring agency. An agency is required to "request offers from as many sources as practicable" even if the need is urgent.

Although the mere existence of patent rights, copyrights, or secret processes, the control of basic raw material, or similar circumstance does not in and of itself justify procurement from a sole source, it may do so in some peculiar instances. Similarly, in many if not most instances, circumstances of procurement of electric power or energy, gas (natural or manufactured), water, or other utility services, may dictate that only one supplier can furnish the service. Furthermore, an agency's standardization program (that only specified makes and models of technical equipment and parts will satisfy the agency's needs for additional units or replacement items) would make only one source available.

During the third millennium, the GAO already has sustained certain protests regarding sole source awards. The Army's plan to make such an award to Rolls–Royce was held not to be based upon accurate evidence and "failed to set forth an accurate estimate of the value of the proposed sole source contract as required ... [and] failed to reasonably demonstrate that only Rolls–Royce has the capacity to perform." The Army again failed to justify a 30,000 unit sole sources within 60 days. A protester showed that the need was limited to only about 14,000 vehicles. The GAO stated, "Contracting officials must act affirmatively to obtain and safeguard competition; they cannot take a passive approach and remain in a noncompetitive position where they could reasonably take steps to enhance competition."

(c) *Unusual and Compelling Urgency*

An agency's need for the supplies or services may be of such an unusual and compelling urgency that the government would be seriously injured unless the agency is permitted to limit the number of sources from which it solicits bids or proposals. This represents another instance when "full and open competition need not be provided for". But the criterion cannot be used because of "the lack of advance planning or concerns related to the amount of funds available to the agency for procurement functions." When agencies are using urgency as a reason to limit competition, they are still required to request offers from as many potential sources as is practicable under the circumstances. Yet an award has been upheld even though the specifications provided under an oral solicitation were so inadequate that only one firm could respond; this was because only that firm could meet the agency's needs within the required time frame. The GAO has held that an agency's decision concerning its time frame or schedule was an improper one.

It has been held that "a decision to make a sole-source award is unreasonable if the agency had adequate time to assess its needs and conduct a more competitive procurement" but failed to do so or otherwise took improper action which created the urgency. Justifications for other than full and open competition based on the urgency exception may be prepared and approved after contract award where these would unreasonably delay the acquisition, provided that they are prepared and approved within a reasonable time after award. Further, recovery of the costs of filing and pursuing a protest is allowed where the protester unreasonably lost the opportunity to compete. Such costs, including attorney fees, were held to be recoverable where an agency failed to show that its urgent circumstances prevented it from requesting offers from as many potential sources as was practicable prior to making a sole award on the basis of urgency.

(d) Industrial Mobilization; Experimental Development; Research Work; Public Interest; National Security; or Expert Services in Litigation

Full and open competition need not be provided for when it is necessary (a) to award the contract to a particular source or sources in order to maintain a facility or supplier available for furnishing supplies or services in case of a national emergency or to achieve industrial mobilization, or (b) to establish or maintain an essential engineering, research, or development capability to be provided by an educational or other nonprofit institution or a federally funded research and development center. See Chapter 35 infra. Further, a contracting officer must, "to the maximum practical extent, eliminate competitive advantage accruing to a contractor possessing Government production and research property."

In addition to the authorization of a procurement action without competition for the reason of national security, there is the "public interest" exception that may be invoked by an agency head. It is nondelegable, and the Congress must be given 30 days notice prior to award. This legislation eliminated or reduced many former restrictions on competitive procurements.

With respect to the project of the New Deal, the Tennessee Valley Authority (TVA), Jim Powell, recently wrote that:

> The TVA remains an unaccountable government monopoly. It is exempt from more than 130 federal laws, including workplace safety laws and hydroelectric licensing laws, and hundreds of laws in the states where it operates (Alabama, Georgia, Kentucky, North Carolina, and Virginia, as well as Tennessee). The TVA is immune from civil liability lawsuits about any wrongful acts it may have committed.

It was also noted that the TVA build nuclear power plants, and in 1998, Ralph Nader reported that "The TVA is by any measure the worst nuclear project in the country ... has the poorest safety record with TVA reactors spending more time on the Nuclear Regulatory Commission's watch list than any other utility."

The justification for other than full and open competition requires approvals in writing for proposed contracts at certain levels by the contracting officer up to the head of an agency or Secretary of Defense. Procurements of simplified purchases under the simplified purchase threshold (see Chapter 13) are justified when the agency reasonably determines that only one source is "reasonably available" and with reprocurements after a termination for default, competition need only be obtained "to the maximum extent practicable."

(e) International Agreements

Other than competitive procedures are also authorized in connection with procurements under memoranda of understanding between the United States and foreign governments and to foreign military sales and where a law authorized procurement from another executive agency. See Chapter 25 infra.

As a result of the Fiscal Year 1990 Defense Authorization Act for DoD, NASA and the Coast Guard, the requirement for justification for use of other than full and open competition for acquisitions under the international agreement exception and their justifications are different from those of civilian agencies (as noted in § 6.3(B)).

§ 6.4 Sealed Bidding and Competitive Proposals

The regulation recognizes several different competitive procedures that fulfill the statutory requirement for full and open competition, including (1) sealed bids, (2) competitive proposals, (3) a combination of competitive procedures (e.g., two-step sealed bidding), (4) selection of sources for architect-engineer contracts in accordance with the provisions of Public Law 92–682 (see Subpart 36.6), and other competitive selection of basic and applied research using a broad agency announcement and peer or scientific review, as well as use of General Services Administration (GSA) multiple award schedules.

Although acceptable procedures for use of sealed bidding and competitive proposals are described in Chapters 14 and 15, infra, this section prescribes a few detailed guidelines. "Sealed bids" must be solicited where four conditions apply to a particular procurement action, namely: (1) time permits the solicitation, submission and evaluation of sealed bids, (2) the award will be made on the basis of price and other price-related factors, (3) it is not necessary to conduct discussions with the responding offerors about their bids due to the clarity of determined specifications and (4) there is a reasonable expectation of receiving more than one sealed bid. Where these conditions do not exist, "competitive proposals" may be requested. Due to "differences in areas such as law, regulations and business practices, it is generally necessary to conduct discussions with offerors relative to proposed contracts to be made and performed outside the United States, its possessions, or Puerto Rico."

Congress enacted CICA in 1984, creating a statutory presumption in favor of competition "except in the case of procurement procedures expressly authorized by statute." A circuit court of appeals has held that Department of Veterans Affairs' sharing agreements with health care facilities for acquisition and joint use of advanced medical technologies, authorized by statute, constitute such "procurement procedures" exempt from public bidding requirements of Competition in Contracting Act.

§ 6.5   Competition Advocates

Another innovation that became law upon enactment of the Competition in Contracting Act was the requirement that the head of an executive agency designate another employee called a "competition advocate for the agency and each contracting activity of the agency." He must be in a position other than that of the agency's senior procurement executive, and not be assigned any duties or responsibilities that are inconsistent with his duties. His job is to challenge barriers to and promote full and open competition by spotting competitive opportunities in the acquisition of supplies and services by the agency. He reviews the contracting operations of the agency and identifies and reports to the agency senior procurement executive opportunities and actions taken to achieve full and open competition in the contracting operations of the agency, as well as any condition or action that has the effect of unnecessarily restricting competition in the contract actions of the agency.

Normally the competition advocate should be provided "with staff or assistance (e.g. specialists in engineering, technical operations, contract administration, financial management, supply management, and utilization of small and disadvantaged business concerns), as may be necessary to carry out his responsibilities." Not being a line officer, he can only make recommendations to the senior procurement executive of the agency. He also may make suggestions for plans for increasing competition as well as a system of personal and organizational accountability for competition, which may include the use of recognition and awards to motivate program managers, contracting officers, and others in authority to promote competition in acquisition.

PART II

ACQUISITION PLANNING

CHAPTER 7

ACQUISITION PLANS— MAKE OR BUY

§ 7.1 Acquisition Plans

Planning a procurement commences as soon as the agency need is identified. This is essential in order to ensure that the government meets its needs in the most effective, economical, and timely manner. It is accomplished by agency procedures establishing criteria and thresholds, of which increasingly greater detail and formality in the planning process is required as the acquisition becomes more complex and costly.

Depending upon the procurement involved, written plans may be necessary to coordinate and integrate the efforts of all personnel responsible for significant aspects of the acquisition. These plans include deciding whether it is more economical to lease equipment or to purchase it. Where a purchase is necessary, cost goals must be established and product life-cycle considered where appropriate. Together with design-to-cost objectives, learning-curves, economic adjustment factors, and delivery or performance-period requirements must be established. The expected consequences of trade-offs among the various cost, capability or performance, and schedule goals must be considered. Most importantly, consideration must be given to how competition will be sought, promoted, and sustained throughout the course of the procurement, and the extent to which sole source-selections may be avoided. See Chapter 6. Where the agency furnishes both government property to contractors (including facilities), as well as government information (such as manuals, drawings, and test data, to be provided to prospective officers and contractors), savings to the taxpayer may result.

An environmental assessment or environmental impact statement, or other environmental-related requirements, may have to be included in solicitations and contracts. In 1995, the regulation was amended to ensure that agency plans embrace environmental considerations (see Chapter 23), and that solicitations for advisory and assistance services are in accordance with prescribed guidelines (see Chapter 37). The plan should also provide for the acquisition of commercial items or, if they are not available or are unsuitable, "nondevelopmental items" to the maximum extent practicable.

The "full and open competition" is not required in many cases (as was noted in Chapter 6). It is only required to "the maximum extent practicable with regard to the nature of the supplies and services to be acquired." An agency's procurement planners (a team which may include fiscal, legal and technical personnel) must ensure that no purchase request is initiated or contract entered into for the performance of an "inherently governmental function by a contractor."

Agencies are to establish standard acquisition plan formats "if desired," and "suitable to" their needs. Their planners also must specify their needs for written paper consistent with the "minimum content standards." In 1994, the Defense Department apparently began its plan to acquire a $3 billion single paperless standard procurement system (SPS) by 2003. It was to serve 43,000 users at 1,100 worldwide sites. A late analysis (both internal and by GAO) showed that SPS costs were excessive and its benefits recessive.

The regulation was modified to implement a statute affecting contracting officers that buy services by explicitly establishing a preference for performance-based contracts or task orders. The written acquisition plan must provide a rationale if performance is based on contract services contemplated on other than a firm-fixed price basis.

There are additional requirements for acquisitions involving bundling. This involves "Consolidating two or more requirements for supplies or services, previously provided or performed under separate smaller contracts, into a solicitation for a single contact." Market research must justify that the agency would derive such substantial benefits. It would justifiably derive measurably substantial benefits if they are equivalent to 10% of the estimated contract value of $75 million or less. But, "a reduction of administrative or personnel costs alone is not sufficient justification for bundling unless the cost savings are expected to be at least 10 percent of the estimated contract value (including options) of the bundled requirements."

Planning the drafting of the proposed contract takes time—particularly the technical portion which can assume the proportions of a telephone book in a large metropolis. Planners, and particularly attorneys, must continually bear in mind the term introduced in 1959 by the late C.P. Snow (Lord Snow) in his Rede Lecture at Cambridge on "Two Cultures and the Scientific Revolution." Snow diagnosed society's intellectuals as unable to speak to each other, having no common language. Each group he called a "culture;" he maintained that scientists can't read literature and that "humanists" can't understand even simple scientific concepts such as the second law of thermodynamics. I found this comment to be quite true in my experience with scientists, engineers and administrators in the field of procurement in the Atomic Energy Commission. Technical people frequently use the same term to mean different things. On occasion they will fail to define terms on the ground that "all technically-trained people will know their meaning"—a conclusion that I discovered was often incorrect and would consume a significant portion of the time. Often it was necessary to include appropriate definitions. Not infrequently, this problem required other changes in the scope of work, but the effort was worthwhile because it was often from the specifications that many legal disputes arose.

§ 7.2   Make or Buy Considerations—OMB Circular A–76

(a) In General

Because it is the policy of the government to "rely generally on private commercial sources for supplies and services," consideration must be given to the two exceptions to this policy in deciding whether to procure or not to procure. The first exception recognizes that some functions are "inherently governmental" and must be performed by government personnel. Many, if not most, levels of government could be run more efficiently by private industry than by or under elected officials. However, by definition, an "inherently governmental function" portion is a policy determination, not a legal determination that had several examples.

The Grace Commission reported in 1983 that the government could save $474 million per year by 1986, if it "privatized" such tasks as food service, firefighting, maintenance, laundry and security, and if Congress did not resist.

When looking at certain aspects of the OMB Circular A–76, reforms aimed at increasing the perception of the procedural "fairness" and reducing some of its "unique procedural burdens" have been addressed.

Inasmuch as government employees are not the intended beneficiaries of the law that is designed to promote contracting out, they lack standing to challenge an agency decision to contract out. However, contractors who have participated in the Air Force's Contractor–Operated Civil Engineer Supply Stores (COCESS) program have been held to have standing to challenge the Air Force's decision to convert the program from contract to in-house operation.

Where the agency includes the A–76 rules in the solicitation to guide the decision on public/private competitions, such solicitations and award decisions are reviewable in a protest. GAO has recognized that only the Department of Defense is precluded by statute from considering "non-cost factors" in a public/ private competition. Under a statute, if a private-sector source can provide services needed by the DoD at a cost lower than the cost of in-house performance, the DoD is required to obtain the services from the private sector unless the Secretary of Defense determines the services must be obtained from military or government personnel.

(b) Determining Availability of Private Commercial Sources

For several decades, the Office of Management and Budget and its predecessors have tried to encourage government agencies to "contract out" when the private sector can provide cheaper service. The Bureau of the Budget Bulletin 60–2, published in 1955, was superseded by Circular A–76 in 1966, and a revision to the latter Circular on May 1, 1979 included the addition of the Cost Comparison Handbook, which provided a method of determining the cost of in-house performance, and contained instructions on how to perform cost comparisons. Both the Circular and its Handbook are revised periodically.

A Congressional Budget Office (CBO) report entitled "Contracting–Out for Federal Support Services: Potential Savings and Budgetary Impact" (published in 1982) showed that

approximately 81 percent of in-house commercial-type work reviewed could be converted to contract performance, resulting in a first-year savings of $335,000,000. These savings would eventually reach $870,000,000, because many of the costs of contracting-out are short-term. According to the CBO, the savings are primarily the result of reduced labor costs. The conversions would result in the elimination of approximately 165,000 Federal jobs.

Congress (particularly in the House of Representatives) often blocked attempted reinforcement of the policy in order to protect Federal employees. In the Veterans' Compensation, Education and Employment Amendment of 1982, Congress barred the contracting out of any activities at a Veteran's Administration health-care facility, unless the VA Chief Medical Director found that the activity was not a direct patient care activity, or that the activity was not incident to direct patient care. The "Edgar Amendment" prohibited the General Services Administration from converting to commercial performance any activity performed by GSA personnel as custodians, security guards, elevator operators, and messengers to protect the jobs of GSA-employed veterans. Thereafter the GSA canceled 14 procurements in which bids had been opened and the agency had decided to award to a contractor, and the GAO upheld these actions under that Amendment. Federal employees displaced by contracting out usually find other jobs in the government. Some states also have severe restrictions on contracting out. In 2002, after noting the nation's 1.8 million federal civilian workers expressed a plan for the private sector to compete for up to 850,000 federal jobs, the proposal was strongly opposed by employee unions.

In instances where an apparent low bidder is a non-profit organization, an amount equal to the Federal, state, and local income taxes that would be paid by the lowest tax-paying bidder is added to the price of the bid, in order to avoid an unfair competitive advantage to the nonprofit organization. Agencies cannot modify, change, or alter the size of their commercial activities solely for the purpose of avoiding cost studies.

The key to a make or buy decision is a comparison of the government's costs with a supplier's prices. An agency's decision to continue work in-house was upheld where the agency accurately made a cost comparison showing that contracting out is less costly. The Office of Management and Budget "Cost Comparison Handbook" prescribes the overall policies and detailed procedures required of all agencies in making cost comparisons between contractor and Government performance. After this period of time, a significant number of changes were made in the regulations and on occasion they were not followed by an agency. For example, in a recent make or buy protest, the GAO refused to reinstate a prospective contractor's initial argument to use in-house employees to perform base operation support services work at Lackland Air Force Base in Texas. The Air Force had twice reversed its own position thereon.

Major improvements occurred during the 1990s when many of them were inserted into Federal Acquisition Regulation (FAR). The current regulation on making cost comparisons between contractor and government performance requires that solicitations and synopses thereof be issued to obtain offers for comparison purposes which "will not result in a contract if Government performance is determined to be more advantageous." Even when the full-time equivalent government employees involved are fewer than those implementing agency guidance, these comparisons may be conducted "if there is reason to believe that commercial prices are unreasonable." It also states that "ordinarily" (at least) agencies "should not incur the delay" in doing so in such cases.

The regulation refers to OMB Circular No. A–76 to note that it provides that each agency "shall establish an appeals procedures for informal administrative review of the initial cost comparison result." This is a review by a higher official of the cost comparison; it does not apply to the selection of one contractor in preference to another. The latter one is subject to the filing of a protest by a contractor (See Chapter 33).

The Federal Activities Inventory Reform Act (FAIR) requires Federal agencies to compile inventories of not inherently governmental activities by June 30 of each year. Such "commercial activities" might be contracted out. They are not required to include cost comparisons. Either the public or private sector have 30 days to challenge the activities on or omitted from these inventories. While private organizations think that the government could save money by making private use of more functions that are not inherent-

ly governmental, unions have disagreed. Contracting officers even considered alerting them of the possibility of
performing a cost comparison "if there is reason to believe
that commercial prices are unreasonable." In 2003, the
Office of Management and Budget (OMB) revised Circular
A–76 to indicate that an interested party may challenge the
inclusion or exclusion of an activity in an agency's FAIR
Act list, including the classification or reclassification of an
activity as either inherently governmental or "commercial"
costs of getting public service are determined by calculations regarding a re-engineered form called the "Most Efficient Organization" ("MEO"). Only the federal manager
who develops the MEO (the "Agency Tender Official" or
ATO) can appeal internally, not unions. On December 22,
2003, the OMB issued a memorandum on long-range competitive sourcing plans, which potentially affect some 850,-
000 federal jobs that have been found to be commercial in
nature.

Conflicts of interest may exist in making determinations
to contract out. The Comptroller General found such a
conflict existed where fourteen of sixteen agency evaluators
involved in the decision held positions that would have been
contracted out under a solicitation. It ruled that the process
was "fundamentally flawed as a result of a conflict of
interest." Although the Office of Government Ethics (OGE)
disagreed that the Air Force's decision to keep the activities
in-house was tainted by a conflict of interest, amendments
to the A–76 Supplemental Handbook in 2000 revised the
issue in favor of GAO's interpretation.

In order to determine the availability of private commercial sources, contracting officers are directed to make all
reasonable efforts to identify such sources and assist in
synopsizing the requirement in the Governmentwide Point
of Entry (GPE) "up to three times in a 90–day period with

a minimum of 30 days between notices." Thus, before bringing an activity in-house, particularly with respect to the fabrication of routine hardware items, the government must first recompute the requirements within the private sector, and if necessary conduct a cost comparison study. However, on April 1, 1996 the Office of Management and Budget published a revised Supplemental Handbook to OMB Circular A-76 that eliminates the requirement for cost comparisons in certain circumstances; namely (1) national security activities, (2) mission critical core activities, and (3) temporary emergency requirements.

A 12 percent overhead rate is required to be applied to government cost estimates for cost comparison studies. Agencies may use a different rate after publishing in the *Federal Register* an explanation of the methodology used in developing the different rate.

(c) Solicitation Provisions and Contract Clause

When private commercial and cost comparison sources are available and a cost comparison is required, the agency personnel who develop the cost estimate for government performance must submit a cost-comparison form to the contracting officer "in a sealed, dated envelope not later than the time established for receipt of initial proposals or bid opening." The contracting officer must issue a solicitation based on the work statement and require "firm offers for the period covered by the cost comparison unless a proper determination to the contrary is made."

A protest challenging an agency's decision not to award a contract under a solicitation issued in accordance with the procedures set out in OMB Circular A-76 has been held to fall within the definition of protest in the Competition in Contracting Act since the act does not require that an award be proposed at the time a protest is filed. A proposed award within the statutory definition is contemplated when a solicitation is issued for cost comparison purposes. Thus, a protest on the Army's failure to perform the "comprehensive documented analysis" of costs and benefits in a solicitation was held to compromise the process and the resulting public/private competition.

Solicitations do not limit award to U.S. offerors. The sealed envelope containing the cost-comparison form on which the cost estimate for government performance has been entered is opened at the public bid opening, where sealed bidding is used, and the apparent result is announced based on the initial cost-comparison form, stating that this result is subject to required agency processing, including evaluation for responsiveness and responsibility. The completed and approved cost comparison analysis is made available to interested parties upon request. A cost comparison conducted after the cancellation of a solicitation can be used to prove that the government had a compelling reason for the cancellation. Even after completion of a cost comparison, an agency should, on being notified of a material change in an offeror's financial condition, reconsider its finding of nonresponsibility, despite the administrative inconvenience involved.

In sealed bidding, solicitations issued for the purpose of comparing the costs of contract or and government performance, contain a clause called "Right of First Refusal of Employment" which states that the government will provide the contractor, within ten days after date of contract award, a list of employees adversely affected or separated as a result of award of a contract. This clause also requires the contractor to report to the contracting officer the names of individuals on the list who are hired within 90 days after contract performance begins.

(d) Appeals

Many interested parties have argued for a process which would permit appeals of agency management decisions, such as the determination of the most efficient and effective in-house organization or whether an activity is a commercial activity or a governmental function. It was also argued that Federal employees should be given the right to appeal decisions to contract out without a cost study. But, the OMB stated that to allow appeals of agency management decisions relating to the in-house organization "would be tantamount to permitting third parties to dictate to agency management. Decisions as to the most efficient and effective in-house organization and whether an activity is governmental or commercial are basic management responsibilities, and management's decisions must be final." Management was required to encourage employee participation in the determination of the most efficient and effective organization during development of the in-house estimate, and the process now permits appeals of the justification to contract out without a cost study. However, the General Accounting Office refused to review a determination under A–76 to contract for services rather than have them performed in-house.

Agencies must establish an appeals or internal procedure for informal administrative review of the initial cost comparison result by an official at the same level as, or at a higher level than, the official who approved that result. However, that procedure is only "to resolve questions concerning the calculation of the cost comparison and shall not apply to questions concerning selection of one contractor in preference to another" (which must be treated as protest against award). The General Accounting Office will not entertain a protest when the administrative appeals procedure established pursuant to OMB Circular A–76 has not been exhausted.

Contractors who have participated in a supply program have been held to have standing to challenge an agency's decision to convert the program from contract to in-house operations and forcing the agency to comply with Circular A–76. A court stated that conversion to government-operated facilities cannot take place "unless a recompetition does not result in reasonable prices, in-house performance is feasible, and the conversion is justified by a cost comparison study performed in accordance with OMB Circular A–76."

(e) GAO Review of Make or Buy Decisions

The GAO does not review all decisions to perform an agency's services in-house. As stated above, the GAO initially refused to review agency decisions on whether to contract-out, initially holding that A–76 was a matter of executive policy and discretion, without establishing any legal rights. But the GAO was concerned that decisions on contracting-out might be detrimental to the procurement system in cases where cost comparisons were erroneous. In 1979, the GAO decided to review A–76 decisions where a solicitation had to be issued to assist an agency in determining whether or not to perform work in-house. That is, where an erroneous cost comparison materially affected an agency's decision, that decision would be overruled, provided that bidders have first raised and exhausted their issues in administrative appeals in the agency involved. However, GAO has held that it cannot recommend that an agency reimburse protest costs incurred in pursuing an administrative appeal of the agency's cost comparison under A–76, because its authority to recommend reimbursement of protest costs does not extend to costs incurred by a protester in litigating in another forum.

After the turn of the millennium, the GAO found a conflict of interest (COI) from an A–76 cost comparison study and sustained a decision to keep work in-house. The COI was held to have "fatally flawed" the Navy's cost comparison with a performance work statement (PWS). Another 2001 decision also dealt with inherently governmental functions in the selection process connected with the award to a services contractor.

The GAO will not hear issues raised by taxpayers, Federal employees, or a union representing the Civil Service employees terminated as a result of contracting out. Thus, the GAO reviews situations in which the procurement system is used for cost comparison purposes and the cost comparison is alleged to be faulty or misleading. It has declined to review an agency's alleged intention to perform services in-house after terminating a contract for default.

Since the beginning of the 21st Century, the GAO has been sustaining A–76 protests at a rate of 53%—in other areas the sustaining rate was only 22%. It has been noted that A–76 cost comparisons "are problematic for agencies."

(f) Review of Make or Buy Decisions by U.S. Courts

The Administrative Dispute Resolution Act of 1996 expanded the U.S. Court of Federal Claims' bid protest jurisdiction—originally limited to preaward protests by the Federal Courts Improvement Act—to include post award protests, and, effective January 1, 2001, terminated the U.S. district courts' concurrent jurisdiction. Accordingly, as of January 1, 2001, protests challenging an agency's contracting out decision can only be brought in the General Accounting Office (under the Competition in Contracting Act) or the Court of Federal Claims. Rather than protesting in either of these, the protest can be sent to the agency together with a request for an independent review "at a level above the contracting officer."

It has been argued that participation by local managers who rely upon the services provided by an in-house activity presents a conflict of interest. However, the Court of Federal Claims held that no such conflict exists. It found no FAR support for this argument and added that it was "unwilling to *hamstring* agencies in this fashion without some better indication that such conduct constitutes a disqualifying conflict." (Emphasis added.) About the same time, the General Accounting Office sustained a bid protest challenging a Navy cost comparison study under Circular A–76, citing flaws in the Navy's decision to retain the work in-house under the FAR standards of conduct.

A union of government employees may oppose the inclusion of particular activities on the list under the Federal Acquisition Inventory Reform Act of 1994 (FAIR) as those not considered "inherently governmental." But the contracting out of Federal worker functions on the basis of "inherently governmental" does not grant such persons standing to challenge the contracting out of their existing Federal jobs based on OMB Circular A–76 cost comparisons.

The office of Management and Budget Circular A–76 states that no funds appropriated will be available to support an A–76, study such as a cost comparison that exceeds 24 months on a single function activity or 48 months after initiation for a multi-function one. A Federal court held that the 48–month limit on the funding of commercial activities runs from the date a study committee is formed.

The Court of Federal Claims dismissed a government employee union's claim challenging the contracting out of jobs at a supply distribution center. It ruled that the displaced Federal workers and their unions lacked standing to challenge a cost comparison under the Federal Activities Inventory Reform (FAIR) Act and Office of Management and Budget Circular A–76, because "Congress did not intend for Federal employees and their unions to be able to challenge cost comparisons." As noted above, the United States Court of Appeals has affirmed the Court of Federal Claims decision.

Similarly, most other U.S. courts have rejected union protests against A–76 cost comparison studies. In 2003, several civilian employees and their union were held by a consent to lack standing to challenge the Air Force's decision, under OMB Circular A–76, to contract out to engineering function at Hanscom AFB.

(g) Commercial Activities Panel

The National Defense Authorization Act for Fiscal Year 2001 directed the Comptroller General of the United States to establish a panel of experts to study the current procedures used to make government sourcing decisions. The Commercial Activities Panel, comprised of government officials, outside experts, union members and contractors, first met in May 2001 and issued its final report in April 2002. The panel voted 8 to 4 to replace the current method of conducting public-private competitions with a new approach modeled on the FAR's "best value" source selection procedures.

§ 7.3 Equipment Lease or Purchase

In addition to "make or buy" decisions, agencies must often make a determination whether to acquire equipment by lease or purchase. This determination is applicable to both the initial acquisition of equipment and the renewal or extension of existing equipment leases. The general policy is to purchase if the equipment will be used "beyond the point in time when cumulative leasing costs exceed the purchase costs." However, leasing may also serve as an interim measure when there is a need for immediate use of equipment to meet program or system goals. In such cases "a lease with option to purchase is preferable," and generally "a long-term lease should be avoided."

§ 7.4 Inherently Governmental Functions

The regulation provides a broad definition of "inherently governmental functions" and provides a list of examples of functions considered to be inherently governmental, or which shall be treated as such, and it also sets forth a list of certain services and actions that are not considered to be inherently governmental functions. "Inherently governmental function" means, "as a matter of policy, a function that is so intimately related to the public interest as to mandate performance by government employees." Nevertheless, its definition is "a policy determination, not a legal determination." In Chapter 1 it is noted that final regulations published in the Federal Register "have the force and effect of law."

An inherently governmental function involves, among other things, the interpretation and execution of the laws of the United States so as to "bind the United States to take or not to take some action by contract, policy, regulation, authorization, order, or otherwise." Contracts themselves cannot be used "for the performance of inherently governmental functions." In Federal procurement activities with respect to prime contracts, inherently governmental functions or those which shall be treated as such include "determining what supplies or services are to be acquired by the government (although an agency may give contractors authority to acquire supplies at prices within specified ranges and subject to other reasonable conditions deemed appropriate by the agency)." These functions include participating as a voting member of any source selection boards; approving any contractual documents, including documents defining requirements, incentive plans, and evaluation criteria; terminating contracts; and participating as a voting member on performance evaluation boards.

Functions generally not considered to be inherently governmental functions include services that involve or relate to "budget preparation, feasibility studies, strategy options to be used by agency personnel in developing policy," and "the development of regulations." It is interesting to note that this list of non-inherently governmental functions also includes services that involve or relate to the evaluation of another contractor's performance, "contractors providing assistance in contract management (such as where the contractor might influence official evaluations of other contractors)," as well as the following:

Contractors working in any situation that permits or might permit them to gain access to confidential business information and/or any other sensitive information.

Contractors providing information regarding agency policies or regulations, such as attending conferences on behalf of an agency, conducting community relations campaigns, or conducting agency training courses.

Contractors participating in any situation where it might be assumed that they are agency employees or representatives.

Contractors participating as technical advisors to a source selection board or participating as voting or nonvoting members of a source evaluation board.

However, the only acknowledgement of this problem is the statement that although they are "not considered to be inherently governmental functions;" however, they "may approach being in that category because of the nature of the function, the manner in which the contractor performs the contract, or the manner in which the government administers contractor performance." More regulatory guidance may be needed in order to prevent the possibility of abuse by government agencies as has happened in the past. See Chapter 3.

CHAPTER 8

GOVERNMENT AND OTHER RE-QUIRED SOURCES OF SUP-PLIES AND SERVICES

§ 8.1 In General

Government agencies are required to obtain supplies and services from or through certain designated sources where possible and where not otherwise provided by law. Such sources include agency inventories, Federal Prison Industries, Inc., the Committee for Purchase from the Blind and Other Severely Disabled, and Mandatory Federal Supply Schedules.

The National Defense Authorization Act for Fiscal Year 2002 requires that market research be conducted regarding price, quality, and time of delivery before a purchase is made from the Federal Prison Industries (FPI); and, unless the FPI item is comparable in all of these areas, competitive procedures must be used. Defense Department contracting officers may unilaterally acquire a product or service competitively once it determines that a Federal Prison industries-provided product or service is not comparable to what is available from the private sector. The General Accounting Office (GAO) has held that it will not review an agency's determination that the FPI's product was not comparable to private sector products because the FPI's enabling statute provides for binding resolution of such disputes by an arbitration board.

§ 8.2   Excess Personal Property

The regulations prescribe that agencies must use excess personal property in their possession as a first source for their needs and those of their cost-type contractors. The General Services Administration (GSA) functions as a "clearing house" of information on the availability of excess personal property by publishing catalogs and bulletins. The GSA also assists other agencies in meeting their requirements for those supply types excepted from reporting as excess by the Federal Property Management Regulations.

§ 8.3   Utilities

Contracts for the acquisition of utility services or charges are long-term and are centrally controlled by the General Services Administration; the GSA has statutory authority to enter into long-term contracts for utility services for periods not to exceed a term of 10 years. These contracts may take the form of an areawide contract or a separate contract. Because utilities are monopolies whose prices and services are regulated by the state where they are located, such utility commodity procurements are normally made by non-competitive methods.

§ 8.4   Ordering From Federal Supply Schedules

The Federal Supply Schedule program, directed and managed by the General Services Administration (GSA), provides Federal agencies with a simplified process for obtaining commonly used commercial supplies and services at prices associated with volume buying. There are both optional use and mandatory use schedules, which are discussed in Chapter 38.

Neither simplified acquisition procedures nor Small Business programs apply to orders properly placed against a Federal supply schedule. Agencies properly issuing orders against a Multiple Award Schedule (MAS) "need not seek further competition." An exception can be made for orders made under schedule Blanket Purchasing Agreements (BPAs), which are not "inconsistent with the applicable schedule contract." Where orders are exceeding the maximum order threshold, the ordering office should seek a price reduction (which reductions may even be available elsewhere). Should the reduction be granted by a schedule contractor under a Blanket Purchase Agreement (BPA), the contractor is not required to pass it on to other than the "individual agency for a specific order." Also provided are procedures for placing orders and obtaining price reductions under GSA federal supply schedule (FSS)contracts, and regarding the "GSA Advantage!" on-line shopping service.

Frequently, agencies will issue a Request for Quotations, with evaluation criteria, to Multiple Award Schedule (MAS) vendors to aid in deciding the best value MAS provider. Where the agency intends to use the vendors' responses as the basis for a detailed technical evaluation and a possible cost/technical tradeoff, it may elect to use an approach that is like a competition in a negotiated procurement. Where the agency uses this approach, and a protest is made against the selection decision, the GAO will review the agency's actions to ensure that the evaluation was fair and reasonable, and consistent with the terms of the solicitation.

Federal penal and correctional institutions also maintain a schedule of products at prices not to exceed current market prices from which agencies may order. In the case of orders from Federal Prison Industries, Inc. (FPI), disputes regarding price, quality, character, or suitability of products are subject to arbitration by a special arbitration board consisting of the Comptroller General of the United

States, the Administrator of General Services, and the Director of the Office of Management and Budget, or their representatives. The decisions of this board are final and binding on all parties.

§ 8.5 Acquisition From the Blind and Other Severely Disabled

A Committee for Purchase From the Blind or Other Severely Disabled is appointed by the President to determine supplies and services to be purchased by all agencies from workshops of such sources. The Committee publishes a Procurement List and establishes fair market prices for items or services required to be purchased from these workshops that are available from GSA stocks as well as the Defense Logistics Agency (DLA) system. The Federal Prison Industries have priority for the purchase of supplies and the Workshops have priority for the purchase of services.

When a workshop for the blind or other severely disabled fails to perform under the terms of an order: (1) the ordering office must make every effort to resolve the noncompliance with the workshop involved and to negotiate an adjustment before taking action to cancel the order. (2) If the problem with the workshop cannot be resolved, the ordering office must refer the matter for resolution first to the central nonprofit agency and then, (3) if necessary, to the Committee for Purchase From the Blind or Other Severely Disabled. (4) Thereafter, if the ordering office determines that it must cancel an order, it must notify the central nonprofit agency and, if practical, request a reallocation of the order. When the central nonprofit agency cannot reallocate the order, that office must grant a purchase exception permitting use of commercial sources. (5) Even this exception, however, is subject to approval by the committee when the value of the purchase exception is $25,000 or more. Some simplification of this procedure would appear to be desirable to prevent the classification of supplies and services as being "suitable" for purchase by the government when, in fact, those supplies or services turn out to be unsuitable for such purchases.

§ 8.6 Acquisition of Printing and Related Supplies

Government agencies that desire to print material normally use the services of the Government Printing Office (GPO) by an interagency order that is not a contract. However, the Joint Committee on Printing (JCP) of the Congress may grant approval for the Public Printer, who heads the Government Printing Office, to contract the work out to private printers. More importantly, the Committee may authorize an agency to either contract for its own work or establish an in-house printing capability. Regulations issued by the Committee require the head of each agency to designate a central printing authority to serve as the liaison with JCP and the Public Printer on matters related to printing. Contracting officers must then obtain approval from their designated central printing authority before contracting for printing or other supplies or services, such as "composition, platemaking, presswork, binding, and micrographics (when used as a substitute for printing)."

§ 8.7 Leasing of Motor Vehicles

With certain exceptions, government agencies are forbidden from preparing solicitations for the leasing of motor vehicles without first certifying that the vehicles requested are of "maximum fuel efficiency and minimum body size, engine size, and equipment necessary to fulfill operation needs." These motor vehicles must also meet prescribed fuel economy standards and, in the case of passenger vehicles (larger than compacts), that they are essential to the agency's mission. The General Services Administration must have advised that it cannot furnish the vehicles. When leasing motor vehicles, the contract must include a statement that the contractor shall perform maintenance on the vehicles unless it has been determined that it will be more economical for the government to perform the work.

CHAPTER 9

CONTRACTOR QUALIFICATIONS

A. RESPONSIBLE PROSPECTIVE CONTRACTORS

§ 9.1 Standards

In Public Contracting, before an award to an offeror can be made it is essential for an agency to consider minimum standards pertaining to its ability to perform. There exist policies, standards, and procedures for determining whether prospective contractors and subcontractors are what is called "responsible." The ability to perform may also be affected by policies pertaining to early testing, qualified products, and first article testing and approval. Furthermore, a potential contractor may be excluded from contracting by debarment, suspension, or declaration of ineligibility and organizational conflicts of interest. However, the Project on Government Oversight (POGO) demonstrated that large government contractors hold some immunity from both the suspension and debarment remedies, apparently many contractors recognize that they must commit a spectacular violation or crime in order to be suspended or debarred. Nevertheless, purchase must be made from, and contracts be awarded to, responsible prospective contractors only. It is effectuated by a prohibition against any purchase or award unless there is "an affirmative determination of responsibility. In the absence of information clearly indicating that the prospective contractor is responsible," the contracting officer must then make a "determination of nonresponsibility." This is because "the award of a contract to a supplier based on lowest evaluated price alone can be false economy if there is subsequent default, late deliveries, or other unsatisfactory performance resulting in additional contractual or administrative costs."

To be responsible, a contractor must have adequate financial resources, a satisfactory record of performance, integrity and business ethics, and the necessary organization, experience, technical skills, and production facility. As regards facilities, the offeror must have the necessary production facilities or the ability to obtain them. A responsibility determination focuses on the bidder's ability to satisfy commitments encompassed in a responsive bid or acceptable proposal. A change in the place of performance was held to raise an issue of responsibility and not of responsiveness, because replacing one facility in the area of consideration with another facility within that area did not render the bid nonresponsive. Although a solicitation might state that the information was to be submitted with the bid, an agency cannot change a matter of bidder responsibility into one of responsiveness by the terms of the solicitation.

A preaward survey is normally required unless the agency has on hand information necessary to make a determination regarding responsibility. However, no such survey should be requested for a contemplated fixed price contract at or below the simplified acquisition threshold (normally $100,000; see Chapter 13) or for acquisition of commercial items (see Chapter 12) unless it can be shown to be cost justified. Preaward surveys being requested when information on hand or readily available is not sufficient; it begins after ascertaining whether the prospective award to a contractor is "debarred, suspended or ineligible".

Under Title III of the 1968 Omnibus Crime Control and Safe Streets Act, an "aggrieved person" "may move to suppress" wiretap evidence in any trial, hearing, or proceeding, on the ground that the communication was "unlawfully intercepted" or intercepted on the basis of an insufficient authorization. An "aggrieved person" is "a person who was a party to any intercepted wire, oral, or electronic communication or a person against whom the interception was directed." It has been held that the process for making a nonresponsibility determination is not a "trial" or a "hearing."

A prospective contractor that is or recently has been seriously deficient in contract performance is "presumed to be nonresponsible" unless a determination is made that the circumstances were beyond the control of the contractor or that it has taken "appropriate corrective action."

Regarding the general standards of responsibility, to some extent in the public eye there once existed the concept that only the financial standard prevails. David Scott, an Apollo 15 astronaut, on blast-off in 1978 was quoted as stating:

> "You just sat there thinking that this piece of hardware had 400,000 components, all of them built by the lowest bidder."

However, assuming competency to one in a government agency who is knowledgeable in the field, he would realize that non-financial requirements for a determination of responsibility of a contractor include all the criteria of responsibility noted above, and many special standards needed for contract performance, have been met. It is only when these standards are ignored, as they sometimes are, that David Scott's worry can arise. Even with competent procurement, he may still, of course, need to worry about the piece of hardware, but then he would have no valid basis for doing so solely because of problems growing out of the making of an award to the lowest responsible offeror—particularly when the agency having developed "the special standards of responsibility" in those purchases where "experience has demonstrated that unusual expertise or specialized facilities are needed for adequate contract performance."

Not infrequently, an owner who has conducted bribery or bid rigging will transfer his interest to a third party under a trust or other arrangement in order to avoid a debarment of his company. However, this will not suffice because the government has no way of knowing whether entrusting the company to a third party will prevent future activities by the owner.

§ 9.2 Subcontractor Responsibility

The normal rule is that prospective prime contractors (and not government agencies) are responsible for determining the "responsibility" of their prospective subcontractors.

Regulations apply to suspensions of prime contractors that may be expected to be awarded subcontracts and establish specific rules for awards of subcontracts to suspended firms, requiring government consent to any award of a subcontract to a suspended "contractor."

Where a determination of a prospective subcontractor's responsibility may affect the government's determination of the prospective prime contractor's own responsibility, the prospective contractor may be required to provide written evidence of a proposed subcontractor's responsibility. When it is in the government's interest to do so, the contracting officer may directly determine a prospective subcontractor's responsibility. A subcontractor may be ineligible because he is on a list of debarred, ineligible, or suspended firms.

§ 9.3   The Time at Which a Responsibility Determination Is Required

The making of the responsibility determination prior to soliciting bids or proposals (pre-qualification of offerors) has generally been viewed as a restriction on competition. Generally, offerors need not be so qualified at time of bid opening. Most aspects of responsibility are such that a contractor need only be able to assure that it will be able to meet the standards at the time of performance. Generally, the agency obtains information regarding the responsibility of prospective contractors after a bid opening or receipt of offers. The requests for information are ordinarily limited to information concerning the low bidder or those offerors who fall within the range for award. The requirement to consider all responsible sources for full and open competition does not mean "that an agency must delay satisfying its own needs in order to allow a vendor time to develop the ability to meet the government's requirements." A "responsible source" is a prospective contractor who is able to comply with the required or proposed delivery or performance schedule. In December 2003, the regulation was amended to preclude placing discretionary orders under existing contractors that have been debarred, suspended, or proposed for debarment, absent a written determination of compelling need.

Although an original solicitation may contain a requirement which the bidder must fulfill in order to be responsive at bid opening time, a subsequent amendment to the solicitation could convert that same requirement into one concerning responsibility which would be evaluated at time of award. Further, the fact that a bidder/protester may have been found responsible by other contracting officers during same period in which it was found to be nonresponsible under a particular procurement does not show that contracting officer acted in bad faith in making a nonresponsibility determination; such determinations are judgmental and it has been held that two contracting officers may reach opposite conclusions on the same facts.

However, in negotiated contracting, especially when research and development is involved, the contracting officer may obtain this information before issuing the request for proposals. This information seeking normally is the action taken as the first step of a "preaward survey." (See subsection 9.1 above) Normally, this is often conducted by an agency office that obtains prospective contractors' financial competence and credit needs, as well as the adequacy of their accounting systems and suitability for use in administering the proposed type of contract.

The contracting officer's signing of a contract constitutes a determination that the prospective contractor is responsible with respect to that contract. That signing cannot also suffice as a record pertaining to those who did not receive an award, when an offer on which an award would otherwise be made is rejected because the prospective contractor is found to be nonresponsible. The contracting officer must sign and place in the contract file a "determination of nonresponsibility," stating the basis for the determination. This record may have special significance for such prospective contractors. Statutes require special treatment of a determination that a small business concern otherwise in line for award lacks certain elements of responsibility.

Procurement regulations specifically prohibit release or disclosure outside the government of the preaward survey report, including information accumulated for purposes of determining the responsibility of a prospective contractor, except as provided in the Freedom of Information Act. On the other hand, the procurement regulation does permit an agency to discuss "preaward survey information with the prospective contractor before determining responsibility." But after award, such discussions are possible only "if it is appropriate." Preaward surveys are not normally made for small orders or when the information on hand is readily available to the contracting officer and is sufficient to make a determination regarding responsibility. If the contemplated contract will be for $25,000 or more but not over $100,000 and involves small business set aside, the contracting officer should award to a single responsible bidder without requesting a survey. A disgruntled bidder cannot complain that an agency improperly found an offeror to be responsible without first conducting a preaward survey, because such a survey is not a legal prerequisite to an affirmative determination of responsibility and these determinations are not generally reviewed by the GAO.

§ 9.4 Review of Responsibility Decisions

Traditionally, both the courts and GAO have declined most reviews of an agency's affirmative determination of responsibility. The Comptroller General's view is that the standards for responsible prospective contractors and the requirements and procedures for responsibility determinations essentially involve a matter of "business judgment;" therefore, the GAO will not review an affirmative determination unless the protester alleges agency fraud or bad faith or the failure to apply definitive responsibility criteria, (i.e., unreasonable application of specific, objective, and mandatory solicitation standards) that measure a prospective offeror's ability to perform a contract. Case law from predecessor courts to the United States Court of Appeals for the Federal Circuit essentially adopted the GAO view.

Recently, the United States Court of Appeals for the Federal Circuit rejected the GAO analogy. In the *Impresa* decision, the court held that a protester had standing to challenge a contracting officer's affirmative determination of the awardee's responsibility, explaining that while contracting officers have wide discretion in making such determinations, that discretion is not absolute. In that case, the contracting officer had made a conclusory finding that the contractor was responsible, even though at least one of its principals had been indicted for bid rigging. The Federal Circuit applied the "arbitrary and capricious" standard for the validity of any contracting officer decision protested under the Administrative Dispute Resolution Act of 1996. The *Impresa* court further ordered a deposition of the contracting officer to explain why he believed the contractor had a satisfactory record of integrity and business ethics.

More uniformity exists between the courts and the GAO on challenges to negative responsibility decisions. Typically, the protester in this situation challenges the agency's adverse responsibility decision, which thereby deprives the firm of the award. One commentator has argued that the *Impresa* case states the correct standard that the GAO should implement by changing its regulation.

§ 9.5 Financial Responsibility

(a) In General

If upon initial examination a prospective contractor's financial ability is doubtful, the contracting officer should attempt to obtain additional information necessary to resolve such doubts. Lack of responsibility does not automatically follow from the filing of a petition in bankruptcy—a rule that is in accord with the law pertaining to private contracts. A contractor's financial condition need only be *adequate* for the performance of the contract.

(b) Accounting Methods

In order to ascertain the financial responsibility of a potential contractor, it may be necessary to examine his accounting statements. In this connection, it is noted that the general rule for income tax purposes is that "taxable income shall be computed under the method of accounting on the basis of which the taxpayer regularly computes his income in keeping his books." Further, if one is engaged in more than one trade or business, he may "use a different method of accounting for each trade or business." But, in spite of these provisions of the Internal Revenue Code (IRC), it must not be assumed by contracting officers that statements of the financial condition received from a potential contractor were necessarily always prepared utilizing the same methods that he used regularly in computing his income for all other purposes. The IRC presently contains numerous "bookkeeping" requirements that mean that lower income for tax purposes must also be so reported for financial purposes to shareholders, creditors, and others. Although the government's contracting officers are not specifically named as beneficiaries of these provisions, they should examine accounting statements that are made for such beneficiaries. If the data supplied is certified pursuant to the Truth in Negotiations Act of 1962, this may act as a substitute for reliance on a statement subject to the sanctions imposed upon income tax returns.

Financial accounting embraces objectives other than income tax accounting and has been described as a system that provides "a continual history quantified in money terms of economic resources and obligations of a business enterprise and of economic activities that change these resources and obligations."

When contracting officers use financial statements in order to make a decision that potential contractors are financially responsible, these statements should meet objectives of reliability and relevance.

(c) *Reliance on Generally Accepted Accounting Principles in Financial Statements*

The only successful general definition of "cost" may be a negative one; that is, it is "not profit." Other more meaningful uses of the word require a more functional analysis. In accounting for the financial responsibility of a bidder or proposer, a contracting officer is likely to receive accounting statements showing solvency and past profits; yet, such a result can be produced by merely increasing the values of the most recent closing inventory. This is because all sums allocated to inventory (rather than expensed) increase net income by a like amount for that period. If such increases are not justified, then a firm may show a profit for the period even though the firm is in fact insolvent at the time the statement is prepared, and hence not financially responsible. This raised a question concerning a contracting officer's ability to rely upon business records based upon "generally accepted accounting principles." In 2001 a Federal Circuit Court of Appeals stated that such principles "tolerate a range of reasonable treatments, leaving the choice among the alternatives to management," and the role of the court in reviewing the accountant's work is limited "to deciding only whether the accountant chose a procedure from the universe of generally accepted accounting principles."

A contracting officer may do very little after receiving such statements. Prior to award, he cannot have an inventory taken of a potential contractor in order to verify that he is not in a "loss position" and may not be a "responsible" contractor. His financial advisors could use comparative statements in order to ascertain the reasonable likelihood of financial responsibility at time of award. He could look for certain statements that may have been submitted to the Securities and Exchange Commission (SEC).

Generally accepted principles must be regarded with some skepticism. This may be illustrated by a case involving defendants who were a senior partner, a junior partner, and a senior associate in an internationally known accounting firm. They were convicted by a federal court in New York of conspiring to knowingly draw up and certify a false and misleading corporate financial statement for Continental Vending Machine Corporation. On appeal the evidence was found to have sustained a jury finding that the accountants knew of looting by the corporate president, that they certified as an asset a receivable whose collectibility was essential but collateralized by securities of the very corporation whose solvency was at issue and failed to reveal a known increase in such receivable.

Defendant asked for instructions which would have told the jury that he could be found guilty only if, according to generally accepted accounting principles, the financial statements as a whole did not fairly represent the financial condition of Continental as of September 30, 1962, and then only if his departure from accepted standards was due to willful disregard of those standards with knowledge of the falsity of the statements and an intent to deceive. The judge declined. On the contrary, he found the "critical test" to be whether the financial statements as a whole "fairly presented the financial position of Continental as of September 30, 1962, and whether it accurately reported the operations for fiscal 1962." Proof of compliance with generally accepted standards was stated to be "evidence which may be very persuasive but not necessarily conclusive."

Generally accepted accounting principles instruct an accountant what to do in the usual case where he has no reason to doubt that the affairs of the corporation are being honestly conducted. Once he has reason to believe that this basic assumption is false, an entirely different situation confronts him. Then, he must 'extend his procedures to determine whether or not such suspicions are justified.'

In the 1980's, public companies no longer indicated that they were distributing "unaudited" statements. They referred to a "reviewed" financial statement; that is one that provides a CPA vague standards in order to give "limited" assurance that there are no more material changes to the financial statements than are necessary in order to bring them into compliance with generally accepted accounting principles. No indication exists that this practice has changed, although with the Enron scandal we may see a change in the auditing of corporations. An "audit" may be an examination resulting in the opinion of an accountant following generally accepted auditing standards. No attorney should assume that a "look-see" by an accountant constitutes an "audit" unless the financial statement so states. Where the accountant's opinion is that the financial statements fairly present the financial position of the firm's books he examined by merely "reviewing" or "compiling" them, then each page of the statements must so indicate under the provisions of Accounting and Review Services No. 1.

(d) Use of Material Related to Projections

Sometimes predictions and forecasts are presented to a contracting officer as indicative of the financial responsibility of a prospective contractor. Often these are conceived in the form of "statistical forecasting"—a field that includes input computation of cyclical and seasonal trends to bolster predictions. Contracting officers may sometimes be misled by their official-looking character; for example data included in statements in order to satisfy Security and Exchange Commission (SEC) Regulations. Until comparatively recently, the SEC's Proxy Regulations predictions of earnings were used as an example of what may be "misleading solicitations" and such projections were excluded from proxy statements and other SEC filings. However, in 1976 the Commission altered its position in order to permit forecasts in field documents. The reasons given for these changes were that "investors appear to want management's assessment of a company's future performance, and some managements may wish to furnish their projections through Commission filings." Investors are risk-takers of a different order than Contracting Officers. Such predictions are of questionable value to the latter, even though the SEC has conditioned its approval of projections on the belief that they are "made in good faith and have a reasonable basis, provided that they are presented in an appropriate format and accompanied by information adequate for investors to make their own judgments." In 2003, the SEC issued amended regulations. See Chapter 42. Even the most carefully prepared and thoroughly documented projections may prove inaccurate. There is a liability for misleading security filings, and for those special instances where the Truth in Negotiations Act (TINA), or similar statutes, become applicable. (See Chapter 15.)

(e) Adequate Disclosure in Consolidated Balance Sheets

Consolidated financial statements of large enterprises may be presented to a contracting officer to show the financial responsibility needed to be awarded a government contract. Consolidated statements are typically used where there is a majority ownership of the voting stock of a subsidiary by the parent company. Questions sometimes arise concerning which corporations are to be consolidated in financial statements. This may be illustrated in agency proceedings under Section 8(d) of the Securities Act of 1933 ("Act") to determine whether a "stop order" should be issued suspending the effectiveness of a registration statement filed by a large research corporation doing business with the U.S. government. That Act imposes upon issuers of registered securities the obligation of making honest, adequate, and timely disclosures in a registration statement and prospectus concerning their corporate business and financial affairs. This is true not only for the benefit of those to whom, and by whom, the securities are proposed to be offered and sold, but also for the entire "market place" to evaluate. Being part of this market place, a Contracting Officer should use these disclosures in discharging his responsibility to evaluate a prospective contractor (or a prime contractor in evaluating a subcontractor).

A contractor's parent company may even have filed for Chapter 11 bankruptcy reorganization without necessitating a finding of nonresponsibility. However, under other circumstances, a bankruptcy filing would not cure such a finding.

§ 9.6   Experience Requirements

The regulation provides limited guidance with respect to the experience needed to bid or propose for a contract. Normally, a potential contractor must have had at least some experience doing similar work, as well as the necessary technical and managerial talent; he cannot merely procure subcontractors with such experience. An awardee's past performance record can even be evaluated as "satisfactory" where the agency did not have on file past performance rating information that it considered sufficient to permit a full evaluation. Thus, with certain exceptions, a prospective contractor's responsibility is also determined on the basis of "relevant performance history." This may be done "when necessary for particular acquisitions" when demonstrated that "unusual expertise" is needed.

The requirement that the product be in public use for a certain period may be essential to satisfy minimum reliability requirements. For example, in one case, an invitation for bids for radio sets was issued by the Department of Justice. The invitation for bid required manufacturers to have five years experience in design and production of similar equipment and that the equipment had been in public use for at least one year. Because the Small Business Administration (SBA) had approved a bidder's capacity, he protested the one-year quantity-in-use experience requirement. However, the Comptroller General upheld the one-year requirement because reliability, not capacity to produce was questioned. The Department of Justice was seeking units that the manufacturer had produced and "demonstrated their reliability under prolonged actual use conditions." The five-year experience requirement for the bidder himself also addressed itself to special standards needed to perform as of the time of award.

A later case involved a solicitation provision that required an offeror to have "an established asbestos abatement business for 5 years." This was held unreasonable because the agency could not justify why other bidders, employing personnel who met the five-year experience requirement, had not been employed by the same corporation for five years.

The government may even make a possibly erroneous judgment of nonresponsibility based upon information received from experts in areas where the contracting officer has little specialized knowledge, and preparation costs for a proposal are not recoverable. After a determination of Lear Sieglar to be nonresponsible, (which precluded the company from receiving an award under a solicitation for Inspection and Repair of C–130 aircraft), Lear Sieglar requested a reconsideration, arguing that the contracting officer looked at some information but ignored that which tended to show responsibility. Although the record led the Comptroller General to believe that "the determination of nonresponsibility is of doubtful validity," it was held that "a contracting officer may obtain information from experts in areas where he may have little or no specialized knowledge, and if he in good faith relies upon such information in all probability, he cannot be held at fault in case he makes an erroneous decision."

The government may reject an offer as unacceptable due to a vendor's inadequate past performance. For example, the Navy reviewed eight of the bidder's previous contracts. Because five of the past performance references reported poor timeliness and quality of performance, the source selection evaluation team gave the offeror an overall negative past performance assessment. The rejection on this ground differs from rejecting the offeror as non-responsible.

The Office of Federal Procurement Policy (OFPP) established requirements for evaluating contractor performance and for using past performance information in the contractor selection process. It does not pertain to procedures used by agencies in assessing performance for purposes of determining fees under award or incentive fee contracts, or to supplant contracting officials' judgments in initiating or conducting debarment and suspension proceedings. It requires all agencies to prepare evaluations of contractors' performance on all new contracts over $100,000 during the performance, and to use past performance information in making responsibility determinations in both sealed bid and competitively negotiated procurements. However, newly established firms are allowed to compete for contracts even though they lack a history of past performance.

Upon request, past performance information should be made available to other Federal procurement activities. However, this information is not provided without the contractor's consent to any private party, except where the agency determines that such information must be released pursuant to a Freedom of Information Act request. It should not be maintained for more than six years without being disposed of or updated. Special requirements exist for Architect/Engineer (A/E) and Construction Contracts.

In denying a protest by an incompetent contractor who had challenged the past performance ratings submitted by an agency, the Comptroller General stated:

> We find from our review that the documentation supports the contracting officer's finding that in a number of significant instances ... the protester failed to comply, at least initially, with clear contract requirements. The fact that there is a disparity in scores given by two reasonably knowledgeable evaluators at issue here is not a basis to object to the propriety of the more recent evaluation; completion of the reference survey clearly involves some degree of subjectivity which logically could produce a difference in point scores.

On the other hand, the GAO found that where an incumbent contractor had an excellent corporate experience and past performance, the agency reasonably could have awarded the contract to the incumbent contractor at a cost premium over a new corporation with no prior corporate experience or past performance.

Finally, in evaluating the past performance an agency may consider a vendors' prior default termination, even though that termination has been appealed to both the Armed Services Board of Contract Appeals and the Federal Circuit.

§ 9.7   Integrity

In interpreting the statute governing procurement by the General Services Administration, the Comptroller General stated that "the phrase 'responsible bidder' in this and similar statutes denotes something more than the ability or capacity of a bidder to perform the contract, and a contracting agency, therefore, may also consider a bidder's record of integrity in deciding whether he is, in fact, a responsible bidder." Thus, a bidder may lack integrity in performing government contracts, causing his elimination from bid consideration. Misconduct of a key employee need not have resulted in a criminal conviction before it could form a proper basis for a finding of nonresponsibility. Where the U.S. Court of Federal Claims did not make a finding that Procurement Integrity Act violations amounted to a breach by the agency of its implied contract to consider an offer fairly and honestly, that court, by enjoining the award, was held to have exceeded its limited equitable authority. Where a bidder had contacted a competitor's employees in an attempt to obtain that firm's proprietary proposal information, the integrity of the competitive bidding process justifies a contracting officer's disqualification of that bidder.

The relationship of a low bidder with another contractor who lacked integrity may also warrant a finding of nonresponsibility and award to the second low bidder. The board of directors of the low bidder empowered another contractor to sign and submit bids on his behalf by signing the name of the president to bid submissions and independently bind him to government contracts. This was held to have "evidenced a longstanding relationship ... which the contracting officer could consider in making his responsible" determination that the protester was nonresponsible. Some corporations acting on their own have forced CEO's to resign in order to maintain their integrity.

In 1992, the President created a new "Executive Council on Integrity and Efficiency" composed of inspectors general. It was charged to identify, and discuss programs' "weakness and vulnerability" to fraud, waste, and abuse, and to develop coordinated, government-wide remedies to "promote economy and efficiency."

§ 9.8   Effect of State Licensing and Permit Requirements on Responsibility

In general, competitive bidding for contracts with the government should be as unfettered by state laws unrelated to public contracting as possible. Thus, possession of a license from a state or local governmental entity might affect responsibility, depending upon whether the license is required by the agency. The U.S. Supreme Court has held that a state could not subject a contractor to state licensing requirements because this would "frustrate the expressed policy of selecting the lowest responsible bidder." Hence, bidders need not possess any state license unless such a license may be needed for work by the government. Although the bidder does not need to have a license at the time he submits his bid, if it is required by the invitation for bids (IFB), then it must have one in order to perform. An IFB may still impose a requirement for a state or local license as an additional requirement pertaining to its responsibility.

The North Carolina Supreme Court has held that a contract illegally entered into by an unlicensed contractor was unenforceable and could not be validated by the contractor's subsequent procurement of a license or by substantial compliance with the licensing statutes. These rulings would not affect the validity of contracts entered into by the United States. However, agencies utilize IFBs that generally require such a license where the legal incidence of the burden of state building code regulations and a municipal building permit requirement is on the contractor and the permit requirement may then become enforceable against its contractor even though the Federal government is the owner of structures to be erected.

B. QUALIFIED PRODUCTS—FIRST ARTICLE APPROVAL

§ 9.21 Qualified Products

Products (but not services) which are "prequalified" (that is, qualified in advance and independently of any specific acquisition action) are included in a Federal or Military "Qualified Products List" (QPL) after they have been examined and tested for compliance with specification requirements. An agency may limit competition for parts to maintain quality and reliability. An agency requirement that such products be on a QPL can be reasonable; however, its determination that bidders have a testing laboratory certification at the time of bid opening has been held to constitute an unjustified prequalification. Such suppliers are derived from two indices: the Index of Federal Specifications and Standards and the Department of Defense Index of Specifications and Standards. Those on the "Qualified bidders list (QBL)" and a "Qualified manufacturers list (QML)" are required to meet virtually the same standards as those applicable to the QPL.

The fact that a product is on one of these lists does not constitute endorsement of the product by the government. It means that the products listed have qualified under the latest applicable specification. If a potential offeror can demonstrate to the satisfaction of the contracting officer that it or its product can meet the standards established for qualification before the date specified for award, it may not be denied the opportunity to submit an offer solely because neither it nor the product is on one of the lists. If its products are qualified and it furnishes evidence of the qualification, it may become eligible for award; however, an award need not be delayed in order to provide a potential offeror with an opportunity to demonstrate its ability to meet the standards specified for qualification. A supplier may use the QPL information for advertising or publicity, if it does not state or imply that the product is the only product of that type qualified or that the government in any way recommends or endorses the product. Within seven years after any qualification requirement is originally established by a civilian agency other than NASA, the qualifications requirement must be revalidated. Products or services may be removed from these lists when they are submitted for inspection or acceptance and do not meet the requirement or if they were previously rejected and the defects were not corrected when resubmitted for inspection or acceptance. A supplier may also be removed for failure to request reevaluation following change of location or ownership of the plant or for its having discontinued manufacture of the product. A special clause is inserted into contracts when components of end items are subject to a qualification requirement.

§ 9.22 First Article Testing and Approval

On occasion it is possible and efficient to reduce the risk and cost to the government by including a provision in a production contract granting the contractor sufficient time in the delivery schedule for acquisition of materials and components, and for production after receipt of what is called "first article approval." This approval ensures that the contractor can furnish a product that conforms to all contract requirements for acceptance. (Before first article approval, the acquisition of materials or components, or commencement of production, is normally at the sole risk of the contractor.) The government is not required to give only an unconditional approval of the first article items, and where the government's conditional approval, though late, did not delay production, the contractor is not entitled to an equitable adjustment for the delay.

In conditionally approving a first article, the government has the right if not the duty to inform the contractor of non-compliance with the specifications noted during testing to ensure that the production will not experience similar deficiencies. However, sometimes government requirements preclude this action and before approval of the first article, the contractor may be authorized to acquire specific materials or components, or commence production to the extent essential to meet the delivery schedule. Under such an authorization, the costs incurred are allocable to the contract for progress payments and termination. By allowing a contractor to use substitute materials, the government does not constructively waive first article testing. The regulations provide for testing to be performed by the contractor, or in the alternative, by the government. In one case, the government promised that it would evaluate a test sample. Its failure to do so was not a breach of the contract and did not excuse the contractor's subsequent default. The contractor proposed, and the government acquiesced, in the testing. Thereafter, when the contractor was subsequently defaulted for late deliveries and substandard contract work, he alleged that the government's failure to report its evaluation of the test tape was a breach of the contract and a contributing factor to his performance failures. But because the contract itself contained no requirement for either the submission or the testing, no breach was found.

C. DEBARMENT, SUSPENSION, AND INELIGIBILITY

§ 9.31   Determination of Nonresponsibility Distinguished; Nonprocurement Suspension and Debarment

The determination of responsibility that is required in order that agencies may award contracts, and consent to subcontracts, has been discussed above. To the extent that the causes for debarment and suspension differ from standards for nonresponsibility, the results of the one must differ from the other. For example, several of the standards for responsibility are peculiar to the needs of a particular procurement, such as the ability to meet a required delivery schedule or having the organizational and technical skills to perform a certain contract. Other standards for responsibility also apply to all contracts such as the requirement of a satisfactory performance record and a "record of integrity and business ethics." All determinations of nonresponsibility are not automatically considered as grounds for suspension or debarment. Nevertheless, some courts hold that determinations of nonresponsibility are the equivalent of or constitute "de facto" debarment.

The debarment of a contractor from participating in programs for a certain period of time does not preclude the Labor Department from imposing a government-wide debarment of the contractor and its officers under a different statute based on wrongful conduct. Individual officers are subject to debarment as government contractors for labor standards violations; however, because they are not subject to strict liability, the government may not debar a corporate officer for willful and aggravated labor standards violations solely on the basis of the corporation's violations and the officer's status. A board of contract appeals has held that the Equal Access to Justice Act provides for the award of attorney fees to a prevailing party in an adversary adjudication in which the government's position was not substantially justified. The statute defines an adversary adjudication as one "required by statute" to be determined after an opportunity for an agency hearing. Because the board hearing is only provided for by a regulation, the board lacks jurisdiction to award attorney fees and costs to a prevailing party in a suspension and debarment hearing.

The common debarment rule of 1988 was for nonprocurement, such as grants, assistance, loans, and benefits programs. In 1995, it became virtually identical with the FAR policies and procedures, except that notices of proposed nonprocurement debarment have no immediate effect on exclusion from government contracting or subcontracting. In 2002, the General Accounting office indicated that it will not continue its review of protests that an agency improperly suspended or debarred a contract, "as the contracting agency is the appropriate forum" for resolving such dispute.

§ 9.32   Debarment and Suspension as Discretionary Acts

The procurement regulations also state that debarment and suspension are "discretionary actions." This is only true in the sense that the debarring official "may" in the public interest debar a contractor for certain causes. The regulation specifies that the existence of a cause for debarment "does not necessarily require that the contractor be debarred." This is because the seriousness of the contractor's acts or omissions and any mitigating factors are considered in making any debarment decision.

There are some signs that agencies are not exercising their discretion. For example, a Defense Department audit found the Army Corps of Engineers and the Naval Facilities Engineering Command were accepting new buildings and other facilities erected despite serious defects, and taxpayer funds were used to repair the work.

These inspection functions were not satisfactorily performed because the Army Corps of Engineers and the Naval Facilities Engineering Command did not require contractors to perform the inspection they were being paid for; did not support their own inspectors in dealing with contractors; and did not debar (disqualify) contractors that continued to build sub-standard structures.

There was an increase in DoD debarment and suspension activity starting in 1980, though by 1987 they had leveled off at some 1,000 suspensions or debarments per year. In 2002 a study by the Project on Government Oversight, a nonprofit watchdog organization, concerned violations occurring between 1990 and 2002 committed by large top government contractors. It was determined that they "enjoy an unfair advantage over smaller contractors in navigating the Federal government's suspension and debarment system." They repeatedly violated the law or engaged in unethical conduct. For example, in 2002, it was reported that

General Electric, which committed 63 violations and alleged violations and paid approximately $982.9 million in fines/penalties, restitution, and settlements; Lockheed Martin, with 63 violations and alleged violations and $231.9 million paid; Boeing, with 36 violations and alleged violations and $358 million paid; Raytheon, with 24 violations and alleged violations and $128.7 million paid; and Fluor, with 19 violations and alleged violations and $70 million paid.

In *Fraud in Government*, the GAO reported that the Justice Department declined to prosecute 61% of all referred government fraud cases. Although criminal prosecution had been declined in almost two-thirds of these cases, administrative action based upon a lesser standard of evidence could appropriately be considered because a criminal case must be proven beyond a reasonable doubt, while a debarment action requires proof by a preponderance of evidence, as in all civil actions. Suspensions have also undergone uneven treatment.

Some courts have required the consideration of mitigating circumstances in order to sustain a debarment or suspension. This may appear to be the cause of discriminatory results, where an agency is like a district attorney who attempts to exercise his discretion in a county by equalizing the characteristics of those whom he prosecutes. The procurement regulation has attempted to accomplish this by providing for the designation of an agency's "debarring official" to impose debarment. Unless the contracting officers throughout the agency send the necessary materials to that official, the system could be unevenly enforced against only those who do send in such materials. Current regulations state, "if a cause for debarment exists, the contractor has the burden of demonstrating to the satisfaction of the debarring official, its present responsibility, and that debarment is not necessary."

The causes for debarment are basically of two types: violation of a civil or criminal statute and violation of the terms of a government contract or subcontract so serious as to justify debarment, such as "willful failure to perform" one or more contracts or "a history of failure to perform, or of unsatisfactory performance of, one or more contracts." In February 1996, President Clinton issued an executive order calling for debarment of contractors who knowingly hire illegal aliens.

In addition, debarment or suspension may result from an offeror's submission of a false certification that he has a drug-free workplace, or his failure to comply with a certification. This may be shown by a number of contractor employees having been convicted of violations of criminal drug statutes occurring in the workplace, which indicates that the contractor has failed to make a good faith effort to provide a drug-free workplace. Although generally debarment should not exceed 3 years, debarment for violation of the provisions of the Drug–Free Workplace Act of 1988 may be for a period not to exceed 5 years.

Intentionally affixing the label "Made in America" or similar inscription may also be cause for debarment or suspension with respect to a product sold in, or shipped to the United States when it was not made there.

In August 1996 the regulation was amended to state "The debarring official may debar a contractor, based on a determination by the Attorney General of the United States, or his designee that the contractor is not in compliance with Immigration and Nationality Act employment provisions." Further, this determination "is not reviewable in debarment proceedings." It remains to be seen whether contracting officers, upon receipt of such determinations from the Attorney General, will automatically debar the offending contractor or else somehow attempt to find a reason to exercise their discretion not to do so.

The regulation lists ten examples of remedial measures or mitigating factors for consideration by an agency in determining whether to debar a contractor. However, it also stated that the existence or nonexistence of any mitigating factors or remedial measures "is not necessarily determinative of a contractor's present responsibility." Once a contractor is debarred, suspended, or proposed for debarment, no agency can renew or otherwise extend the duration of current contracts, or consent to subcontracts, with him unless the agency head or a designee authorized representative states, in writing, "the compelling reasons for renewal or extension." In 2001 an appellate court held that a False Claims Act whistle-blower was entitled to share in the proceeds of a suspension and debarment settlement between a contractor and the government.

§ 9.33   List of Parties Excluded from Federal Procurement and Nonprocurement Programs

(a) In General

The General Services Administration (GSA) compiles and maintains a current consolidated list of all parties Excluded from Federal Procurement and Nonprocurement Programs. In this connection it is noted that the definition of "contractor" on this listing includes persons or entities that contract with the government indirectly through others or who may reasonably be expected to act as agents or representatives for another contractor. Such listing constitutes debarment of all divisions or other organizational elements of the contractor, unless the debarment decision is limited by its terms to specific divisions, organizational elements, or commodities. A contractor's debarment becomes effective throughout the executive branch of the government, unless an acquiring agency's head or a designee states in writing the compelling reasons justifying continued business dealings between that agency and the contractor; and debarred or suspended contractors are excluded from receiving contracts and no agency can solicit offers from, award contracts to, or consent to subcontracts with these contractors. Such contractors are also excluded from conducting business with the government as agents or representatives of other contractors. Parties excluded from non-procurement programs are found on the same listing. A contractor whose suspension is overturned on appeal is not entitled to damages under the Federal Tort Claims Act (FTCA), because the agency's decision to investigate and suspend the contractor falls within the discretionary functions exception to the FTCA.

(b) Effect of Listing on Existing Contracts or Subcontracts

Agencies may continue contracts or subcontracts in existence at the time the contractor was debarred or suspended, unless the acquiring agency's head or a designee directs otherwise. But, agencies cannot renew current contracts or subcontracts of debarred or suspended contractors, or otherwise extend their duration, unless the acquiring agency's head or a designee states in writing the compelling reasons for renewal or extension. Contractors may not enter into a subcontract in excess of $25,000 with a contractor that has been disbarred, suspended, or proposed for debarment "unless there is a compelling reason to do so." A contractor who intends to subcontract with such a party must notify the contracting officers in writing before entering into that subcontract. The regulation also addresses the placement of orders under existing contracts and agreements with contractors that have been debarred, suspended, or proposed for debarment.

D. PROCEDURES FOR DEBARMENT AND SUSPENSION

§ 9.41 In General

Agencies are required to establish procedures governing the debarment decisionmaking process that afford the contractor (and any specifically named affiliates) an opportunity to submit, in person, in writing, or through a representative, information and argument in opposition to the proposed debarment. Where a contractor is able to persuade a court to overturn its debarment, it may then obtain its attorney fees and expenses under the Equal Access to Justice Act (EAJA), consistent with the statutory criteria.

The action of an agency in debarring a contractor from the agency's projects does not preclude, on ground of res judicata or collateral estoppel, the Department of Labor (DOL) from imposing government-wide debarment of the same contractor and its officers under different statutes than those in the agency's proceeding.

§ 9.42 Notice to the Contractor

A debarment is initiated by advising the contractor (and any specifically named affiliates) by certified mail, that debarment is being considered, the reasons for the proposed debarment (in terms sufficient to put the contractor on notice of the conduct or transaction(s) upon which it is based) and of the cause(s) relied upon. It is also informed that within 30 days after receipt of the notice, it may submit information and argument in opposition to the proposed debarment, including any additional specific information that raises a genuine dispute over the material facts. It receives a copy of the agency's procedures governing debarment decisionmaking and is informed of the potential effect of the proposed debarment.

Effective October 1, 1988, twenty-seven agencies issued a common rule for debarment of grantees that closely parallels debarment procedures for procurement programs. It applies to all nonprocurement programs, except certain entitlement programs. These procedures grew out of the decisions of many courts that required sufficient notice to permit a contractor to prepare for a hearing.

In actions not based on a conviction or judgment, the party may request a fact-finding hearing. If the debarring official determines that there is a genuine dispute on material facts, the matter is referred to a fact-finding official.

The contractor has an opportunity to appear with counsel, submit documentary evidence, present witnesses, and confront any person the agency presents. The agency will make a transcribed record of the proceedings available at cost to the contractor upon request, unless the contractor and the agency, by mutual agreement, waive the requirement for a transcript. This is done because debarments and suspensions are subject to judicial review, a result which grew out of a number of court decisions which held that the sanction imposed by the government may cause a contractor economic hardship. A recommendation by a wage and hour administrator of the Department of Labor (DOL) for debarment for a violation of the Service Contract Act is not subject to judicial review until the Secretary of Labor has acted on a request for relief from being placed on the list. Due process became a requisite in the "suspension process."

§ 9.43   The Hearing

No hearing is required when there is the concern that such a proceeding may prejudice a prosecutorial action. In one case, there was adequate evidence to support a suspension and a formal determination of an official's discretion that significant injury would result if a hearing were to be held. The court pointed out that:

> There may be reasons why the Government should not be required to show any of its evidence to the contractor, particularly reasons of national security, or, more likely, the concern that such a procedure may prejudice a prosecutorial action against the contractor. The Government may also be concerned that a suspended contractor may seek a proceeding not so much to obtain reinstatement as a bidder, but in order to obtain a discovery not generally provided to criminal defendants.

As a result of this action, the former regulations were modified to allow for a hearing in the "usual" case and to provide that where, for investigation or other reasons, a hearing cannot be held, the contractor may be given the opportunity to present and the agency to consider "information or argument in opposition to the suspension ... in writing or through representation." The Sixth Circuit Court of Appeals found that these regulations effectively accommodated "these conflicting interests by requiring the decision of a top level administrator in accordance with specifically articulated standards before the suspension may be issued and permitting the suspended bidder to submit information and argument in opposition to suspension."

The Supreme Court has upheld the simultaneous pursuit of civil, criminal and administrative remedies ("parallel" proceedings), provided they are done with care. Although no stay of civil proceedings is required pending the outcome of criminal proceedings, in its discretion a court may stay civil proceedings, including civil discovery "when the interests of justice seem to require such action."

A "debarring official" is defined as one who is authorized "to impose debarment;" but the regulation indicates that he also decides whether, after receiving the contractor's submission, a genuine dispute exists over material facts. If so, he may refer the matter to another official for findings of fact. That official's findings are final, unless the debarring official determines them to be "arbitrary, capricious, or clearly erroneous." This rule grew out of a case in which the U.S. Court of Appeals for the Federal Circuit held that it is not improper for the official who recommended a suspension to preside over a subsequent hearing thereon. "Preponderance of the evidence" is the evidentiary standard for debarment. The debarring official then determines whether debarment should be imposed and its duration. Only where there is a genuine dispute over material facts may a contractor facing debarment insist upon cross-examining the government's witnesses.

Under the procedures, the debarring official can decide whether the contractor is entitled to "additional proceedings" (a hearing) where the debarring official's evidence might be subject to cross-examination. Because the agency and the contractor may strongly disagree whether there is a disputed issue of material fact, the officer will weigh the evidence carefully before deciding against additional proceedings. The existence of a conviction based upon the statutes may help him in many instances—particularly where he has read the contractor's arguments and found that they did not add to the court's view, or raise any genuine dispute over material facts. To do otherwise may permit a contractor to delay the process in order to obtain significant contracts, only thereafter to be suspended or debarred. In such event, the contractor knows that the contracts entered into during the delay will stand unless the head of the acquiring agency directs otherwise. In this connection, it is noted that the U.S. Court of Appeals for the Federal Circuit decided a contractor who has been temporarily suspended is not automatically entitled to a trial-type administrative hearing. "A full-blown, trial-type hearing is not necessarily the process due a temporarily suspended contractor with a protected liberty interest where the government's interest in protecting an ongoing criminal investigation is considerable." The government's failure to permit a suspended contractor to cross-examine FBI agents involved in an ongoing criminal probe was held not to constitute a due process violation. It has also been held that a agency did not violate due process when it failed to provide a pre-suspension hearing for a contractor that had been indicted on state fraud charges. The court held that the agency was not obligated to stay a suspension action against an indicted contractor until the criminal case was over, because otherwise, the government could suspend only unindicted contractors.

In awards over $100,000 a contractor must execute a certificate disclosing whether he is presently suspended, debarred or proposed for debarment, and any convictions or civil judgments involving efforts to obtain or perform state or local contracts, and whether he has been terminated for default within the previous three years. Where there is no assurance that the owner's alleged bribing and bid rigging activities on behalf of the company will not continue, the transfer of an owner's interest to a third party under a trust agreement is not enough to avoid a debarment.

§ 9.44 The Decision

It has been proper for a procuring agency to allow contractors against whom debarment proceedings were pending to participate in a new procurement up to the time of award. This is because it would then be a simple matter to make award elsewhere.

The debarring official's decision may be made on the basis of a conviction or without such a conviction. In actions based upon a conviction or judgment, or in which there is no genuine dispute over material facts, the debarring official makes a decision on the basis of all the information in the administrative record, including any submission made by the contractor. He must do this within 30 working days after receipt of any information and argument submitted by the contractor, unless he extends this period for "good cause." Additional proceedings are necessary as to disputed material facts. Written findings of fact are prepared and the official must base the decision on the facts as found, together with any information and argument submitted by the contractor and any other information in the administrative record. In any action in which the proposed debarment is not based upon a conviction or civil judgment, the cause for debarment must be established by a "preponderance of the evidence" in a manner similar to the standards of the civil courts.

The regulation specifically provides for imputing to a contractor the "fraudulent, criminal, or other seriously improper conduct of any officer, director, shareholder, partner, or employee when the conduct occurred in connection with the individual's performance of duties for or on behalf of the contractor, or with the contractor's knowledge, approval, or acquiescence." The contractor's acceptance of the benefits derived from the conduct is "evidence of such knowledge, approval, or acquiescence." It has been argued that debarment and suspension proceedings may normally hurt small businesses more than large businesses because the cause of the sanction more frequently takes place at a relatively low level in a large corporation but at a much higher level in a small one.

If the debarring official decides to impose debarment, the contractor and any affiliates involved must be given prompt notice by certified mail, referring to the notice of proposed debarment; stating the period of debarment, including effective dates, and advising that the debarment is effective throughout the executive branch of the government. Conversely, if debarment is not imposed, the official so notifies the contractor and any affiliates involved, by certified mail, return receipt requested. Although debarment is for a period commensurate with the seriousness of the cause(s), generally, a debarment should not exceed three years. Further, where suspension precedes a debarment, the suspension period is considered in determining the debarment period. Where the debarment is extended for an additional period, it must be determined that an extension is necessary to protect the government's interest, and it may not be extended solely on the basis of the facts and circumstances upon which the initial debarment action was based.

The debarring official may reduce the period or extent of debarment, upon the contractor's request, supported by documentation, for reasons such as newly discovered material evidence, "reversal of the conviction or judgment upon which the debarment was based, a bona fide change in ownership or management, or elimination of other causes for which the debarment was imposed."A court of appeals has noted that:

A debarment need not be proportional to the severity of a prior criminal sentence, for a criminal sentence is a statutory sanction quite distinct from a debarment. A criminal sentence constitutes punishment for past wrongdoing. In contrast, a debarment is designed to insure the integrity of government contracts in the immediate present and into the future. Toward that end, the maximum term of debarment may be, under certain conditions present here, justifiably imposed even though the criminal sentence is relatively more moderate.

Similarly, following an agency's debarment decision a contractor is not normally entitled to a de novo judicial review unless the agency's decision lacks a rational basis. Thus, this decision differs from that of a contracting officer under the Contract Disputes Act. (See Chapter 33)

A whistleblower who shared in proceeds owed to the government under the False Claims Act (FCA) was held entitled to also share in the suspension or debarment settlement of a contractor—even though the Justice Department itself lacked authority to bring a debarment action. The court also pointed out that guidance in possible conflicts of interest was applicable.

§ 9.45   Suspension

Suspension is somewhat like debarment, in that both are based on the violation of a single statute or regulation. Suspension is an action imposed on the "basis of adequate evidence, pending the completion of investigation or legal proceedings, when it has been determined immediate action is necessary to protect the government's interest." The proceedings, results, and statutory causes are virtually identical to debarment except that only a suspension may be used upon evidence of an indictment for violation of the criminal or civil statutes involved. However, a suspension is for a temporary period pending the completion of investigation and any ensuing legal proceedings. The suspending official is not required to consider remedial measures or mitigating factors. If legal proceedings are not initiated within 12 months after the date of the suspension notice, the suspension is terminated unless an Assistant Attorney General requests its extension, in which case it may be extended for an additional six months. In no event may a suspension extend beyond 18 months, unless legal proceedings have been initiated within that period.

A contractor may be suspended if indicted for fraud, related criminal offenses, or for "any other offense indicating a lack of business integrity or business honesty that seriously and directly affects the present responsibility of a government contractor or subcontractor." Further, the government "may suspend a contractor suspected, upon adequate evidence," of having committed any of these offenses. Adequate evidence means that the government must have information sufficient to support the reasonable belief that a particular act or omission has occurred. One supplier challenged a suspension decision for reason that the government had actually made five small purchases thereafter even though a criminal investigation was pending. A large contract was involved, and its suspension was still held as "cogent and reasonable."

A suspension may also be imposed for "any other cause of so serious or compelling a nature that it affects the present responsibility of a government contractor or subcontractor."

Where an agency suspected an individual authorized to sign bids and contracts for a firm of bribing government employees, and had adequate evidence to impute the contractor's misconduct to the individual, a suspension of the firm was upheld pending a complete investigation. Where a contractor has previously been suspended based on unrebutted allegations of misconduct contained in a civil lawsuit brought by another entity, that contractor may properly be excluded from a competition. This is because it may be suspended upon suspicion of misconduct upon a showing of adequate evidence. Agencies assessing the adequacy of evidence should consider "how much information is available, how credible it is given the circumstances, [and] whether or not important allegations are corroborated and what inferences can reasonably be drawn as a result."

§ 9.46 Use of Nolo Contendere Judgment as Evidence

The Office of Federal Procurement Policy (OFPP) defined conviction to include a conviction entered upon a plea of nolo contendere, as an admission of improper conduct sufficient for debarment. Formerly, the regulations defined a "conviction" to include "one entered upon a plea of nolo contendere." The Federal Rules of Criminal Procedure would not generally admit such evidence, nor would the Federal Rules of Evidence. It may be argued that while a nolo contendere plea does provide evidence of probable improper conduct, some consideration of the facts upon which the plea was based may be necessary for a debarment. Peter Kiewit Sons' Co. was charged with bid rigging on a series of Mississippi River construction projects. Kiewit pleaded nolo contendere, and paid $400,000 in fines and civil penalties but it continued to receive awards of construction contracts. When prior to the FAR this practice was criticized by Senator Carl Levin of Michigan, the Corps of Engineers ordered its offices not to award contracts to Kiewit, pending review of debarment reports. A district court judge attempted to prevent the Corps from blocking such awards until Kiewit had exhausted its administrative remedies and the Army had issued a final decision. The U.S. Court of Appeals for the District of Columbia reversed, holding that there was insufficient evidence of congressional interference in the Army's administrative debarment process to justify a court's decision to block those proceedings. The appellate court noted that "Had Kiewit exhausted its administrative remedies, judicial review might well have proven unnecessary.... This initial determination of what constitutes sound business practice for the United States Department of Defense requires the 'discretion' and 'experience' of an administrator. A court is poorly suited to make such a decision."

Nevertheless, a circuit court of appeals held in 1992 that a plea agreement between a government contractor and the U.S. Attorney bound the entire government and hence prevented the Defense Department from debarring the contractor as a result of the plea. However, agencies in the executive branch may continue current contracts notwithstanding suspension of debarment.

§ 9.47 De Facto Debarment

(a) In General

In spite of the injunction in the regulations that agencies establish procedures governing the debarment process "that are as informal as is practicable," the essential elements of these procedures are quite strict. But what about different procedures which do not result in a contractor appearing on a consolidated list of those who are debarred, suspended and ineligible for award of government contracts for a period of time? These potential contractors are denied the right to perform one particular contract. Usually this is because of an agency's decision that the contractor was nonresponsible with respect to criteria peculiar to the particular procurement action, such as having inadequate financial resources, experience, or technical experience or equipment to perform the resulting contract. These standards are not causes for debarment.

For example, suspension of a small business after the Navy failed for nearly five months either to reject its bids or refer them to the Small Business Administration for certificate of competency because of its inadequate performance of prior contracts was held to result in a de facto debarment. The court stated that:

> The circumstances give rise to a reasonable inference that the Navy's delays in failing to act on [the firm's] bid ... were not due to the Navy's continuing efforts to satisfy itself as to [the firm's] competence and responsibility in performing the work, but represented a method of de facto debarment ... prior to the time the Navy had adequate evidence to support such action.

The Navy had awarded three of the four disputed contracts to other firms, and the bidder was held to be entitled to injunctive relief. The Claims Court stated that "monetary damages, limited to bid preparation costs, would be inadequate to compensate (the firm) for loss of contract if it was successful on the merits," and the Navy was barred from going ahead with performance of the disputed contracts. Bid preparation costs are compensation, and no bidder has a right to the award or any property interest in a contract with the government.

Courts have considered two threshold questions when determining if an agency action has resulted in a de facto debarment: (1) whether the procedures surrounding the actions giving rise to the de facto debarment were in compliance with governing debarment regulations and, if so, (2) whether these regulations satisfy minimum constitutional requirements.

For example, an agency finds that a company is nonresponsible for award because it has previously been "an administrative burden" and persistently seized opportunities to demand exorbitant change orders that also raised questions of fraud. A de facto debarment may thereafter occur. An actual debarment occurs only after a company has been given adequate notice of the charges against it and allowed an opportunity to respond. A contractor that failed to reply to a pay survey requested by the Department of Labor's Office of Federal Contract Compliance Program was debarred under a consent decree. Yet, as noted above, some agencies are often hesitant about commencing debarment proceedings.

A circuit court of appeals has held that where a de facto debarment results from an agency's determination that a contractor lacked integrity, the Fifth Amendment requires that notice be given of the charges and an opportunity to rebut them. A contractor who had been found nonresponsible under two solicitations argued that this constituted a de facto debarment for which he was entitled a notice as such. However, it was held that no de facto debarment occurred where the determinations of nonresponsibility were based upon a lack of compliance with environmental laws.

(b) Low Bidders Not Receiving Awards

Two divergent decisions by different members of the Claims Court concerned low bidders who did not receive the award. In the first case, the denial was because it was determined that the plant manager (named "Outlaw") lacked integrity, a determination in which the Small Business Administration (SBA) concurred. The Speco Corporation then asked for an "injunction" presumably against an award being made. The Court held that it lacked authority to enjoin a determination of the SBA, or to order the Defense Department to withhold award from another bidder that would be equivalent to enjoining the effectivity of a decision statutorily reserved to the SBA. The second and subsequent decision (by a different judge) concerned the Defense Department's rejection of the bid of Related Industries at a price of $7 million for sleeping bags because its president and sole shareholder was a consultant to a former contractor who lacked integrity. Related sought a declaratory judgment that he was qualified. This judge refused to follow the *Speco* decision by another judge of the same court and in reviewing the merits found that the SBA had failed to include lack of integrity in its notice to Related. The judge found that the contracting officer would not award "any contract" to Related (without including the background for this judicial statement in the opinion) and found a de facto debarment to have occurred without proper notice having been given to Related under due process. The Defense Department was then enjoined from awarding to anyone other than Related until the proper notice was given and, until Related or the president "are properly debarred or suspended." However, a contracting officer need not await actual debarment before denying award to an apparent low bidder on grounds of lack of integrity. Such proceedings may be analogous to the case denying a stay of disciplinary proceedings against attorneys or judges pending their trial on criminal charges.

The U.S. Court of Appeals for the Federal Circuit (CAFC) has ruled that the Small Business Administration's denial of a certificate of competency to a small business concern is subject to judicial review. There, the Defense Personnel Support Center (DPSC) issued a solicitation inviting small business firms to submit sealed bids for a contract to manufacture 38,900 women's Army coats. Cavalier was the apparent low bidder and a pre-award survey was conducted by Defense Contract Administration Services (DCAS). DCAS recommended against awarding the contract to Cavalier, citing Cavalier's (1) prior unsatisfactory performance of other government contracts, (2) inability to control production scheduling, (3) inability to maintain adequate quality control, and (4) lack of financial capacity. The contracting officer then rejected Cavalier as nonresponsible and referred the matter to the Small Business Administration (SBA). The SBA determined that Cavalier was entitled to a Certificate of Competency (COC) enabling it to receive the contract award, but two days later, Cavalier received a letter stating that an offer to lend Cavalier $150,000 was being rescinded. The SBA withdrew the COC.

Cavalier filed suit against the government in the Claims Court seeking injunctive relief and asserting that its rejection was part of a de facto debarment and therefore illegal. The government moved for summary judgment, citing Speco Corp. v. United States. Cavalier defended, citing Related Industries, Inc. v. United States. The CAFC upheld the position of the *Related* decision that the SBA's denial of a COC is reviewable. The Circuit Court held that even the statute, which specifically gave to the SBA "final disposition" of the competency certification, was only final with respect to a decision certifying a contractor to the procurement officer as responsible. "The SBA's refusal to issue a COC does not prevent the contracting officer from later reversing himself, on the basis of new evidence." Hence, the Claims Court had jurisdiction to entertain Cavalier's complaint. The appellate decision stated: "We recognize that the Claims Court cast the gravest doubt on the merits of Cavalier's case, but it did so in the course of what it designated an advisory opinion or dicta."

(c) Effect of Nonresponsibility

A finding of nonresponsibility in connection with a procurement action does not constitute a de facto debarment unless the contracting officer's decision was effectively being used to bar the contractor from all further government contract work. The determination of whether a contractor has been effectively barred from any further government contract work involves a number of factors: (1) whether other persons or government agencies were apprised of the contracting officer's finding of nonresponsibility; (2) whether the information circulated was for the purpose of preventing the contractor from securing future contracts with the government; (3) whether circulation of the information stigmatized the contractor; and (4) whether the contractor has lost any government business attributable to the contracting officer's determination.

(d) De Facto Debarment Versus Formal Debarment

Creation of the de facto debarment by the courts was intended to serve the purpose of bridging the gap between prolonged or excessive findings of nonresponsibility and formal debarment or suspension proceedings. By applying the same procedural safeguards to de facto debarment as formal debarment, some courts have virtually made the two equal. But, there were no clear guidelines as to when findings of nonresponsibility or investigations end and de facto debarment begins. A a contractor is not entitled to damages under the Federal Tort Claims Act for its unlawful de facto debarment.

A change has described when a prospective contractor shall be presumed to be nonresponsible, in a section making no reference to applicable causes for debarment, stating "A prospective contractor that is or recently has been seriously deficient in contract performance shall be presumed to be nonresponsible." Exceptions are if the contracting officer determines that the circumstances were properly beyond the contractor's control, or that he has taken appropriate corrective action. Past failure to apply sufficient tenacity and perseverance to perform acceptably is "strong evidence of nonresponsibility." The applicable cause for debarment may be based upon a preponderance of evidence of "wilful failure to perform one or more contracts" or "a history of failure or of unsatisfactory performance" of them.

E.   ORGANIZATIONAL CONFLICTS OF INTEREST

§ 9.61   In General

An organizational conflict of interest (OCI) may result when factors create an actual or potential conflict of interest on an instant contract, or when the nature of the work to be performed on the instant contract creates an actual or potential conflict of interest on a future acquisition. Organizational conflicts of interest are not limited to any particular kind of organization (whether profit or nonprofit) or kind of procurement action. However, the regulation points to certain types of contracts where conflicts of interest are more likely to occur; namely, contracts involving "management support services; consultant or other professional services; contractor performance of or assistance in technical evaluations; or systems engineering and technical direction work performed by a contractor that does not have overall contractual responsibility for development or production."

There are two underlying principles in determining whether a significant potential conflict exists and, if it does, in developing an appropriate means for resolving it. First, the existence of "conflicting roles that might bias a contractor's judgment." Second, preventing unfair competitive advantage (e.g., where a contractor competing for award possesses (a) proprietary information obtained from "a government official without proper authorization" or (b) source selection information relevant to the contract but not available to other competitors).

A contractor that provides systems engineering and technical direction services may not receive an award unless the contractor has overall contractual responsibility for system development. If a contractor furnishes specifications for nondevelopmental items to be used in a competitive procurement, it may not also furnish these items "during the initial production run." There are some exceptions. For example, the contractors may be the sole source of supply. Contractors are also prohibited from providing technical evaluations of other contractors' offers or products or advisory and assistance services, from evaluating their own products or activities, or those of a competitor, without "proper safeguards to ensure objectivity."

In order to avoid a potential Organization Conflict of Interest (OCI), offerors frequently construct "mitigation plans" detailing how their procedures would prevent or mitigate conflicts. The contracting officer is required to award the contract to the apparent successful offeror unless an OCI is determined to exist that cannot be avoided or mitigated.

The regulation directs contracting officers to analyze planned acquisitions in order to identify and evaluate potential organizational conflicts of interest and to do so as early in the acquisition process as possible in order to "avoid, neutralize, or mitigate significant potential conflicts to them before contract award." It is mandatory that the potential conflicts be identified and recorded. Thus, where the Air Force based its work on a system that had been installed by EDS, a contractor under an earlier contract, it was held that "due to its status" as an earlier contractor, EDS "possessed information other offerors did not." The result was that EDS, through no fault of its own, enjoyed "an unfair competitive advantage." If "a significant potential organizational conflict" is known before a solicitation is issued, then the contracting officer is required to take a course of action for resolving the conflict. In this connection, certain clauses must be inserted in solicitations. The Court of Federal Claims has held that a subcontractor is bound by the conflict of interest clauses in a prime contract, even if the subcontract or task orders issued under it do not contain the clauses.

In order to avoid a situation in which the contractor could draft specifications favoring its own products or capabilities, where a single contractor drafts complete specifications for nondevelopmental equipment, he should be eliminated for a reasonable time from competition for production based on the specifications. Participation in the preparation of a proposal directly conflicts with the regulation's prohibition against his being able to supply these services in most instances. Thus, where a contract proposal on a draft project paper was prepared for an agency and it led directly to a statement of work for a follow-on technical assistance contract, the proposer was ineligible for award of that contract.

Contracts involving technical evaluations of other contractors' offers of products or consulting services should not be awarded to a contractor that would evaluate or advise the government concerning its own products or activities, or those of a competitor, "without proper safeguards to ensure objectivity and to protect the Government's interests."

In those instances where a contractor gains access to proprietary information of other companies in performing a contract for the government it must agree with the other companies to protect their information from unauthorized use or disclosure for as long as it remains proprietary. It must also agree to refrain from using the information for any purpose other than that for which it was furnished.

In Johnson Controls World Services, Inc., the GAO sustained an OCI protest because the awardee's proposed subcontractor possessed comprehensive historical data on maintenance activities at the facility that was not available to the other offerors and gave the awardee an unfair competitive advantage. The GAO found that the awardee's subcontractor had failed to establish adequate procedures to prevent interaction between its personnel possessing the data and those involved in proposal preparation. Additionally, the GAO found that the subcontractor, under its own contract with the agency, would have been evaluating the awardee's team and making workload allocation recommendations to the agency that could have benefited the awardee. In a subsequent protest, the GAO upheld the agency's proposed corrective action to require the awardee to terminate its teaming arrangement with the subcontractor and to release the historical data to all of the offerors for revised proposals.

F.   CONTRACTOR TEAM ARRANGEMENTS, DEFENSE PRODUCTION POOLS AND RESEARCH AND DEVELOPMENT POOLS

§ 9.71   In General

Production or research and development pools and contractor-team arrangements do not necessarily involve conflicts of interest. A team arrangement of firms may be desirable from both a government and industry standpoint in order to enable the companies involved to complement each other's unique capabilities and offer the government the best combination of performance, cost, and delivery for the system or product being acquired. The adversary competition among and within U.S. corporations has sometimes compared unfavorably with the team spirit of the Japanese.

A "contractor team arrangement," as used in the regulation is often where a "potential prime contractor agrees with one or more other companies to have them act as its subcontractors under a specified government contract or acquisition program." "Companies involved normally form a contractor team arrangement before submitting an offer." Of course, the government holds the prime contractor "responsible for contract performance, regardless of any team arrangement between the prime contractor and its subcontractors." Hence, this may result dispute between the prime and subcontractor as noted in Chapter 44, state law has been appealed in many cases. Certain "presubcontract teaming agreements," often lack most important details, enforceable or not according to state law.

Although these arrangements are sanctioned by the procurement regulations, this does not authorize contractor team arrangements in violation of antitrust statutes or limit the government's right to pursue its policies on competitive contracting, subcontracting, and component breakout after initial production or at any other time. The government may hold the prime contractor fully responsible for contract performance, regardless of any team arrangement between the prime contractor and its subcontractors, and others. The first challenge by the AntiTrust Division of the Justice alleged that a teaming arrangement on a 1992 Army contract for Combined Effects Munition systems was anticompetitive within the meaning of Section 1 of the Sherman Act. This was because it had the effect of eliminating competitive bidding between the teammates, by reducing the number of bidders from two to one, and raising the price of the single bid the defendants submitted. In the consent decree settling the case, the defendants agreed to pay approximately $4 million to the government and not to team on future such procurements on which the government sought competition.

When contracting with a production or R & D pool, the pool is in general treated the same as any other prospective or actual contractor. Such contracts are exempt from the "manufacturer or regular dealer" requirement of the Walsh–Healey Public Contracts Act. Although a pool member may submit an individual offer, independent of the pool, it will not be considered by the agency.

A federal district court has held that one of two contractors in a joint venture may pursue government contracts outside its joint venture.

CHAPTER 10

MARKET RESEARCH

§ 10.1 Market Research

Part 10 has been one of the replaced by policies and procedures, establishing the requirement for market research as the first steps in the acquisition process; and, as an element in the later steps of describing the agency's need (see Chapter 1, describing agency needs), developing the overall acquisition strategy and identifying terms and conditions unique to the item being acquired.

When consolidating two or more requirements for supplies or services ("bundling" them) under the complex definition in FAR 2.101 for this concept, the agency should do so only after consulting with the Small Business Administration (SBA) procurement center representative (PCR) or the SBA Office of Government Contracting area office serving the locale of the procuring activity. (See Chapter 13.) At least 30 days before release of the solicitation, notification of the government's intention to bundle "must" be made to any affected incumbent small business concerns.

Market research is to be conducted to determine if commercial or nondevelopmental items are available to meet an agency's needs or could be modified to do so. This requires that the agency contact individuals in government and industry by publishing requests for information in technical, scientific or business journals, "querying government data bases," reviewing catalogs, and holding presolicitation meetings. If such market research indicates that commercial or nondevelopmental items might not be available to satisfy an agency's needs, the agency must then "reevaluate the need" and "determine whether the need can be restated to permit commercial or nondevelopmental items to satisfy the agency's needs." Where that need may be met in the commercial marketplace, the procedures described in Chapter 12, Acquisition of Commercial Items are to be used. If not, then the procedures described there may not be used, and, if a notice is required to be published through the Governmentwide Point of Entry (GPE), the notice must include a statement that the government does not intend to use the procedures for commercial items for the acquisition.

The rules increased the amount of the micro-purchase threshold and the simplified acquisition threshold and provide expanded access to streamlined procedures for procurements of supplies or services by or for an executive agency that are to be used to facilitate defense against or recovery from terrorism or nuclear, biological, chemical, or radiological attack.

The regulation was also amended to add the querying of commercial databases that provide information relevant to the agency acquisition as a technique for conducting market research. The data base for use by multiple agencies is at www.contractdirectory.gov.

CHAPTER 11

DESCRIBING AGENCY NEEDS

§ 11.1 In General

The procurement process begins when a need exists for a product or service, at which time a description thereof is developed. In order to ensure full and open competition and be cost and environmentally effective, acquisition of commercial products by the government is preferable and they are ordinarily less expensive than are items fabricated according to specifications. Such procurement begins with a description of the government's needs stated in functional terms in sufficient detail so that market research and analysis can be used to help determine whether commercial products, distribution systems, and logistics support are available to fill those needs. Agencies continually conduct market research and analysis as needed to assure adequate competition and that the government's needs are met in a cost effective manner. The acceptability of commercial products to meet government needs will depend upon reliability, performance, and logistics support requirements, as well as cost.

When acquiring energy-using products, agencies are required to buy energy-efficient products and services if they are life cycle cost effective. They are directed toward Internet sources for more detailed information on ENERGY STAR and other energy efficient products for design, construction, renovation, or maintenance of public buildings that will include energy using products.

The Office of Federal Procurement Policy (OFPP) Act Amendments of 1988 established the position of "Commercial Products Advocate" to make recommendations to the OFPP Administrator regarding government acquisition of commercial products. The Advocate is to make recommendation to the Administrator regarding changes to regulations that will encourage the acquisition of commercial products. For extensive guidance on commercial item purchasing, with some departures from ordinary procurement rules, see Chapter 12.

The government's order of precedence for requirements documents, as well as the concept of market acceptance, commences with those required by law, followed by "performance-oriented documents." In lower rank are design-oriented documents, standards, and specifications issued by the government. This orientation toward performance was inhibited by a culture that overemphasized design by the buyer.

"Market acceptance" is the quality analog of the test for reasonableness of price used for over 3 years as an exception to the need for cost or pricing data; namely, "established catalog or market prices of commercial items sold in substantial quantities to the general public." With it, there is no need for "cost or pricing data." Normally, such items may meet an agency's minimum needs. Its use only becomes inappropriate when new or evolving items are needed. The danger is that a requirement may be written to feature a product peculiar to one manufacturer. Products of other manufacturers may actually meet, or can be modified to meet, the agency's minimum needs.

In a solicitation, there is added a provision to address the use of "voluntary consensus standards" in accordance with the requirements of Office of Management and Budget (OMB) Circular A–119.

§ 11.2   Selecting Specifications or Descriptions

(a) In General

The government, finding it economical to prepare exact specifications and standards for most of the services and products it repeatedly purchases, defines these standards and specifications. Standards are descriptions that establish engineering or technical limitations and applications for materials, processes, methods, designs, and engineering practices or criteria deemed essential to achieve the highest practical degree of uniformity in materials or products, or interchangeability of parts used in those products. Specifications are intended to be clear and accurate descriptions of the technical requirements for a material, product, or service, including the procedure by which it will be determined that the requirements have been met. They also include preservation, packaging, packing, and working requirements.

The Administrator of the General Services Administration (GSA) prepares specifications and standards covering products commonly used by government agencies. Similarly, the Secretary of Defense prepares and controls military specifications and standards unique to DoD. The market research, as well as the development and use of specifications and purchase descriptions, must specify need in a manner designed to achieve full and open competition in acquisition. Restrictive positions or conditions can be used only to the extent necessary to satisfy minimum agency needs. Further descriptions of agency requirements must be stated whenever practicable in terms of functions to be performed or performance required.

(b) Design Specifications

Insertion of provisions in a government contract specifying dimensions imports a warranty that if the specifications are complied with, the execution of the project will be adequate. This is called a design warranty and it has been extended to supply contracts. It applies to contracts calling for the contractor to perform work strictly in accordance with government specifications with the contractor having no responsibility for the design of the product or the preparation of the specifications.

For example, the contractor manufactured the chemical DDT and delivered it in the metal containers specified in the contract. The contract contained a requirement that the DDT would not deteriorate over a certain length of time. When deterioration was discovered, it was demonstrated that it was due to the chemical reaction of the DDT to the metal containers that were specified for use by the government. The contractor was therefore relieved of liability for the defective DDT. The court stated

> The plaintiff urges that, because of a mutual mistake as to a material fact, the parties made a contract that was impossible of performance. It says that, since the government prepared the contract that specified that the liquid should be shipped in metal containers, it implicitly represented that if the specifications were complied with, satisfactory performance would result. We think that, in the instant situation, that is a correct statement.

> We think that when the government, through one of its important agencies, orders the production of a specified thing by specified means, it would be a rare instance when the supplier could reasonably be expected to investigate for himself whether compliance with the specifications would, in fact, produce the desired result.

Where a contractor substituted its own specifications without notifying the Navy that it had identified a problem with the Navy's specifications, it cannot recover increased costs based on a claim that the problem made the Navy's specifications defective. In a recent case, a contractor sued for $5 million in damages after showing that the Air Force had made an error in the specifications. However, it was shown that the contractor had been maintaining the area for 10 years. Since it must have been aware of the actual acreage, the court denied the recovery, stating that the contractor could not recover because it made an affirmative decision to bid on a specification that it knew to be inaccurate.

(c) Performance Specifications

Performance specifications are inherently more competitive than design specifications, although not infrequently they are used together in the same contract. Design specifications must be distinguished from "performance" specifications (where no contractor warranty is implied). Whenever the contractor retains the responsibility for the means and methods selected to achieve the end result, no warranty by the government is implied. It then becomes similar to those instances where impossibility is alleged even though the contract called for development or manufacture of a product in accordance with performance specifications (rather than design specifications). There the contractor has the contractual responsibility for preparing the detailed design of the product to meet the performance specification. It therefore has a large amount of discretion in manipulating all aspects of the product in meeting the performance specifications. Where a performance specification is used, the contractor always has the responsibility of preparing a detailed design that meets the performance requirements.

The contractor has assumed the risk of impossibility when it agrees to prepare such design. In one case, the contract called for the furnishing of a digital data recording system to meet certain specific performance requirements. The contractor had suggested the contract specification requirements after extensive negotiations in the technical area and the contract embodied his suggestions. A board found that the contractor had "full knowledge of being confronted with perilous scientific development and with hazardous manufacturing achievement" and therefore that he had assumed the risk of unsuccessful performance. Thus, it is clear that the intention of the parties at the time the contract was entered into is the controlling factor. In the first GAO decision that addressed the issue of commercial versus detailed specifications, it upheld a performance specification in a commercial item solicitation as adequately describing the product sought to enable potential bidders to intelligently prepare their bid. Because it can be argued that the use of performance or design specifications is (or may be) inherently restrictive in some degree, the rule is that such specifications cannot be unreasonably restrictive.

Federal agencies are required, to the maximum extent practicable, to state requirements with respect to an acquisition of supplies or services in terms of (1) functions to be performed, (2) performance required, or (3) essential physical characteristics.

(d) Double Dimensioning

Not every government contract can be placed in such black and white terms as a design specification or a performance specification contract, and these terms need not be "so mutually exclusive" where both types are used.

Where both design and performance specifications appear in the scope of work, these are often called "double dimensions." In this connection, specific language is often needed where the government intends to place responsibility on the contractor to meet both dimensions. Thus, contracts may call for the contractor to perform work strictly in accordance with government specifications with the contractor having no responsibility for preparation of the design specifications or performance or test requirements which the product is required to meet. The parties later find that when the product is manufactured in accordance with the design specifications, it will not pass the tests or meet the performance requirements. In such a case, the contractor has been relieved by the former Court of Claims of liability for the defective product.

The same court noted that, where the government did not prescribe the "manner" in which the material involved therein should be prepared or treated in order to meet the requirements set out in the contract specifications, "the responsibility rested on the [contractor] to meet the requirements of the specifications by the use of such methods as he might deem to be appropriate for that purpose."

Where the contract calls for development or manufacture of a product in accordance with performance specifications, the contractor has the responsibility for preparing the detailed designs to meet the performance specification. It therefore has a large amount of discretion in manipulating all aspects of the product in meeting the performance specifications. The contractor has the responsibility of preparing a detailed design that meets the performance requirements and assumes the risk of impossibility when it agrees to prepare such design.

Where the contract contains both design and performance specifications, the intention of the parties at the time the contract was entered into is the controlling factor governing the question of the assumption of risk. The Comptroller General has ruled that a request for proposals to manufacture air conditioners for the government may place all risk of discrepancies, errors, or deficiencies in design or technical data upon the contractor even though specifications and drawings are to be furnished by government. In the case of existing impossibility to meet both, the duty of the promisor depends on whether he has assumed the risk of the existence of facts creating the impossibility.

In this connection it should be noted that the default clause for fixed-price supply contracts provides that if, after termination, it is determined that the contractor was not at fault, or that the default was excusable, the rights and obligations of the parties shall be the same as if the termination had been issued for the convenience of the government. In such event the contractor is paid substantially all of his costs, normally those that are allowable for uncompleted work, and settlement costs (plus profit) in accordance with the regulation and the provisions of that clause. Accordingly, it would appear to be essential that the government in awarding contracts (or possibly the prime contractor in awarding subcontracts) with both design and performance specifications make a determination whether or not to include a provision thereon. The clause could provide that the Seller (contractor) has assumed the obligation to deliver product that meets the design, process, and performance requirements, and all risks resulting from his failure to do so or any incompatibility among them. Buyer, (government or prime contractor) may in its discretion issue change orders to facilitate performance by Seller, and in such event, there would be an upward adjustment in the price; however, if such change causes a decrease in the cost of performance of the work, an appropriate downward equitable adjustment would be made in purchase order price. In making this determination, consideration of criteria such as the following may be useful:

1. Did the basic design originate with the contractor?

2. If so, did the government materially modify this design?

3. If the contractor's design was materially modified, has the item previously met the performance specifications?

4. Did the design originate with another government contractor?

5. If so, has the item previously met performance specifications?

In this connection a question is often raised whether the government had "superior knowledge" vital to a performance of the contract but which is unknown and not reasonably available to the contractor who is thereby misled. In such a case, the government must disclose such superior knowledge or be held liable for breach of contract.

The government's implied warranty of the adequacy of its design specifications is based on the correctness of the specifications rather than any presumed "superior knowledge" in the sense of greater expertise.

Where the government adopted a specification prepared by and for the industry for its own use, members of that industry rather than the government possessed superior knowledge. But the fact that the affected industry may have participated in the development of a particular specification may not relieve the government from responsibility therefor. Each situation requires inquiry into the extent of responsibility for the specification. Where such knowledge is not unique to the government, or where the contractor either has employees with such knowledge or, if not, failed to consult experts, then no duty of disclosure by the government arises.

§ 11.3   Acquiring Other Than New Material

A change has been that agencies must not require virgin material (or supplies composed of or manufactured using virgin material) unless compelled by law or regulation or unless such material is vital for safety or meeting performance requirements of the contract. For agency purchases of printing and writing paper, an Executive Order establishes minimum recovered material content standards (material discarded for recovery having completed its life as a consumer item). A "Material Requirements" clause has been included in all supply contracts, except for commercial items. The supply contractor is required to provide supplies that are new, as defined by the clause, except as the contract otherwise requires virgin material or supplies. If the contractor determines to provide unused former government surplus property, or used, reconditioned, or remanufactured supplies, then the proposal must describe the material completely. The Contracting Officer must approve such use before it is furnished by the contractor. A violation may lead to liability under both the contract and the False Claims Act. Specifications must be developed "in such manner as is necessary to obtain full and open competition." Potential suppliers have to be informed as fully as possible of what are the needs in an unambiguous manner, in order to foster true competition. It is not always possible to prepare specifications that have no uncertainties. This is one reason why design specifications "are generally inappropriate if an agency can state its minimum needs in terms of performance specifications which alternate designs could meet."

§ 11.4   Delivery or Performance Schedules

Nothing seems to induce higher costs for government procurement more than tight delivery schedules, which often cause a procuring office to protect itself by making delivery earlier than necessary. Many procurement specialists defend themselves against the higher costs they pay (beyond the costs of commercial procurements) by pointing to such schedules over which they claim to have no control. The regulations require agencies to "ensure that delivery or performance schedules are realistic," and point out that unreasonably tight schedules tend to restrict competition, and "may result in higher contract prices." If timely delivery or performance is unusually important to the government, liquidated damages clauses may be used. One solution which may be applied in many instances is for the agency seeking supplies or services to set forth a required delivery schedule and to allow an offeror to propose an alternative delivery schedule (for other than A–E or construction contracts.) The agency may also indicate that it "desires" delivery by a certain time but "requires" delivery by a specified later time.

§ 11.5   Liquidated Damages

If liquidated damages are to be inserted into the contract, they must be "a reasonable forecast of just compensation."

A contractor will weigh the possibility of its having to pay liquidated damages at the time his bid is being prepared. If it seems more likely than not that this will occur, he may consider adding some contingent amount to the overall bid to protect himself—particularly if he believes that his competitor may increase his price in a like fashion; for this reason, the government can only use liquidated damages clauses when the time of delivery or performance is such an important factor in the award of the contract that the government may reasonably expect to suffer damage if the delivery or timely performance is delinquent, and "the extent or amount of such damage would be difficult or impossible to ascertain or prove."

Since the end of World War II, the law no longer has looked with disfavor upon liquidated damages provisions in contracts. If they represent fair and reasonable attempts to fix compensation for anticipated losses caused by a breach of contract, their validity has usually been upheld. Liquidated damages provisions serve a useful function when the damages are uncertain in nature or amount or are immeasurable. Liquidated damages clauses must represent a good faith attempt to measure damages in advance, and must not be so large as to constitute a "penalty." The regulations provide that liquidated damages are to be used where the extent or amount of such damage would be difficult or impossible to ascertain or prove. All agencies have considered the probable effect on such matters as pricing, competition, and the costs and difficulties of contract administration on a case-by-case basis, since liquidated damages fixed without any reference to probable actual damages may be held to be a penalty, and therefor unenforceable.

Boards of Contract Appeals have denied recovery of liquidated damages where they determined that the amounts thereof were not reasonable forecasts of the anticipated damages. The regulation provides that where a liquidated damages clause is to be used in a contract, consideration must be given to the "appropriate rate(s)" of liquidated damages to be included in the solicitation.

Where an agency's regulations require the inclusion of a liquidated damages provision in a contract and this has not been done, the clause cannot be incorporated by operation of law because the lack of agreement by the parties on a rate of damages precludes any assessment. An agency may use a maximum amount or a maximum period for assessing liquidated damages, if these limits reflect the maximum probable damage to the government. Such damages are used in cost-plus-fixed-fee contracts. Following a breach by the contractor, the agency must take reasonable steps to mitigate the damages (such as action to obtain performance by the contractor), or to terminate the contract and obtain the delivery or performance elsewhere within a reasonable time. This is imperative "to prevent excessive loss to defaulting contractors and to protect the interests of the government."

Acquiescence in a contractor's late performance may be characterized as a forbearance to default; it does not result in a waiver of the right to assess liquidated damages. Historically, the Comptroller General had the power to remit part or all of amounts owing as liquidated damages under certain circumstances. Under the current regulation the head of the agency may reduce or waive the amount of liquidated damages assessed under a contract, if the Commissioner, Financial Management Service approves.

Where the contract provides for liquidated damages for delay in performance and the government is responsible for the delay, the contractor may consider that the government is entitled to no liquidated damages. The Supreme Court has held that "since the contractor agreed to pay a specified rate for each day's delay not caused by the government, it was clearly the intention that it should pay for some days' delay at that rate, even if it were relieved from paying for other days because of the government's action." Since liquidated damages are determined at time of making a contract, they may be received if at the time of completion of the work the government suffered no actual damages, provided that the parties at the time of contracting reasonably contemplated that damage would flow from a delay in performance.

Guidance from the commercial world can be useful. The Uniform Commercial Code (UCC) refers to "the anticipated or actual" loss caused by the breach. This provision has been used to uphold a liquidated damages clause that was "reasonable with respect to either (1) the harm which the parties anticipate will result from the breach at the time of contracting or (2) the actual damages suffered ... at the time of the breach." Although the UCC does not control government contracts, Federal courts and boards do rely on its principles for analogous authority where persuasive.

§ 11.6 Priorities, Allocations, and Allotments

A special statute has been enacted in order to keep certain defense and energy production programs on schedule and maintain an administrative means of promptly mobilizing the nation's economic resources in the event of war or national emergency. This law provides that priorities may be used to require contractors to accept and perform "rated orders" (i.e., orders required to be supported with rating and allotment authority) in preference to other orders, and that materials and facilities may be allocated for defense and energy production purposes. The Office of Industrial Resource Administration, Department of Commerce (DOC) was given the responsibility for establishing the basic priorities and allocations rules. This resulted in a series of regulations and orders called the Defense Materials System and the Defense Priorities System.

Any solicitations that will result in the placement of rated orders or Authorized Control Material orders (any delivery order for controlled material as distinct from a product containing controlled material) must have special clauses inserted to appropriately apprise the vendors that the procurement will be subject to priority system. A "rated order" means a prime contract for any product, service or material (including controlled materials) placed by a Delegate Agency under the provisions of the Defense Priorities and Allocations System (DPAS) in support of an authorized program and which requires preferential treatment, and includes subcontracts and purchase orders resulting under such contracts. All rated orders (symbolized by "DO" and "DX") have precedence over unrated orders; DX orders take precedence over DO orders.

§ 11.7 Variations in Quantity

Fixed-price supply and construction contracts may authorize variation in the quantity of required items. In supply contracts, the variation is stated as a percentage that may be an increase, a decrease, or a combination of both. Unless an agency regulation specifies otherwise, permissible variations may not exceed plus or minus 10%. Quantities delivered in excess of those specified may be retained without compensating the contractor. In supply contracts, the clause is only required to be used where a variation in quantity is authorized. Above $250, the excess quantities may be returned at the contractor's expense or retained and paid for at the unit price.

In construction contracts, an equitable adjustment shall be made upon demand where the variation is estimated and actual quantity exceeds 15%.

CHAPTER 12

ACQUISITION OF COMMERCIAL ITEMS

§ 12.1 In General

The general definition states that commercial items are for "purposes other than governmental purposes" means purposes that "are not unique to the government." Its policies are applicable to all acquisitions of commercial items above the micropurchase threshold ($2,500 for supplies and services, $2,000 for construction), except acquisitions made using the Standard Form 44, the imprest fund governmentwide commercial purchase card, or directly from another Federal agency. The definition of "commercial item" at FAR 2.101 was revised in several respects by a final rule published October 22, 2001. The rule replaced the requirement that a commercial item must be of a type "customarily used for nongovernmental purposes" with the requirement that the item be of a type "customarily used by the general public or by non-governmental entities for purposes other than governmental purposes." The phrase "purposes other than governmental purposes" is defined as "purposes that are not unique to a government." Additionally, the revised definition provides that a "standalone" service (i.e., a service not in support of a commercial item) may be considered a "commercial item" only if it is offered or sold in the commercial marketplace "based on established catalog or market prices." The rule also revised the ancillary services provisions to clarify that the ancillary services need not be provided by the same vendor or at the same time as the commercial item. The rule added definitions of the terms "catalog price" and "market price" which, with one notable exception, are substantially similar to the definitions in the now-repealed "established catalog and market price" exception of the Truth in Negotiations Act (TINA). However, while the TINA definition of market price required substantiation through "data from sources independent of the manufacturer or vendor," the new commercial item definitions require that the market price be substantiated "through competition or from sources independent of the offerors." (See Chapter 15.)

On December 3, 2001, DoD released a new "Commercial Item Handbook" designed to provide "further guidance on sound business strategies for acquiring commercial items" and to be used as a "practical reference tool." The Handbook emphasizes the broad definition of "commercial item," and stresses that acquisition professionals must begin each acquisition by conducting market research to determine whether the supply or service is commercially available and consider a Government-unique contract only after careful consideration of the commercial item definition and market research information.

The requirements of other parts of the FAR apply to commercial items to the extent they are not inconsistent with Part 12. That is, agencies must use the policies in Part 12 in conjunction with those applicable to solicitation, evaluation, and award prescribed for Simplified Acquisition (see Chapter 13), Sealed Bidding (see Chapter 14), and Negotiated Procurements (see Chapter 15).

§ 12.2 Special Requirements for Commercial Items

The "special requirements" for the acquisition of commercial items include market research already discussed in

Chapter 10, and the methods for describing agency needs discussed in Chapter 11. A standard form is to be used for such items. Agencies are requested to allow offerors to "propose more than one product that will meet a government need." Reasonableness of price and financing are to be determined by policies completely set forth elsewhere (Chapters 15 and 32) as are the applicable policies regarding technical data.

Contracts and subcontracts for the acquisition of commercial items are exempt from Cost Accounting Standards requirements when these contracts and subcontracts are firm-fixed-price or fixed-price with economic price adjustment, if the price adjustment is not based on actual costs incurred.The definition of a "commercial item" does not specifically cover all items found in catalogs or the market place. Yet, it has been broadened to indicate coverage of services for installation, maintenance, repair, training, "and other services" if the offer uses "[t]he same work force . . . providing such services to the general public."

This concept has given rise to the argument that both "time and materials" (T & M) and "labor hour" (LH) types of contracts should be treated as commercial items, rather than different "types of contracts" (see Chapter 16). That is, they should also be exempt from cost accounting requirements. While the "use of any other contract type to acquire commercial items is prohibited," an LH type is not used to procure such an item. The true variables in LH contracts are the hours to perform the work. The GAO upheld the Navy's determinations that travel management services were not "commercial items" in a procurement.

§ 12.3 Solicitation Provisions and Contract Clauses

Although wording of standard provisions and clauses has been prescribed for use in the acquisition of commercial items, contracting officers are allowed to tailor solicitations and contracts in order to meet the needs of the particular acquisition and the marketplace for that time which is consistent with commercial practices.

The new regulation offers guidance in three areas where the prescribed terms and conditions either do not reflect customary practice for a particular market or differ from those contained elsewhere in the FAR; namely, acceptance, termination, and warranties. It notes that the government has the right to refuse acceptance of nonconforming items without any clause to that effect. This is because the "general law of contracts" often applies to government contracts in the absence of a statute or agreement to the contrary. (See Introduction.) One of the new clauses authorizes the termination for convenience, a clause peculiar to government contracting: the contractor is paid for the percentage of work performed prior to the notice of termination "using its standard record keeping system," rather than the cost accounting standards (CAS) (discussed in Chapter 30) or the contract cost principles (discussed in Chapter 31). Under Federal law, contracts for commercial items include clauses "determined to be consistent with commercial practice." The "termination for cause" clause states that the government shall not be liable "for supplies or services not accepted" and upon such a termination, the contractor becomes liable "for any rights or remedies provided by law." It adds a noncommercial clause entitled "Termination for the Government's Convenience"—a diminished type of which normally only appears in government contracts. Thereunder, the contractor receives a percentage of the price of his work done "prior to the termination notice plus reasonable charges" that he can demonstrate using his "standard record keeping system." The government is denied the right to audit, but it enjoys certain implied warranties, such as the implied warranty of merchantability, contained in the standard clause.

§ 12.4 Applicability of Certain Laws to Purchases of Commercial Items

The regulation identifies the applicability of certain laws to the acquisition of commercial items. It also contains the list of laws determined to be inapplicable to executive agency prime contracts for acquisition of commercial items. This list has been expanded to also include those laws that have been revised in some manner to modify their applicability to commercial items. Agency unique laws, determined to be inapplicable to prime contracts that are not addressed in the FAR, may be addressed separately by the respective agencies. Also listed are laws determined to be inapplicable to subcontracts for commercial items. This list has been expanded to include those laws that have been "amended to eliminate or modify their applicability to either contracts or subcontracts" for commercial items.

The regulation also contains procedures for the evaluation and solicitation of contracts for commercial items. These procedures may be tailored at the discretion of the contracting officer. When using simplified acquisition procedures (See Chapter 13), the agency is not required to describe the relative importance of the evaluation factors. Where the agency follows negotiation procedures (see FAR Part 15), fairness can require that the agency disclose the relative weight of the factors.

Only laws are cited in the FAR. The Uniform Commercial Code (UCC) is a state law. Nevertheless, the Federal Acquisition Streamlining Act of 1994 (FASA) mandated that to the maximum extent practicable, government contracts for the acquisition of commercial items must contain only those clauses "that are determined to be consistent with standard commercial practices." The UCC could be applied by analogy—particularly with respect to subcontracts (see Chapter 44). In connection with prime contracts, an appellate court has noted that if law does not address an issue, courts should look to appropriate alternative sources of law. Accordingly, adjudicators, the courts and the GAO, sometimes cite the UCC as such an alternate source of the common law. These references can only be made with respect to the law concerning the sale of commercial goods and not to the procurement of services. FAR clauses govern over the UCC, which covers many areas, and most of the clauses may be modified by the contracting officer to be consistent with commercial practice.

The Consumer Product Safety Commission (CPSC) seeks recalls of products subject to a "substantial product hazard." Most companies generally avoid having their products fall within that category and the Commission will undertake a recall voluntarily of products under investigation. Its reports may be announced with or without an incident and most of those are not followed by civil penalty actions. That part of the Federal Acquisition Regulation governing "Contract Quality Assurance" specifies that "[w]hen acquiring commercial items ... , the Government shall rely on contractors' existing quality assurance systems as a substitute for Government inspection and testing ... unless customary market practices for the commercial item being acquired include in-process inspection."

PART III

CONTRACTING METHODS AND CONTRACT TYPES

CHAPTER 13

SIMPLIFIED ACQUISITION PROCEDURES

§ 13.1 Procedures for Simplified Acquisitions, and Small Business Set Asides

Pursuant to the Federal Acquisition Streamlining Act (FASA) of 1994, simplified procedures are provided in the regulations for certain purchases in order to reduce "administrative costs and improve opportunities for small business concerns and small disadvantaged business concerns." Policies and procedures are prescribed for the acquisition of supplies and services, including construction and research and development, the aggregate amount of which does not exceed the simplified acquisition threshold: $100,000, except for contracts made and performed, or purchases to be made, outside the United States in support of a contingency, humanitarian, or peacekeeping operation, in which case the simplified acquisition threshold is $200,000. Special procedures are to be used when acquiring architect-engineer services (see Chapter 36) and commercial items exceeding the simplified acquisition threshold but not exceeding $5 million (see § 13.6).

Under these simplified procedures, agencies are given maximum flexibility. That is, they have "broad discretion in fashioning suitable evaluation procedures." Agencies making simplified acquisitions may provide that they inspect items or services acquired the same way, as they must for other purchases (see Chapter 46). Other FAR parts that may be adapted include regulations governing sealed bidding (see Chapter 14), contracting by negotiation (see Chapter 15), and acquisition and distribution of commercial products (see Chapter 12).

With certain narrow exceptions, supplies or services with an anticipated dollar value exceeding $2,500 and not exceeding $100,000 must be reserved exclusively for small business concerns by using set-asides. For purchases over $2,500, quotations must be made so as to "promote competition to the maximum extent practicable." Requests for quotations should be solicited "orally to the maximum extent practicable" for contract actions not expected to exceed the simplified acquisition threshold, provided oral solicitation is more efficient than soliciting through available electronic commerce alternatives and notice is not required. However, "an oral solicitation may not be practical for contract actions exceeding $25,000" (which certain exceptions). There may be solicitations connected with the Telephone Consumer Protection Act (TCPA) of 1991. The contracting officer is required to comply with the public display and notice requirements unless (1) acquisition computer network (FACNET) or the single, Government-wide point of entry is used or (2) an exception in FAR 5.202 applies. Additionally, when acquiring commercial items, a combined synopsis/solicitation may be used.

Paper solicitations for contract actions not expected to exceed $25,000 should only be issued when obtaining electronic or oral quotations is not considered economical or practical. Solicitations for construction contracts over $2,000 shall only be issued electronically or by paper solicitation. Solicitation of at least three sources may be considered to promote competition to the maximum extent practicable if the contract action does not exceed $25,000. The provision under the simplified procedures authorizes solicitation from one (1) source "if the contracting officer determines that the circumstances of the contract action deem only one source reasonably available (e.g., urgency)." If only one source is solicited, a notation is made to explain the absence of competition. In 2003, the GAO decided that where an invitation for bids under a simplified acquisition procedure had no provision expressly providing that quotations must be received by a certain date, an agency's decision to exclude an offeror's bid as "late" was improper. Further, the U.S. Court of Federal Claims ruled that an agency was not prohibited from revising its RFQ or obtaining revised quotations or proposals without discussions under this procedure.

Contracting officers may evaluate quotations or offers based on price alone or price and other factors (e.g., past performance). Evaluation of other factors may be based on "such information as the contracting officer's knowledge, previous experience, or customer surveys." Further, standing price quotations may be used in lieu of obtaining individual quotations each time a purchase is contemplated. The buyer should ensure that the price information is current and that the government obtains the benefit of maximum discounts before award is made. Notifications to unsuccessful suppliers are given "only if requested."

For purchases within the simplified acquisition threshold, the agency may solicit from a single source if it determines "that the circumstances of the contract action deem only one source reasonably available" (e.g., emergency, etc.). The reasons may be limited to the contracting officer's personal knowledge of the item being purchased, if any, or any other reasonable basis. Procurements for commercial items under the simplified acquisition procedures are not subject by regulation to the requirement for "discussions" (see Chapter 15). This applies where the agency decides to accept a revised quotation from the low-priced vendor without conducting discussions with the other vendors. This can deprive vendors of any right to have the government point out deficiencies in their quotations for the same reason; namely, there is no need to conduct discussions with prospective contractors when using simplified acquisition procedures.

The regulation sets forth a portion of the common law by stating that a quotation is not an offer that can be accepted to form a binding contract.

§ 13.2   Blanket Purchase Agreements (BPAs) and Indefinite Delivery Orders

Agencies are encouraged to seek opportunities to cooperate to achieve simplified purchase efficiency and economy through the use of indefinite delivery contracts that are placed by several contracting or ordering offices in one or more executive agencies. Where there is a wide variety of items in a broad class of goods to be purchased but the exact items, quantities, and delivery requirements are not known in advance, blanket purchase orders (BPAs) may be used by establishing "charge accounts" within available funds. Such orders are generally made with firms from which numerous individual purchases will likely be made in a given period where, for example, past experience has shown that certain firms are dependable and consistently lower in price than other firms dealing in the same commodities. They are often established with Federal Supply Schedule contractors "not inconsistent with the terms of the applicable schedule contract." Although the regulation states that competitive sources should be given an equal opportunity to furnish the supplies or services, it also states that BPAs should be made with firms "from which numerous individual purchases will likely be made in a given period." Individual purchases and a BPA are limited to $5 million for commercial items, but this limit does not apply to Federal Supply Schedule contractors. A BPA's existence "does not justify purchasing from only one source or avoiding small business set asides." It has been held that a blanket order that aggregated $50,000 or more each year does not constitute a single contract for purposes of requiring that a contractor maintain written affirmative action plans; the agreement contemplated individual government purchases made through separately negotiated "calls" or "requisition documents." If no binding agreement results, an abuse may occur when an agency pays a revised price current in the year of delivery rather than the price in effect when the order was placed. The Air Force has stated that such annual price revision added over $100 million to spare-parts costs at a particular plant; later, the Secretary of Defense banned further use of the redeterminable basic ordering agreement.

§ 13.3   Unpriced Order Procedure

The unpriced order is one issued when the price of supplies or services is not established at the time of issuance of the order. The procedure is used to support the government's need to repair equipment and "determine the nature and extent of repairs." A monetary limitation is placed upon the order that may be subject to adjustment when the repair is completed.

The general law of sales contracts (as exemplified by the Uniform Commercial Code) provides that under certain circumstances a contract in which the price was not fixed calls for the payment of a reasonable price. UCC § 2–204(3), for example, provides that a contract for sale does not fail for indefiniteness "even though one or more terms are left open if the parties have intended to make a contract and there is a reasonably certain basis for giving an appropriate remedy."

UCC § 2–207(3) provides that "conduct by both parties which recognizes the existence of a contract is sufficient to establish a contract for sale even though the writings of the parties do not otherwise establish a contract." It consists of "those terms on which the writings of the parties agree, together with any supplementary terms incorporated under other provisions of the Code." The UCC is state (and is not Federal) law and its approaches may or may not apply to government contracts; but it may apply to subcontracts. Where a small item or a spare part under open price terms is not rejected, the *goods* are accepted; however the seller's *price* has not been accepted. That price becomes negotiable and the fact that the parties cannot reach agreement as to the price does not necessarily obligate the buyer to pay the amount claimed by the seller. Restitutionary relief then becomes available to the supplier and he receives a "reasonable price" which might be lower than his asking price.

The remedy of ceasing to do business with contractors who overcharge may present a serious problem to the government in instances where the contractor is not on a List of Parties Excluded from Procurement and Non-procurement Programs. Under the "full and open competition" requirements (See Chapter 6), the government does not have the same flexibility to cease doing business with a contractor, as private or commercial businesses have to cease doing business with *their* private customers or with the government.

An unpriced order or a Blanket Purchase Agreement (BPA) may be used in the fast payment procedure. These may be used for material available at only one source for which cost cannot readily be established or exact prices are "not known." Thereafter, the invoice price must be reviewed and, "if reasonable," processed for payment.

§ 13.4   The Government Commercial Purchase Card

The government-wide commercial purchase card may be used by contracting officers by a certification of appointment. Other individuals may be designated for micro-purchases without such a certificate. Agencies "should not limit" the card to micro-purchases. They "should encourage use of the card in greater dollar amounts." Since 1995, these cards have been used to place orders under a Blanket Purchasing Agreement (BPA) and make payments when the contractor agrees to accept payment thereunder.

Reforms during the late 1990s were alleged to have "expanded the use of flexible commercial-like purchases which permit large classes of transactions to avoid scrutiny and avoid competition and oversight." The "most dramatic example" was claimed to have been the widespread use of the government's purchase card.

The General Accounting Office (GAO) has reported that during the last several years, credit card fraud has surpassed $1 billion per year. In 2003, the Navy cancelled all of its 22,000 purchase cards after learning that hackers had gained access to approximately 13,000 Navy purchase cards.

§ 13.5   Fast Payment Procedure, Imprest Funds

Another procedure available for fast payment is designed to reduce lead-time to consignees and to improve supplier relations by expediting payment for purchases up to $25,000. It applies to payment to be made for supplies received and accepted based on the contractor's submission of an invoice that constitutes a certification that the supplies have been delivered to "a post office, common carrier, or point of first receipt by the government." The contractor agrees to replace, repair, or correct supplies not received at the destination, damaged in transit, or not conforming to purchase agreements. The procedure allows (rather than mandates) use of fast payment procedures and specifically describes the conditions that would justify the procedure. It is used where deliveries of supplies are to occur at locations where there is both a geographical separation and a lack of adequate communications facilities between government receiving and disbursing activities.

Imprest funds may be used for purchases "in relatively small amounts" of cash, which may be made orally and without competition.

§ 13.6   Micro–Purchases

Nowhere but in the Federal government would one consider the acquisition of supplies or services up to $2500 not as "small"; but rather as "micro-purchases." Nonetheless, a new subsection has been added to the FAR to designate them in accordance with the Federal Acquisition Streamlining Act. Micro-purchases of construction are limited to $2000 because of Davis–Bacon Act requirements (see Chapter 22).

Like imprest funds, so-called micro-purchases may be awarded without soliciting any competitive quotations. This is done where the contracting officer has information to indicate that the price may be reasonable. A Government-wide commercial purchase card may be used to make micro-purchases.

§ 13.7   Test Program for Certain Commercial Items

The FAR authorizes the use of simplified procedures for the acquisition of supplies and services in amounts greater than the simplified acquisition threshold but not exceeding $5 million (including options), "if the contracting officer reasonably expects, based on the nature of the supplies or services sought, and on market research, that offers will include only commercial items." This revision vests contracting officers with additional procedural "discretion and flexibility, so that commercial item acquisitions in this dollar range may be solicited, evaluated, and awarded in a simplified manner."

The U.S. Court of Federal Claims held that an agency must inform offerors in the solicitation whether it is involving the Subpart 13.5 test program and simplified acquisition procedures, in spite of the fact that there is no such express requirement in the FAR. The court stated that, "[s]implified acquisition procedures relax many of the FAR requirements and grant contracting officers broad discretion, but they do not grant a contracting officer unfettered discretion."

CHAPTER 14

CONTRACTING WITH SEALED BIDDING

A. THE PURPOSE AND OPERATION OF SEALED BIDS

§ 14.1 In General

A primary method of contracting that employs competitive bids, public opening of bids, and awards is "sealed bidding." This has been traditional for public bodies; in the Federal government, use of the advertised bid method has been required by statute since the commencement of the Civil War. It was formerly called "formal advertising."

Competitive bidding is essential to efficiency and its use is not limited to the free world. Communist China found that its construction industry, "one of the country's most mismanaged and inefficient, has been chosen to pioneer even more fundamental reforms—the success or failure of which will guide the later restructuring of the entire economy." Plans were announced whereby all major construction contracts will be awarded on the basis of public bidding by competing state, and collectively owned, companies. In the free world, large corporations changed from a practice of negotiating agreements with a limited number of suppliers, to competitive bidding.

The purposes of sealed bidding is to give all qualified contractors the opportunity to compete for government contracts while avoiding favoritism, collusion, or fraud and to obtain for the government the benefits of competition. The judiciary itself finally initiated some use of bidding procedures: In 1989 U.S. District Judge Walker in San Francisco required sealed bids from any of the 25 plaintiff law firms that had filed actions and wished to lead the litigation. Four firms complied.

Advertised bidding procedures of public bodies are often considered to be very mechanical in their operation which is conducted by low-level clerical personnel pursuant to rules automatically applied. This view has been generally rejected because the matter of competitive bidding for government contracts is not one in which the contract must always automatically be awarded to the lowest bidder.

Because, in many procurements, the lowest bid is not an unreasonable price, the item offered does meet the specifications, and the bidder is a responsible one, the process often appears to be automatic. When any of these factors are missing, a knowledge of the law particular to this area becomes paramount, and the operation ceases to be a clerical job.

An appellate court has ruled that the selection and supervision of contractors is a discretionary function. Where an employee was killed while performing a timber-cutting contract between his employer and the U.S. Forest Service, his widow sued the government claiming that the Forest Service was negligent. The majority ruled that "the selection of contractors is clearly a discretionary function within the scope of the discretionary function exception."

B. REQUIREMENTS OF SEALED BIDDING

§ 14.11 In General

Procurement by sealed bidding involves the following basic steps: (a) preparation of the invitation for bids, describing the requirements of the government clearly, accurately, and completely, without unnecessarily restrictive specifications or requirements which might unduly limit the number of bidders the term ''invitation for bids'' (IFB) means the complete assembly of related documents (whether attached or incorporated by reference) furnished prospective bidders for the purpose of bidding; (b) publicizing the invitation for bids through the Governmentwide Point of Entry (GPE) (formerly Commerce Business Daily), or otherwise, distribution to prospective bidders, posting in public places, and other such means as may be appropriate, in sufficient time to enable prospective bidders to prepare and submit bids before the time set for public opening of bids; (c) submission of bids by prospective contractors, which may include electronic bids, if authorized; (d) public opening and evaluation of bids without discussions by bidders; and (e) awarding the contract to that responsible bidder whose bid, conforming to the invitation for bids (that is a responsive bid), will be most advantageous to the government ''considering only price and price-related factors.'' When the method of contracting is by sealed bidding, a firm-fixed-price contract must result.

Effective December 28, 1989, FAR authorized the use of facsimile equipment for the submission of bids, proposals, acknowledgments to solicitations, and modifications or withdrawals of bids. However, agency procedures may prohibit or restrict such use. Facsimile equipment has the capability of duplicating text or graphic information, transmitting the information over telephone lines to another fax machine, and reproducing both printed and handwritten material. After scanning a document, a fax machine converts the information into an electronic code and sends it over a telephone line to a receiving fax machine that is compatible with the sending machine. The signature on a fax may be transmitted; although an unsigned faxed bid modification must be rejected as nonresponsive, agencies may request the apparently successful offeror to provide the original signed bid.

Sealed bidding is distinguished from the other method called "negotiation"—a term used to characterize a "contract awarded using other than sealed bidding procedures," when the agency uses "competitive proposals" or "other competitive procedures." (See Chapter 15)

Sealed bidding is to be used whenever certain conditions apply which were discussed above in connection with competitive requirements; namely, time permits the solicitation and evaluation of bids, award will be made on the basis of price or price related factors, no discussions with offerors are needed, and it is reasonable to expect receipt of more than one bid. Solicitation mailing lists must be established by contracting activities to assure access to adequate sources of supplies and services. Under the Competition in Contracting Act, when these conditions are met, an agency must use sealed bidding procedures and lacks the discretion to use competitive negotiation as an alternative method.

§ 14.12   Price Related Factors

The term "price related factors" requires regulatory guidance. If such factors exist, they must be included in the solicitation. For example, there may be foreseeable costs or delays to the government resulting from such factors as differences in inspection, locations of supplies, and transportation if bids are requested on f.o.b. origin basis. Transportation costs to the designated points shall be considered in determining the lowest cost to the government; changes may be requested by the bidder in the terms of the invitation for bids, which may be made if the change does not constitute a ground for rejection; advantages or disadvantages to the government might result from making more than one award. The contracting officer assumes, for the purpose of making multiple awards, that $500 would be the administrative cost to the government for issuing and administering each contract awarded under a solicitation. Individual awards are for the items or combinations of items that result in the lowest aggregate cost to the government, including the assumed administrative costs. Factors such as state and local taxes may need to be considered and, if supplies are of foreign origin, then it may be necessary to consider application of the Buy American Act or any other prohibition on foreign purchases.

The GAO has ruled that the submission of a below-cost or low-profit offer is not illegal. An offer of $0.00 for certain contract line items did not violate the terms of the solicitation in a fixed-price environment.

§ 14.13   Restrictive Specifications

The regulation states, "Unnecessarily restrictive specifications or requirements that might unduly limit the number of bidders are prohibited." Use of specifications that are designed by, or are the property of, a prospective bidder may restrict competition more than necessary for minimum needs of an agency and violate the law. For example, after the Navy requested bids for office desks, Business Services Corporation protested the rejection of its low bid and the award to another on the ground that the specifications were proprietary; they were "written around" specifications of a desk offered by one company in violation of a regulation which required that specifications state only minimum needs, describe supplies in a manner which encourages competition, and eliminate restrictive features. The General Services Administration recommended revision of the specifications, but the Navy ignored the recommendation and purchased desks from the seventh highest out of eight bids received because it wanted a superior product not related to its minimum need for desks. Although the specifications were found to be restrictive, at that time the Comptroller General merely told the Navy to avoid such mistakes in the future. When a protester challenges a specification as unduly restrictive of competition, the agency must establish that the restrictions imposed were reasonably related to its needs; the protester retains the considerable burden of showing that the requirements complained of are clearly unreasonable. This is because discretion must be accorded to a procuring agency in determining its needs; and government procurement officials familiar with the particular conditions under which equipment has to be used are in the best position to know the government's actual needs and to draft appropriate specifications. The Comptroller General held that where the basis of the protest is simply the protester's disagreement with the agency's technical opinion and the protester's position is supported by its expert's technical advice, the protester has not necessarily met its burden of proof to establish that the agency's position regarding its technical needs is unreasonable.

Agencies may ignore patent rights in awarding a contract because a statute expressly authorizes the government to disregard patent claims when awarding a contract. A patent indemnity clause is normally inserted in sealed bid contracts for supplies or services sold in the commercial open market.

Agency contracting activities must establish solicitation mailing lists to assure access to adequate sources of supplies and services except for small or nonrecurring purchases. Federal agencies are also authorized to remove names of bidders from such lists when they do not bid after two consecutive solicitations.

Procedures concerning display of bids in a public place, releases to newspapers and trade journals, and synopsizing in the Governmentwide Point of Entry (GPE), which have been discussed above. Except where preinvitation notices are used, such information cannot be released outside the government before solicitation, and, even within the government, information is restricted to those having a "legitimate interest." Telegraphic bids will not be considered unless permitted by the invitation. Significantly, previous regulations have been changed in order to permit consideration of a telegraphic bid that is telephoned into the contracting agency, in certain instances.

§ 14.14   Unbalanced Bids

The term "unbalanced" is applied to bids on procurements which include a number of items as to which the actual quantities to be furnished are not fixed, in which a bidder quotes high prices on items he believes will be required in larger quantities than those used for bid evaluation, and/or low prices on items of which he believes fewer will be called for. If their prices for any line items are "materially unbalanced," bids may be rejected as nonresponsive.

In 1999, the U.S. Court of Federal Claims denied a postaward bid protest alleging that the awardee's bid was unbalanced. It found that although it was mathematically unbalanced, it was not materially unbalanced and that the protester's bid was more unbalanced.

Agencies sometimes anticipate the possibility of unbalanced bids when unit prices are solicited by specifying that bids with unbalanced first article prices could be rejected. Where, despite this warning, the protester submitted a bid with inflated first article prices (unit prices for first articles many times greater than the unit prices for production items), the bid was held to be materially unbalanced and rejected.

Bids submitted in response to two similar invitations concerning rental and maintenance of washers and dryers for a one-year base period and two option years were held to be mathematically unbalanced because the base prices were 459% and 308% higher than the option year prices. The bids were also materially unbalanced because the bids would not result in the lowest cost to the government until well into the option periods and there was no guarantee that both options would be exercised. The GAO has also upheld the rejection of a bid as unbalanced where the unit price for ten first articles was a thousand times greater than that for 100,000 production items.

The applicable part of the regulation in Part 14, "Sealed Bidding," authorizes bid rejection for "unreasonableness of price," including "individual line item prices," and particularly where the prices for line items are "materially unbalanced." The same criteria became applicable to "negotiated contracts" in order to emphasize risks associated with unbalanced pricing of "start up" work on option quantities of separate items. (See Chapter 15)

§ 14.15   Bidding Time—Generally

In order to obtain reasonable bids, it is obvious that a prospective bidder must be given a reasonable time after issuance of the solicitation and before bid opening in order to prepare and submit a bid consistent with the needs of the government. The time must be at least 30 calendar days when a synopsis is required for a proposed contract. This is because, by using an unduly limited bidding time, some potential sources may be precluded from bidding or forced to include amounts for contingencies that could be eliminated with additional time.

§ 14.16   Bidding Time—Late Bids or Late Withdraw-
al of Bids

Pursuant to applicable regulations, consideration of a bid is generally prohibited unless received on or before the bid opening date. An agency may designate regular mail, electronic commerce, or facsimile (electronic equipment that communicates and reproduces both printed and handwritten material) for the transmission of a bid in response to an invitation for bids (IFB). If no time of day is specified, it is by 4:30 p.m. local time of the date due. Any bid not received on time at the proper location will not be considered "unless received before award is made." Although the agency may accept the late bid, that would "not unduly delay the acquisition." When an electronic bid is authorized, it must be received at the initial point of entry to the government infrastructure "not later than 5:00 p.m. one working day prior to the date specified for receipt of bids."

It was held that a bid which was hand-delivered after the time shown on the clock in the room where bids were received was late. It was also known that the clock was one minute, 37 seconds ahead of "official phone number standard time." The Comptroller General noted there was no regulatory requirement that the clock's time be verified and he stated "in this case, we believe that the bid opening officer's determination that the time for bid opening had arrived based on the time shown on the bid opening room wall clock was reasonable because of the very small alleged variation between the wall clock and the actual time."

In another case, a potential bidder did not receive the Invitation until one day after bid opening. The government was not required to reject the bids it had in fact received because the other bids represented adequate competition at reasonable prices, and the notice of the solicitation was published in the Commerce Business Daily (now Governmentwide Point of Entry), was held to provide constructive notice of the procurement to the disappointed would-be bidder.

When a bid is received late and cannot be considered, the bidder may be notified and the bid is held unopened. In 1999, the regulation was amended to provide uniform guidance regarding receipt of late sealed bids.

§ 14.17 How a Bid Becomes Irrevocable Without Consideration

The mere request by a buyer to a bidder that the latter maintain his offer during a specified period, and the bidder's assent thereto, is considered insufficient to bind the bidder to his promise in jurisdictions where the common law prevails. The bidder is able to renege on his promise so long as his withdrawal is received by the buyer before award is made.

The principal object of sealed bidding procedures is to obtain, where possible, a binding contract between the lowest responsive and responsible bidder and the purchaser. An offer may be modified or withdrawn at any time up to the moment of acceptance, but not afterwards. Unlike typical contracts for which this rule was designed, contracts resulting from competitive bidding generally require that rights of modification and withdrawal do not continue during an appreciable interval prior to acceptance in order to permit proper evaluation of the bids and to ascertain the lowest responsible bidder. A bidder may agree that he will not withdraw or modify his bid during this interval. The invitation to bid and other form documents used by the Federal government are explicit in forbidding withdrawal after the time set for opening. Similar provisions can be found in forms used at state and local levels. The bidder may argue that he did not receive consideration for this agreement.

The Federal government, with billions of dollars continuously being invested in sealed bid procurements with no statute specifically prohibiting a low bidder from withdrawing his bid after opening and prior to award. Such a rule has also been declared by the Attorney General who ruled that a bidder on a government contract cannot withdraw his bid before a reasonable time is allowed the government for acceptance. The Comptroller General has held that where such a bid has been withdrawn, the bidder's deposit is forfeited. The courts have used their power to declare public policy a substitute for legal consideration in the case of public bidding procedures.

C. OPENING OF BIDS AND AWARD OF CONTRACT

§ 14.31   In General

Bids received before the time set for the opening of bids should remain unopened in a locked bid box or safe. Information concerning the identity and number of bids received is made available only to government employees on a "need to know" basis. If a sealed bid is opened by mistake (e.g., because it is not marked as being a bid), the envelope is signed by the employee who opened it, and delivered to a designated official. The official then immediately writes on the envelope an explanation of the opening, the date and time opened, the number of the invitation, signs and reseals the envelope. This is because by statute and regulation all bids must be publicly opened at the time stated in the invitation. And "examination of bids by interested persons shall be permitted if it does not interfere unduly with the conduct of government business." It is the bid-opening officer who decides when the time set for opening bids has arrived and personally and publicly opens all bids received before that time. If practical, the bids are read aloud and then recorded. The purpose of the public opening requirement is to protect both the public interest and bidders against any form of fraud, favoritism, or partiality. Such openings are vital to one goal of the procurement process: that it is conducted in a manner as should leave no room for any suspicion of irregularity. Material exempt from disclosure under the Freedom of Information Act is to be excluded from the bid abstract.

§ 14.32   Rejection of Bids

After bids have been opened, award must be made to that responsible bidder who submitted the lowest responsive bid. If all bids are to be rejected, there must be a compelling reason to do so. If there are changes to be made in the IFB after it has been issued and some bids have been submitted, all bidders should be notified and, if necessary, the time for submission of bids should be extended in order to permit bidders to evaluate the modification. "As a general rule," after the opening of bids, an invitation should not be cancelled and readvertised due solely to increased requirements for the items being acquired. Award should be made on the initial invitation for bids and the additional quantity should be treated as a new acquisition. It may happen after opening and prior to award that the solicitation did not correctly identify the specifications; in such event, the invitation must, of course, be cancelled. This is also true where no responsive bid has been received from a responsible bidder. If only one bid is received, the invitation may be cancelled unless the contracting officer can determine the bid price to be reasonable. He may also notify the bidder in a sealed bid acquisition that "negotiations will be conducted."

When a bid is accompanied by descriptive literature, and the bidder imposes a restriction that prevents the public disclosure of such literature, the restriction may render the bid nonresponsive unless the requirement for descriptive literature is waived.

If after bid opening the government discovers that a solicitation has overstated its minimum needs, it is not necessarily obligated to cancel and resolicit; it is a matter in the discretion of the contracting agency.

Administrative discretion of the government which results in bid rejection and re-solicitation renders all original bids ineffective. This is illustrated by a case where a low bid of $105,403 was submitted by Cannon Diamond Drilling Co. for exploratory drilling and water testing. The next low bid was $226,696. Cannon alleged an error of $22,500 but failed to support the error with sufficient evidence for correction. In view of the disparity between the bids and the possibility that the other bids were excessive, all bids were rejected and new bids were obtained: $148,185 from Cannon, who received the award, and $208,158 from the second low bidder. Another bidder protested on the ground that Cannon's new bid contained modifications of eleven items in addition to the one on which correction was requested on its prior bid. In holding against the protestor, the Comptroller General pointed out that rejection of bids and readvertisement has never been countenanced "merely for the purpose of affording the bidders an opportunity to better the prices of their competitors." Rejection of all bids is "discretionary" with the government when it "administratively determined" that the lowest acceptable bid is in excess of the amount for which the government should be able to obtain the supplies or services sought. In such instances, the original bids have been held to be "no longer material or effective for any purpose whatsoever."

A prime example of a difference between Federal and state procurement rules may be found in a case where a court held that an affirmative action plan that requires rejection of a low bid on a public contract because of the bidder's failure to meet a 10 percent minority set aside goal violates California's procurement laws. MGM submitted the low bid to Alameda County that indicated that MGM would subcontract less than one percent of the work to minority firms. The bid was rejected by the county as nonresponsive to the county's 10% minority subcontractor goal. MGM charged that the county's plan violated California law requiring that the award be made to the lowest responsible bidder and violated constitutional provisions on equal protection and due process. The court agreed with MGM.

Where there is no apparent prejudice to other bidders, the Comptroller General has on several occasions allowed cancelled invitations for bid to be reinstated.

The Comptroller General has also ruled that the rejection of all bids does not render the original bids ineffective for all purposes; he has authorized the reinstatement of a cancelled invitation in instances that had shut out competition by other lower bidders.

§ 14.33   Bid Guarantees

When a bid guarantee is required and a bidder fails to furnish the guarantee in accordance with the requirements of the invitation for bids, the bid will normally be rejected. Thus a bid which included a promise to submit an irrevocable letter of credit as a bid guarantee upon acceptance has been held nonresponsive where the bidder's bank approved a standby letter of credit, but conditioned delivery of the letter upon acceptance of the bid. "By its terms, the bank's letter contemplated delivery at some future time of what the IFB specifically required to be submitted contemporaneously with the bid." Bids were rejected by the Navy on construction contracts as nonresponsive because the individual sureties submitted on a bid bond pledged the same assets. The Navy took the position that the failure to have separate pools of assets for each surety detracts from the joint and several liability of the sureties. But because the bidders submitted an affidavit which disclosed a net worth which was more than adequate to cover the requirement that each surety have a net worth at least equal to the penal amount of the bond, the Comptroller General held the bid bond legally sufficient to establish the joint and several liability of the sureties.

§ 14.34   Modification or Withdrawal of Bids

Bids may be modified or withdrawn by written or other authorized method provided that that notice is received in the office designated in the invitation for bids "not later than the exact time set for opening of bids." The bid may be withdrawn in person by a bidder or its authorized representative before that time.

§ 14.35   Rejection of Individual Bids—The Requirement of Responsiveness

As a result of the policy favoring competition, any bid that fails to conform to the essential requirements of the invitation for bids has to be rejected by the soliciting agency. These essential requirements include failure of a bid to conform to the applicable specifications. The GAO also followed the policy against non-responsive bids concerned with a solicitation for construction of a DC power supply. Each of six bidders concluded that the other five were nonresponsive because they deviated from specifications in the IFB that were detailed design-type in some areas and broad performance-type in other areas. The Comptroller General held that the specifications were not sufficiently clear as to assure that full and free competition would be obtained. He recommended using the two-step advertising method. However, he refused to disturb the award because it would delay the program. In some circumstances, his conclusion as to the deficiency of the specifications could result in a refusal to grant relief to aggrieved bidders.

A bid may be rejected as nonresponsive for lack of detail required by the invitation. The bid of Empire Gas Engineering Co. to the National Space Agency was rejected for lack of data required to be furnished by the invitation for bids (IFB). The bidder had submitted a sketch without the detail required by the invitation; such lack of sufficient detail on the design of an item justified rejection of the bid. This case may be distinguished from one where information was requested in the invitation for bids regarding the location of the bidder's physical facilities and his credit rating, both of which the bidder neglected to provide as of the time of the bid opening. The case involved the bidder's responsibility— a concept different from responsiveness; it can be determined after bid opening without giving one bidder an unfair competitive advantage over another. Whether a matter raises an issue of responsiveness or responsibility may depend upon the purpose for which information in a bid is to be used.

If a bid received by electronic data interchange is unreadable to the degree that conformance to the essential requirements of the invitation for bids cannot be ascertained, the contracting officer immediately shall notify the bidder that the bid will be rejected unless the bidder provides clear and convincing evidence of the content of the bid originally submitted and the unreadable condition of the bid that was caused by government software or hardware error, malfunction, or other government mishandling.

A bid must also be rejected which fails to conform to the delivery schedule or imposes conditions that would modify requirements of the invitation or limit the bidder's liability to the government; it would be prejudicial to other bidders if a single bidder were allowed to protect himself against future changes in conditions, such as increased costs, to state that his price is that in effect at time of delivery (which would allow the bidder to avoid price competition entirely), or if the bidder were to limit the rights of the government under any clause in the solicitation or resulting contract. An acknowledgment to the invitation for bids which extended the bid acceptance period from 60 to 90 days could be rejected even though the bidder had inserted "60 days" in the bid form blank for proposing a bid acceptance period.

The rejection of a bid as nonresponsive may involve exercise of expertise and hence some discretion on the part of agency personnel. It has been held that such a rejection should not be overturned unless "no rational basis" exists for the agency's determination.

§ 14.36 Necessity of Authority to Waive Requirements

(a) Lack of Authority to Waive Requirements, Vested Rights

Unlike the purchasing agent of a private corporation seeking competition in its procurement, the contracting officer of a public body has been held to lack the authority to waive specifications in bidding without receiving adequate consideration therefor. This is called the "Vested Rights Doctrine" and is illustrated by the case of Prestex, Inc. v. United States. The Army requested bids on white duck cloth on the basis of samples, and awarded a contract to Prestex without testing the samples. The sample was tested and rejected when found not to meet specifications. Prestex refused the Army's request that it comply with the specifications, claiming that they were modified when Prestex submitted its sample and subsequently received the award. Prestex resold his product elsewhere and sued the United States for excess costs—the difference between market price and government contract price. In granting judgment for the United States, the former Court of Claims found the contract to be invalid because the contracting officer lacked authority to waive substantial specification requirements with respect to the yarn's weight, thread count and sizing content. The plaintiff then claimed recovery on the basis of quantum meruit, but was unsuccessful because none of his cloth had been accepted or used and the United States was not unjustly enriched in any way.

In deciding whether a bid is responsive, an agency may rely on descriptive literature indicating that an item fails to meet specifications. A failure to consider other available literature that indicates the bid is responsive has been held to constitute a breach of the government's implied contract to consider bids fairly, and a permanent injunction barring award to another bidder has been granted for such inaction. The agency was held to the standard of being required to request all relevant data and where it had obtained data indicating a possible problem with engine performance (and raising doubts regarding bid responsiveness), the Claims Court stated that the agency "irrationally refused" to request all relevant data then available from the bidder, adding that "when a contracting officer solicits literature, he has a duty to obtain all relevant literature."

The waiver of a bidder's failure to acknowledge an amendment to an invitation to bid may be authorized; the amendment has a negligible effect on price, quantity, quality or delivery terms. Nevertheless, the Comptroller General refused to follow his earlier precedents on the Davis–Bacon Act amendment to increase prices by $1,000 on a $418,000 project. The Comptroller General stated that "Although the impact of a wage rate revision might be minimal relative to the bid price, it may well be significant to the employees that the Davis–Bacon Act is designed to protect. Giving the bidder such control over the bid's acceptability compromises the integrity of the competitive procurement system."

(b) Informalities Which May Be Waived by the Government—Minor Informalities

A requirement of an invitation for bids (IFB) is material if it could affect the price, quantity, quality, or delivery. Where a bid variation has no effect or negligible effect on elements, it is not material and the relative standing of bidders remains unaffected. The bid is still responsive in such a case and the low bidder may be requested to delete objectionable conditions from a bid provided those conditions do not go to the substance, as distinguished from the form, of the bid, or work an injustice on other bidders.

The decision concerning informalities depends on the circumstances and is generally within the reasonable discretion of the contracting officer. For example, the Corps of Engineers sought bids for Capehart housing with maximum usable construction not to exceed $11,213,592. The low bid was by D & L Construction Co. at $11,211,000. D & L did not include the source of its financing as required by the IFB, and its bid was rejected as non-responsive. D & L protested but the project was readvertised. Then Bateson, the next low bidder, protested an award to any bidder but Bateson. This protest was denied because failure to provide a source of financing (as required by the invitation) was found to be an informality that could be waived.

Although an informality might be subject to waiver, the government need not waive it, and the contracting officer has authority to award the contract to the next low bidder. This could lead to possibly arbitrary results. For example, United States ex rel. Brookfield Construction Co. v. Stewart concerned bids for the construction of an underground garage for an additional House Office Building. One of the requirements was that every proposal be accompanied by a bond for at least ten percent of the bid amount. The plaintiffs, due to an inadvertent error, submitted less than a ten percent bond. Although they were the low bidders, the architect of the capital rejected their bid and the plaintiffs sought mandamus to require that an award be made. The court declined, holding that it could not compel executive action unless the executive official was acting in excess of his statutory authority.

A bid may be held nonresponsive merely because the bidder failed to check a box—such as one certifying that only items from an approved list of vendors would be used.

A large quantity of minor errors may still result in a responsive bid. An agency may make assumptions that result in making a bid responsive where the assumptions are adverse to the bidder and he is still low. Similarly, a failure to provide enough information for the government to perform a comparison between domestic and foreign materials does not require a rejection of the bid where the government can obtain the information and the relative standing of the bidders remains unchanged. Nevertheless, a failure to execute certifications with respect to Equal Opportunity and Affirmative Action Programs may be waived as an informality. One United States District Court held that the government can, without prior hearing, withhold an award to a low bidder for refusing to adopt a seniority system designed to provide affirmative action relief to women pursuant to Executive Order 11246. The requirements of the Order were seen as tantamount to contract specifications; neither the Fifth Amendment nor the Executive Order required the government to offer a hearing to a potential contractor concerning whether it could comply with the specifications of a contract. The nonresponsibility determination was predicated upon the present inability of the company to comply with the equal employment clause of the prospective contract.

The creation of a corporation following the submission of a bid by that "corporation" has been permitted as an "informality" where the bidder himself did not attempt to retain the option of avoiding the government's acceptance of its bid.

The GAO stated that the signature on the certificate bid package was sufficient to show a bidder's intent to be bound by its bid, even if the bid itself was unsigned.

§ 14.37 Responsiveness to Public Policy

In Northeast Construction Company v. Romney, an invitation for bids was issued including provisions of the so-called "Washington Plan," which required a prospective contractor to specify his estimated total employment under the proposed contract in designated trades over a four-year period as well as the percentage of minority group employees to be included. (This was a prerequisite to eligibility for award of a construction contract costing in excess of $500,000 by an order promulgated by the Secretary of

Labor on June 1, 1970, implementing Executive Order 11246.) Northeast Construction Company was the low bidder by $47,145. Northeast failed to supply the written goals requiring equal employment opportunity by contractors for minority manpower employment, but two days after bid opening, this information was supplied. When Northeast was declared ineligible for the contract award, an action was commenced in the District Court that granted a preliminary injunction. This was reversed by the Court of Appeals because the District Court's conclusion of law that Northeast "was likely to succeed on the merits" was held to be an erroneous legal premise in this case. The appellate court held that procurement officials must comply with Labor Department regulations mandating the information that must be contained in the bids when filed. A procurement official can be held to have acted unreasonably if he follows this mandate where the information pertinent to minority utilization goals has been made a question of responsiveness. The Court noted that usually the "experience" of the bidder is a matter of "responsibility", which is determined after bid opening and prior to award. But the court determined this to be an "occasion when it rises to the level of responsiveness of the bid." The Secretary of Labor's regulation had specified that bidders must submit the plan "prior to bid opening." Judge Leventhal did not believe a procurement official "can be held to be unreasonable if he follows his mandate." He stated that the disappointed bidder should have sued the Department of Labor "to enjoin that department from persisting with its regulation."

In one case a low bid was rejected by the former Atomic Energy Commission (AEC) because it was determined to be nonresponsive to the bid conditions in the solicitation, setting forth affirmative action and equal employment opportunity requirements. The bidder had failed to execute the certification and to submit an affirmative action plan. It was AEC's position that if awarded the contract, the bidder would not have been found to perform in accordance with the bid conditions. The Comptroller General found the fact that the bidder failed to sign the certification which would expressly have committed him to comply with the provisions, as well as his failure to submit an affirmative action plan, created doubt as to whether he intended to meet the bid conditions.

In 1999, the Court of Federal Claims (COFC) emphasized that not all errors require rejection of an award. However, the same year in another case, the U.S. Court of Appeals for the Federal Circuit (CAFC) ruled that a protester was prejudiced by the agency's award of a contract based on the price of an offer that did not meet certain mandatory solicitation requirements:

> But while price differential may be taken into account, it is not solely dispositive; we must consider all the surrounding circumstances in determining whether there was a substantial chance a protester would have received an award but for a significant error in the procurement process.

In this connection, the CAFC also referred to its previous decision which had held that, following an alleged error in the procurement process, the protestor failed to establish a reasonable likelihood that it would have been awarded contract absent disputed communications.

§ 14.38   Award

(a) In General

An award constitutes an acceptance of a bid "and the bid and the award constitute the contract."

The award process in government procurement differs from that in private exchanges due to the fact that government contracts are formed according to an extensive set of rules, comprised for the most part of statutes, executive orders, regulations and agency internal procedures. These rules prescribe the steps the parties are to take during the award process, including the proper solicitation to be used in each circumstance, the contents of the solicitation, the correct manner of response to the solicitation, the period within which a response must be made, and how the response will be evaluated. An award is made by written notice, within the time for acceptance specified in the bid or an extension, and to that responsible bidder whose bid, conforming to the invitation, will be most advantageous to the government considering price and the price-related factors included in the invitation. An award cannot be made "until all required approvals have been obtained." A bidder may offer an acceptance period that is shorter than the one requested. In one case the invitation for bids did not contain a mandatory bid acceptance period and the bidder chose to limit its bid acceptance period to 14 calendar days from bid opening. When the agency took more than 14 days to make the award, the Comptroller General held that the bidder could not extend its bid period and that acceptance of the bid would afford the bidder an unfair advantage. Although acceptance in sealed bidding is only by the government (and thus may differ from acceptance under the UCC), the question of whether "additional terms" become part of the contract may depend upon the circumstances. Identical counterparts to this system of rules cannot be assumed to exist in private contract law; the distinctions are not always as obvious as might at first appear, certain differences are peculiar to Federal procurement law and often differ from the law pertaining to procurement by the state and local governments.

The Comptroller General has consistently held that preservation of the integrity of the procurement system outweighs cost savings to the government. Thus, even though it would cost the government $71,000 to terminate two improperly awarded contracts in a $2.3 million procurement; he held it to be necessary to preserve integrity. A contract award is to be made by written notice, within the time for acceptance to that responsible bidder whose bid, conforming to the invitation, "will be most advantageous to the government, considering only price and price-related factors included in the invitation."

Acceptance must be accomplished within the reasonable time specified in the Invitation. The duration of the bid acceptance period is essentially a matter of intent and it will remain open as long as the parties have expressed their intent to accept the award. Where a bidder agreed to be bound when his bid was accepted within 90 days from the date for receipt of bids, government acceptance of the bid created a valid contract, despite the bidder's attempt to withdraw his bid after opening.

As in the case of the common law governing private contracts, in government contracts the acceptance must conform to the offer and where the offer specifies a written acceptance, an attempted oral acceptance is ineffective. Where the time for acceptance is contained in the offer, the government lacks authority to accept the offer unilaterally after expiration of this time, without obtaining the consent of the offeror.

(b) Approvals After Award

At common law contracts for purchase and sale may contain a provision whereby one or both parties are given a period of time to consult their attorneys or with superiors prior to being bound by the contract. A notice of an invitation for bids (IFB) that certain approvals by the government are required after acceptance of a bid makes the subsequent approvals of acceptance of the bid unconditional; the contract may be avoided if the approvals are not thereafter obtained. In U.S. v. National Optical Stores Co., the defendant bid for the purchase of a former VA Hospital. The IFB stated that acceptance of a bid was subject to credit approvals and to avoidance if the sale conflicted with anti-trust laws. A bid was accepted subject to these approvals that were later obtained. When the contractor failed to make the next down payment, the government resold the property and sued for excess costs. Although the contractor asserted that the government did not unconditionally accept its bid, he was held to be bound because the so-called conditions in the invitation were agreed to when he submitted his bid and the acceptance of the bid was unconditional, being in complete conformity with such bid.

(c) *Time of Acceptance—The Mailbox Rule*

The current regulation states: "Award shall be made by mailing or otherwise furnishing a properly executed award document to successful bidder." This would appear to be a confirmation of the common law rule that unless an offer otherwise provides, a contract is formed at the time an acceptance is transmitted. This is made clear by the statement that "the award is an acceptance of the bid, and the bid and the award constitute the contract" unless this result were to be contradicted by some specific statement in the bidding documents.

The former Court of Claims sought to postpone the common law rule with respect to the time when a contract becomes effective. In Rhode Island Tool Co. v. United

States, a bidder made a mistake, notified the government thereof by telephone, and asked for withdrawal. The invitation form then in use stated "the successful bidder will receive Notice of Award at the earliest possible date, and such Award will thereupon constitute a binding contract between the bidder and the government without further action on the part of the bidder." Although the receipt did not show whether the notice of award was mailed before or after this telephone conversation, the award was received by the mistaken bidder after the conversation, who then supplied the tools and sued to recover for the mistake. In granting judgment for the bidder, the court noted that in 1885, the Post Office changed its rule to permit senders to retrieve mail. The sender, it said, "retains the right of control up to the time of delivery ... and acceptance." Under the older regulations, when a letter was deposited in the mail, a sender lost all control of it, the Post Office becoming, in effect, the agent of the addressee. Under the 1885 regulations, the sender retained the right of control up to the time of delivery. The majority, therefore, permitted the plaintiff to recover for unilateral mistake where he had notified the buyer of the mistake and withdrew his bid prior to actual receipt of the notice of award but after notice of award had been mailed. However the overwhelming majority of the and state courts support the "mailbox" rule, begun in 1818 by the Court of Kings Bench in Adams v. Lindsell.

It has been suggested that the court should have first attempted retrieval prior to praising "progress" in this manner. Mail carriers are trained to push mail forward and the practical problems of attempting to retrieve a letter are very real. Because the Court of Federal Claims and U.S. Court of Appeals for the Federal Circuit adopted the former Claims Court holdings as binding precedent, most changes are less likely from that portion of the judiciary concerned with government contracts, than from the drafters of the FAR.

(d) Less Than Three Bids Received and the Problem Where a Single Bid Is Received

The regulation states that where fewer than three bids have been received, "Award shall be made notwithstanding the limited number of bids." In such instances, the contracting officer must first examine the situation to ascertain the reasons for the small number of responses. It has been argued that an award should be made in these circumstances because that bidder did not know that he would be alone and that no one else would submit a bid. However, any award made is a procurement without price competition. This part of the regulation can only protect the taxpayer in such instances with procedures applicable to sole source procurements for ascertaining that the price is reasonable; this procedure may necessitate cost or price analysis. Some companies submit bids to be able to remain on an agency's solicitation mailing list; when they "fail to respond to two consecutive invitations" to bid, their name has generally been removed from that list unless the firm makes a specific request to be retained on the lists. Because "negotiation" with a single responsible source is authorized where "no other type of supplies or services will satisfy agency requirements," where a single, sealed bid is received, the procurement could be subject to the requirements for a negotiated one including a cost or price analysis where applicable. The current regulation prescribes the use of price analysis as a guideline with respect to the reasonableness of the price after sealed bidding by following the analysis required for negotiated contracts. "The benefit of competition to both the government and to the public in terms of price and other factors is directly proportional to the *extent* of competition.''

§ 14.39   Withdrawal on the Ground of Mistake Discovered After Opening But Before Award

(a) Burden of Discovery and Proof

Regulations frequently require verification of a bid by a contracting officer in cases where he has reason to believe that a mistake may have been made. A bid is permitted to be either withdrawn or corrected after bid opening and prior to award, provided that the bidder submits clear and convincing evidence of a mistake. Earlier the Comptroller General had attempted to shift the burden of proof by holding that if, after bid opening and before award, a bidder claimed that he made a mistake in his bid, the withdrawal would be permitted unless the contracting officer showed that he made no error or else alleged error in bad faith.

(b) Where a Bid May Be Withdrawn

The general rule forbidding withdrawal of bids prior to award is distinguishable from certain exceptional cases where an honest error by the bidder might cause him to suffer beyond his natural expectations. The exceptions to this rule clustered about the principle that the buyer could not take advantage of an inherent but honest error on the part of the bidder. Because manipulation of working papers may exist, corroboration of the evidence may be required.

Agencies may accept the submission of originals or copies of worksheets as sufficient to comply with the requirement of ''clear and convincing evidence'' when such worksheets themselves show the alleged error. Some bidders could prepare two sets of worksheets after the opening of bids decide that they had bid much too low (or they may have received another and bigger job but cannot do both). Agencies require sworn statements regarding the preparation of these worksheets from several employees wherever possible.

§ 14.40   Mistakes in Bids

(a) *Necessity of Disclosure of Suspicion When Requesting a Verification of Bid*

After the opening of bids, agency personnel must examine all bids for mistakes. Where there is reason to believe that a mistake may have been made, they must request from the bidder a verification of the bid, calling attention to the suspected mistake and then give the bidder a reasonable time to respond to the request for verification.

Most problems concern the adequacy of the contracting officer's request for verification. United States v. Metro Novelty Manufacturing Co. established the standard for determining the contracting officer's request for verification. The contract was for the supply of gilt cap and gilt collar ornaments. Metro's bid on both items was about 130% lower than the next lowest bids. Before award, the contracting officer telephoned Metro's president and asked that the bid be verified, saying nothing else. Metro's president verified the bid by letter. After award he withdrew on the ground of "mutual mistake." The government's defense was that Metro's verification of its bid precluded reliance on a mutual mistake argument. The court held that verification of the bid did not foreclose a mutual mistake argument because the government was under an affirmative duty of disclosure, stating that the "plaintiff, however, did not put defendant on notice of the mistake which it surmised."

A Board of Contract Appeals has held that even a bid very much lower than another bid must be verified. It held that a bid 35% lower than the government estimate and lower than the next low bid by a large amount should be verified and rejection of the bid as nonresponsive might constitute arbitrary and capricious action. The award of the contract to another resulted in damages for bid preparation costs to the aggrieved party. The current regulation specifies that where the bidder fails or refuses to furnish evidence in support of a suspected or alleged mistake, the contracting officer shall consider the bid as submitted unless the amount of the bid is so far out of line with the amounts of other bids received, or with the amount estimated by the agency as reasonable, or there are "other indications of errors so clear, as to reasonably justify the conclusion that acceptance of the bid would be unfair to the bidder or to other bona fide bidders."

Where a contractor unreasonably relied upon a subcontractor's intention to provide a product not in conformance with the solicitation, the U.S. Court of Federal Claims ruled that the contract might be rescinded because these documents were attached to papers which government officials were required to review. The government must give a more reasonable review than is required of the contractor. The court stated, "[t]heir failure to perform that duty cannot excuse the government from the consequences that would flow if they had done so."

(b) Clerical vs. Judgmental Mistakes

A clerical mistake, apparent on the face of the bid, may be corrected by the contracting officer at any time before award provided he has first obtained from the bidder a verification of the bid intended. The types of obvious mistakes include misplacement of a decimal point; incorrect discounts (for example, 1 percent 10 days, 2 percent 20 days, 5 percent 30 days); reversal of price f.o.b. destination and price f.o.b. origin; and mistake in designation of unit. A court held that a contracting officer acted unreasonably by refusing to permit the low bidder in a two-step bid submission to amend a 50–page bid that mistakenly omitted one page regarding the minimum bid acceptance period. In this case the bidder's intent could readily be inferred elsewhere. A bidder cannot allege a mistake and later decide to waive it in order to receive an award based upon his original bid. An alleged $18 million made as a result of using the wrong algorithm was held not to be a unilateral mistake that would justify reformation because it was not a "clear cut clerical or arithmetical error, or misreading of the specifications."

In an all-or-nothing bid on several items being offered for sale by the government, the contractor typed "36" where he wanted to bid on Item 35. He then sent in his worksheets and other evidence tending to provide that he had made a mistake. After he was denied the right to correct his bid (because a correction would have displaced an otherwise high bidder), he offered to stand by his mistake, pay the bid price, and take the goods. He was not permitted to do so because such a waiver would prejudice the new high bidder. The current regulation does not permit a bidder to withdraw or modify "all or none" qualifications after bid opening "since such qualifications are substantive and affect the rights of other bidders."

There have been many cases denying relief for mistake in bid on the grounds that the mistake was one of "mistake in judgment." It is often said that where there is a "mistake in judgment," there is no "mistake" because the contractor fully intended to make the bid it made. A government claim of mutual mistake in the overtime rate under its lease of a building was denied because it was a mistake in judgment; the General Services Administration had agreed to pay a rate that was "absurdly high." The rate was part of a lease agreement that included many other provisions and it was paid for several years before the government called a halt. This has prevented contractors from using a mistake in bid doctrine to obtain relief for mistakes in the business judgments that go into the formulation of the bid or offer price and which constitute the essence of price competition.

(c) Comparison With Information From Outside Sources

A contracting officer may be charged with constructive notice of mistake on the basis of information derived from outside sources. One outside source of information is the contractor himself. If the contracting officer does not utilize the information furnished by the contractor in evaluating the bid, he is obligated to consider another outside source of information, including the fair market value of the items to be supplied. If the items have no fair market value or if the fair market value of the items rapidly fluctuates, it cannot be used as a touchstone for determining whether the contracting officer should be charged with constructive notice of the mistake. On the other hand, if the fair market value of the items can be convincingly established, relief may be available to the contractor in cases where there is a wide discrepancy between the fair market value of the items and the low bid submitted.

(d) Comparison With Government Estimates

In construction and other work, the government prepares its own contract price estimate. The contracting officer may be charged with constructive notice of a mistake if bid prices are out of line with the estimate. A discrepancy between the government's estimate and the low bid may be offset by the consistency of the low bid with the other bids submitted. In other cases, especially where only two bids have been received, the discrepancy with the government's estimate may become the critical factor in deciding that constructive notice should attach. In Allied Contractors, Inc. v. United States, Allied's low bid was $20,000 and the other bids were $49,918; $60,531; $70,000; $95,000; and $122,000. The government's estimate of the project's cost was $19,000. After award, Allied brought suit to reform the contract upward to an amount which it said was the amount it should have bid and would have bid except for the mistake. The former Court of Claims refused to reform the contract, holding that there was no mutual mistake. Since Allied's bid nearly coincided with the government's estimate, the 250% discrepancy with respect to the next lowest bid was irrelevant and did not put the contracting officer on constructive notice of any mistake.

In C.N. Monroe Manufacturing Company v. United States, the court held that the government should have known of a mistake when plaintiff's bid was $3.91 per unit. Plaintiff mistakenly omitted an item. The second low bid was $6.40 per unit, and the other bids ranged from $18 to $300 per unit. A 13% price disparity between the contractor's bid and the other submitted bid did not impute knowledge of the mistake to the contracting official where the contractor's bid was less than 1% lower than the government's estimate. In many cases the government's estimate may be incorrect. Even where the estimate had been assiduously prepared, it was held reasonable to require the contracting officer to check low bids that were out of line with the other bids in view of the fact that the estimate was not the only guide for determining whether constructive notice of a mistake should have been imputed.

In addition to making contract price estimates, the government makes estimates for other purposes. These other estimates usually do not impart notice of a mistake to the contracting officer. In one case the low bid was $8.00 per unit. The next lowest bids were $8.20 per unit and $11.11 per unit. After award, the bidder alleged a mistake and claimed that the contracting officer had constructive notice because the government had made a fund allocation of $25.60 per unit. The Comptroller General refused to grant the low bidder relief, holding that the fund allocation was for budgetary control purposes and was not intended to be an estimate of the contract price.

(e) *Comparison With Prior Procurements*

An indicator of possible mistake might be derived from a history of procurement of the same or similar items by a government agency at substantially higher prices. A comparison of current bids with bids under prior procurements ordinarily is not required of the contracting officer if the government's estimate did not signal that a possible error had been made in the computation of the low bid.

(f) *Other Mistakes Disclosed Before Award*

Corrections of bids are often allowed, as are withdrawals in connection with mistakes in bids alleged after opening of bids and before award. Agencies have authority to permit correction of bids if they are responsive to the invitation. Bids may not be corrected in order to "make them responsive." If the bid is responsive, and the bidder provides "clear and convincing evidence" both of the existence of the mistake and the bid actually intended, an agency head may make a determination "permitting the bidder to correct the mistake." If this correction would result in displacing one or more lower bids, such a determination shall not be made unless the existence of the mistake and the bid actually intended are "ascertainable *substantially* from the invitation and the bid itself" (emphasis added). If the alleged mistake evidence is not "clear and convincing, a higher official may permit a withdrawal of the bid, or the agency head may determine that the bid be neither withdrawn nor corrected."

The Federal system is clearly more helpful to bidders and less advantageous to taxpayers than systems in effect in some states. For example, California enacted a statute providing that, in order for a bidder on a public contract to be relieved of his bid, he must establish satisfactorily that he gave the public entity written notice within five days after bid opening of the mistake, specifying in the notice "in detail" how the mistake occurred; that it made the bid materially different than he intended it to be; and that the mistake was made in filling out the bid and not due to error in judgment, such as carelessness in inspecting the site of the work or in reading the plans or specifications. Under this statute, even where a mistake is "clerical" and a city has been notified thereof prior to award, no relief is possible if the bidder did not send written notice of mistake within five days after the bid opening specifying in detail how the mistake occurred.

§ 14.41 Problems Arising From Multiple Bites at the Apple

(a) In General

Situations sometimes occur where a bidder appears to have possible choices between withdrawing his bid and standing on an erroneous bid. For example, the Army invited bids for repair of engines. The low bid was $40,221; the next low bid was $47,920; and the two highest bids were over $50,000. When the low bidder, Ramirez Enterprises, was requested to confirm its bid in writing, it then claimed error growing out of a mistake and requested its bid be increased by $3,898. The full transportation costs of at least $8,000 would have increased its bid above the next low bidder and it was advised by the Army that it could withdraw its bid. When it refused, it was told its bid would be disregarded. Ramirez protested and the protest was denied because "by reason of its own mistake, [Ramirez] could choose after other bids were disclosed between (1) withdrawing its bid on the ground of mistake, seeking correction thereof; or (2) standing on the erroneous bid, as seemed to be in its best interest." Therefore, to accept Ramirez's erroneous bid was held to be "contrary to the principles of competitive bidding."

Occasionally a bidder alleges error that would, if corrected, enable him to become the low bidder. Unless the error is apparent on the face of the bid, the Comptroller General has denied permission to correct a bid downward, to displace another bidder, on the ground that this would do too much violence to the competitive bidding system. Dorman Helicopters, Inc. submitted a low bid of $135,762 to the Navy for containers. Industrial Metal Fabrication Co. was the next low bidder at $152,098, and alleged an error after bid opening, offering to reduce his bid by about $20,000 to $131,098, which would make him the low bidder. Dorman protested and his position was sustained because, even though Industrial could correct its bid prior to award by submitting convincing evidence of its error and of the intended bid, this was not permitted to "displace a low bidder." This result was held necessary to "maintain the competitive bidding system," a standard which had been given a higher priority than the financial gain to the taxpayer on any single transaction.

A low bidder alleging a mistake which if corrected would continue to make him the low bidder, will be closely examined, the upward correction will usually be denied, and the low bidder may be permitted to withdraw his bid. For example, Teledyne, a low bidder on a Navy procurement for linear shape charges, alleged a mistake in the unit bid price that, if corrected, would have resulted in Teledyne's price of $4.76 being the low bid. When the correction was denied, and the contract awarded to another, Teledyne protested stating that it would accept the contract at the original unit bid price of $3.76. The original figure did not appear on the worksheets and Teledyne failed to clearly and convincingly establish its intended bid. At no time prior to the award did Teledyne clearly indicate to the Navy its willingness to accept the contract at the original bid price if the correction was denied. The Comptroller General stated that, if Teledyne were permitted to reinstate its original bid (which it could not substantiate), this would be "contrary to the principles of competitive bidding." A low bid is a low bid regardless of whether or not it may be substantiated.

Although documents furnished by a bidder clearly establish that a mistake has been made in his bid, he will not be permitted to correct the mistake if analysis of those documents reveals that more than one possible bid was intended. In one case, the low bidder on a contract to furnish mess attendant services was permitted to withdraw but not modify his bid even though he had presented clear and convincing evidence that a mistake has been made. The documentation he supplied to support the existence of the mistake permitted interpretation of at least two other possible bids, in addition to the bid he claimed he intended, the worksheets were susceptible of more than one interpretation, and each method of analysis resulted in a different intended bid price. Correction of the amount requested would have increased his bid to within less than one-half of one percent of the next lowest bid.

(b) Mistake After Award

At common law, if the contractor seeks to withdraw from a contract after award or to reform the contract, he will usually be denied unless the error in making the contract is mutual. If a contractor's discovery and request for correction of a mistake in bid is not made until after the award, under certain circumstances it may be processed either within the agency itself or under the "Disputes" procedures or both. The regulation requires that correction of such mistakes may be made "only on the basis of clear and convincing evidence that a mistake in bid was made." A circuit court of appeals has held that a bidder's uncorroborated, post-bid-opening statement did not meet this standard.

The correction of such a mistake by the agency is possible, if correcting the mistake would be favorable to the government without changing the essential requirements of the specifications. This is accomplished by contract modification. Agencies are authorized to make a determination to rescind or to reform a contract so as to either delete the items involved in the mistake or to increase the price. However, in the latter case the price, as corrected, cannot exceed that of the next lowest acceptable bid under the original invitation for bids. Such determinations may be made only on the basis of "clear and convincing evidence" that a mistake in bid was made, and either mutual or, if unilaterally made by the contractor, "so apparent as to have charged the contracting officer with notice of the probability of the mistake."

(c) Apparent or Obvious Mistakes

One type of mutual mistake occurs where the contractor may be able to show that the contracting officer was on actual or constructive notice of the possibility of mistake prior to the time of award. "Constructive notice" is said to exist when the contracting officer should have known of the contractor's mistake. This usually happens when apparent or obvious mistakes have been made and are discovered by comparing the contractor's bid with information from outside sources or with government price estimates or with bids under prior procurements, as well as by examining the disparity in bids under the procurement in question.

A clear case of constructive notice exists when the mistake is patent on the face of the bid itself. Examples are when the unit price is irreconcilable with the total price, the unit price multiplied by the total number of units does not necessarily equal the total price, or when the prices for different amounts of the same items are illogical (the bid price to supply paint in one gallon containers, when multiplied by five, was lower than the bid price to supply paint in five-gallon containers).

Although the internal bid inconsistencies described above have been deemed sufficient to charge the contracting officer with notice of the mistake, there is a class of internal bid inconsistencies where the courts and the Comptroller General have declined to grant relief to the contractor alleging an obvious or apparent mistake. This occurs where the contract is to be awarded in the aggregate with a number of bid items. It has been held that the contracting officer was not required to compare bid prices on individual items to try to detect mistakes.

§ 14.42   Discounts and Price Adjustments

(a) Prompt Payments Discounts

"2–10, Net 30" is a common offer by a supplier to permit the government to save 2% of the price (which may amount to significant sums) merely by making payment within 10 days. Unlike the practice in private procurements, the current regulation prohibits prompt payment discounts from being considered in the evaluation of bids, even though any discount offered will form a part of the award, and will be taken by the agency's payment center if payment is made within the discount period specified by the bidder. In certain instances, it may be less costly to use more than 10 days for inspection of the product, or for other purposes than to pay quickly and seek legal recourse against the supplier later. In other instances, the discounts could be the most significant difference between two or more bids from suppliers whose record for reliability with respect to the products involved may permit use of the "Fast Payment Procedure."

(b) Economic Price Adjustment or Escalation

In the late 1970s inflation began to run rampant and continued until the early 1980s when it greatly diminished. As a result, many suppliers considered it necessary to include clauses proposing economic price adjustments with a price ceiling. In such instances the bid is to be evaluated on the basis of the maximum possible economic price adjustment of the quoted base price and, if eligible for award, the bidder will be requested to agree to the inclusion in the award of an approved economic price adjustment clause that is subject to the same ceiling. If the bidder will not agree to an approved clause, the award may be made on the basis of the bid as originally submitted. If the bids contain economic price adjustments with no ceiling, there is no price competition and they are rejected "unless some other clear basis for evaluation exists."

The government itself may propose an economic price adjustment in the invitation for bid. In such instances, and provided that no bidder takes exception to the provisions, bids are evaluated on the basis of the quoted prices "without the allowable economic price adjustment being added." When a bidder increases the maximum percentage of economic price adjustment stipulated in the invitation (or limits the downward economic price adjustment provisions of the invitation) the bid must be rejected as nonresponsive. If the successful bidder offered a lower ceiling, that would be reflected in the award.

§ 14.43   Attempted Withdrawal After Acceptance

The Federal approach to the firm offer problem is to give the rules of acceptance retrospective effect; no bidder who has made an error in computing his bid and complains after acceptance may withdraw as a matter of right.

After bid opening, an attempted withdrawal by the low bidder amounts to an anticipatory breach of contract. The government may then elect either to sue for damages at the moment of the repudiation, or await non-performance before commencing an action. If the government were forced to await nonperformance (e.g., nondelivery of the goods or noncommencement of construction at the time indicated in the contract schedule), the bidder might withdraw his repudiation and commence performance. The government, for an extended period of time, would have been uncertain as to whether or not the bidder would choose to perform. The Federal government would be able to treat an attempted withdrawal by a low bidder, after bid opening, as an anticipatory breach, by making an award to the bidder after the attempted withdrawal.

§ 14.44   Equal Low Bids

When two or more low bids are equal in all respects, the government has set up a system of priorities for award to small business concerns that are also labor surplus area concerns, other small business concerns, other business concerns that are also labor surplus area concerns, and other business concerns. Only where if two or more bidders "still remain equally eligible" after application of these priorities is an award to be made "by a drawing by lot limited to those bidders." After the award is made, the contractor will perform "in accordance with the circumstances justifying the priority used to break the tie or select bids for a drawing a lot."

§ 14.45 Protest Against Award

The procedure for protests against award after sealed bidding is essentially the same as for protests against award in negotiated procurement; both procedures are covered in Chapter 33, "Protests, Disputes, and Appeals."

D. TWO–STEP SEALED BIDDING

§ 14.61 In General

As noted above, sealed bidding requires that an agency's requirements must be described "clearly, accurately, and completely" in the solicitation. There are situations where the agency desires to obtain the benefits of sealed bidding when adequate specifications are not available. This is desirable where the agency hopes to develop a sufficiently descriptive statement of its requirements so that subsequent acquisitions may be made by conventional sealed bid procurement procedures. The method is especially useful in technical proposals for "complex items." It is called "two-step sealed bidding," an approach designed to promote maximum competition while preventing the elimination of potentially qualified producers from the competitive base.

Of the two steps, Step One is unique; it consists of public notice of the request for submission, evaluation, and (if necessary) discussion of a technical proposal. No pricing is involved since the objective is to determine the acceptability of the supplies or services offered. The evaluation is of the technical approach in a "broad" sense. Step One is the proper step for clarification of questions relating to technical requirements. The acceptance of a firm's technical proposal under Step One does not bind the government to accept that firm's Step Two bid if the bid is nonresponsive. Step Two is identical to all other aspects of sealed bidding except that it involves the submission of sealed priced bids by only those who had submitted acceptable technical proposals in Step One. There is no synopsis in the Governmentwide Point of Entry or public posting as an acquisition opportunity. Bids submitted in Step Two are evaluated and the awards made like any other sealed bid procurements discussed above. Where an agency fails to establish ground rules for testing, it cannot reject a bidder based on adverse test results obtained during the second step.

Agencies may use two-step sealed bidding in preference to negotiation when available specifications are not definite or complete or may be too restrictive to permit full and free competition without technical evaluation and discussion. On the other hand, definite criteria must exist evaluating technical proposals from more than one source that will result in a firm-fixed-price contract (with or without economic price adjustment). While the government may proceed with the second step without requesting further information from any offeror, it may request additional information from offerors of proposals that it considers reasonably susceptible of being made acceptable, and may discuss proposals with their offerors. Further, an agency may permit multiple technical proposals to be submitted. An agency may also conduct its own tests before award. In order to treat all competitors equally, any other bidder in line for award should have his product undergo the same tests.

The evaluation of proposals is placed into one of three categories: acceptable, reasonably susceptible of being made acceptable, or unacceptable. Upon receipt of two or more acceptable proposals, the agency may either proceed to Step Two or first request bidders whose proposals may be made acceptable to submit additional clarifying or supplementing information after the deficiencies in the proposal are identified and a deadline is fixed for the resubmission. When a technical proposal is found unacceptable (either initially or after clarification), the offeror is notified of the basis of the determination and that a revision of the proposal will not be considered. An agency's failure to list all deficiencies in a proposal during Step One technical discussions of a two-step procurement is not prejudicial to an offeror whose proposal is almost completely deficient.

CHAPTER 15
CONTRACTING BY NEGOTIATION

As negotiator, a lawyer seeks a result advantageous to the client but consistent with requirements of honest dealings with others. As an evaluator, a lawyer acts by examining a client's legal affairs and report about them to the client or to others.

Preamble: ABA Model Rules of Professional Conduct (2002).

A. GENERAL REQUIREMENTS FOR NEGOTIATIONS

§ 15.1 In General

Competitive standards in negotiated procurements were not to be relaxed; offers were required to be solicited from all such qualified sources deemed necessary by the contracting officer to assure full and free competition. Many agencies were more concerned with justifying negotiated sole-source procurements than in making competitive procurements, although some slight improvement occurred in one or two of the years immediately preceding enactment of the Competition in Contracting Act of 1984. The reason for this was that exceptions to competition were more available. The "loosest" exception to formal advertising requirements was found in a regulation that permitted negotiation for "supplies or services for which it is *impracticable to secure competition* by formal advertising." Some studies concluded that savings could exceed $2 billion and initial steps were taken by the Office of Federal Procurement Policy. However, no policy letter could delete exceptions to formal advertising contained in the statutes. The Competition in Contracting Act (CICA) was introduced in the U.S. Congress for reforming the tendency of the Federal bureaucracy to limit competition. Agencies were required to publish a 30–day advance notice of proposed awards in the Commerce Business Daily (now Governmentwide Point of Entry) if they were above a threshold amount to be set by the Office of Federal Procurement Policy. The maximum threshold would then be $25,000. All agencies would be required to include, in their solicitations for both sealed bids and competitive proposals, a list of the evaluation factors which they expected to have a bearing on the selection for award, and the relative order of importance of each of these factors. Detailed records would be required of the noncompetitive contracts awarded, including the name of the contracting officer who approved each award.

In part 15, several substantive changes were made effective on January 1, 1998. The majority of contracting expenditure infused innovative techniques into the source selection process, simplified the acquisition process, incorporated changes in pricing and unsolicited proposal policy, facilitated the acquisition of best value products and services, emphasized the use of effective and efficient acquisition methods, and revised the sequence which was to be presented to facilitate use of the regulation. Since the turn of the 3rd millennium, a number of these declarations have begun to be challenged.

§ 15.2   The Competitive Requirement

It is interesting to note that the Nobel Prize for Economics for 1983 was awarded to Gerrard Debreu for research confirming Adam Smith's theories of the competitive market in the 18th century.

In addition to attempts to increase the effectiveness of the competitive requirement, the government prosecuted those who rigged bids in order to thwart it.

§ 15.3 Similarities Between Negotiation and Sealed Bidding

In commercial contracting where sealed bids are not used, typically a buyer, such as a governmental agency, will issue a purchase order after receiving quotations from a prospective supplier concerning goods or services which may be sold. The purchase order becomes the first document containing a promise in the form of an offer to buy. Unless it is accepted by the seller, no contract will arise. In government contracts, the award is made by the government as the buyer, whether by sealed bids or by negotiation, each with their competitive aspects. Today, with few exceptions, contracts must be awarded on a competitive basis by both methods.

By definition, any contract awarded without using sealed bidding procedures is a negotiated contract. Unlike sealed bidding, negotiation is a procedure that includes the receipt of proposals from offerors, permits bargaining, and usually affords offerors an opportunity to revise their offers before award of a contract. "Bargaining includes persuasion, alteration of initial assumptions and positions, and give and take, and may apply to price, schedule, technical requirements, type of contract, or other terms of proposed contract." The lowest price must be included in the evaluation by the agency of the proposals submitted "when best value is expected to result from the selection of the technically acceptable proposal with the lowest evaluated price."

The exceptions to competitive requirements have been discussed above. An agency head (or a delegee) may convert from sealed bidding to negotiation procedures and an invitation for bids may then be cancelled provided that prior notice of intention to negotiate and a reasonable opportunity to negotiate is given to each responsible bidder that submitted a bid in response to the invitation. The GAO stated that "if [the agency's intent to negotiate] applied to bids rejected as nonresponsive, bidders who did not meet all material requirements and may have been able to bid lower than they otherwise would, could not offer a higher price for adhering to all such requirements in the negotiation phase."

It is difficult for a protester to challenge an agency's determination that sealed bids were appropriate for a particular procurement. A protester's argument that safety in surveying an exposure of unexploded ordnance was far more important than price was rejected because the record did "not show that the agency's determination is unreasonable."

§ 15.4 Examination of Records by the Comptroller General, the Procuring Agency, and by the DCAA

When awarding a contract without the use of sealed bids, an agency is required by statute to insert a clause authorizing examination of a contractor's records by the Comptroller General of the United States with a few exceptions. The exceptions include nonnegotiated contracts and contracts below the Simplified Acquisition Threshold (normally $100,000). This clause gives the GAO only the right to examine—not the right to do anything else. Since 1980, the Comptroller General need no longer sustain his right to access by suing for specific performance; instead, he may utilize his subpoena power.

A clause grants the Comptroller General the right to inspect records that "directly pertain" to the contracts. The Supreme Court held in Bowsher v. Merck and Co., Inc., that the Comptroller General has statutory authority only to inspect the contractor's records of direct costs, and not certain indirect costs. The majority held that the words "directly pertain" were a limitation, and permit the Comptroller General to inspect only certain cost records such as direct material, labor, or manufacturing costs. Often no distinction between direct and indirect costs is found in the applicable statutes (or their legislative history), which date from the Korean War. Nevertheless, a congressman was concerned with the original bill, which granted the Comptroller General access to "pertinent records involving transactions related to the contract".

In the *Merck* case, the Comptroller General had sought to examine indirect costs of government contracts awarded to the pharmaceutical company at catalog prices for standard commercial products that were exempt from the cost or pricing data requirements of the Truth in Negotiations Act. The opinion of Justice O'Connor, for the five-member majority, rejected the government's argument that Merck's indirect costs are directly pertinent ... "because Merck uses the payments made under these contracts to defray indirect expenses". The court only emphasized the importance of direct costs as a subject to be examined to determine excessive profits. The dissenters remarked that access to indirect costs was overwhelmingly important because direct costs constituted only nine percent of the contract costs, and it was obvious that attention should have been directed there and "[i]n some instances indirect costs have a critical bearing on the makeup of the contract price." The indirect cost/direct cost test creates an artificial distinction restricting the government's ability to examine price data that are subject to the control of and manipulation by a company's management. The Court was analyzing the Comptroller General's inspection authority as a question of statutory interpretation rather than one concerning the intention of the parties with respect to a clause in their contract. The Court stated:

> [a]ny impediment that our holding places in the path of the GAO's power to investigate fully government contracts is one Congress chose to adopt, and any arguments that this situation be changed must be addressed to Congress, not the courts.

In the 1980s, the Eighth Circuit Court of Appeals upheld the right of a district court to enforce the statutory subpoena power of the GAO and the district courts did not defer to boards of contract appeals or the Court of Federal Claims under the doctrine of primary jurisdiction. The court noted that, unlike *Merck*, this case involved a cost-type contract and the records were "directly pertinent" to the contract. In a parallel proceeding, the Court of Appeals for the Federal Circuit concurred with the Eighth Circuit, ruling that a board of contract appeals lacks jurisdiction to review the merits of a subpoena being sought by the Comptroller General.

In addition to the Comptroller General, who for most purposes is responsible to the Congress, the right of the contracting agency to examine and audit accounting books and other documents is set forth in a clause required in all negotiated contracts exceeding the simplified acquisition threshold (normally $100,000). The need for this requirement is obvious in cost-reimbursement, incentive, time-and-material, labor-hour, or price redeterminable contracts in order to assure that the documents reflect all costs claimed to have been incurred in performing such contracts. This need may be less evident in fixed-price contracts. Where pursuant to the Truth in Negotiations Act, the contractor has been required to submit cost or pricing data in connection with pricing the contract or any modification thereto (over $550,000), the right to examine is needed. The clause also grants the agency the right to inspection at all reasonable times of the contractor's plants, or parts of them, engaged in performing the contract and to pass down the requirement in all subcontracts over $100,000.

In the Department of Defense (DoD), the Defense Contract Audit Agency (DCAA) provides accounting and financial advisory services regarding the negotiation, administration and settlement of contracts and subcontracts to all DoD components responsible for procurement and contract administration.

A U.S. Court of Appeals has held that the Department of Defense Inspector General (DoD IG) could subpoena internal audit reports from a contractor and could authorize the Defense Contract Audit Agency (DCAA) to review those reports as part of the DoD IG's investigation, including internal audits paid for by the government. The DCAA is not entitled to perform internal audits not related to defense contracts. A court has held that the DCAA could also subpoena the income tax returns, financial statements, and supporting schedules of a defense contractor. A Board of Contract Appeals has held that an agency may reasonably require that a company have a DCAA—audited cost accounting system in order to receive an award of a cost—reimbursable contract.

A contractor is not entitled to receive an unedited version of a contract audit from the Defense Contract Audit Agency under the Freedom of Information Act. This is because it was prepared as part of the government's decision-making process and as such is protected from disclosure in order to encourage open and frank communication between agencies.

Where the government inadvertently destroyed pre-award audit reports and price negotiation memoranda that the contractor needed in connection with its defense against the government's claim, no sanctions may be imposed upon the government. Similarly, the government has no liability under the Federal Tort Claims Act for the DCAA's alleged audit malpractice.

§ 15.5   1997 Amendments to FAR Part 15

The 1997 amendments to FAR Part 15 made significant changes in negotiated procurement practices.

A new section called "Tradeoff Process" became appropriate for an award to "other than the lowest priced offeror or other than the highest technically rated offeror." It requires that the solicitation state whether "all evaluation factors other than cost or price, when combined, are significantly more important than, approximately equal to, or significantly less important than cost or price."

The Air Force chose a lower-priced proposal by Northrop Grumman Corporation over a technically superior but higher-priced proposal by ITT Federal Services Corp. in awarding a support services contract. The court stated that the Air Force "reasonably determined that the cost savings of $4.5 million or 8.4 percent in selecting Northrop was not offset by the superior characteristics of ITT's Management Technical Proposal." Where an agency rejected a protester's highest-rated proposal without considering its significant technical superiority and without comparing it to each of three awardees' lower-rated proposals, the awards were ruled invalid by the Comptroller General.

When using the tradeoff process, the evaluation factors and significant subfactors that establish the requirement of acceptability must be set forth in the solicitation. When using the lowest price technically acceptable process, tradeoffs are not permitted.

Oral presentations by offerors may substitute for written information and may occur at any time during the acquisition process. If discussions occur after the competitive range is determined, special standards must be met.

Another new section, called the "Advisory Multi–Step Process" continued the authority of an agency to publish presolicitation notices and that information may be "limited to a statement of qualifications and other appropriate information (e.g., proposed technical concept, past performance, and limited pricing information)." This process "should not be used for multi-step acquisitions that result in the offerors being required to submit identical information in response to the notice."

The agency is required to evaluate all of the responses it receives in accordance with the criteria stated in the notice, and then (a) advise each offeror in writing either that it will be invited to participate in the resultant acquisition or, based on the information submitted, that it is unlikely to be a viable competitor; and (b) inform all of the offerors that, "notwithstanding the advice provided by the government in response to their submissions, they may participate in the resultant acquisition."

B. REQUESTS FOR PROPOSALS AND REQUESTS FOR QUOTATIONS

§ 15.11 In General

Solicitations for negotiated contracts are called Requests for Proposals (RFPs), or Requests for Quotations (RFQs). They are used in negotiated acquisition to both communicate requirements to prospective contractors and to solicit proposals or quotations from them. Virtually all these requests must be made in writing and should contain the information necessary to enable prospective contractors to prepare proposals or quotations properly.

In addition to describing the government's requirements and anticipated terms and conditions that will apply to the contract, the solicitation may authorize offerors to propose alternative terms and conditions, including the contract line item number (CLIN) structure. If such alternative CLIN structures are permitted, the agency's evaluation approach should take into consideration "the potential impact on other terms and conditions or the requirements (e.g., place of performance or payment and funding requirements)."

Solicitations are generally sent to all prospective contractors only when there is a definite intention to award a contract, except that under certain circumstances they may be used for information or planning purposes. Where an agency synopsized the procurement in the Commerce Business Daily (now Governmentwide Point of Entry) and distributed the RFP to 15 former prime contractors, its inadvertent failure to provide a previous subcontractor with a solicitation copy did not require the agency to resolicit. However, a failure to solicit an offer for a follow-on contract from the holder of the existing contract has been held to require resoliciting the follow-on procurement.

Unlike a quotation, a proposal is an offer; use of a request for proposals is permitted when it is reasonable to expect prospective contractors to respond with offers and may anticipate negotiations after receipt of offers. Presolicitation notices and conferences may be used as preliminary steps in negotiated procurements in order to locate interested services and aid prospective contractors in later submitting proposals without undue expenditure of effort, time and money. The notice may indicate that it will be followed by a presolicitation conference.

Amended solicitations are prescribed. If a proposal of interest to the government involves departure from the stated requirements, the agency must amend the solicitation, "provided this can be done without revealing to the other offerors the alternate solution proposed or any other information that is entitled to protection." The regulation also provides that where, in judgment of the contracting officer, based on market research or otherwise:

> an amendment proposed for issuance after offers have been received is so substantial as to exceed what prospective offerors reasonably have anticipated, so that additional sources likely would have submitted offers had the substance of the amendment been known to them, the contracting officer shall cancel the original solicitation and issue a new one, regardless of the stage of the acquisition.

Once a competitive range is established, a request for a final proposal revisions (FPR) (formerly known as requests for best and final offers (BAFO)) is issued advising offerors that an award will be made "without obtaining further revisions."

§ 15.12   Uniform Contract Format

The uniform contract format, facilitates preparation of the solicitation and contract, as well as reference to and use of those documents by offerors and contractors. In essence, solicitations to which the uniform contract format applies include the Schedule (Part I, the solicitation or contract form, description of work and price, packaging, inspection and any special requirements), the contract clauses (required by law or regulation or peculiar to the contract called Part II) and a list of attachments or exhibits (called Part III). A final section constitutes representations and instructions (called Part IV) that is retained by the agency and not physically included in the resulting contract.

Although contracting by negotiation differs from sealed bidding in many respects (but not all of them), the "uniform contract format" is identical for both of these.

§ 15.13   Late Proposals and Modifications

Offerors are responsible for submitting offers, and any modifications thereof, to reach the government office designated in the solicitation on time. Unless the solicitation states a specific time for receipt, it is 4:30 p.m. local time for the designated government office on the date that proposals are due. Proposals and modifications to them that are received in the designated office after the exact time specified are "late." They are then considered only if they are received before award is made, and the circumstances (including acceptable evidence of date of mailing or receipt at the government installation) meet the specific requirements. Late proposals and modifications that are not considered are held unopened if identified. When a late proposal or modification is received and it is clear from available information that it cannot be considered for award, the contracting officer promptly notifies the offeror that it was received late and will not be considered.

When a competitive range is established, a request for a final proposal is issued advising offerors that an award will be made without obtaining further revisions. Where an amendment is proposed after offers have been received that is so substantial "as to exceed what prospective offerors reasonably could have anticipated, so that additional sources likely would have submitted offers" had its substance been known to them, the original solicitation must be canceled "regardless of the stage of the acquisition."

§ 15.14　Disclosure and Use of Information before Award—Restrictions on Disclosure

Before the receipt of proposals, the exchange of information among all parties is encouraged, provided it is consistent with procurement integrity requirements. After issuance of the solicitation, the contracting officer is the focal point of exchanges with potential offerors. To avoid creating an unfair competitive advantage, when specific information necessary for the preparation of proposals is disclosed to one or more potential offerors, it must be made publicly available as soon as possible, but no later than the next general release of information. However, information provided in response to a particular offeror's request cannot be disclosed if doing so would reveal that offeror's confidential business strategy or the information is otherwise protected under the procurement integrity requirements or exempt from disclosure under the Freedom of Information Act. Additionally, the agency's personnel may not reveal an offeror's technical solution or any information that would compromise his intellectual property to another offeror.

However, the regulation now states:

If award will be made without conducting discussions, offerors may be given the opportunity to clarify certain aspects of proposals (e.g., the relevance of an offeror's past performance information and adverse past performance information to which the offeror has not previously had an opportunity to respond).

If a competitive range is to be established, communications must "be held with offerors whose past performance information is the determining factor preventing them from being placed within the competitive range." Written notice must be given to unsuccessful offerors of their exclusion from the competitive range and these offerors may request a debriefing. Communications with offerors before the establishment of the competitive range are called "exchanges." Subsequent communications with those offerors within the competitive range are called "discussions" and these must include deficiencies, "significant weaknesses, and other adverse past performance information to which the offeror has not yet had an opportunity to respond."

C.   UNSOLICITED PROPOSALS

§ 15.21   Agency Procedures

Unsolicited proposals are advantageous for government agencies that often do obtain innovative or unique methods or approaches to accomplishing their missions from sources outside the government. They are advantageous to private companies because unsolicited proposals may be used as a marketing technique for marketing research and unique products. Often the government will desire follow-up procurements after it has funded research and will make an award based on a contractor's unsolicited technical proposal. Such a contractor is in an advantageous position if he has established his technical capability in the area of funded research or development. Upon funding, the contractor may be given access to beneficial government data as well as technical data available to the government from other sources and may find an unsolicited proposal to be a very advantageous beginning. If no immediate award is forthcoming, the government's future recognition of its effort may be helpful to the firm. Where a firm is attempting to break a competitor's unique position on a line of contracts with a particular department or agency, an unsolicited proposal may direct a government department's attention to a different technology, and thus cause that department to modify its current approach on a given procurement. An "unsolicited proposal" is a written proposal that is submitted to an agency on the initiative of the submitter for the purpose of obtaining a contract with the government and which is not in response to a formal or informal request (other than an agency request constituting a publicized general statement of needs). An agency is not authorized to make express contracts obligating appropriated funds for the purchase of suggestions; no express contract or implied contract could then be authorized. Although the regulations provide that late proposals and modifications of proposals must be held unopened until after award, some contractors have used the "unsolicited proposal" (as distinguished from a "bid" or "offer") to apprise the government of a new approach. This is because the government will then be able to consider a new technical approach to the government's needs before making an award.

Where an unsolicited proposal is submitted to an agency and appropriately marked with a restrictive legend and later the agency issues an invitation for bids that discloses proprietary technology contained in that unsolicited proposal, such action constitutes a breach of the government's obligation to maintain the confidentiality of proprietary data. Agencies are directed to encourage potential offerors to contact their personnel before making extensive efforts on the submission of unsolicited proposals. Advertising material, commercial product offers, contributions, or technical correspondence are not unsolicited proposals; a valid unsolicited proposal must be innovative or independently originated and developed by the offeror, without government supervision and include sufficient detail to permit a determination that government support could benefit the agency's mission responsibilities. Beginning in 2002, "agencies must evaluate unsolicited proposals for energy-savings performance contracts."

All agencies must establish procedures, including assurance of accountability, for controlling the receipt, evaluation and timely disposition of proposals. These procedures include controls on the reproduction and disposition of proposal material, in particular data identified by the offeror as subject to duplication, use, or disclosure restrictions.

A favorable comprehensive evaluation of an unsolicited proposal "does not, in itself, justify awarding a contract without providing for full and open competition" unless a resolution of the synopsis requirement and certain sole source requirements are met.

One portion of the regulation states that an agency "need not" submit a notice (synopsis) of the proposal to the Governmentwide Point of Entry (GPE) that "would improperly disclose proprietary information associated with the proposal." However, when considering the negotiation of a contract, the regulation specifically prohibits the use of any data or other part of an unsolicited proposal unless the offeror agrees to the intended use. The agency must place a cover sheet on the proposal with a notice setting forth its "use of data limited, unless the offeror clearly states in writing that no restrictions are imposed on the disclosure or use of the data contained in the proposal."

§ 15.22 The Uniqueness Problem in Unsolicited Proposals

Where a proposal appears to meet the agency's mission requirements in a unique way, a comprehensive evaluation will be performed.

The regulation states that a contracting officer may commence negotiations following a favorable comprehensive evaluation and "the agency technical office sponsoring the contract supports its recommendation with facts and circumstances that preclude competition," and furnishes the necessary funds. The regulation has been revised to require compliance with the synopsis requirements in FAR subpart 5.2 so that potential competitors may consider sending in a proposal prior to an award being made to the unsolicited proposer.

Upon receipt of an unsolicited proposal, the government may solicit more proposals. In some instances, the government could essentially incorporate some of the unsolicited proposal in a Request for Proposals (RFP) and seek competition. Because the government may not wrongfully disclose to others confidential information that has been included in an unsolicited proposal, such RFP's must be tailored to exclude such information. This method could be used in instances where no truly confidential information need be disclosed in solicitation. Possible alternatives for the agencies to consider include the award of a small sum of money for bringing the idea to the government's attention. However, it might be difficult to structure the amount to be equal to the necessary incentives in many cases. If so, consideration might be given to either the purchase of any confidential data rights, or the next alternative. Possible alternatives also include a developmental contract for a limited sum of money (with a clause giving some data rights to the government) might be awarded to the proposer. However, this contract award may be subject to the objection that the proposer has a "head start" which may become enough to eliminate competition for a significant period of time; if the proposer's first attempts are successful, the government agency's "time restraints" on the procurement of many items may preclude the seeking of further competition for them. That is, once an agency finds that the contractor's first contract produces a few items which work well, the agency may find a need for many more of them in a time frame which generally precludes competition and necessitates a sole course procurement on the basis of "public exigency."

Sometimes after a request has been issued, an unsolicited proposal is received which is of interest to the agency, but involves "a departure from stated requirements." In such a case, the agency must amend the solicitation "provided this can be done without revealing to the other offerors the alternative solution proposed."

The circumstances permitting other than full and open competition for a responsible single unsolicited source is currently authorized with companies that have "unique capabilities," with limited rights in patent or "secret processes," and when the agency head determined that the agency's standardization program "only specified makes and models of technical equipment and parts" that satisfied the agency's need.

D. SOURCE SELECTION

§ 15.31   In General

In Western society, for the purpose of efficiency in the allocation of scarce resources, it is essential to select sources by procedures designed to maximize competition, while at the same time attempting to minimize the complexity of the solicitation, evaluation, and the selection decision.

In evaluating proposals to each acquisition and including only those factors that will have an impact on the source selection decision, best value must be included as an evaluation factor in every source selection. While the lowest price or lowest total cost to the government is properly the deciding factor in many source selections, in certain acquisitions the agency may select the source whose proposal offers the greatest value to the government in terms of performance and other factors. The award of a cost-reimbursement contract is made primarily on the basis of estimated costs (as has not infrequently been done in the past), has encouraged the submission of low estimates and increased the possibility of cost overruns. However, a solicitation stating that offers would be evaluated based on delivery rather than price has been held to violate the statutory requirement that price must be considered in any negotiated procurement.

Dual sources have often been solicited where large or continuing procurements are involved for specially fabricated items. When doing so, the agencies must utilize the safeguards normally applied in evaluating non-competitive procurements including submission of certified cost or pricing data; contractors' cost representations; "should cost" evaluations of contractors' proposals and technical evaluations of contractors' proposals. Agencies cannot assume that adequate price competition exists when two contractors submit bids or proposals on a dual-source contract. Neither of the sources has an implied-in-fact contract to continue dual-sourcing because a contractor's rights under the existing contracts are a matter of contract administration. The qualifications of agency evaluators are not subject to challenge; these are within the agency's discretion.

§ 15.32   Disclosure of Mistakes before Award

Unlike the case of sealed bids, the matter of mistakes of the offeror in negotiated procurement is generally handled by the procedures set forth below. Errors in the agency's solicitation are normally handled by the issuance of amendments. Mistakes in the contractor's proposal are processed in accordance with the procedures for mistakes in bids.

Minor informalities or irregularities and apparent clerical mistakes are handled in the same manner as they are in connection with sealed bids. However, unlike the sealed bid situation, other mistakes are usually resolved during discussion concerning information that is essential for determining the acceptability of a proposal and may even provide an opportunity for its revision. Such cases fall into two categories: (1) the agency suspects a mistake, advises the offeror thereof and requests verification, or (2) the offeror alleges a mistake in its proposal, in which case he is advised that he may withdraw the proposal or seek correction.

If a proposal received in electronic format is unreadable to the degree that conformance to the essential requirements of the solicitation cannot be ascertained from the document, the contracting officer immediately must notify the offeror. Furthermore, the GAO has held that "an agency cannot eliminate a technically acceptable proposal from consideration without first considering the relative cost of that proposal to the government." But, agencies must realize that "Proposals may be withdrawn by written notice at any time before award."

§ 15.33 Proposal   Evaluation   and   Competitive Range

A more recent evaluation factor is founded on *past performance* with subfactors. An offeror without a record of relevant past performance "may not be evaluated favorably or unfavorably." Except in that instance however, past performance "shall" be evaluated in all source selections for negotiated competitive acquisitions "unless the contracting officer documents the reason past performance is not an appropriate evaluation factor." The regulation repeats that "past performance need not be evaluated if the contracting officer documents the reason past performance is not an appropriate evaluation factor for the acquisition." Thus, the mandatory statement requiring its evaluation may be eliminated either by the unavailability of information on past performance or by simply documenting in some way why it is "not an appropriate evaluation factor." The regulation also states "that comparative assessment of past performance information is separate from the responsibility determination." Professor Schooner stated that GAO had warned agencies "of the chilling effect upon contractors prompted by the government's broadened use of past performance evaluations, and recent guidance has attempted to constrain improper behavior." The GAO recently upheld several agency decisions acting upon the new standards.

The regulation details instructions regarding "price analysis" (the examination of a proposed price without evaluating its separate cost elements and proposed profit), "cost realism analysis," "information to support proposal analysis," "subcontract pricing consideration," "profit," and "price negotiation." These prenegotiation objectives establish the government's initial negotiation.

A proposal is assessed by: (1) using cost or price analysis for determining reasonableness as well as the offeror's understanding of the work and ability to perform the contract; and (2) a technical evaluation. In 1997, two new sections were added to Part 15. The first states that the source selection authority (SSA) decision shall be based on a comparative assessment of proposals against all source selection criteria in the solicitation. While the SSA may use reports and analyses prepared by others, the source selection decision shall represent the SSA's independent judgment. However, the rationale for the selection decision "need not quantify the tradeoffs that led to the decision." The second refers to "cost realism" analysis, which is supposed to be a process "independent" of the evaluation of specific elements of each offeror's cost estimate to determine if they are "realistic for the work to be performed." The effectiveness of these additions must be documented.

Proposal evaluation is followed by written or oral discussion with all proposers who are in the "competitive range." That range is determined based on cost or price and other factors stated in the solicitation. The goal is to include all proposals that are the "most highly rated proposals." However, the Comptroller General has described his standard of review for the determination of competitive range as "a matter primarily within the discretion of the procuring agency, and we will not overturn that determination in the absence of clear evidence that it had no reasonable basis or is in violation of Federal procurement laws or regulations."

An agency may not eliminate technically qualified offerors from competition without considering price and all the evaluation criteria stated in the solicitation. Nevertheless, the evaluation factors are generally "within the *broad discretion* of agency acquisition officials" (emphasis added).

In certain circumstances, the solicitation may notify offerors that award might be made without discussion. Unpriced technical proposals rarely are solicited and evaluated to determine which are acceptable to the government, or could, after discussion, be made acceptable. In those instances, after discussion, price proposals are solicited for all the acceptable technical proposals that offer the greatest value to the government and an award is made to the low responsible offeror, either with or without discussion. Written or oral discussion need not be applied in acquisitions in which the solicitation notifies all offerors that the government intends to evaluate proposals and make award without discussion. Furthermore, unlike the procedures for use of sealed bids, the offeror who alleges a mistake that cannot be corrected may simply withdraw without producing any further evidence of the mistake.

The current regulation states that contracting officers are to include in the competitive range only "the most highly-rated proposals, unless the range is further reduced for purposes of efficiency," which substantially increased the government's ability to limit the competitive range. Interpreting for the first time the revised competitive range standard, the GAO ruled that an agency need not retain in the competitive range a proposal which "has no realistic prospect of award"—in spite of the fact that it was the most highly rated and its exclusion leaves only one offeror in the competitive range. It also held that an agency might, after reevaluation, reinstate a proposal where this is consistent with the solicitation's evaluation factors.

As of July 1, 1995 agencies have been required to consider a contractor's past performance in awarding negotiated contracts over $1 million, and to begin evaluating contractor performance on all contracts over $1 million; $500,000 beginning July 1, 1996; and $100,000 beginning Jan. 1, 1999. Where the agency documents the reason past performance "is not an appropriate evaluation factor," it need not use it. Firms lacking relevant past performance history, or where information on past performance is not available, "may not be evaluated favorably or unfavorably on past performance."

The GAO has sustained a protest and declared a proposal evaluation unreasonable where an agency gave "overwhelming emphasis" to past performance, and this emphasis was inconsistent with the solicitation criteria. Since October 1, 1995, at a minimum the solicitation must clearly state the significant evaluation factors, such as "cost or price, cost or price-related factors, past performance and other non-cost or non-price-related factors, and any significant subfactors, that will be considered in making the source selection, and their relative importance." The solicitation must also inform offerors of minimum requirements that apply "to particular evaluation factors and significant subfactors." This is a significant improvement in the regulation. In the past, the Comptroller General held that agencies did not have to disclose subfactors if they were "sufficiently related to the stated criteria so that offerors would reasonably expect them to be included in the evaluation."

§ 15.34 Point Scores

Point scores are often used to evaluate negotiated procurements with respect to items where the cost figures submitted will not apply, such as "enthusiasm" for the work to be done. The regulation has been augmented to provide that "[e]valuations may be conducted using any rating method or combination of methods, including color or adjectival rating, numerical weights and ordinal rankings." A contracting agency must be able to substantiate a reason for point scores awarded, or else the evaluation may be found to be defective. Where the GSA ignored an incumbent contractor's relevant past performance information in awarding a follow-on combined guard services contract, a post-award protest was sustained. The Comptroller General ruled that the completion of contract performance as a whole—rather than of particular incidents of interest to agency evaluators—determines when the three year limit on consideration of past performance information begins to run.

Even though the technical scores are 10 percent apart, they may be regarded as "technically equal," and an award may then be made to the lower-ranked offeror where significant cost savings might be achieved. In one case, the agency used an evaluation scheme that gave technical merit and cost approximately equal values. But it was held that the agency need not give equal weight to the percentage differentials between offerors' technical scores and proposed costs. The GAO has pointed out that technical point ratings are merely guides for decision-making and too much reliance should not be placed on them. The selecting official must determine what a difference in evaluation point scores might mean in terms of performance and what it would cost the government to take advantage of them. This does not mean that the weighted evaluation criteria are changed or ignored, since the importance of price is always accentuated when other factors, in the good faith judgment of procurement officials, do not clearly identify one proposal as most advantageous to the government. A contracting officer's determination that there is no significant technical difference between proposals with a 14.4 percent difference in technical point scores was held to be reasonable. When an agency gave different scores for technical merit, and the differences reflected substantive differences in quality, it was unreasonable to find the offers technically equivalent.

Where technical factors are rated as the most important evaluation criteria, an award to the offeror whose technical proposal is rated lower (and whose costs also are lower) must be justified by the agency. In a negotiated procurement, the government is not required to make award to the lowest priced, technically acceptable offeror unless the RFP specifies that price will be the determinative factor for award.

Where a point system is used and an award made based on an improper evaluation, that award will not be overturned unless a protestor can demonstrate that he was in fact prejudiced. It has been held that a technically acceptable proposal may be excluded from the competitive range if it is 44 percent higher in price than the lowest technically acceptable proposal. The solicitation informed competitors that award might be made based on initial proposals and without discussions and that offerors "may" be provided the opportunity to submit best and final offers. It also reserved the right to reject even technically acceptable offers if they had no reasonable chance for award. The agency was not required to conduct discussions with all technically acceptable offerors and it had a reasonable basis for excluding the proposal from competition. In another case, the term "responsiveness" was held as proper to show that an offer that failed to address 133 of 200 sub-items, and received only 21 of a possible 100 evaluation points, was outside the competitive range.

Evaluation of points for exceeding an agency's minimum requirements (enhancements) can affect competition adversely unless they are noted as subfactors in the solicitation. Some agencies conduct cost/technical tradeoffs seeking to determine "greatest value" where there is no requirement that the contract be awarded based on the low price. The approach could also place a premium upon setting forth evaluation factors in the solicitation in order to avoid possible use of subjective evaluation factors by the agency, unless an "aesthetic" evaluation factor is involved and is specifically indicated in the solicitation. The evaluators' point scores are "merely aids for selection officials" and are not binding on them. They are bound "only to the tests of rationality and consistency with the established evaluation factors."

§ 15.35   Written and Oral Discussion

Discussions are not required when the agency reasonably determines that the award will be made on the initial offers. This is if (1) the solicitation notifies all offerors of the possibility that award might be made without discussion; and (2) the award is in fact made without any written or oral discussion with any offeror. If award will be made without conducting discussions, offerors may be given the opportunity "to clarify certain aspects of proposals (e.g., the relevance of an offeror's past performance information and adverse past performance information to which the offeror has not previously had an opportunity to respond)". The U.S. Court of Federal Claims stated that even though a solicitation is labeled a negotiated procurement, if the agency tells bidders there will be no discussions, it is in effect a sealed bid procurement and the rules in Part 14 apply. The decision by the Navy not to discuss costs with bidders has been held adequate, noting that a downward cost adjustment may not affect award.

Otherwise, written or oral discussion must take place with all responsible offerors who submit proposals within the competitive range. Where written or oral discussions are required, then the agency personnel must also control all discussions, point out deficiencies and significant weaknesses, attempt to resolve any uncertainties concerning the technical proposal and other terms and conditions of the proposal, and call the offeror's attention to any suspected mistakes as specifically as possible without disclosing information concerning other offerors' proposals or the evaluation process. The offeror should be provided a reasonable opportunity to submit any cost or price, technical, or other revisions to its proposal that may result from the discussions.

These obligations formerly placed a burden upon agency technical personnel, who must be trained to conduct the discussions so as to avoid helping an offeror bring his proposal up to the level of the others or disclosing information that results in improvement of a competing proposal (called "technical leveling" or "transfusion"). The former prohibition against technical leveling is absent from the new rules. They only prohibit the government from revealing "an offeror's technical solution" which includes "unique technology, innovative and unique uses of commercial items, or any information that would compromise an offeror's intellectual property." Contracting officers are required to "establish a common cut-off date only for receipt of final proposal revisions" which must be in writing.

An agency was held to have failed to conduct meaningful discussions with an offeror, where the agency did not give the offeror a chance to provide additional information on material points. The GAO has held that unequal discussions, where one competitive range offeror is advised of areas in which its proposal is believed to be deficient, but another competitive range offeror is not, do not satisfy the requirement for meaningful discussions. Nevertheless, these discussions are not to be used to cure deficiencies or "material omissions or materially alter technical or cost elements of a proposal."

In one case, NASA negotiated a satellite contract with General Electric Co. (G.E.) after an evaluation in which G.E. scored 687 points and Fairchild 686 points. The evaluation board found the companies technically equal and estimated that the cost difference was minor. G.E. proposed a cost about 2% lower than Fairchild. Fairchild protested pointing out that, unlike G.E., it only had 1 week to prepare the proposal. G.E. received an extra week. Fairchild claimed that if another week had been granted, it could have cut costs more than 2%. The Comptroller General held that a situation prejudicial to Fairchild was created by the different dates allowed for submission. He also noted that some of Fairchild's costs could have been "leaked" to G.E. during the extra time allowed G.E. and stated it was not conclusive that there was no evidence of a leak. There was, however, a situation created wherein a leak, which might have affected the results of the competition, could have occurred. Accordingly, NASA was requested to reconsider the proposed award to G.E.

These discussions may stop when a proposer has been informed of the deficiencies in his proposal and given the opportunity to correct them. The government is not obligated to assist him in increasing his overall score or to reopen negotiations after a best and final offer is submitted. The U.S. Court of Appeals for the Federal Circuit, in reversing the Claims Court, has held that the mere potential for improprieties in competitive negotiations does not justify issuing an injunction against an award.

When an agency determines that only one proposal has a reasonable chance to be selected for award, the competitive range may be revised after exchanges (which are negotiations) so that only the highest rated offeror remains. In such circumstances, an agency, in its discretion, may make more than one competitive range determination.

§ 15.36   Final Proposal Revisions

At some point, it is necessary to cut off all discussions in order to move toward an award. Fairness requires that all proposers be so notified along with information concerning whether they are still within the competitive range and given an opportunity to submit a final proposal revision (FPR).

Under the former rule, multiple rounds of "best and final offers" were possible, albeit discouraged. The rationale was that reopening discussions without a justification tended to compromise the integrity of the procurement system by creating price leaks. If the agency has a reasonable basis for reopening discussions, the GAO will deny the protests. If the discussions are reopened, the contracting officer shall issue an additional request for FPRs to all offerors still within the competitive range. Requests for FPRs are not required to use specific words.

The regulation requires agencies to evaluate total cost. Accordingly, where the Department of Health and Human Services (DHHS) failed to evaluate the full range of costs (the developmental services costs to be incurred under the contract) and where the solicitation provided for evaluation of "total costs," an award to a higher-priced, higher-rated firm was held unreasonable.

§ 15.37   Debriefing of Offerors on Awards Based upon Competitive Proposals

The contracting officer must award a contract to the successful offeror by furnishing the executed contract or other notice of the award to the offeror. He must also notify, in writing or electronically, each offeror whose proposal is determined to be unacceptable or whose offer is not selected for award. Upon his written request, any offeror must be debriefed and furnished the basis for the selection decision and contract award. This may be done orally, in writing, by electronic means, or any other method acceptable to the contracting officer who will normally chair the meeting. Debriefings must include a summary of the rationale for eliminating the offeror from the competitive range well as an "evaluation of significant elements of the offeror's proposal," and will not disclose the quantity or identity of other offerors or any evaluation of them. It will not include point-by-point comparisons of the debriefed offeror's proposal with those of other offerors or reveal any information exempt from release under the Freedom of Information Act. Post-award debriefings are limited to those whose written request for a debriefing is received by the agency within three days of the offeror having been notified that it was not selected for award, either because the offeror was excluded from the competitive range or because award was made to another offeror. To the maximum extent practicable, the debriefing should occur within five days after receipt of a written request. Post-award debriefings should include "overall evaluated cost or price (including unit price) and technical rating, if applicable, of the successful offeror and the debriefed offeror."

The regulation directs that the post-award notice must to include "unit prices of the award." Although the term "unit price" is not defined, if the listing of any stated such price is not "impracticable," they must be made "publicly available, upon request." It also states "no offeror's cost breakdown, profit, overhead rates, [or] trade secrets" are to "be disclosed to any other offeror." However, an offeror had objected to the right of NASA to make such a release. Other provisions state that debriefings shall not reveal any information "exempt from release under the Freedom of Information Act," including "financial information that is privileged or confidential." In 1999, this right was denied by the Circuit Court of Appeals for the District of Columbia. The court held that the government did

> not claim that it or NASA has any independent legal authority to release line item pricing information ... [and that if] commercial or financial information is likely to cause substantial competitive harm to the person who supplied it, that is the end of the matter for the disclosure would violate the Trade Secrets Act.

The following year, the Department of Justice issued a memorandum to the Freedom of Information Office noting that this was "case specific and record specific" and did "not set forth a new rule of law or categorical nondisclosure principle." Further, it noted that agencies may be able to rely on these portions of the regulation as "mandatory authority" to release unit prices without notice to the submitter. Another part of the regulation states that government personnel shall not use "any data, concept, idea, or other part of an unsolicited proposal as the basis ... for a solicitation or in negotiation with any other firm ... and shall not disclose restrictively marked information in an unsolicited proposal" under certain conditions, namely, where the labeling of each page containing restricted data with the legend:

> Use or disclosure of data contained on this sheet is subject to the restriction on the title page of this proposal.

The offeror's failure to do this was found to be fatal to his claim of wrongful dissemination of his data.

In adding the pre-award debriefing requirement of the Clinger–Cohen Act, the Congress expressly recognized that it may not be in the government's best interests to conduct a debriefing until after the award. As noted above, post-award debriefings are limited to those within the competitive range who received notices three days after the date of contract award and were not selected. Furthermore, "to the maximum extent practical," it should occur within five days after receipt of a written request. An agency is not to provide the pricing information of an unsuccessful offeror to the potential awardee during a solicitation.

E. MAKE–OR–BUY PROGRAMS OF PRIME CONTRACTORS

§ 15.51   In General

The past two decades have massive increases in privatization in the many countries of the world. Policies and procedures of the government with regard to its primary reliance on private commercial services for supplies and services are discussed above. The Federal Acquisition Regulation (FAR) points out that "some functions are inherently governmental and must be performed by government personnel." By way of analogy, a government agency desires that a prime contractor remain responsible for managing contract performance, including planning, placing, and administering subcontracts as necessary to ensure the lowest overall cost and technical risk to the government. That agency also must control certain management decisions that include the right to review and agree upon the contractor's make-or-buy program when necessary to ensure negotiation of reasonable contract prices, satisfactory performance, or implementation of socioeconomic policies. In 1997, this provision was expanded and definition was inserted for

"Make item," an item or work effort "to be produced or performed by the prime contractor or its affiliates, subsidiaries, or divisions." The "make-or-buy program" constitutes that part of a prime contractor's plan identifying those items to be produced or work efforts to be performed in the contractor's facilities and those to be subcontracted. A contracting officer must "evaluate and negotiate proposed make-or-buy programs as soon as practicable after their receipt and before contract award." He "may" incorporate the make-or-buy program in negotiated contracts for major systems (see Chapter 34) or their "subsystems or components, regardless of contract type."

The head of an agency has been held to have the authority to overturn a decision to cancel a contract award in favor of performing the work in-house. This is because a contrary decision would result in a "situation in which the responsible officer would be divested of the power to correct erroneous decisions of his subordinates." Prospective contractors may be required to submit make-or-buy programs for all procurements without sealed bids whose estimated value is $10 million or more. The information required from a prospective contractor is confined to those major items or work efforts that would "normally require company management review of the make-or-buy decision because they are complex, costly, needed in large quantities, or require additional facilities to produce." Normally the program would only include items or work efforts "estimated to cost less than (a) 1 percent of the total estimated contract price or (b) any minimum dollar amount set by the agency, whichever is less."

The proposed program of the prime contractor is evaluated and negotiated as soon as practicable after its receipt and before the contract award. An agreement will not normally be reached on proposed "make" items when the products or services are not regularly manufactured by or provided by the contractor and are available.

After agreement is reached, the contracting officer may incorporate the make-or-buy program in contracts for major systems or their subsystems or components; he may also do so for other supplies and services if the contract is a cost type contract in which the contractor's share of the cost is less than 25 percent, where it is determined that technical or cost risks justify review and approval of changes or additions to the make-or-buy program. A standard clause is inserted in the contract governing any changes or additions to the make-or-buy program. An agency may be requested to redo its cost comparisons when a project is submitted showing that the government's failure to follow established procedures had a material effect on the comparison. For example, an agency's calculations of direct labor costs under a cost comparison solicitation for base operations and maintenance service were not in sufficient detail to determine how it had arrived at its in-house estimate or if the Service Contract Act or Davis–Bacon Act were misapplied in estimating its in-house costs. Depending upon the results, such a recomputation may, or may not, need to result in cancellation of the Request for Proposals.

In 1991, an appellate court ruled that the decision by an agency to contract out work formerly done by government employees is reviewable under the Administrative Procedure Act (APA). An issue arose concerning whether the decision was "committed to agency discretion by law." The court found that the mandatory character of the Office of Management and Budget's Circular A–76 permitted the review under the APA in order to authorize review of contracting out decisions. These decisions must be regarded with considerable attention to ascertain whether they may lack specific support in the Circular.

F. PRICE NEGOTIATION

§ 15.61   Cost or Pricing Data—Generally

Although cost or pricing data may be essential for an agency to carry out its mandate to purchase supplies and services from responsible sources at "fair and reasonable prices", no cost or pricing data need be submitted where there is "adequate price competition." The criteria for whether price competition exists, if offers are solicited, requires at least two responsible offerors who can satisfy the government's or prime contractor's requirements (in the instances where subcontractor cost or pricing data are required) and who independently contend for a contract or subcontract. Standards for exceptions from cost or pricing data requirements may exist where there was a reasonable expectation that two or more responsible offerors, would submit priced offers in response to the solicitation's expressed requirement, even though only one offer is received from a responsible offeror, under certain conditions; namely, the reasonableness of this expectation must either (a) reflect a reasonable comparison with current or recent prices for the same or similar items under contracts that resulted from adequate price competition, or (b) it must be approved at a level above the contracting officer.

Other data becomes necessary in other instances, including modifications of prime and subcontracts, whether or not the initial agreement was awarded based on sealed bids. In accordance with provisions of a statute, the regulation (1) exempts suppliers of commercial items under Federal contracts from the requirement to submit cost or pricing data; (2) provides for the submission of information other than cost or pricing data to the extent necessary to determine price reasonableness; and (3) may remove specific audit authorities pertaining to information provided by commercial suppliers.

Although some agencies had issued policy memoranda thereon prior to the 1960's, the Truth in Negotiations Act of 1962 for the first time provided a statutory mandate that the Department of Defense, the National Aeronautics and Space Administration, and the Coast Guard require a prime contractor or any subcontractor to submit and certify cost or pricing data under certain circumstances. Such data specifically includes such factors as vendor quotations, non-recurring costs, information on changes in production methods and in production or purchasing volume, data supporting projections of business prospects and objectives and related operations costs, unit-cost trends such as those associated with labor efficiency, make-or-buy decisions, estimated resources to attain business goals, and information on management decisions that could have a significant bearing on costs.

The Act's requirements are applied to all executive agencies. Unless exempted, cost or pricing data are required before awarding a contract which is not based upon sealed bids and which is expected to exceed $550,000, and before the modification of any sealed bid or negotiated contract— whether or not it was awarded after obtaining sealed bids and whether or not cost or pricing data were initially required—when the modification involves a price adjustment expected to exceed that limit. A $251,000 modification resulting from a reduction of $451,000 and an increase of $200,000 is a pricing adjustment exceeding $550,000. This requirement does not apply when unrelated and separately priced changes for which cost or pricing data would not otherwise be required are included for administrative convenience in the same modification.

Even though an item qualifies for exemption from the requirement for submission of cost or pricing data, the agency must make a price analysis to determine the reasonableness of the price and any need for further negotiation. Such data is also required before awarding a subcontract at any tier, if the contractor and each higher tier subcontractor have been required to furnish certified cost or pricing data, provided that the subcontract amount is not waived. In addition to the data itself, there is required a certificate of current cost or pricing data, in a specified format, certifying that to the best of the submitter's knowledge and belief, the cost or pricing data were accurate, complete, and current as of the date of final agreement on price.

When cost or pricing data are required, the contracting officer should request field pricing assistance (which may include an audit review by the cognizant contract audit activity) before negotiating any contract or modification resulting from a proposal in excess of $550,000. However, he is restricted from requesting a pre-award audit of indirect costs if the results of a recent audit are available.

A price negotiation memorandum (PNM) must clearly document for the government the major cost element of the contractor's proposal, the field or other pricing recommendations, and how the contracting officer used this information to establish the government's negotiation position and reach the agreement. Further, any direction from external sources that has a significant bearing on the contract action must be documented in the PNM and a contracting officer cannot waive the cost or pricing data requirement.

§ 15.62   Exemptions From or Waiver of Submission of Cost or Pricing Data

As noted above, an agency will not require submission of cost or pricing data when it determines that prices are based on adequate price competition—that is, after solicitation, two or more responsible offerors that satisfy the government's requirements independently submit price offers responsive to the solicitation.

There has been an exemption where the prices are based on established catalog or market prices of commercial items sold in substantial quantities to the public. The regulation since 2000 exempts all such commercial items. In order to qualify for this exemption, the terms of the proposed purchase, such as quantity and delivery requirements, should be sufficiently similar to those of the commercial sales so that the catalog or market price will be fair and reasonable.

Any price set by law or regulation (such as a utility price) is already controlled and hence is exempt from an agency's requirement for submission of cost or pricing data. Waivers of requirements for submittal of prime contractor cost or pricing data do not automatically waive requirements for subcontractors, unless also included in the waiver by the head of the contracting activity (HCA).

§ 15.63   Defective Cost or Pricing Data

Before agreement on price, if the agency learns that any cost or pricing data submitted are inaccurate, incomplete, or non-current, the agency must immediately bring the matter to the attention of the prospective contractor (whether the defective data increases or decreases the contract price). It must then negotiate, using any new data submitted, or making satisfactory allowance for the incorrect data. An error in estimating future general and administrative (G & A) rates has been held to be judgmental and not factually defective cost or pricing data. However, should information respecting incorrect data as of the date of final agreement on price given on the contractor's (or subcontractor's) certificate of current cost or pricing data come to the agency's attention after award, then the government is entitled to a price adjustment, including profit or fee, of any significant amount by which the price was increased because of the defective data. This may be ensured by contract clauses which give the government the right to price adjustments for defects in cost or pricing data submitted by the contractor, a prospective subcontractor, or an actual subcontractor. Upon suspecting erroneous data after award, the agency must first request an audit. Then only if the audit reveals that the certified data were defective may the agency evaluate the profit-cost relationships. The contract will not be repriced solely because the profit was greater than forecast or because some contingency specified in the submission failed to materialize. When an audit indicates defective pricing, the agency must determine whether or not the data submitted were defective and relied upon, and then give the contractor an opportunity to support the accuracy, completeness, and currency of the data in question. A defective pricing claim may be asserted by the government more than six years after the final contract payment. This is because the statute of limitations does not apply to appeals from a contracting officer's final decision asserting a government claim under the Contract Disputes Act.

If both the contractor and the subcontractor submitted cost or pricing data, the government has the right to reduce the prime contract price if it was significantly increased because a subcontractor submitted defective data. Under cost-reimbursement contracts and under all fixed-price contracts (except firm-fixed-price contracts and contracts with economic price adjustment), payments to the subcontractor that are higher than they would be had there been no defective subcontractor cost or pricing data become the basis for disallowance or nonrecognition of costs. Where a prime contractor prepares a report analyzing a subcontractor's cost proposal, the report constitutes cost and pricing data that should be disclosed to the government. In one case, however, the board found other information so that there was no overstatement of the contract price, and therefore no defective pricing.

Changes made in both the False Claims Act (with respect to burden of proof and "qui tam" actions by private citizens, (see Chapter 3)) and the Truth in Negotiations Act include the imposition of penalties on overpayments and government entitlement to interest on its overpayments from the date of the overpayment to the date of repayment. Where the contractor knows it submitted defective data, he becomes liable for an additional amount equal to that of the overpayment.

A board of contract appeals has held that it would not stay a board proceeding involving a government claim of defective pricing so that the government could pursue an investigation based upon the same audit report as the contracting officer's final decision finding there was defective pricing.

The Truth in Negotiations Act prohibits certain contractor defenses when defective pricing has occurred, allows contractor offsets to price reductions otherwise due the government and prohibits such offsets in other situations. In connection with defective cost or pricing data, an offset "for any understated cost or pricing data submitted in support of price negotiations, up to the amount of the government's claim for overstated pricing data" are covered in the regulation if the contractor certifies the amount requested. In 1999, a contractor who failed to provide accurate pricing information to GSA contract negotiators before award of a five-year road building contract, and overcharged for road building equipment by not offering GSA the same discounts it provided other customers, agreed to pay the government $1.9 million to settle the claims.

In April 1993, the Defense Inspector General's Office issued the "Truth in Negotiations Act (TINA) Handbook," to aid contracting officers in processing defective pricing reports. It included synopses of laws, regulations, boards, courts, and General Accounting Office (GAO) cases. A later report by the General Accounting Office to the Senate Committee on Governmental Affairs stated that the Department of Defense's deterrent features of the Truth in Negotiations Act do not recover most of the defective pricings identified by audit, do not assess penalties, and underutilize the interest provisions of the Act.

§ 15.64   Factual and Judgmental Data Distinguished

The failure to submit engineering studies and cost analyses prepared and used by a contractor, or which tended to show that a subcontractor's quotation was unreasonably high, has been held to give the government a right to a price reduction. The reasoning was that such data constituted the

type of facts which prudent buyers and sellers would reasonably expect to have a significant effect on the price negotiations and are data which could reasonably be expected to contribute to the sound estimates of future costs as well as to the validity of costs already incurred.

To the extent that the data reasonably affects "costs already incurred," it is factual and verifiable. Nevertheless, the reference to the contribution that the data was expected to have on "estimates of future costs" may possibly be "judgmental-type" data and, if so, it is not "cost or pricing data" as defined in the regulation. It has been held that a "profit plan" with targets and projections for use in training and in motivation of sales people need not be disclosed. The government had to establish that the failure to disclose the plan resulted in a higher contract price. If the data is factual and would be "reasonably available" within a contractor's or subcontractor's organization on matters significant to contractor management and to the government, it must be disclosed. Facts cannot always be distinguished from judgment in their exposition. Decisions defining cost or pricing data have construed the term "factual" to include some judgmental data such as internal corporate analysis, reports and studies. Congress confirmed this approach by an enactment stating that some judgmental data must be disclosed.

Cost estimates are not cost data. Hence, it has been held that cost estimates submitted by a guard services contractor in support of his proposal were not cost data subject to the operation of the contract's defective cost or pricing data clause which applied only to inaccurate or false cost data submitted by the contractor. This was emphasized by a board of contract appeals in 1992 in a case that concerned whether an agency was entitled to a price reduction for the contractor's failure to provide Estimated Standard Labor Hours reports. The contractor denied that the reports were cost or pricing data. The issue was whether the "fact" that an estimate has been made makes it cost or pricing data. The Board decided that factual information can be verified and audited. The report was based on estimates made by industrial engineers or test engineers as a "pure judgment" matter and the data need not be disclosed. Applicable guidance at the time defined cost or pricing data as "all facts as of the time of price agreement that prudent buyers and sellers would reasonably expect to affect price negotiations significantly.''

Cost or pricing data is to be submitted by the contractor under the forms mentioned in the regulation. A prospective contractor cannot fulfill its obligations by making available to the agency its books and records without specific identification of the data. A board ruled that the government could recover interest on the overcharges the contractor made that constituted inaccurate pricing data. The interest recovery was made retroactive to the date the contractor received the overpayments until the date they were repaid.

§ 15.65   The Certificate of Cost or Pricing Data

As soon as practical after agreement on the price of any contract where cost or pricing data is required to be submitted, the contractor must execute a certificate stating that the data are accurate, complete, and current as of the date of that agreement. This constitutes a representation as to the accuracy of the data on which any estimate is based and the basis of liability for failure to disclose data whenever the agency relied upon it. As regards the reliance factor, prior regulations pointed out that

> In the absence of evidence to the contrary, the natural and probable consequence of defective data is an increase in the contract price in the amount of the defect plus related burden and profit or fee; therefore, unless there is a clear indication that the defective data were not used, or were not relied upon, the contract price should be reduced in that amount.

This had been implied into the regulation and results in a shift to the contractor of the burden of going forward with the evidence, while at the same time permitting him to shift the burden back by locating evidence of nonreliance. Under the Truth in Negotiations Act, submission of current cost or pricing data is mandatory and cannot be waived by the contracting officer; the fact that a contractor submitted no certificate of cost or pricing data for option quantities is no defense or prerequisite to the government's claim to a reduction in the contract price where it has been overstated.

The current regulation requires that in arriving at a price adjustment, the agency must consider the "extent to which the government relied upon the defective data." The amount of recovery, through the price reduction clause, of a contractor's cost overstatement includes the appropriate burden and profit, or fee. This may differ somewhat from recovery for defective pricing prosecuted as false statements under other civil statutes or the criminal law. For example, under the False Claims Statute, the government may recover three times the amount of actual damages (treble damages). (See Chapter 3.)

G. NEGOTIATION SKILLS

§ 15.71 In General

During and since World War II, the United States has consistently negotiated more contract value than it has by sealed bids. The regulations do not tell one "how to negotiate;" they do discuss what information or limits are required or involved if negotiation does take place.

Legal negotiating is an art involving skills that, historically, were rarely taught in law schools, in spite of the fact that this is what most lawyers do. The negotiation process applies to contracts as well as the settlement of lawsuits. The literature on negotiation is large.

Unlike private negotiations, the government during contract formation must accept the contractor for negotiation or competitive purposes so long as he is within the competitive range and is willing to discuss if it has affected in any way his prior performance.

Some experienced negotiators may attempt to obtain as much information as possible and disclose as little as they can concerning their side. However, due to Truth in Negotiations laws and regulations, this approach is somewhat outdated due to cost or pricing data if the estimated price is above the threshold with regard to such data.

§ 15.72 Adjudication Distinguished

A contractor's administrative costs by its attorneys may be recoverable, as distinguished from those connected with adjudication. While citing the Contract Disputes Act (CDA), the Court of Appeals for the Federal Circuit stated "costs incurred in connection with the prosecution of a CDA claim" were not recoverable. Under FAR Part 33, Disputes and Appeals, such a claim refers to "a written assertion by one of the contracting parties seeking, as a matter of right, the payment of money in a sum certain, the adjustment or interpretation of contract terms." The Federal Claims Court has held that expenses for a consultant to assist a contractor in negotiating disputed claims with the government were unallowable because "negotiations are a reasonably expected part of contractor's prosecution of a CDA claim."

§ 15.73 Negotiation as a Legal Specialty

It has been held that performance in a business capacity is not protected by attorney-client privilege under New York law, not in accordance with national rules pertaining to ethical conduct.

The American Bar Association's (ABA's) Model Rules of Professional Conduct 2003 Edition applies to lawyers both in and out of government service. Model Rule 1.11, Special Conflicts of Interest for Former and Current Government Officers and Employees, states that a lawyer who has formerly served as a public officer or employee of the government (and not as a trial lawyer) may "not otherwise represent a client in connection with a matter in which the lawyer participated personally and substantially as a public officer or employee, unless the appropriate government agency gives its informed consent, confirmed in writing, to the representation."

A government lawyer may not participate in a matter in which he had participated personally and substantially while in private practice or nongovernmental employment, unless the appropriate government agency gives its *informed consent*, confirmed in writing. However, he "may have authority under applicable law to question such conduct more extensively than that of a lawyer for a private organization in similar circumstances. Thus, when the client is a governmental organization, a different balance may be appropriate between maintaining confidentiality and assuring that the wrongful act is prevented or rectified, for public business is involved." Finally, it is professional misconduct for a lawyer to state or imply an ability to influence improperly a government agency or official or to achieve results by means that violate the Rules of Professional Conduct or other law.

(a) Absence of a Complete "Good Faith" Requirement During Negotiations

Neither the common laws nor the Uniform Commercial Code (UCC) requires the use of total good faith during negotiations—barring fraud and deception. During negotiation, the parties are allowed to take the best advantage they can, in order to reach an agreement favorable to their own side. Except with regard to actions taken pursuant to laws and regulations, there is no more legal duty to negotiate a public contract in good faith than is the case with private contracts, (although there are some exceptions such as a letter of intent which may create the duty to negotiate in good faith toward a final contract). The parties must consider and balance short-term gain in language bordering on prevarication against the long-term loss of credibility generated as a result of mistakes.

(b) Confusion Between Morals and Rules of Professional Responsibility

A client has the right to pursue a malpractice action against his lawyers for failing to carry out his instructions in negotiating a contract, even though the client cannot prove the other party to the contract would have accepted the terms the client wanted.

The second edition of the Encyclopedia of Bioethics—five volumes on a subject which includes the modern law—contains the statement that "Law's influence on bioethics has been so pronounced as to be unmistakable, yet so pervasive as sometimes to be unnoticed . . . a perfect legal solution may not exist for all legal bioethical dilemmas." Nevertheless, at the turn of the third millennium, Deborah Rhode, former senior counsel for the House Judiciary Committee, wrote a volume in which she stated, "In essence, *lawyers need to assume greater moral responsibility for the consequences of their professional conduct.*" (Emphasis added.)

Science and other developments offer a significant amount of the evidence concerning why changes in ethics remain in great need of attention, as well as the methods by which they might be accomplished. This evidence must include that derived from various cultures, religions, and their connections with the sciences. Early in the 20th century, an American philosopher stated, "The problem with putting the values that are present in our culture to use in our culture can sometimes be undermined by the conclusions of modern science." At the end of 20th century, Nobel Laureate Feynman stated, "It seems to me that there is no scientific evidence bearing on the Golden Rule." Thereafter he wrote that "it must lie outside science because it is not a question that you can answer only by knowing what happens; you still have to judge what happens in a moral way."

Many people appear to define "ethics" to be the same as "morals," and most of the latter are derived from their religion. However, the judiciary generally requires recognition of its "wall of separation" from religion. Thus, a lawyer for a plaintiff may request a jury "Please do unto my client as you would have him do unto you." If so, he may be held to violate the "Golden Rule" prohibition. Similarly, an argument that asks the jury to place itself in the defendant's shoes is improper when used with respect to liability on the issue of damages.

(c) Model Rules of Professional Conduct in Negotiations

Major changes occurred in the ABA Model Code of Professional Responsibility, adopted on August 12, 1969; and Canons of Ethics, adopted by the American Bar Association on August 27, 1980; and most significantly in the Rules of Professional Conduct, which the ABA adopted in August, 1983. The original canons were viewed as essentially moralizing statements about honesty. The current rules in the Model Code are more largely Disciplinary Rules written in a more statutory form in order to be enforced in disciplinary proceedings. These rules have been considered for adoption by the states.

(d) Confidential Information of Employees and Former Employees; Disqualification Because of Relationship With Former Client

The Supreme Court in Upjohn v. United States held that the attorney-client privilege applies when the client is a corporation and assumes the privilege's existence and applicability. The attorney-client relationship by itself does not raise a presumption of confidentiality, whereas an agency counsel's acts are usually those within the privilege. Such a privilege belongs to the United States and it may be waived by the government.

The Restatement of the Law governing lawyers has a section prohibiting a lawyer from acting on behalf of a client with respect to "a matter in which the lawyer participated personally and substantially while acting as a government lawyer or officer unless both the government and the client consent to the representation" under several limitations and conditions. If such a lawyer acquires confidential information that concerns the governmental client or employer, he may not represent another public or private client in certain circumstances. A Circuit Court of Appeals has ruled that the obligation to preserve client confidence exists not only with respect to information that falls within the category of the attorney-client evidentiary privilege, but extends to all knowledge and information acquired from the former client.

Great ethical thinkers have recognized that "interesting moral choices are not those between good and evil, but those between good and good."

H. OTHER REQUIREMENTS

§ 15.81 Unit Prices

Because of the enactment of the Defense Procurement Reform Act of 1984 and the Small Business and Federal Procurement Competition Enhancement Act of 1984, new regulations were issued to require that "unit prices are in proportion to the item's base cost (manufacturing or acquisition costs)." When procuring without full and open competition, or if adequate price competition is not expected, offerors must then identify in their proposals those items of supply which they will not manufacture or "to which they will not contribute significant value." This information will be used to determine "whether the intrinsic value of an item has been distorted through application of overhead and whether such items shall be considered for breakout." A clause entitled "Integrity of Unit Price" is to be inserted in all contracts except small purchases or those involving construction, architect engineer, utility services, service contracts, and contracts for petroleum products.

It has been held that a contractor's "unit price rates" are not protectable as confidential information under the Freedom of Information Act. The contractor claimed that disclosure of the rates would cause potential harm to the contractor's competitive position. An appellate court upheld an agency's determination that the aggregate figures composing the unit price rates are made up of a number of fluctuating variables, preventing calculation of the profit margin.

§ 15.82 Unbalanced Offers

Much of the material devoted to "unbalanced offers" resulted from the impact of two cases discussed in Chapter

14 above. Offers must be analyzed to determine whether they are unbalanced with respect to prices or separately priced line items. This may increase performance risk and could result in payment of unreasonably high prices. For example, the greatest risks concern the price for first article tests or test items compared to the price for the production units, or the prices for options in relationship to the prices for the basic requirement. Such offers may be mathematically unbalanced based upon prices that are significantly less than cost for some contract line items and significantly overstated in relation to cost for others. If so, they may be rejected.

In order to determine if offers are materially unbalanced, agency personnel use price analysis techniques. The regulation describes techniques that can be used to determine if an offer is unbalanced. These include comparing all offers to determine if the offerors have significantly higher prices for the first articles than for the production units while considering whether the government or the contractor will perform the first article test. The technique suggested for evaluating a single offer is to compare the relationship of first article prices to prices for production items. The evaluated price is the aggregate of estimated quantities to be ordered under separate line items of an indefinite-delivery contract. If the prices of the offer are unbalanced, the associated risks to the government must be considered to determine the competitive range and in making the source selection decision. This information will indicate whether unreasonably high prices are being requested while the contract is being performed. If so, and the award is made to that contractor, he may possibly receive an illegal advance payment or an interest-free loan and the offer may be rejected if determined to be an "unacceptable risk."

§ 15.83   Profit—Generally

Profit or fee objectives represent "that element of the potential total remuneration that contractors may receive for contract performance over and above allowable costs." This element and the estimate of allowable costs "together equal the government's total prenegotiation objective." The payment of a profit is in the government's interest not only to "stimulate efficient contract performance," and to attract the best capabilities of qualified large and small business concerns to government contracts, but also to maintain "a viable industrial base."

Statutes impose fee limitations based upon a percentage of estimated costs. For experimental, developmental, or research work performed under a cost-plus-fixed-fee (CPFF) contract, the fee cannot exceed 15 percent of the contract's estimated cost, excluding fee. For other such contracts, the fee cannot exceed 10 percent of the contract's estimated cost, excluding fee, except that for Architect Engineer (A–E) professional services, the fee for production and delivery of designs, plans, drawings, and specifications cannot exceed 6 percent of the estimated cost of construction of the public work or utility, excluding fee.

§ 15.84   Profit—Structured Approaches to Profit or Fee Objectives

Subject to the authority of agencies to implement or supplement the FAR and in order to provide a discipline for ensuring that all relevant factors are considered, agencies making noncompetitive contract awards over $100,000 totaling $50 million or more a year must use a structured approach for determining the profit or fee objective in all procurements requiring cost analysis; they may prescribe specific exemptions for situations in which mandatory use of a structured approach would be "clearly inappropriate"—an undefined term. Agencies may use one another's structured approaches.

The first factor in a structured approach must concern the complexity of the work and the resources required for performance. "Greater profit opportunity should be provided under contracts requiring a high degree of professional and managerial skill." This requires consideration of the number of subcontracts to be awarded and administered, whether established sources are available or new sources must be developed and whether material will be obtained through routine purchase orders or through complex subcontracts requiring detailed specifications. Additional considerations include the diversity of engineering, scientific, and manufacturing labor skills required and the amount and quality of supervision and coordination needed to perform the contract task, and how much the indirect costs and general and administrative costs (G & A) contribute to contract performance. A significant factor is the degree of cost responsibility and associated risk that the prospective contractor will assume under the type of contract being negotiated. The contractor has the greatest incentive and cost risk in a firm fixed price contract and assumes the "least cost risk in a cost-plus-fixed-fee level-of-effort contract," as well as in time-and-materials, and labor-hour agreements.

In Federal contracts, greater profit opportunity may be provided contractors who have displayed unusual initiative such as those involving small business concerns "owned and controlled by socially and economically disadvantaged individuals, women-owned small business concerns, handicapped sheltered workshops, historically underutilized business zone areas, and energy conservation."

Consideration must also be given to any contribution of contractor investments to performance and independent development efforts relevant to the contract end item without government assistance.

§ 15.85 Pre-award and Post-award Notification; Protests

Offerors whose proposals are excluded from the competitive range and/or otherwise eliminated from competition award are notified thereof. They may request a pre-award debriefing within 3 days after receipt of the notice. Where such a firm asks that debriefing be made after award, he will be debriefed.

Although a considerable amount of information is included in the pre- or post-award notice, when a contract is awarded on a basis other than price, unsuccessful offerors are furnished the basis for the selection decision and contract award. Debriefing includes the offeror's costs or prices, but not trade secrets, manufacturing processes or other confidential business information.

Mistakes disclosed after award are treated substantially the same as those where sealed bids are used.

The subject of protests is discussed in detail in Chapter 33.

§ 15.86 Should–Cost Analysis

Where an initial production has taken place and a new one is awarded, then a "should-cost analysis" must be considered. It reevaluates the contractor's existing workforce, methods, materials, facilities, or management and operating systems in order to identify uneconomical or inefficient practices "(including plant-wide overhead and selected major subcontractors)." This is done by a government team and a separate audit report is required which is used in negotiations. Thereafter, the administrative contracting officer receives a report of "correction or disposition agreements reached with the contractor" and a "follow-up plan to monitor the correction of the uneconomical or inefficient practices" is established.

On January 26, 1996, guidance was issued on overhead should-cost reviews for contractors, expanded the circumstances under which the government may require the submission of subcontracting plans, and increased the threshold for performing contractor purchasing system reviews.

CHAPTER 16

TYPES OF CONTRACTS

A. INTRODUCTION

§ 16.1 Selecting Contract Types

The first useful way to group government contracts is according to the objects for which they are made. There are contracts for supplies, construction, services, research, and for acquisition of real property. Although such a classification is helpful, it is not sufficient; a new classification was the method of making a contract (that is, by sealed bids or by negotiation) and the method by which a contractor is to be reimbursed (fixed price or cost-type contracts). Fixed price contracts may be further broken down into firm fixed price contracts and fixed price contracts with escalation, with price redeterminations, and incentives. Similarly, cost-type contracts may be with or without a fixed fee, and with or without incentives.

In deciding upon the types of contract to be used in any procurement, in acquisitions other than those made under simplified acquisition procedures (see Chapter 13), the parties must examine the risks involved in performance. Government policy concerning the specific type of contract to be used is determined by the degree of risk in contract performance resulting from its complexity, stability of design, quantity of items purchased, duration of performance, and other features. As the uncertainties become more significant, cost-type contracts tend to be employed in order to accommodate those uncertainties and to avoid placing too great a cost risk on the contractor.

Both public bodies and contractors think in terms of the risk of nonperformance. Although the government as a buyer always strives to place more of this risk with the contractor, it cannot always do so without also paying too high a price for contingencies involved. The government is willing to reduce this risk by using contract-types according to a classification which begins with those cost-type contracts, for which the contractor has virtually no risk or incentive, and ends with firm fixed price agreements, where the contractor bears a large measure of the risks and has the maximum incentive to perform.

	Need	*Type of Contract*
(1)	Basic Research	Cost, CPFF (fixed fee)
(2)	Applied Research	Cost, CPFF
(3)	Exploratory Development	Cost, CPFF
(4)	Advanced Development	CPFF, CPAF (award fee)
(5)	Engineering Development	CPFF, CPAF, CPIF (incentive fee)
(6)	Operational System Development	CPIF, CPAF, FPI
(7)	First Production	FPI (fixed price incentive)
(8)	Follow-on Production	FPI, FPP
(9)	Supply	FPP (fixed price production)
(10)	Supply	FFP (firm fixed price)

The fixed price type of contract maximizes both potential risks and profit to the contractor. It has the maximum incentive without using the word "incentive." Price adjustment clauses may be included for identified contingencies, such as the cost of materials or labor, and such clauses lower the risk to a contractor, although there exists a monetary ceiling on the amount of any adjustment. (See

§ 16.13, infra.) Within the category of fixed-price contracts are certain variants according to the particular need that must be considered by the government, including requirement contracts, indefinite quantity or option contracts, basic and blanket ordering agreements, and multi-year contracts. Basic ordering agreements contain clauses applying to future contracts that will be awarded to the contractor during a particular period.

Selecting a contract type requires sound judgment with the goal of only placing a reasonable risk upon the contractor while, at the same time providing him with "the greatest incentive for efficient and economical performance." Therefore, a firm-fixed-price contract must be used as a matter of policy whenever the risk involved is "minimal or can be predicted with an acceptable degree of certainty" because it "best utilizes the basic profit motive of business enterprise." Other types of contracts are to be considered when a reasonable basis for firm pricing does not exist. For firm-fixed price type contracts, documentation showing why the particular contract type was selected is required for major systems and research and development contracts. The Department of Defense is prohibited from using a fixed-price type contract for a developmental program absent a written determination that the level of program risk permits realistic pricing and that the use of a fixed-price type contract permits an equitable and sensible allocation of program risk between the government and the contractor.

Often the type of contract will change over a period of time so that, while it may be necessary to commence with the cost-type contracts during early phases of a program, these can be succeeded or modified with experience to use of firmer priced agreements as the risks become more manageable. There should be no quantity production without a concurrent cost risk shift to the contractor and consideration of a fixed price type of contract. However, this result may often be difficult to attain because of time restraints imposed by the government.

Contracts awarded through sealed bidding must be firm-fixed-price contracts or fixed-price contracts with economic price adjustment. Agencies are required to use firm-fixed-price contracts or fixed-price contracts with economic price adjustment for the acquisition of commercial items. Professional services are customarily sold at a standard billing rate per hour; agencies must either force-fit the services into a firm-fixed-price contract or forego use of policies and procedures for acquiring commercial items (See Chapter 12).

§ 16.2   Transfer of Costs from Fixed Price Contracts to Cost–Type Contracts

Where a government agency is considering a fixed price contract in the same plant or location where there is a cost-type contract by the same or another agency, there will exist an incentive for the contractor to transfer reimbursable costs to the cost-type contract. Although the administrator of the fixed price contract may count upon a contractor's integrity, the taxpayer has an increased interest in the separation and control of accounting for the allocation of costs in such instances with prior review of the contractors' accounting methods; if this cannot be achieved, the fixed price contracts should not be awarded. Otherwise, a fixed-price contractor is not prevented from performing a cost-type contract at the same site as part of a joint venture.

§ 16.3   Fixed–Price Contracts—Generally

The most frequently used form of government contract is the fixed price type. Such contracts provide the maximum incentive to a contractor to reduce costs because the more they are below the fixed price, the higher becomes his profit. Where the price is not subject to any adjustment on the basis of the contractor's cost experience during performance (absent a contract clause to the contrary), it is called a "firm-fixed-price contract" and typically used for all commercially available products; but it should also be used where design or performance specifications are being used and the reasonableness of price may be established by adequate price competition and comparisons with prior purchases of the same or similar supplies or services made on a competitive basis.

§ 16.4   Fixed–Price Contracts—Economic Price Adjustment

Where the performance period is lengthy and there is serious doubt concerning the stability of material prices or labor cost, a fixed-price contract may also include an economic price adjustment clause.

In order to reduce contingency costs (included in the contract price), the regulation requires use of a clause setting forth upward and downward revision of the stated contract price upon the occurrence of certain contingencies. The risks are reduced by the inclusion of escalation provisions in which the parties agree to revise the stated prices upon the happening of a prescribed contingency. The Court of Appeals for the Federal Circuit held that the Economic Price Adjustment (EPA) clause is not unconscionable even if it may result in a reduction of price. An EPA clause based on a published price index rather than established prices, a cost index, or actual costs of labor or material is invalid.

These clauses provide for upward or downward revision of the contract price of three types: the first and second types of the price adjustments are based on increases or decreases up to 10% from an agreed-upon level in published or otherwise established prices of specific items or the contract end items. Of course, a base level must be established from which adjustments will be made in all cases. The third type is based on increases or decreases in labor experienced during contract performance or based on standards or indices that are specifically identified in the contract. Consideration is also to be given to the appropriateness of selected indices, such as the Consumer Price Index (CPI), which may increase due to some items (such as housing) which may be completely unrelated to contract products. There is a 10% limit on increases, but this limit may be exceeded by obtaining approval from the government. The use of a clause providing for adjustment based on cost indices of labor or materials is normally only appropriate when the contract involves an extended period of performance with significant costs to be incurred beyond 1 year after performance begins, the amount subject to adjustment is substantial, and the economic variables for labor and materials are too unstable to permit a reasonable division of risk without this type of clause.

Performance of the parties in a manner contrary to a contract's terms and other evidence could lead to reformation of the contract in order to conform to the actual intention of the parties. In one case the contractor, although aware of price changes, continued to bill the government and accept payment at prices higher than the prices in the EPA clause. The government was held entitled to a price reduction even though it asserted its right very late. In absence of a mutual mistake, the contract cannot be reformed above the maximum price increase in the contract, regardless of the amount of cost increases to the contractor.

On occasion, it is possible to negotiate a fair and reasonable firm fixed price for an initial period, but not for subsequent periods of contract performance. In such instances, a fixed-price contract with prospective price redetermination may be used which provides for a firm fixed price for an initial period of contract deliveries and prospective redetermination of the price for subsequent periods of performance. The initial period should be "the longest period for which it is possible to negotiate a fair and reasonable firm fixed price." Each subsequent pricing period should be at least 12 months. A ceiling price based on evaluation of the uncertainties involved in performance and their possible cost impact should provide for "assumption of a reasonable proportion of the risk by the contractor."

In research and development contracts estimated at $100,000 or under, a variation is possible by use of a fixed-ceiling-price contract with retroactive price redetermination; this provides for a fixed-ceiling price and retroactive price redetermination within the ceiling after completion of the contract. Such contract type is less used because, like a cost-type contract, it provides the contractor "no cost control incentive except the ceiling price" and fails to provide him with incentives promoting management effectiveness and ingenuity.

Where the work cannot be clearly defined and it is desired that a contractor merely investigate or study in a specific research and development area and then render a report showing the results achieved, a firm-fixed-price, level-of-effort term contract may be used with payment being based on the effort expended rather than on the results achieved.

Finally, it may be determined by an agency that the nature of the supplies or services being acquired and other circumstances of the acquisition are such that the contractor's assumption of a degree of cost responsibility will provide a positive profit incentive for effective cost control and performance. A fixed-price incentive contract may be negotiated that provides for adjusting profit and establishing the final contract price by a formula based on the relationship of final negotiated total cost to total target cost. The incentives on technical performance and/or delivery can have a meaningful impact on the contractor's management of the work. Where the parties can negotiate at the outset a firm target cost, target profit, and profit adjustment formula that "will provide a fair and reasonable incentive and a ceiling that provides for the contractor to assume an appropriate share of the risk," then a fixed-price incentive (firm target) contract may be appropriate. The target profit should reflect any assumption by the contractor of a considerable or major share of the cost responsibility under the adjustment formula. If adequate cost or pricing information to establish a firm target is reasonably expected to be available at an early point in contract performance, then successive targets may be used.

When meeting a required delivery schedule is a significant government objective, delivery incentives are considered. These will also specify the application of the "reward-penalty structure" in the event of government-caused delays or other delays beyond the control, and without the fault or negligence, of the contractor or subcontractor. Multiple incentives that address the reduction of costs and delivery schedules or the attainment of performance characteristics are also possible where properly structured to "motivate the contractor to strive for outstanding results in all incentive areas." These compel trade-off decisions to be made among the incentive areas; emphasizing only one of the goals may jeopardize control over the others.

B. COST–REIMBURSEMENT CONTRACTS

§ 16.11 In General

In many procurements, the uncertainties involved in contract performance do not permit costs to be estimated with sufficient accuracy to use any type of fixed-price contract. In such instances, a cost-reimbursement type contract may be used which provides for payment of allowable incurred costs, to the extent prescribed in the contract based on an estimate of total cost for the purpose of obligating funds. The contracts also include a ceiling that the contractor "may not exceed (except at its own risk)" without the approval of the agency. Such a contract can be used only when the contractor's accounting system is adequate for determining costs applicable to the contract and they can provide appropriate surveillance during performance to assure that efficient methods and effective cost controls are used. Because of these difficulties, use of cost-type contracts is restricted to those instances where, due to the significant risks involved, it is impractical to obtain supplies or services of the kind or quality required without the use of this contract type. Contract cost principles applicable to cost-type contracts are discussed below.

Cost-type contracts are of several types. For research and development work, particularly with nonprofit educational institutions or other nonprofit organizations (as well as agreements for a contractor to run a facility), they may provide for cost-reimbursement with no fee. These are called "cost contracts." When the contractor agrees to absorb a portion of the costs, he does so only within the expectation of substantial compensating benefits. He receives no fee and is reimbursed only for an agreed-upon portion of its allowable costs. This is called a cost-sharing contract. In these types of contracts, care must be taken by the agency to determine both the adequacy of the contractors accounting system for determining costs and efficiency of methods used to control them.

§ 16.12   Cost–Plus–Fixed–Fee Contracts (CPFF)

An agency to pursue development and testing of a product cannot practically use a cost-plus-incentive fee or cost-plus-award fee (CPAF) contract. In such instances they more often settle upon a cost-plus-fixed-fee contract (CPFF). This is a cost-reimbursement contract that provides for payment to the contractor of a negotiated fee fixed at the inception of the contract. Like all cost-type contracts, determinations must be made respecting the adequacy of the accounting system of the prospective contractor and his ability to monitor costs.

The CPFF contract may take one of two forms: completion or term. In the completion form, a goal or target is set and an end product specified. This may be a final report of research accomplishing the goal or target within the estimated cost as a condition for payment of the entire fixed fee, or the agency may require more effort without increase in fee, provided the government increases the estimated cost.

The term form of CPFF contract obligates the contractor to devote a specified level of effort for a stated time period. The fixed fee is payable at the expiration of the agreed-upon period. The completion form is preferred over the term form whenever the work (or specific milestones for the work) can be defined well enough to permit development of estimates within which the contractor can be expected to complete the work. Both completion and term types permit contracting for efforts that might otherwise present too great a risk to contractors; and neither type gives the contractor a significant incentive to control costs. The fixed fee does not vary with actual cost, but it may be adjusted as a result of changes in the work to be performed under the contract. This contract type also may give some incentive to increase costs by way of seeking such changes.

§ 16.13   The Fixed Fee

Not all cost-type contracts involve payment of a fixed fee; those that do present particular problems. Though no precise rules exist for negotiating the fixed fee, cost alone is not a true measure and the fixed fee may be influenced by the amount of alleged risk involved. Determination of a fair and reasonable profit or fee is a matter of judgment, based on consideration of all factors that affect performance of the contract.

The fixed fee is computed as a percentage of the total estimated cost. The fee may be as high as 15% of estimated costs for experimental, development or research work, exclusive of fee, and limited to 10% of such costs for other work. The fee may be equitably adjusted when the contracting officer orders changes that cause a material increase or decrease in the amount or character of the work. The factors for determining fees describe the manner in which a profit objective under a cost-reimbursement type contract is negotiated; they involve considerations with respect to the cost responsibility of the contractor, the reliability of his estimates, and the complexity of the project.

Cost contractors normally incur some expenses of the type considered unallowable. Although the contractor's non-governmental customers in effect accept a pro rata share of many costs that are ordinary business expenses, some expenses must be recouped from another source. Contractors may be expected either to recoup them through the fixed fee or to reduce their unallowable costs.

§ 16.14   Approval of Costs

The government endeavors to include in its cost-type contracts the principle that certain items are allowable only to the extent approved by the contracting officer, even when some of these costs are normally considered costs of doing private commercial business. Contractors may object to this approach, which gives them no real assurance of reimbursability when unallowable costs are incurred and the approval is after-the-fact.

The Comptroller General stated that the word "approval," as used in statutes and regulations, included "the ratification or confirmation of a thing already done, as differentiated from the word 'authorized' which contemplates the giving of permission prior to the act." If "prior approval" is required by contractual terms or regulations and the expense has already been incurred, subsequent approval by the contracting officer cannot always make the cost reimbursable under the contract, without additional consideration to the government from the contractor to support a modification or without a broad indemnity clause in the contract.

§ 16.15   Applicability of Cost Principles

While many of the provisions found in cost-type contracts are similar or identical to those found in fixed-price agreements, the provisions pertaining to allowable and unallowable costs are largely peculiar to cost-type contracts and often create some difficulties during negotiation. The same cost principles are applicable in negotiation and in administration of fixed-price contracts and contract modifications when cost analysis is performed.

Cost principles are made a part of a cost-reimbursement contract. The contract cost principles not only apply for purposes of reimbursement under cost-reimbursement contracts, but they also apply to fixed-price contract terminations and settlements.

§ 16.16   Problems Inherent in Cost–Type Contracts

Cost-plus-percentage of cost contracts (CPPC) were used extensively in World War I with unfortunate, if predictable, results. Their principal incentive for the contractor was to increase costs in order to increase his profit. Such contracts have been made illegal from World War II onward. They have been replaced by contracts in which the fee is fixed in advance. Years ago the Department of Defense noted that CPFF contractors are indifferent about effecting economies and stated, "because of the lack of incentive, the cost-plus-a-fixed-fee contracts are the contract type we least prefer. We use it ... not sparingly, but grudgingly." In the same testimony, the Department found it essential to add that: "This least-favored type of contract has been used, during the past fiscal year, in contracts obligating more dollars than obligated by any of the various fixed-price type of contracts." (Later on more controls were introduced regarding allowable costs.)

The thoughts of management have thus been directed toward new business to a large extent on the basis of a cost-plus-a-profit on all items produced. They can be easily attracted to a CPFF contract in an economy where their costs are continually increasing and profits per unit are diminishing or likely to do so with respect to their commercial products—if the drain on labor and facilities caused by such a contract does seriously jeopardize their commercial (non-government financed) endeavors. Commercial enterprises will often become CPFF contractors in order to enter a field and gain know-how without financial risk during the precommercial production period.

§ 16.17   The Responsibility of a Cost–Type Contractor

(a) In General

The term "responsibility" as used in this section emphasizes financial responsibility for recovering costs incurred in performing a contract for a profit. In a fixed-price contract, management has an incentive to attempt to increase its anticipated profit by effecting economies. This cannot be done on a cost-plus-a-fixed-fee contract where the fee is fixed in advance. As labor and material costs increase more than the amount of dollars which management can save through increased efficiency, there occurs the "profit squeeze" and management is often happy to negotiate a CPFF agreement which is not subject to the profit squeeze since the fee is fixed regardless of cost changes and management can ignore pressure to effect the economies it would obtain if the work were performed on a fixed-price basis. A cost-type contractor's legal responsibility could be affected by different types of written and unwritten provisions in these contracts. They are of three types: (1) written indemnity provisions, tending to decrease responsibility and functioning; (2) general responsibility derived from unwritten limitations applicable to cost-type contractors; and (3) written provisions tending to increase the responsibility of the cost-type contractor. Let us briefly examine the first two here; the third involves unallowable costs (discussed in Chapter 31) and the "limitation of cost" clause (which is discussed in Chapter 32 below).

(b) Indemnity Provisions Covering "Business Risks" and All Costs "Incident" to Cost–Type Contracts

In the past, cost-type contracts sometimes contained indemnity provisions that would bear upon almost all the financial responsibility of the contractor—a corporate executive's dream. The former Court of Claims held that such a clause does not require responsibility—but simply that the cost was incurred "incident" to the contract—which was tantamount to being an expense which would not have been incurred "but for" the cost-type contract.

Such a clause is known as "business risk" indemnity; its applicability was not limited to particular losses and expenses that are typically insurable risks (for personal injury, death, or property damage arising out of performance of the contract). The more recent CPFF agreements that contain indemnity provisions are limited to particular losses and expenses; the general lack of contractor responsibility discussed above no longer apply to CPFF contracts.

(c) The General Responsibility of Cost–Type Contractors

The Comptroller General had indicated that there existed certain general rules of responsibility applicable to all cost-type contracts when the agreement itself is silent on particular items in question. He set forth five general rules of reimbursability in the absence of specific contract language: The item of cost incurred must (1) be "reasonably incident" to work, (2) not "presumed (to be) included in the fixed fee," (3) "serve a useful purpose in fulfilling contract requirements," (4) not result from the absence of due care by Contractor management and (5) the contractor may not be reimbursed for any cost incurred "in contravention of the law." A CPFF contractor who discharged certain employees and then reinstated them with back pay was denied reimbursement for the back wages on the ground that the United States received no tangible benefit from the expenditure even though the contracting officer had approved the expenditure as a reimbursable item incurred by the contractor in the performance of his work. The Comptroller General found that the contracting officer had exceeded his authority since "manifestly the terms of the contract may not be construed as imposing upon the government cost incurred as a result of the contractor's own fault or folly." It is also impossible to escape from restrictions placed upon those funds in appropriation acts. Authority to purchase on a CPFF basis does not suspend statutory restrictions with respect to the purchase from appropriated funds of typewriters or passenger-carrying vehicles.

Later, the Armed Services Board of Contract Appeals rendered some decisions that seemed to place a stricter burden upon the government of showing that a contractor's conduct was "unreasonable." These decisions indicated an outer limit beyond which a cost-type contractor could not expect reimbursement. They also seemed to assure him that if he avoided folly or illegality while reasonably attempting to perform and incurred expenses not presumed to be covered by the fixed fee, he would normally be able to recover those costs not made unallowable by law or specific provision of the contract.

§ 16.18   Conversions From Fixed Price to Cost–Type Contracts and Vice Versa

Downward conversion from a fixed price to a cost-type agreement with a concurrent reduction in risk to the contractor in the past has been referred to as a major defect in military procurement; it may result in a bailout that includes payment of a significant profit to a contractor for correcting his own mistake under a fixed price contract. In private industry this could result in management turnover and possible reorganization of the business.

Conversions from cost-type to fixed price may be upward when they are made with respect to quantity production contracts following a development contract that only produced prototypes. The effect of conversion before final payment "might possibly be construed as nullifying, or rendering ineffective, any audit action this office might take to ascertain the amounts paid to the contractor." Where almost half or more of the work is completed at the time of a pending conversion, the contractor may be in a better position during negotiations than the government because the cost records may not yet reflect all his knowledge with respect to the cost of completing the work. Such conversion should not occur under these circumstances. This is a principal reason why letter contracts (discussed below) are to be definitized as early as possible.

§ 16.19   The Cost–Type Contractor as an Agent of the Government

If a cost-type contractor were expressly made an agent of the government, it would appear that, like a contracting officer who is an agent of the government, he could only bind the government for actions which are authorized. Although it has been held that there is no general authority to assess charges against agents of the government for losses sustained by third parties as a result of error, or even neglect of duty by the government agent, when a person becomes an agent by contract, the terms and conditions of the contract would govern his liability as an agent. Such a relationship can be established by a contract that expressly makes the prime contractor an agent for the government, or impliedly does so. The government seldom contracts in this manner even though there are often significant tax advantages for doing so. If he is not a government agent and has no exemption from such taxes, they are reimbursable costs (See Chapter 29). The tax advantages to the government in making contractors agents seldom have bearing on a contractor's responsibility.

An agent is subject to a duty to his principal to act solely for the benefit of the principal in all matters connected with his agency, a duty not necessarily attaching to independent contractors. He has a duty not to bring disrepute upon his principal, and to give information relevant to the affairs entrusted to him. An agent to buy and sell is subject to a duty to the principal to be loyal and to obtain terms that best satisfy the principal's purposes. Generally, government agencies have felt that the possible disadvantages are predominant over the possible advantages that may accrue from making cost-type contractors agents of the government. These disadvantages are of various sorts: where the principal is disclosed, the agent is not even a party to the subcontracts he makes (unless the parties agree otherwise). The agent is not liable for nonperformance, unless he misrepresents that he has authority to make a subcontract which is in fact beyond his authority; the signature of the agent as being "on behalf of," "for," or "as agent of" creates the inference that only the principal (and not the agent) is a party to the transaction.

Where agency exists, liability of the principal must be disaffirmed in order that the principal (government) be not solely subject to liability or even only concurrently or jointly liable with the agent-contractor. If the government is to place the responsibility on the prime contractor for its subcontract activities, the contract document should so specify. In the alternative it may be agreed that the disclosed or partially disclosed principal (government) alone be liable, or that both agent and principal are liable thereon.

The liabilities of the United States may be increased if a contractor becomes the agent of the government, since a general agent may make the principal liable even for those of his acts that are forbidden by the principal if they are "usual or necessary actions."

A disclosed or undisclosed principal may be liable for unauthorized representations of his agent (not representations pertaining to his authority) in actions brought for breach of contract or rescission if the contract is otherwise authorized. One of the government's major concerns is how to take advantage of the concept without becoming ensnarled in its inconveniences, and such inconveniences may result in a decrease in responsibility of management of a cost-type contractor.

The increased use of cost-type contracts since World War II has constituted a revolution in government procurement in peacetime that will probably continue. The challenge to government is to enforce the government's duties and prerogatives in the administration of the contract. Inasmuch as the government takes virtually all the risk in cost-type agreements, it is recognized that it must exercise certain controls to protect the public's funds. No form of contract more severely tests the relationship between industrial management and government administration than the very flexible CPFF contract; a government official should not be judged principally upon "how well he gets along with" the manager of a cost-type contractor. In the author's experience, some agencies have evaluated their contract administrators in this fashion.

C. INCENTIVE CONTRACTS

§ 16.31 In General

Because a cost-plus-fixed-fee (CPFF) contract provides the manager of a contractor with little motivation to decrease costs in order to earn the fee, cost and fee incentives were devised to motivate contractor efforts and discourage inefficiency and waste. This is generally attempted by use of predetermined incentives on technical performance or delivery with (a) concurrent increases in profit or fee provided only for achievement that surpasses the targets, and (b) decreases provided to the extent that such targets are not met. Thus, incentive contracts include a target cost, a target profit or fee, and a profit or fee adjustment formula tied to the relationship between actual reimbursable costs incurred by the contractor and the target costs; where they meet, the contractor receives the target profit or fee. The regulation expressly permits the use of award-fee provisions as performance incentives in fixed price contracts.

In lieu of cost, the target may be a specific performance characteristic of a specific product such as the range of a missile, an aircraft speed, an engine thrust, or vehicle maneuverability. These incentives may be particularly appropriate in major systems contracts (see Chapter 34), both in development (when performance objectives are known and the fabrication of prototypes for test and evaluation is required) and in production (if improved performance is attainable and highly desirable to the government). The incentives on individual technical characteristics must be balanced so that no one of them is exaggerated to the detriment of the overall performance of the end item. Performance tests must be devised and the degree of attainment of performance targets tests must be measured and coordinated with engineering and pricing specialists. In particular, the parties must agree explicitly on the effect that contract changes (e.g., pursuant to the changes clause) will have on performance incentives.

§ 16.32   Cost–Plus–Incentive–Fee Contracts (CPIF)

When a cost-reimbursement contract is necessary for development and test programs and a target cost and a fee adjustment formula can be negotiated "that are intended to motivate the contractor to effectively manage costs," a cost-plus-incentive-fee contract (CPIF) is appropriate. If it is highly probable that the required development of a major system is feasible and the government has established its performance objectives, the contract may also include technical performance incentives. Such a cost reimbursement contract specifies a target cost, a target fee, minimum and maximum fees, and a fee adjustment formula. Upon completion of the contract, the formula provides, within limits, for increases in fee above the target fee when total allowable costs are less than target costs, and decreases in fee below the target fee when total allowable costs exceed target costs. When total allowable costs are less than the range of costs within which the fee-adjustment formula operates, the contractor is paid total allowable costs, plus the minimum or maximum fee. In one case, despite incurring nearly $1 billion in cost overruns on the International Space Station program, the contractor still received the minimum incentive fee—two percent of the negotiated target cost. The actual and projected cost overruns on the prime contract had grown from $783 million to $986 million.

If a high maximum fee is negotiated, the contract may also provide for a low minimum fee in order to provide an incentive for the contractor to manage the contract effectively. The type of private agreement negotiated with the Corning Co. back in the 1930's for the world's largest telescope mirror disk (200 inch) was described as follows:

If the two-hundred-inch could be successfully cast, there would be further orders for additional 60–inch mirrors and other special-purpose mirrors. Hale agreed that if the project were to go ahead, the final price to the Observatory Council would be computed on a "cost plus" basis. The "plus" was a 10 percent profit that Corning would bill only after the disks were figured into mirrors and accepted by the Observatory Council.

§ 16.33 Cost–Plus–Award–Fee Contracts (CPAF)

Where it is not feasible to devise predetermined objective incentive targets applicable to cost, technical performance, or schedule, and the contractor can be motivated toward exceptional performance, a cost-plus-award-fee (CPAF) contract may be used. This type of contract provides for a fee consisting of a base amount fixed at inception of the contract plus an award amount (fee) that the contractor may earn in whole or in part during performance and that is sufficient to provide motivation for excellence in such areas as quality, timeliness, technical ingenuity, and cost-effective management. The amount of the award fee is determined by the contracting officer's "judgmental evaluation of the contractor's performance" against the criteria stated in the contract. This amount is made "solely at the discretion of the government." The criteria and rating plan should be established to motivate the contractor toward improved performance in the areas rated, but without sacrificing at least minimal acceptable performance in all other areas. The evaluation is conducted at stated intervals during performance, so that the contractor will periodically be informed of the quality of its performance and the areas in which improvement is expected. Partial payment of the fee must generally correspond to the evaluation periods. These evaluations take additional administrative effort on the part of the agency.

D. INDEFINITE–DELIVERY CONTRACTS

§ 16.41 In General

(a) ID/IQ Contracts

Indefinite-delivery contracts may be used to acquire supplies (by the issuance of a delivery order) or services (under a task order) when the time or quantities thereof are not known at the time of award. Such contracts will provide for appropriate cost or pricing data for an estimated quantity of supplies or services. Agencies are not precluded from making multiple award indefinite delivery contracts for architect-engineer services.

One indefinite delivery contract, called a "requirements contract," provides for flexibility in the actual purchase deliveries or performance as requirements materialize during a specified period. It states an estimated total quantity of the quantity ordered and, if feasible, a maximum limit of the contractor's obligation. There are possible limitations on the use of requirements contracts for advisory and assistance services.

It has been held that an agency breached a requirements contract by using its own personnel to perform some of the services rather than obtaining the services from the contractor. This opinion found that the agency's officials were "unnecessarily burdened in their efforts to administer the contract because Appellant was so confrontational and argumentative about contract requirements and because he refused to act in a professional manner." As pointed out by the dissent, the contract's statement of work stated that the contractor was to perform field reviews "on an as-needed basis." Although the contract states a realistic estimated total quantity, this estimate is not a representation to the contractor that "the estimated quantity will be required or ordered, or that conditions affecting requirements will be stable or normal.'' The agency may obtain the estimate from records of previous requirements and consumption, or by other means, and should base the estimate on the most current information available.

The regulation requires the agency to ''state a realistic estimated total quantity in the solicitation.'' Where the agency cannot show that its quantity estimates are realistic from the historical information and anticipated orders, the GAO has held that the solicitation should be canceled. However, it is still only an estimate, and the Comptroller General held that a contractor was not entitled to be reimbursed for overhead expenses where the government's estimate of a board services to be supplied under a requirements contract turned out to be wrong by 55%.

An indefinite-quantity contract provides for the government to order more than a nominal quantity of supplies or services stated as numbers of units or values not to exceed a maximum limit. The regulation states that: ''It is inadvisable for an agency to commit itself for more than a minimum quantity.'' Such a contract should be used ''only when a recurring need is anticipated.'' Except for advisory and assistance services, the agency must, ''to the maximum extent practicable, give preference to making multiple awards of indefinite-quantity contracts under a single solicitation for the same or similar supplies or services to two or more sources.'' It has been held that an agency can terminate for convenience an indefinite delivery, indefinite quantity (ID/IQ) contract without having ordered the guaranteed minimum quantity.

The contract may also state the total maximum limit of the contractor's obligation to deliver and the government's obligation to order. The minimum quantities that the government may order under each individual order and the maximum that it may order during a specified period of time must be included. Maximum and minimum limits for indefinite-quantity contracts may be expressed as a number of units or dollar value. Effective April 25, 2000, the regulation was amended to require that indefinite-quantity contracts require the government to order and the contractor to furnish at least a stated minimum quantity of supplies or services, which must be "more than a nominal quantity but should not exceed the amount the government is fairly certain to order."

To the extent practical, the agency must give preference to making multiple awards of indefinite-quantity contracts under a single solicitation for the same or similar supplies or services to two or more sources. The regulation was changed by adding a requirement that agencies must not employ allocation or designation of any preferred awardee(s) that would result in less than "fair consideration being given to all awardees prior to placing each order." Now "a task-order contract and delivery-order contract ombudsman" must be designated by the head of each agency. He must be a senior official who is "independent of the contracting officer." Although he may be the agency's competition advocate, he reviews complaints from contractors and must ensure they are afforded a "fair opportunity to be considered, consistent with the procedures in the contract."

(b) Requirement Contracts

The most recent disputes seem to involve decreases in orders from the amounts estimated to be ordered where the agency failed to notify the contractor of the "most current estimate available." However, information available after the contract has been executed is something not covered by the regulation. One case held that the government did not breach a contract when it reduced its requirements under a vehicle maintenance and repair services agreement because, "the only limitation upon the government's ability to vary its requirements under a requirements contract is that it must do so in good faith." Similarly, in 2001, a contract for commercial leasing of vehicles was held to be neither a requirements contract nor an indefinite-quantity contract; the Board held that the contractor was entitled to be paid only for services actually ordered and provided.

A solicitation for construction services that does not obligate the government agency to order work from any individual contractor and that provides for no guaranteed minimum per contractor was held to be neither a binding requirements contract nor a binding indefinite quantity contract. A requirements contract necessarily obligates the government to purchase exclusively from a single source. Where a contract clause purported to bind the government to order "all" its requirements from each awardee but also stated that the obligation applies "except as this contract otherwise provides"—the aspects of a requirements contract have been held "trumped" by other contract provisions.

Requirement agreements for consultant services (now called "advisory and assistance services" and covered in Chapter 37, infra) have sometimes been abused by the government (see Chapter 37). Such agreements are to last only 3 years up to the amount of $10,000,000; these limits may be ignored if the contracting officer determines that such services are "necessarily incident to, and not a significant component of, the contract."

E.　TIME–AND–MATERIALS, LABOR–HOUR CONTRACTS AND LETTER CONTRACTS

§ 16.51　Time-and-Materials (T & M) and Labor–Hour (LH) Contracts

When it is not possible at the time of placing the contract to estimate accurately the extent or duration of the work, or to anticipate costs with any reasonable degree of confidence, a time-and-materials (T & M) contract may be used. Under this type of contract, payment is made for labor on the basis of (1) direct labor hours at specified fixed hourly rates that include wages, overhead, general and administrative expenses, and profit and (2) materials at cost, including, if appropriate, material handling costs as part of material costs. When included as part of material costs, material handling costs must be clearly excluded from the labor-hour rate. These contracts provide an incentive for the contractor to increase costs so as to increase profit. Government direct surveillance of contractor performance is required to give reasonable assurance that efficient methods and effective cost controls are being used. It can only be used where no other contract type is suitable and the contract includes a ceiling price that the contractor exceeds at its own risk.

It has been held that the government was not estopped from invoking the ceiling price limitation under a time and materials contract even though it had reason to believe the contractor was approaching an overrun condition but gave no notice to the contractor. The contractor did not establish that notwithstanding that knowledge, the government demanded continued performance by cure letter, the contractor was not aware of the facts, and relied to its detriment on the government's action.

A labor-hour (LH) contract is a variation of the time-and-materials (T & M) contract, differing only in that materials are not supplied by the contractor. Although T & M contracts can have results similar to the illegal cost-plus-percentage-of-cost (CPPC) agreements, the Comptroller General has upheld their legality when a dollar ceiling had been fixed in advance.

§ 16.52 Letter Contracts

A letter contract is a written preliminary contractual instrument that authorizes the contractor to begin immediately manufacturing or services. It must include a price ceiling during the remaining negotiations for a target date for when a definitive contract is executed. The letter contract should be as complete as feasible under the circumstances. It must also contain a negotiated definitization schedule including dates for submission of the contractor's price proposal, required cost or pricing data, and, if required, make-or-buy and subcontracting plans. It should also include a date for the start of negotiations, and the earliest practicable target date for definitization. This definitization is to be within 180 days after the date of the letter contract or before completion of 40 percent of the work to be performed, whichever occurs first. It is a form of incomplete agreement that is authorized when performance must begin prior to the time to complete a formal definitive contract. Letter contracts do not have a firm price, but they do contain a number of standard contract clauses, a limitation on the government's liability plus a clause stating that the parties will negotiate in good faith toward execution of a definitive formal contract by a specified date.

Letter contracts have been held to be binding agreements. If, after exhausting all reasonable efforts, the parties fail to reach agreement as to price or fee, a contract clause requires the contractor to proceed with the work while the contracting officer unilaterally determines a reasonable price or fee in accordance with regulations pertaining to price negotiation and cost principles that are subject to appeal as provided in the disputes clause. Following the ordering of the minimum quantity specified in a letter contract for advertising services, the government let it expire and neither definitized it nor issued a termination for convenience. This was upheld. The contractor was limited to payment for the orders issued but not for its preparation for future orders.

F. BASIC AGREEMENTS AND BASIC ORDERING AGREEMENTS

§ 16.61   In General

When a substantial number of separate contracts may be awarded in the future to a contractor during a particular period and significant recurring uncertainties have been experienced, then a "basic agreement" may be used. This agreement is not a contract, but it contains contract clauses applying to future contracts between the parties during its term. It also contemplates separate future contracts that will incorporate by reference or attachment the required and applicable clauses agreed upon in the basic agreement. Like the letter contract, the basic agreement also contains a limitation of government liability. Unlike the letter contract, the basic agreement provides for discounting its future applicability upon 30 days' written notice by either party; it may be changed only by modifying the agreement itself and not by a contract incorporating the agreement. Discounting or modifying a basic agreement does not affect any prior order issued under the basic agreement. It is subject to requirements pertaining to competition. Such agreements may continue for several years, although annual reviews are required.

Thus, when specific items, quantities, and prices are not known at the time the agreement is executed, but a substantial number of requirements for the type of supplies or services covered by the agreement are anticipated to be purchased from the contractor, a so-called basic ordering agreement may be used to expedite contracting for such uncertain requirements for supplies or services. Like the basic agreement, it is not a contract and it contains items and clauses applying to future contracts (orders) between the parties during its term and methods for pricing, issuing, and delivering future orders. Because basic agreements do not give rise to an enforceable contract, the Court of Federal Claims does not have jurisdiction of a breach of contract claim based on the government's termination of a basic agreement.

No damages would be awarded under a basic pricing agreement that obligated an agency "only to the extent of individual orders actually placed under this agreement," and provided that "each order that the agency places and that contractor accepts becomes an individual contract." Similarly, it must not state or imply any agreement by the government to place future contracts or orders with the contractor or be used in any manner to restrict competition. Indeed, before issuing an order under a basic ordering agreement, the agency must either obtain competition or determine that it is impracticable to obtain competition. If an order is issued, failure to reach agreement on price before its price is established is a dispute under the Disputes clause.

PART V

GENERAL CONTRACTING REQUIREMENTS

CHAPTER 28

BONDS AND INSURANCE

A. BONDS

§ 28.1 In General

Agencies may impose bonding requirements as a means to secure fulfillment of the contractor's obligation where needed to protect the government's interest. Although most frequently used in construction contracts, bonds have been imposed in service contracts where the continuous operation of services is necessary.

§ 28.2 The Bid Bond

In Federal procurement, bid bonds are not required by statute; they are only called for by regulations where bids exceed a minimum amount—although they may be required in connection with contracts for lesser amounts. Formerly agencies could only require a bid guarantee when a performance bond or a performance and payment bond was required. However, agencies may now require separate bid bonds as bid guarantees for construction contracts.

The amount of a bid guarantee must be adequate to protect the government from loss should the successful bidder fail to execute further contractual documents and bonds as required. The bid guarantee amount must be at least 20 percent of the bid price but not exceed $3 million. When a bid guarantee is required, the solicitation contains a statement to that effect, and provides sufficient details for bidders to determine the amount of the bid guarantee as well as the clause that contains a requirement for a bid guarantee, and the clause is substantially the same as that used for negotiated contracts. Should the bid bond expire prior to the acceptance period, the bidder will have eliminated himself from the competition. Similarly, conditional bid guarantee is unacceptable and renders the bid itself nonresponsive and subject to rejection.

With certain exceptions, the failure of an offeror to submit a bid guarantee requires rejection of the bid. For example, unless the agency determines that acceptance of the bid would be detrimental to the Government's interest, the requirement for a bid must be waived when only one offer is received; in that case, the furnishing of the bid guarantee may be required before award. Also, following a mistake in his bid, the bidder can increase the bid guarantee to the level required for the corrected bid. Further, although the bid cannot exceed the quantity covered by the bid guarantee, it "is sufficient for a quantity for which the offeror is otherwise eligible for award." These "predetermined informalities" are to be waived by the contracting office.

A surety's right to recover under subrogation is limited to the contract balance at the time the government was notified of the surety's interest where a formal takeover agreement exists between the surety and the government whereby the surety assumed performance of the contract after default; a surety who completes the contract can also assert claims for additional work and resulting price adjustments.

But, in the absence of a formal takeover agreement, a surety is not in privity with the government, and also is not a "contractor" within the meaning of the Contract Disputes Act. In view of the fact that there is no express or implied contract between a surety and the government, the government has no duty to notify a bid and performance bond surety that its principal had made an error in the bid or that the principal had elected to perform the contract at the underbid price rather than withdraw the bid.

The surety has normally executed a takeover agreement upon the failure of a contractor to perform. The Claims Court has held that the Contract Disputes Act becomes applicable to the surety when he signs the takeover agreement and becomes a contractor.

§ 28.3 Payment and Performance Bonds for Construction Contracts

The Miller Act requires performance and payment bonds for any construction contract exceeding $100,000 for construction work in the United States. This requirement may be waived for as much of the work as is to be performed in a foreign country upon finding that it is impracticable for the contractor to furnish such bond, or as otherwise authorized by the Miller Act or other law. For construction contracts with a value between $25,000 and $100,000, the contracting officer is required to select two or more of the following payment protections: (1) a payment bond, (2) an irrevocable letter of credit, (3) a tripartite escrow agreement with a Federally insured financial institution, (4) a certificate of deposit from a Federally insured financial institution, and (5) a security deposit in the form of either a U.S. bond or note or a cashier's check, or currency in an amount equal to the penal sum of the bond.

Although the Miller Act requires the government to insist that its contractors furnish payment bonds, it says nothing about what happens when the contractor fails to furnish the bond. It has been held that a prime contractor's failure to secure the payment bond does not render the government liable to subcontractors when the prime contractor does not pay them.

Unless the contracting officer determines otherwise, the penal amount of performance bonds must equal "100 percent of the original contract price; and if the contract price increases, an additional amount equal to 100 percent of the increase." Under certain conditions, the amount of security to support a bond may be reduced.

A surety's rights and remedies are limited to the contract that it took over and completed upon the default of a contractor. Further, it has been held that a surety cannot recover bond losses from funds due to a contractor from the government on unrelated work under the doctrine of equitable subrogation. A surety cannot stand in the shoes of a contractor and demand payment of reprocurement costs where the surety has not completed the contract. This is because it would have no equitable basis to stand in the place of the defaulted contractor until after it made payment according to the demand.

The government's early release of retained percentages of progress payments does not release the surety from its obligations under the performance bond. Fireman's Fund Insurance Co. v. United States involved a contract with the Army to build a pressure recovery system for the high energy laser system test facility at White Sands Missile Range. Fireman's Fund issued a performance bond. The construction contract provided for periodic progress payments to Westech Corporation, the contractor, and for 10 percent of the estimated amount due to be retained from each progress payment until completion and acceptance of the work, unless the contractor made satisfactory progress during the payment period. When the contractor experienced cash flow problems, he asked for and received a release of some retainages. The contractor notified the surety of payment problems between the contractor and its subcontractors, but Fireman's Fund did not notify the government that payments to Westech should be withheld until five months after the government had released the retainages. The Court of Appeals for the Federal Circuit held that the government did not depart from the provisions of the contract in releasing the retainages, and the surety was not discharged from its obligations under the bond stating "it is irrelevant whether the surety claims a right to funds during performance of the contract, or after it is completed when the government functions as a 'stakeholder' of funds owed but not yet paid. In either event, notice by the surety is essential before any governmental duty exists."

It has also been held that where an arbitration agreement exists only in the contract between the subcontractor and the general contractor, there is no agreement between the plaintiff subcontractor and the defendant surety obligating the surety to arbitrate the claim of the subcontractor. The provision in the Miller Act for exclusive Federal jurisdiction over suits against sureties constitutes an "external legal constraint foreclose[ing] arbitration." However, when used in conjunction with the Federal Arbitration Act, agreement of the parties, may confer Federal jurisdiction where payment has not been made within one year from the last date labor was performed or materials provided. The filing of a demand for arbitration is not the filing of an action. The Federal Arbitration Act provides for a stay of court proceedings pending arbitration. Arbitration awards are difficult to challenge absent fraud or corruption (with the exception when "arbitrators exceeded their powers.") An attorney's fees are recoverable against a surety in a Miller Act proceeding.

Where a prime contract does not require the contractor to obtain a payment bond, it has been held that the prime contractor is not liable to a second tier subcontractor for work performed under the subcontract.

To maintain an action to collect on a payment bond for work completed but unpaid, section 2(a) of the Miller Act requires that notice of the claim be given to a bonded contractor within 90 days after completion of the work. It has been held that this notice is not satisfied if the notice is not received until after the 90–day period expires.

An appellate court has held that where a construction contractor has defaulted, and the surety has completed the contract, the surety may, under the doctrine of equitable subrogation, set off the loss it incurred in completing the contract against funds owed the contractor by the government under another completed contract. The court reasoned that had it completed the contract (in lieu of the surety), the government could have offset any losses it might have incurred against the funds it owed the contractor under the other contract. The defaulting contractor should not "be better off simply because the surety, rather than the government, completed a contract and thereby incurred damages." The dissenters stated, "the government's right of setoff, to which the surety is now held to succeed, is nonexistent. Unless and until the government itself performed the defaulted contract, which it did not do, it had no 'setoff' against the contractor. The surety, who asserts only a right to step into the shoes of the government, has no government shoes in which to step." It has been noted that the bonds should be modified to state that the surety's subrogation rights are those of the government "under the contract." Where a surety has completed a contract following a termination for default, its financial interest does not justify allowing the surety to intervene in the contractor's appeal seeking to convert a default termination into one for convenience. In 1994, the Court of Federal Claims ruled that the Contract Disputes Act does not apply to an equitable subrogation claim of a performance bond surety that executes a takeover agreement following the contractor's default. This is because the subrogation claim neither arises under the takeover agreement nor relates to it; the surety's right of subrogation derives from the duties under the bonds.

As regards the ability of a general contractor to assert a recoupment defense against a supplier, when sued on a Miller Act bond for materials supplied to subcontractor (to reduce payment to extend materials were defective), the Circuit Courts of Appeal are in conflict. The Ninth Circuit has held that where the supplier has a contract with a subcontractor but not with a prime contractor, the Miller Act forbids the general contractor from taking "offsetting" deductions. The First Circuit has held that a prime contractor was entitled to assert a right of recoupment against an unpaid supplier of a subcontractor, making a broad statement that "disallowing recoupment would seem to give the supplier 'rights' to which his contract would not entitle him." It has also been held that public policy prevents an agency from making an enforceable agreement to release a Miller Act bond upon final acceptance of all work under the contract prior to payment to all subcontractors.

§ 28.4 Payment and Performance Bonds for Other Than Construction Contracts

Although agencies do not normally require performance and payment bonds for other than construction contracts, there are instances where they may be required to protect the government's interest. E.g., where a contractor sells assets to or merges with another concern, the government, after recognizing the latter concern as the successor in interest, may desire assurance that it is "financially capable." Another instance is where substantial progress payments are made before the commencement of delivery of end items. Annual performance bonds only apply to non-construction contracts and these must provide a gross penal sum applicable "to the total amount of all covered contracts."

The Miller Act requires most general contractors for construction to provide the government with performance and payment bonds pertaining to the work to be performed; persons in privity of contract with the prime contractor, and suppliers in privity of contract with a subcontractor, who have furnished labor or materials in the prosecution of the work provided for in the government contract, have the right to sue on such payment bond for the amount owing for the services or materials so furnished. The Act states that subcontractor suits on payment bonds "shall be brought" in U.S. district court "for any district in which the contract was to be performed and executed and not elsewhere." However, it has been held that this provision does not confer exclusive jurisdiction on Federal courts to determine a surety's liability; a state court's determination of a principal's liability may be given preclusive effect in a Miller Act suit against a surety. In order for persons furnishing services or materials to a subcontractor and having no contractual relationship with the prime contractor to perfect their right of action upon the payment bond of the prime contractor, they must give written notice to the prime contractor within 90 days from the date on which the last of the labor or material was furnished. When the contract contains an advance payment provision and a performance bond is not furnished, advance payment bonds may be required. In similar manner, if a contract provides for patent indemnity, patent infringement bonds may be required whenever a performance bond is not furnished and the financial responsibility of the contractor is unknown or doubtful.

Although payment bonds protect subcontractors and suppliers, agencies are barred from withholding payments due contractors or assignees during contract performance because subcontractors or suppliers have not been paid. However, where, after completion of the contract work, the government receives written notice from the surety regarding the contractor's failure to meet its obligation to its subcontractors or suppliers, the final payment may be withheld. The surety must agree to hold the government harmless from any liability resulting from withholding the final payment; it will be authorized upon agreement between the contractor and surety or upon a judicial determination of the rights of the parties. The Miller Act no longer requires the Comptroller General to determine and certify the final settlement date of such contracts; a law was enacted amending the Miller Act to transfer the responsibility for furnishing certified copies of Miller Act payment bonds from the Comptroller General to the Federal agency that awarded the contract.

With respect to construction subcontracts, the surety generally executes the bonds by an attorney and certifies as to the authority of the person executing the bond on behalf of the surety company. The agency is required to provide information regarding the name and address of the surety to subcontractors on payment bonds under contracts for other than commercial items upon request.

§ 28.5 Sureties

In order to ascertain that corporate sureties are used which protect the government, the only corporate sureties acceptable for bonds furnished with contracts performed in the United States, its possessions, or Puerto Rico are those which appear on the list contained in the Department of the Treasury Circular 570 entitled "Companies Holding Certificates of Authority as Acceptable Sureties on Federal Bonds and Acceptable Reinsuring Companies." A subcontractor cannot sue the government for negligence in approving the sureties in the event that the prime contractor's securities have insufficient assets.

Following the award of a construction contract at a price of $28,000, a contractor cannot lower his bid to $25,000 in order to avoid the bond requirement, because the ensuing contract cannot be unilaterally modified by the contractor.

Individual sureties must execute the bond and the net worth of each individual must normally equal or exceed the penal amount of the bond. Furthermore, any person required to furnish a bond to the government has the option, instead of furnishing a surety or sureties on the bond, of depositing certain United States bonds or notes in an amount equal at their par value to the penal sum of the bond. A duly executed power of attorney and agreement authorizing the collection or sale of such United States bonds or notes in the event of default of the principal on the bond must accompany the deposited bonds or notes.

However, a provision in an invitation for bids (IFB) that bonds executed by individual sureties would be acceptable only upon deposit with the contracting officer of cash, bonds, or notes of the United States equal to the amount of the guarantee is appropriate. This is because the regulation authorizes class deviations.

A contractor may not act as his own surety. The Comptroller General has ruled that where a surety is called upon to answer for its principal's default, the surety is subrogated to any funds due or to become due under the contract, and this subrogation right relates back to the date of the bond. Therefore, a performance bond surety which completed contract performance after the contractor's default had priority to proceeds of an Armed Services Board of Contract Appeals' award over the prime contractor and the contractor's assignee bank.

A surety's right to recover under subrogation is limited to the contract balance at the time the government was notified of the surety's interest. Where a formal takeover agreement exists between the surety and the government, whereby the surety assumes performance of the contract after a contractor's default, a surety who completes the contract can also assert claims for additional work and resulting price adjustments. But, in the absence of a formal takeover agreement, a surety is not in privity with the government, and also is not a "contractor" within the meaning of the Contract Disputes Act.

When a construction contract was terminated for default, the surety entered a takeover agreement; after the work was complete, the contracting officer and the Armed Services Board of Contract Appeals denied its claim. This ruling was affirmed by the Court of Appeals for the Federal Circuit because the surety was not a "contractor" as defined by the Contract Disputes Act.

B. INSURANCE

§ 28.11 In General

With several exceptions, the Cost Accounting Standards (CAS) are mandatory for use by all executive agencies and contractors and subcontractors for negotiated contracts and subcontracts in excess of $500,000. The FAR requires any contractor subject to Cost Accounting Standard 416 to obtain insurance, by purchase or self-coverage, for the perils to which the contractor is exposed, unless the contract contains an indemnification provision or specifically relieves the contractor of liability for loss of or damage to government property. There are exceptions where the contract specifically relieves the contractor of liability for loss of or damage to government property. Whether or not contracts are subject to those cost accounting standards, contractors are required by law and regulation to provide insurance for certain types of perils (e.g., workers' compensation). Insurance is mandatory also when commingling of property, type of operation, circumstances of ownership, or condition of the contract make it necessary for the protection of the government. Agencies may establish risk-pooling arrangements designed to use the services of the insurance industry for safety engineering and handling of claims.

In fixed priced contracts, the government is not ordinarily concerned with the contractor's insurance coverage except in special circumstances such as where the contractor is engaged principally in government work, government property is involved, or the work is to be performed at a government installation. On the other hand, cost-reimbursement contracts (and subcontracts, if the terms of the prime contract are extended to the subcontract) ordinarily require insurance.

Special provisions set forth minimum amounts of liability insurance required in cost-type contracts and for contractors proposing a self insurance program.

Special clauses are inserted into contracts for "work on a government installation" obliging the contractor to provide "minimum amounts of insurance required in the contract." Cost reimbursement contracts contain a clause requiring the contractor to maintain worker's compensation and other insurance concerning liability to third persons.

C. GOVERNMENT CONTRACTORS AND LIABILITY FOR THEIR PRODUCT

§ 28.21   In General

This volume is not generally concerned with tortious actions. Yet it will be shown that contract law is intertwined and this will be discussed. It might be argued that no "tortious act" has been alleged in a complaint where plaintiffs, by applying a tort label, attempt to convert a claim for breach of a contractual representation into a tort claim. It has been stated that

> The law of torts and the law of contracts are said to protect different interests. A plaintiff may recover in contract because the defendant has made an agreement, and the law thinks it desirable that he be held to that agreement . . .

> Where the conduct alleged breaches a legal duty which exists "independent of contractual relations between the parties" a plaintiff may sue in tort. If the only interest at stake is that of holding the defendant to a promise, the courts have said that the plaintiff may not transmogrify the contract claim into one for tort. But if in addition there is an interest in protecting the plaintiff from other

kinds of harm, the plaintiff may recover in tort whether or not he has a valid claim for breach of contract.

This explains neither why punitive damages are available for tort claims but rarely for contract claims nor how the legal duty that is a predicate to tort liability can exist "independent of contractual relations between the parties" when the duty arises out of the promissory relationship. In the latter connection, a quite different view has been taken by one of the so-called "active" courts.

The American Law Institute approved Section 402A of the Restatement of the Law of Torts (2d) dealing with strict products liability. The Institute wrote that those engaged in the business of selling defective products are strictly liable if the product is in a defective condition, is unreasonably dangerous, and causes injury to person or property. Thereafter, case law followed § 402A of the Restatement, although the Supreme Court had held that strict liability is inapplicable to claims brought against the government under the Federal Tort Claims Act.

§ 28.22 The So–Called "Government Contractor Defense"

Several courts began to recognize the so-called "government contract or defense" or "government specifications defense." This resulted from rulings that permit the contractor who is sued by a third party to assert a defense that the harm was caused by defective specifications of the government, and that the contractor complied with those specifications. The Federal circuit courts of appeals split on the issue of whether the government contractor defense is limited to military contracts or applies more broadly to any product procured under a Federal government contract.

In 1988 the Supreme Court held 5–4, in Boyle v. United Technologies Corp., that a contractor who manufactures military equipment based on "reasonably precise," government-approved specifications is not liable for injuries resulting from defects in the equipment. As a result, the manufacturer of the equipment will not be held liable if (a) the government approved reasonably precise specifications, (b) the equipment conformed to them, and (c) the supplier warned the government about any dangers that were known to the contractor but not to the government. The procurement of equipment by the government is an area of "uniquely Federal interest," and a state law (that held government contractors liable for design defects in equipment) presented a significant conflict with Federal policy.

In 1996, the Supreme Court again had occasion to consider the contours of the government contract defense, but failed to resolve the issues on which the lower courts have split because it affirmed the lower court's holding on an alternative ground. Although the Court did not reach the government contractor defense, it described the defense in relatively expansive terms, observing that: "The government contractor defense, which many courts recognized before the Agent Orange settlement, but which this Court did not consider until afterward, shields contractors from tort liability for products manufactured for the government in accordance with government specifications, if the contractor warned the United States about any hazards known to the contractor but not the government."

The Federal courts of appeals have held that the government contractor defense applies to state law failure-to-warn claims as well as to the design defect claims alleged in *Boyle*. The circuits differ in their application of the defense to claims based on a failure to warn.

The effect of approval of design specifications was the issue in Trevino v. General Dynamics Corporation. A contractor was equipped with a diving chamber designed by the contractor. The court held that government approval of the design specifications amounted to no more than a "rubber stamp", and it ruled out the defense because the approval must constitute a discretionary function pursuant to the Federal Tort Claims Act. Such functions were delegated by the government to the contractor, and the court stated "[w]hen the government merely accepts, without any substantive review or evaluation, decisions made by a government contractor, then the contractor, not the government, is exercising discretion." Courts in some other cases have held that the government's participation in and approval of design specifications went far enough beyond a rubber stamp so that the government contractor defense could be applied.

The question of design vs. manufacturing defects has caused courts to find both ways. Where the government's design was found faulty, the contractor was exonerated; if otherwise, it was held liable. To be exonerated, the contractor who is aware of dangers in his product must inform the government about them. If he does, then he may be exonerated; otherwise he is not.

Following the death of an Air Force major in an airplane accident, his widow sued the manufacturer for wrongful death under Texas law. She claimed strict liability for, and negligence in, the design and manufacture of the aircraft. An appellate court reversed a summary judgment in favor of the manufacturer which had been based upon the government contract or defense. The court stated that it could not determine if the defect was a "manufacturing defect" instead of "non-conformity with government specifications."

It appears that the courts are slowly working out the government contract defense parameters without legislation in spite of the dissent of Justice Stevens in the *Boyle* opinion where he concluded that Congress, not the Supreme Court, should balance "the conflicting interests in the efficient operation of a massive governmental program and the protection of the rights of the individuals." It has been held that there was insufficient Federal interest to support the removal of a personal injury action against a government contractor from a state court to a Federal court. The court found that asbestos is no longer used in the design and manufacture of equipment and the action cannot interfere with a Federal program concerning products with asbestos.

CHAPTER 33

PROTESTS, DISPUTES, AND APPEALS

A. PROTESTS

§ 33.1 In General

Obviously one cannot seek a remedy for breach of contract until a contract exists. Unlike private contracts, government contracts to a greater extent are the subject of public policies in connection with how these contracts are awarded. The written objection by one who would be economically affected by an agency's solicitation or award of a contract is called a "protest." The protestor is called an "interested party" who is the actual or prospective offeror whose direct economic interest would be affected by the award or failure to award a contract.

The Comptroller General has rendered opinions noting a number of considerations concerning the determination of an interested party. These include the party's relation to the procurement and prospective prime contractors; but not to subcontractors, suppliers, or organizations that do not submit offers to an agency's solicitations.

As of January 1, 2001, protesters have three fora in which to bring a pre- or post-award protest: (1) the contracting agency, (2) the General Accounting Office (GAO), and (3) the U.S. Court of Federal Claims (COFC). Effective August 8, 1996, the Clinger–Cohen Act terminated the authority of the General Services Board of Contract Appeals to hear information technology protests, leaving the GAO as the sole governmentwide administrative protest tribunal. The Administrative Dispute Resolution Act of 1996 (ADRA), which took effect on December 31, 1996, significantly expanded the scope of the COFC's protest jurisdiction and extended it to include post-award protests. The ADRA also terminated the U.S. District Court's protest jurisdiction, effective January 1, 2001. As a result, the COFC is the sole judicial forum in which protests may be brought, and the U.S. Court of Appeals for the Federal Circuit is the sole forum for appellate review.

Typically, protesters claim that the solicitation or award decision violates an applicable statute or regulation; that the agency improperly excluded the protester from the competitive range; that the agency engaged in improper discussions with other offerors or failed to conduct meaningful discussions; that the source selection evaluation was irrational, arbitrary, or not conducted in accordance with the solicitation; or that the awardee is not responsible or qualified to perform the work, or its offer was not responsive to the solicitation.

Contracting officers are required to consider all protests, whether pre- or post-award, and whether submitted to the agency or the GAO. If the head of an agency determines that the solicitation, proposed award, or award does not comply with applicable statutes or regulations, the agency may take any action that could be recommended by the Comptroller General in connection with a GAO bid protest, pay appropriate costs, and require the awardee to reimburse the government's costs when a post-award protest is sustained as a result of the awardee's intentional or negligent misstatement, misrepresentation, or miscertification.

§ 33.2   Protests to the Contracting Agency

In addition to the general requirement that contracting officers consider all protests, Executive Order 12979 establishes policies designed "to ensure effective and efficient expenditure of public funds and fair and expeditious resolution of protests to the award of Federal procurement contracts:"

The Executive Order has been implemented by the regulation. An agency protest must be filed, in writing, with the contracting officer or other official designated in the solicitation, by an interested party, and concern (1) the terms of a solicitation, (2) the cancellation of a solicitation, or (3) an award or proposed award of a contract. Adopting the definition established through GAO decisions, the regulation defines an "interested party" as "an actual or prospective offeror whose direct economic interest would be affected by the award of a contract or by the failure to award a contract." As is the case with GAO and COFC protests, agency protests alleging deficiencies apparent in the solicitation must be filed before bid opening or the closing date for receipt of initial proposals. In all other cases, protests must be filed not later than 10 calendar days after the basis of the protest is known or should have been known, although an agency may, for good cause shown, consider an untimely protest that raises issues significant to the agency's acquisition system. Protesters may request an independent review of their protest at a level above the contracting officer. Agencies are required to use their best efforts to resolve protests within 35 days after the protest is filed.

§ 33.3   Protests to General Accounting Office (GAO)

(a) In General

Since 1921, the Comptroller General (GAO) has been deciding government contracts cases under the Budget and

Accounting Act of 1921, which granted him authority to settle and adjust "[a]ll claims and demands whatever by the government of the United States or against it, and all accounts whatever in which the government of the United States is concerned, either as debtor or creditor." The statute gave the GAO settlement authority, but no express authority to decide bid protests.

The statute also states that in settlement of public accounts, "[b]alances certified by the General Accounting Office . . . shall be final and conclusive upon the Executive Branch of the government." The Comptroller General is authorized to render a decision, upon the application of the head of an executive department, or other establishment not under any of the executive departments, or a disbursing officer, upon any question involving a payment to be made by them or under them, which decision, when rendered, "is conclusive on the Comptroller General in settling the account containing the payment." By deciding an award protest, (that is, by determining in advance the validity of a potential contract), unauthorized payments of public funds may be avoided. Such adjudication of award protests by the GAO has been agreed upon in a number of court decisions. Further, an appellate court has held that courts should not overturn an agency's decision to follow the GAO's recommendation on a contract award unless it is irrational.

For more than 80 years, the GAO has been ruling upon complaints by proposers in negotiated and sealed bid procurements prior to contract awards. However, with the enactment of the Competition in Contracting Act of 1984, Congress for the first time gave specific statutory authority for hearing and deciding bid protests, and a direction to revise its bid protest regulations. The GAO reported a 16% increase in its docket for the first quarter of FY 2004, with

383 new filings who represent "the highest they have been for at least five years."

A protesting party can look to several adjudicators for consideration of his protest. For example, he may begin with the contracting agency by asking the contracting officer to decide the matter or he may ask the Comptroller General to provide a decision prior to award. This procedure protects the bidder or proposer who may materially change his position to his detriment in reliance on the award. Often a protestor will seek and simultaneously commence an action in a Federal court because in the past, at least, the likelihood of obtaining relief from the GAO in the form of stopping the procurement and forcing a reprocurement by the agency seemed rather slim.

Disappointed bidders and offerors constitute the bulk of protestors; sometimes other protesters claim to have a direct enough interest, but they seldom succeed. The General Accounting Office (GAO) generally closes an increasing number of bid protest cases. Prior to a 1982 enactment, the GAO did not have authority to obtain records of contracts. Under the General Accounting Office Act of 1982, the Comptroller General may compel production of Federal and nonfederal records when an executive branch agency or other organization refused to comply with the request for records. Under this statute, the GAO has subpoena power to enforce its right of access to a contractor's in-house estimate of direct costs, and the Federal district courts have jurisdiction to enforce the subpoena and jurisdiction to interpret a contract's Access to Records clause.

(b) Unpublished Opinions

The majority of Comptroller General opinions have been unpublished. The decisions are generally available within

24 hours after redaction on the GAO web page and such decisions can be cited.

(c) Limitations on GAO Protest Jurisdiction

The General Accounting Office (GAO) will not consider antitrust contentions by displaced bidders because "such a requirement upon the contracting officers of the government would impose an intolerable burden and would inordinately delay the procurement process." The Office will not review protests regarding grantee awards until the protester has exhausted his administrative remedies. In general, the GAO will not review bid protest evidence that has been withheld by an agency and later submitted in an attempt to seek reversal of an adverse protest decision. Protests of awards made to subcontractors by prime contractors will not normally be considered and reservation by a governmental agency of the right to approve the subcontract does not bestow any such right. An exception is when the prime contractor, acting as the government's purchasing agent, requests an advance decision involving a subcontract being considered; in such instance the government is in control of the procurement to the same extent as if it were a direct purchase. In a similar manner, where the government becomes directly involved in a particular procurement, protests have been considered by the Comptroller General. In order for a protest to challenge an agency's decision to perform services in-house (in lieu of contracting out), a protester must show that the agency violated OMB Circular A–76 and that the violation materially affected the agency's cost comparison.

The GAO will normally refuse to decide issues that are or were before a court. Similarly, the GAO refuses to consider a patent infringement issue because "the exclusive remedy for a patent holder who claims patent infringement by the government or by a government contractor who acts with authorization or consent of the government is a suit against the government in United States Court of Federal Claims.'' In the absence of a showing of possible fraud or bad faith on the part of procurement personnel, the GAO would not review a protest that concerns a contractor's responsibility.

Although the General Accounting Office (GAO) acknowledges the doctrine of res judicata (that the valid judgment of a court on a matter is a bar to a subsequent action on that same matter before the GAO), in many instances it has refused to regard as stare decisis the view of any court (other than the Supreme Court). This is particularly true where the claimant is arguing that some minority viewpoint represents (in the claimant's opinion) a ''trend'' for future decisions, as was frequently done by the American Law Institute beginning with its Restatement Second of the Law.

(d) *The Procurement Protest System and the Deficit Reduction Act*

The independence of the GAO from contracting agencies helps to assure both taxpayers and contractors that their protests will be considered free from possible bias in favor of a particular procuring agency. The Justice Department argued that permitting the GAO to exercise more than an advisory role would violate the separation of powers doctrine because the Comptroller General is a ''Legislative Officer.'' Effective January 15, 1985, under the Deficit Reduction Act of 1984, there began a somewhat newer ''procurement protest system,'' governing ''an alleged violation of a procurement statute or regulation.''

The Comptroller General prescribes the procedures for filing protests and he is authorized to use his audit powers to "verify assertions made by the parties." The Comptroller General only recommends relief, but an agency must report to him within 60 days if it has not fully implemented those recommendations, and he then reports all such instances to Congress on an annual basis. Further, when a protest is sustained, the Comptroller General may declare that the protester should receive the costs of filing the protest, including reasonable attorneys' fees, and bid and proposal preparation costs; the agency is directed to pay such amounts from its appropriations. He does not have exclusive jurisdiction over protests.

(f) Protests Before and After Award

Protests concerning alleged improprieties in a solicitation, which are apparent prior to bid opening or the due date for initial proposals, must normally be filed with the GAO prior to such opening time (or time for receipt of proposals). Otherwise, the protest must be filed within 10 calendar days after "the basis of the protest is known or should have been known, whichever is earlier." However, where a protest is initially filed with a contracting agency, then the protest to the GAO must be made within 10 calendar days of learning the "initial adverse agency action."

The GAO must notify the contracting agency within one day of the filing of a protest and, if award has been made, the agency must notify the contractor "immediately." If no award has been made, all bidders or offerors must be notified who "appear to have a substantial and reasonable prospect of receiving an award if the protest is denied." No bond need be posted. However, where a contractor is directed to stop performance due to the filing of a protest after award, the government may be required to reimburse the awardee for costs incurred as a result of the protest.

(i) Protective Orders

The report of the agency to the GAO can be subject to a protective order which may be requested by any party in order to limit the release of specified documents to the protester or other interested parties. "Consultants," retained by counsel appearing on behalf of a party, may be permitted access to documents under the protective order. Objections by any party to application for access must be filed within two days of receipt of a copy of the protective order request. The GAO must decide within five days of receipt of the contracting agency's report whether the document will be withheld or released, or that a particular party be included or excluded from the order.

Individuals seeking access to documents covered by a protective order must submit an application to the GAO certifying that they are "not involved in competitive decision making in connection with Federal procurements." Violations may result in sanctions including a referral to appropriate bar associations or other disciplinary bodies by the GAO and other remedies such as breach of contract, can be filed by the party whose information was improperly disclosed. Attorneys who do not serve in other capacities with their clients usually simply file the GAO's models (and thus force the opposing counsel to support an objective that that attorney was not involved in competitive decisionmaking). Corporate counsel, on the other hand, must provide more information and GAO scrutiny is increased. The GAO itself may disclose information in its decision where it no longer would give a competitive advantage to other parties. The GAO may dismiss protest allegations that do not state a valid basis for protest, do not contain sufficient detail, or are untimely. It may also accelerate the protest schedule and/or issue a summary decision resolving the protest.

(l) Matters Pending in Court or in Default Terminations

The Comptroller General will not consider a matter pending before a court unless the court has issued a temporary restraining order or preliminary injunction to stay the procurement action or award pending issuance of his decision, or the court expresses a desire to obtain the views of the Comptroller General prior to deciding the case.

The fact that a default termination was on appeal to the agency's board did not bar the General Accounting Office (GAO) from deciding whether the contracting officer conducted the reprocurement according to the required procedures. This was because whether the default termination was justified was not the issue in such a protest; the issue was, for example, the propriety of a sole source reprocurement.

(m) Attorney's Fees on Protests

In those instances where counsel for a protestor could not provide a reasonable estimate of the fees allocable to the portion of the protest on which the protester prevailed (and the parties could agree on the matter), the GAO determined the amount.

Under the Federal Acquisition Streamlining Act (FASA), no protester may recover "costs for attorneys' fees that exceed $150 per hour unless the agency determines (on the recommendation of the Comptroller General) that an increase in the cost of living or a special factor such as the limited availability of qualified attorneys justifies a higher fee" or consultant fees "that exceed the highest rate of compensation for expert witnesses paid by the Federal government."

§ 33.6 Protest Jurisdiction of the U.S. Court of Federal Claims and U.S. District Courts

(a) The Traditional Standing to Sue Rule

Traditionally, under Federal law, a low bidder who did not receive an award could not sue in equity to compel the Federal procurement agency to make the award to him. Until 1970, the General Accounting Office constituted the swiftest, most economical and only forum to decide pre-award cases. But presently, even though it remains quick (and sometimes inexpensive), it is no longer the only forum because of judicial and statutory actions.

(b) The Partial Change Beginning in 1970

Beginning in 1970 some Federal courts indicated a willingness to consider award protests. The change started with the case of Scanwell Laboratories, Inc. v. Shaffer. There, a low bid was submitted by Cutler Hammer, Inc., who received the award. Scanwell Laboratories, as second low bidder, alleged that the apparent low bid was nonresponsive, and sought to have the contract declared null and void under applicable procurement regulations and as a violation of section 10 of the Administrative Procedure Act (APA) of 1946. That section states that "a person suffering legal wrong because of agency action, or adversely affected or aggrieved by agency action within the meaning of a relevant statute, is entitled to judicial review thereof." The Court of Appeals ruled that explicit requirements of the bid had been waived by the agency, and the resulting allegation of arbitrary misconduct was sufficient to give the plaintiff standing to sue under the Administrative Procedure Act that makes the doctrine of sovereign immunity inapplicable. While an agency's administrator has the discretionary power to reject all bids if he deems such action to be in the public interest, he may not award a contract illegally under the guise of discretionary action.

Later in that same year, the Supreme Court did set forth new criteria for determining standing to sue under the Administrative Procedure Act (APA), which were not applied in the *Scanwell* decision. These criteria require a determination of (a) whether the plaintiff alleges that the challenged action has caused him injury in fact, economic or otherwise; (b) whether the interest sought to be protected by the complainant is arguably within the "zone of interests" to be protected or regulated by the statute or constitutional guarantee in question; and (c) whether judicial review is precluded by statute.

Other decisions have been rendered, subsequent to *Scanwell*, which limit its application to bid protests on other grounds. In Simpson Electric Company v. Seamans, the plaintiff brought an action to enjoin the award of a contract to another, and to compel the awarding of it to himself. Although the Federal district court agreed that the award that had been made to the other person was illegal and that the contract should have been awarded to the plaintiff, it refused injunctive relief. The court stated that "[m]andatory relief by way of injunction is not required to preserve the integrity of the bid process since a declaration of rights with the liability of damages that will flow therefrom will suffice."

(c) Federal Courts Improvement Act and "New" Courts

The Contract Disputes Act of 1978 did not authorize boards to resolve bid protests. However, in 1982 the Federal Courts Improvement Act created the U.S. Claims Court and gave it jurisdiction with the following language: "To afford complete relief on any contract claim brought before the contract is awarded, the court shall have exclusive jurisdiction to grant declaratory judgments and such equitable and extraordinary relief as it deems proper, including but not limited to injunctive relief." In 1983, the new Court of Appeals for the Federal Circuit (CAFC) interpreted the word "claim" so as to limit its authority to grant equitable relief to disappointed bidders only when a claim is made before contract is awarded.

In 1992 the Federal Courts Administration Act renamed the Claims Court the Court of Federal Claims. The Administrative Dispute Resolution Act of 1996 (ADRA) expanded the bid protest jurisdiction of the U.S. Court of Federal Claims (COFC) to include challenges "to a solicitation by a Federal agency for bids or proposals for a proposed contract or to a proposed award or the award of a contract or any alleged violation of statute or regulation in connection with a procurement or a proposed procurement." Both the U.S. Court of Appeals for the Federal Circuit and COFC broadly construed the COFC's bid protest jurisdiction under the ADRA. In 1999, the Federal Circuit held that the phrase "any alleged violation of statute or regulation in connection with a procurement or proposed procurement" was broad enough to encompass challenge to an agency's override of the automatic stay. The COFC subsequently held that it had jurisdiction to review an agency's refusal to suspend contract performance following an agency protest. The COFC has also held that it has jurisdiction to consider a challenge to an agency's procurement of services under an existing contract. However, the COFC has held that it does not have jurisdiction to consider the validity of the Randolph–Sheppard Vending Stand Act or Department of Defense implementing regulation because its ADRA jurisdiction is over actions challenging the government's compliance with procurement laws and regulations, not the validity of such laws and regulations. Those claims must be brought in the U.S. district courts.

Protests at the COFC are different from protests at GAO in three important respects. First, the COFC has adopted a somewhat broader test of "interested party" than the Competition in Contracting Act (CICA) definition applied by GAO. The GAO Bid Protest Regulations define "interested party" as "an actual or prospective bidder or offeror whose direct economic interest would be affected by the award of a contract or by the failure to award a contract." By contrast, the COFC has applied the more liberal Administrative Procedure Act test. However, the court has held that a contract awardee does not have an unconditional right to intervene in a lawsuit brought by an unsuccessful offeror challenging the award. This is because the applicable statute only gives the court jurisdiction over an "interested party" and "refers only to the party filing the action and making the challenge to the award." However, the United States Court of Appeals for the Federal Circuit ruled in favor of an unsuccessful bidder who filed a postaward bid protest over a contract for supplying centrifugal fuel oil purifiers to the Navy. The COFC held that the government's error in awarding Naval contract to another bidder whose proposal was technically noncompliant, due to failure to comply with particular vibration test requirement, was prejudicial to the unsuccessful bidder.

The COFC has applied more liberal timeliness rules than the GAO for post-award protests. Although the COFC, like the GAO, requires that protests challenging terms of the solicitation must be filed before bid opening or the time set for receipt of proposals, it has no express rules for post-award protests. However, as of October 2001 the COFC had not sustained a single one of the 26 postaward protests filed that year. The COFC has also applied a more deferential "arbitrary or capricious" standard of review.

(d) *Jurisdiction of United States District Courts*

As a result of the Administrative Dispute Resolution Act of 1996, the U.S. District Court lost their protest jurisdiction on January 1, 2001. As a result, the U.S. Court of Federal Claims is the sole judicial forum in which protests may be brought.

§ 33.7 Damages for Refusal to Properly Consider a Bid and Bid Preparation Costs

Limits on the government's discretion to refuse consideration of a bid were suggested in the decision of the Court of Claims in Heyer Products Co. v. United States, which indicated that the Federal government might be forced to accept the offer of the lowest responsible bidder or respond in damages where the discretion has been abused. In a case, following rejection of his low bid and acceptance of a higher bid, the low bidder brought suit alleging that the contracting officer had taken arbitrary action in bad faith. The court, in denying a motion by the government to dismiss the complaint on the ground that it did not state a cause of action, held that although the Armed Services Procurement Act of 1947 conferred no rights on an unsuccessful bidder, the government impliedly "agreed" that each bid invited would receive fair and impartial treatment. Damages would be awarded to cover preparation expenses incurred.

This decision could not logically be limited to cases of arbitrary action or bad faith on the part of a government official since the only basis for awarding damages would appear to be that the lowest responsible bidder has some right to a good-faith consideration of his bid. If so, it may be fair to ask whether the lowest responsive and responsible bidder can ever be rejected in good faith. If the government in good faith decides not to go ahead with a given project, it may reject all bids. However, where one bid is accepted and other lower bids are rejected on the grounds of lack of responsibility, the rejected bidders have a right to damages if they can show bad faith on the part of the government. The *Heyer* case introduced two ideas: first, that the court has jurisdiction on the basis of a sort of agreement of this kind implied in law; and second, that a government supplier has standing to contest an administrative award to another bidder. In similar manner, where a prime cost-type (management) contractor for the Department of Energy (DOE) arbitrarily determined that a potential subcontractor was not responsible, the subcontractor was held to be entitled to recover his proposal preparation costs.

Without either arbitrary action or bad faith on the part of the government agency, the canceling of a request for proposals (RFP) is a discretionary act and an offeror is not entitled to any preparation costs.

The Claims Court has held that a recommendation by the GAO that a protestor be awarded bid preparation costs is not binding on that court, stating that the GAO relied on protest decisions "which have no force of law in this circuit."

To prevail in a preaward case, a plaintiff has to show either that there was no rational basis for the agency's decision in a matter committed primarily to its discretion, or the procurement procedure involved a clear and prejudicial violation of applicable statutes or regulations. A claimant must pursue a bid protest decision or else the General Accounting Office will not consider a claim for proposal preparation costs.

Protest costs were not limited to costs that would be allowable under contract cost principles of government contracts. Further, there was no ceiling on allowable protest costs based on the dollar value of the underlying procurement, and there was no correlation between the dollar value of a contract and the complexity or importance of issues involved.

The Claims Court rendered a very questionable decision by granting a permanent injunction against an agency on the grounds that the bidder would be irreparably injured by an award to another and there was no adequate remedy at law, because a suit for damages would result only in recovery of bid preparation costs. In the making of public contracts, recovery of the cost of bid preparation has been held to be an adequate remedy at law. Yet, the Claims Court appeared to be equating (rather than balancing) remedies for breach of contract with those involved in the making of contracts.

B. DISPUTES AND APPEALS

§ 33.21   In General

Often criticized, disputed, and litigated, government contracts generally ought to be well-drafted, with input from both industrialists and lawyers drafting and redrafting them for more than a half century. Also, such contracts frequently serve as models for private contracts. Unlike a private contract (where the parties may be somewhat more reluctant to sue because such action could result in the possible loss of future business between them), the government contractor knows the government has a continuing need for products, supplies, and services and except in rare instances the government would not refuse to do business even though suits may have been brought in the past. The rise in the government's demand for information on a bidder (or offeror) with regard to his past performance has resulted in some reduction in lawsuits.

An entity that is a nonappropriated fund instrumentality (NAFI) in general is outside the scope of the Contract Disputes Act CDA.

§ 33.22 Law Controlling the Validity and Interpretation of Government Contracts

Most private contracts are controlled by the law of the state in which they were made or are to be performed, in accordance with conflict of laws principles. This is true whether suits concerning these contracts are adjudicated in state or Federal courts. There is a major difference between private and government contracts because, with few exceptions, the latter are governed by Federal law regardless of the place of execution or the place of performance. On August 18, 1821, President Thomas Jefferson wrote to Charles Hammond stating:

> The federal judiciary is ... working like gravity by night and by day, gaining a little today and a little tomorrow, and advancing its noiseless step like a thief over the field of jurisdiction until all shall be usurped from the states, and the government of all be consolidated into one (i.e. federalization) (Emphasis Added).

It is important to know what law governs a contract. The absence of Federal statutes leaves a choice between the Federal common law and state common law or statutes. In the famous case of Erie R. Co. v. Tompkins, Justice Brandeis for the Supreme Court interpreted the word "laws", appearing in section 34 of the Judiciary Act of 1789, to include state decisions on matters other than those encompassing statutory interpretation. As a result, the Federal common law, in the commercial area, was dealt a severe blow, but it was far from a deathblow. On the contrary, whenever the Federal government is directly involved in a commercial transaction, Federal law will apply. The Federal government is one of delegated powers. Where there has been an express delegation in the Constitution, Federal law should govern in place of state law, unless the Congress expressly made state law applicable to a given set of circumstances.

Where the "Federal interest" is very direct, the law is clear. Five years after the Erie case, the Supreme Court decided the case of Clearfield Trust Co. v. United States, which involved the law governing the right of the United States to recover the amount of a check drawn on the Treasurer of the United States and paid by him when presented, with a forged endorsement. Justice Douglas, for the majority of the Supreme Court, stated, "the rule of Erie R. Co. v. Tompkins ... does not apply to this action. The rights and duties of the United States on commercial paper that it issues are governed by Federal rather than local law. In absence of an applicable Act of Congress it is for the Federal courts to fashion the governing rule of law according to their own standards."

Later cases have virtually extended the rule from the "paper it issues" to the contracts it makes and have led to the generally accepted view that prime government contracts are to be interpreted according to the "general law of contracts" without limitation by the law of any particular state.

A circuit court of appeals declared: "We assume that, in accordance with frequent pronouncements by the Supreme Court and by this Court, the prime contract, being a contract with the government, is governed by Federal law'' and the Federal common law is very much alive whenever the Federal government directly contracts because, as previously noted, of the fact the Federal government is one of delegated powers. This Federal common law is the ''general law of contracts'' throughout the United States, as distinguished from that in any one state or in a few states. Thus many portions of Article 2 of the Uniform Commercial Code, which includes trade usage, may be a source of Federal common law for contracts for the sale of goods because it is essentially the law in forty-nine states. However, the UCC approach within a state has sometimes been changed by statute, regulation, or contract. Where the change is by a Federal court alone, this may become more troublesome.

The former Court of Claims had stated that the Federal contract law ''should take into account the best in modern decision and discussion.'' However, the use of the term ''best'' is not the test used by the Supreme Court. Further, it is not only of no guidance, but it is often a mere substitute for the phrase ''in the judge's bias.'' Different relief has been granted under Federal government contracts by Federal courts than has been granted under private or commercial contracts by the majority of state courts (which follow the general law of contracts) under similar or analogous circumstances. Some of these differences were due to a prescribed contract clause, a statute or regulation, or minimum Federal interest so that the law of a specific state may be incorporated into the Federal law. The former Court of Claims and its successor courts tend to *cite themselves* more often than other courts which would be more representative of the general law of contracts in the United States. This tendency is analogous to the fact that some Federal courts of appeals in diversity cases have preferred citing their own previous diversity decisions rather than state court decisions, even though the latter are more authoritative.

In 1991, the U.S. Supreme Court held that Federal courts of appeals must give de novo review to district court determinations of state law. A district court had applied the substantial performance doctrine to a student's diversity-based contract action against a Rhode Island college, even though that doctrine had only been applied to construction contracts by the Rhode Island Supreme Court. The First Circuit Court of Appeals affirmed, citing "the customary appellate deference accorded to interpretations of state law made by *Federal judges* of that state." However, the Supreme Court reversed and required "independent" appellate review of such legal issues. The court noted that this would support the goal of Erie R. Co. v. Tompkins to discourage forum shopping.

By using the general law applicable to most states, more certainty and uniformity would exist in the general law of Federal contracts. In this connection, the courts cannot always assume that the Restatement (Second) of Contracts represents the general law. The American Law Institute (ALI) became reoriented toward a more "legislative" approach with the initiation of the Second Restatement. A statutory or regulatory change could achieve a standard that would actually be applied by Federal tribunals in order to aid in the quest for more uniformity and certainty by those who are dealing with both governments. Such change would also tend to reconcile the divergence of the law applicable to subcontracts under prime contracts with the Federal government in instances where the law of a particular state would not apply because of the partial absence of a Federal interest.

We have now reached a special point in history with respect to government contracts that arrived ago in *Erie v. Tompkins*, wherein the Federal common law concerning commercial contracts was abolished. During this period, such a common law has arisen again; Federal courts are now acting in nondiversity cases as they did during the century preceding *Erie* (1938), when they developed a Federal common law utilizing any approach that pleased them, which resulted in significant divergences from state law. Requiring these courts to follow the law of the state in which they sit was a great advance and eliminated almost a century's accumulation of contrary caselaw. A similar advance in nondiversity cases involving government contracts has become a vital and complex force affecting our economy during the last half-century. It would appear that (except in very rare instances) there is little justification for refusing to follow the "general law of contracts" and thus applying different legal principles to contracts with the Federal government.

Subcontractor disputes and the choice of law governing subcontractors are discussed below in connection with subcontracts.

§ 33.23   Contract Claims

In government contracts, post-award remedies are sought by making a written demand or assertion called a "claim." The Contract Disputes Act (CDA) of 1978 does not define the terms "dispute" or "claim;" however, the term "claim" is defined in the regulation. Requests for relief seeking extraordinary emergency authority to facilitate the National Defense (under Public Law No. 85–804) are not claims within the Contract Disputes Act of 1978 or the Disputes clause. A board of contract appeals has held that the claim of a contractor, to expenses incurred to have its product placed on the Qualified Products List in order to be able to bid on a contract, was a valid claim under the Contact Disputes Act. This, the board said, was because the relief sought clearly "relates" to the contract the contractor later bid for and won. A board ruled that a contracting officer's letter seeking repayment of almost $1.2 million allegedly overpaid for improper dredging was a government claim from which the contractor properly appealed.

A contracting officer's demand for liquidated damages was held to be a government claim even though the demand did not state that it was the contracting officer's final decision. However, a contracting officer's "final decision" that concluded with an offer to discuss the matter further was not truly final, and therefore did not start the running of the 90–day appeal period.

The date of its submission by a contractor is important because if it proves to be valid, that is the date from which the government must pay interest. Where a claim exceeds $100,000, it must be accompanied by a certification that it was made in good faith, by supporting data that are accurate and complete to the best of the contractor's knowledge and belief, and by an amount requested that accurately reflects the contract adjustment for which the contractor believes the government is liable.

For many years, the definition of a claim was a source of considerable litigation as a result of the Federal Circuit Court's decision in Dawco Construction, Inc. v. United States, where the Court stated that a contractor's demand for money is not a claim under the CDA unless the parties are in dispute over entitlement and the amount requested at the time the demand is made. This was interpreted by one Claims Court judge to mean that a claim only existed "when the parties clearly have abandoned negotiations." By contrast, the Armed Services Board of Contract Appeals (the ASBCA) has stated that "[t]he 'impasse' and 'abandon[ment of] negotiations' tests for the existence of a 'dispute' can lead to perverse results, inconsistent with" the Contract Dispute Act's (CDA) purpose of seeking resolution of contract disputes by negotiations before instituting litigation. Indeed, "[i]nsistence on both parties having abandoned negotiations for a claim or dispute to exist can encourage one of the parties to drag out negotiations indefinitely."

In Reflectone Inc. v. Dalton, the Court of Appeals for the Federal Circuit noted that there was no independent statutory requirement that a matter "in dispute" be a proper claim. The court determined that the existing FAR definition of a claim did not require that a matter, not a routine request for payment, be in dispute. In the year 2000, it ruled that a contractor's termination settlement proposal does not ripen into a claim until the parties have reached an "impasse" creating a dispute. However, there need not be a pre-existing dispute for the contracting officer to render a final decision on a claim arising under a termination for convenience.

The submission of a termination settlement claim with the added statement that it would be altered as the claimant acquired additional documents was held not a demand for a sum certain. Citing its *Reflectone* decision, the U.S. Court of Appeals for the Federal Circuit overturned a U.S. Court of Federal Claims' dismissal for lack of jurisdiction of a contractor's lawsuit seeking additional compensation arising from a termination for convenience. A contractor's "final invoice" for costs allegedly incurred before its convenience termination was held not to be a claim.

Not infrequently, a contractor may seek to amend its claim to incorporate new factual allegations. However, where such an amendment contradicts the facts set forth in its original claim, it constitutes a new claim that must first be submitted to the contracting officer before it can be appealed.

Where a contractor has previously amended his complaint, he may not again amend it in order to assert another theory of recovery (and to substantially increase the amount claimed) unless it is established that the increased amount is based on further information not reasonably available when the original claim was filed.

On October 13, 1994, President Clinton signed into law the Federal Acquisition Streamlining Act (FASA) which, inter alia, created a new six-year statute of limitations on the submission of CDA claims by contractors and the government. As to contracts awarded after October 1, 1995, a claim must be submitted to the contracting officer within six years after it accrued unless the parties have agreed to a shorter time.

Similarly, absent such an agreement, the contracting officer must issue a written decision on any government claim initiated against a contractor within six years after accrual of that claim.

§ 33.26   Settlement Authority

(a) In General

With few exceptions, the contracting officer is authorized to either decide or settle all claims arising under or relating to a contract subject to the Contracts Disputes Act. However, the contracting officer's authority does not extend to "the settlement, compromise, payment, or adjustment of any claim involving fraud."

The government was not bound by a settlement agreement entered into by a government's attorney, who did not first obtain the contracting officer's approval; an appeal by a contractor was reinstated when the contracting officer objected to the settlement.

In one case, a contractor and the government attorney notified a board by telephone that they had settled. The board then dismissed the appeal with prejudice subject to reinstatement if the settlement was not effectuated. As a government employee, the attorney was without authority to bind the government. Later, the contracting officer received an additional estimate substantially reducing government liability and refused to approve the settlement. This refusal was upheld.

A client might be counseled to "agree, for the law is costly." In some cases he might also consider existing Federal procedural rules which make it easier for judges to impose fines on lawyers pursuing frivolous suits. A statute affects proceedings brought "unreasonably or vexatiously." The U.S. Court of Appeals for the Seventh Circuit ruled that Federal courts might award attorneys' fees as a sanction against a plaintiff that files a frivolous lawsuit, even after the case is voluntarily dismissed.

The possibility of settlement should be considered in government contract claims and disputes as in other types of dispute. This is because it is the government's policy "to try to resolve all contractual issues by mutual agreement at the contracting officer's level."

The offer of judgment provisions of Federal Rule of Civil Procedure 68 shift to the party who rejects a settlement offer, the costs incurred after the making of the offer if the judgment finally obtained by the offeree is not more favorable than the offer. This can be an inducement to settle because this rule does not apply to cases that end in settlement instead of entry of judgment. The Supreme Court has approved simultaneous negotiation of liability on the merits and liability for attorneys' fees.

Where court approval is required, it has been stated that "[o]nce a claim—whatever its jurisdictional basis—is initiated in the Federal courts, we believe that the standards by which that litigation may be settled ... are preeminently a matter for resolution by Federal common law principles, independently derived." The government is not bound by a settlement agreement reached by counsel for the parties that was not ratified by the contracting officer. In the United States, the rule that "costs shall be allowed as of course to the prevailing party," helps to encourage the making and acceptance of settlement offers.

(e) The Settlement Contract and Its Enforcement

Settlement agreements are contracts that must meet certainty requirements in order to be enforceable. The settlement should be in writing, if it is within the state's statute of frauds. This may well be the case with most subcontracts at various tiers as discussed below. Federal Courts have inherent power to enforce settlement agreements where Federal jurisdiction exists over the case or controversy (and in the case of a prime contract, which is controlled by Federal law).

Settlement contracts involve the execution of a release that may set forth a list of claims reserved. The former Claims Court held that it has jurisdiction over construction contract claims reserved by an executed release. The Claims Court ruled that a contractor "may properly increase the value of its claims notwithstanding how it valued them at the execution of the release. If it should appear at a later date that [the contractor] has presented a 'new' claim, as opposed to 'clarifying' the claims it reserved, that claim will be dismissed with prejudice and with costs to the [government]." A Federal district court has held that a settlement agreement requiring a party to withdraw a motion for sanctions against the opposing party does not deprive a Federal district court of authority to impose sanctions pursuant to Fed.R.Civ.P., Rule 11 against an opposing party's lawyer for filing a frivolous claim.

The settlement agreement is also subject to judicial review where it would violate laws requiring competitive bidding. In one case a settlement agreement was executed by the Justice Department under the attorney general's litigation authority and discretion. Nevertheless, the court stated that the attorney general's authority to settle litigation "stops at the walls of illegality."

§ 33.27   Contracting Officer's Conference, Decision, and ADR

(a) In General

The Contract Disputes Act states that "all claims by a contractor against the government relating to a contract shall be ... submitted to the contracting officer for a decision." The Act contemplates the fact that government contractors will submit their claims in writing to contracting officers (COs) of the agencies with whom they are contracting, who will then decide their claims.

Normally, a contractor is afforded an opportunity for an informal conference with the agency involved. The purpose of such a conference is to consider the possibility of disposing of the claim by mutual agreement, or by use of Alternative Dispute Resolution (ADR). This conference (which often precedes ADR) may be held within a period of about thirty days of the request for such conference, or later by mutual agreement between the contractor and the agency. Such a conference will also enable the agency to detect differences at an early point and to correct decisions that may not be in accord with procurement regulations.

Under the Contract Disputes Act (CDA), the contracting officer must, if so requested in writing, issue a decision for claims of $100,000 or less within sixty days of receiving the request from the contractor that a decision be rendered within that period (or within a reasonable time after receipt of the claim, if the contractor does not make such a request). For contractor certified claims over $100,000, the decision must be rendered within sixty days or the contracting officer must notify the contractor within that period of the time within which a decision will be issued. By statute, the contracting officer lacks authority to render a final decision on a claim for money damages that is already the subject of pending litigation.

The standard Disputes clause obliges the contractor to continue performance pending final resolution of any claims arising under the contract. Agency procedures may determine that a provision is necessary so that the contractor remains obligated to continue performance pending final resolution of any claims arising under a provision related to the contract and comply with any decision of the contracting officer.

(b) Interest on Claims

Interest on amounts found due contractors is payable from the date the contracting officer receives the claim. This was a major change in the law because in the absence of constitutional or statutory provisions, interest does not run on a claim against the United States unless the contract so provides. Interest is paid at the rate established by the Secretary of the Treasury.

Interest can also accrue on claimed costs that had not yet been incurred. The timing of the due date of interest on a judgment awarding attorneys' fees has split among a number of Federal circuit courts between the date of a judgment which either (a) quantifies the fee award or (b) unconditionally entitles the prevailing party fees.

(c) Alternative Dispute Resolution (ADR)

Beginning in the mid 1980's, the Corps of Engineers and other agencies started expanding the Contract Officers' Conference into what they call a "mini-trial." It is not a trial, but rather an exchange of information following a denial of a claim by the contracting officer. In one case, the contractor was given approximately three and one-half hours to make his case-in-chief; the government then had ninety minutes for cross-examination of witnesses, followed by ninety minutes for redirect questioning, and a one-hour roundtable question-and-answer session. An impartial lawyer then summarized what he thought were the strengths and weaknesses of each party. The following day, settlement negotiations commenced and were completed within twelve hours. In two days, the parties accomplished what might have taken weeks of hearings before a board of contract appeals and months of waiting for a decision. Principal differences from the Contracting Officer's Conference appear to be that in the so-called "mini-trial," the contractor may believe he knows what the decision will be from the material he has presented the government, and hence he may have an incentive to reveal more information, and perhaps there is the unknown factor of the influence of the third party's summary.

The Administrative Dispute Resolution Act (ADRA) was signed into law by the President on November 15, 1990. Thereafter, each agency was required to adopt a policy on the use of Alternative Dispute Resolution (ADR) in connection with formal and informal adjudications, rulemakings, enforcement actions, licensing proceedings, contract administration, litigation, and must designate a senior official as "dispute resolutions specialist."

On May 1, 1998, the President established an Interagency Alternative Dispute Resolution Working Group as "part of an effort to make the Federal Government operate in a more efficient and effective manner, and to encourage, where possible, consensual resolution of disputes and issues and controversies involving the United States, including the prevention and avoidance of disputes."

After the turn of the millennium, a person with experience with these changes indicated that his reservations with regard to the ADR movement "is the public's diminished access to and scrutiny of settlements." He also found this particularly troubling given the number of experienced agency counsel that express their belief that their agencies today willingly pay out larger settlements to comply with the "spirit" of their agency's ADR initiatives and mandates.

§ 33.28   Appeals to Boards of Contract Appeal

(a) In General

Many consider that "[j]ustice is what we get when the decision is in our favor;" when not in our favor, an appellate process may be needed. The Contract Disputes Act of 1978 established a statutory basis for boards of contract appeals within an agency. The existing boards were retained. Agencies must consult with the Administrator for Federal Procurement Policy, and the agency may then make a determination from a workload study that the volume of contract claims justifies establishment of a full-time agency board. The agency may determine that its procurement claims are insufficient to justify a board; it may arrange for appeals to be decided by a board of another agency or submit its cases to the Administrator for such placement.

Because the members of the Armed Services Board of Contract Appeals (ASBCA) and other such boards are appointed and can be removed by the agencies that are parties to contract disputes on which the boards issue decisions, questions arose concerning their independence. In 1985, the GAO completed a study that concluded that the Armed Services Board of Contract Appeals was operating independently, even though its members were not completely insulated from all agency pressures. The Board's decisions are generally made by a majority vote from the opinions of five members, called Administrative Judges (AJs). New members must have a minimum of five years of public contract law experience prior to voting. The chairperson and two vice-chairpersons are chosen from among Board members to serve for a two-year term, unless removed sooner or reappointed for an additional term. The chairperson has delegated authority to assign disputes to the recorder, who assigns disputes among the divisions based on caseload. Unlike Federal judges, the chairperson conducts Board members' annual appraisals using standards similar to those established for the Senior Executive Service. However, these appraisals are not reviewed by DoD officials.

Any appeal from the contracting officer's decision to a board of contract appeals must be made within ninety days from its receipt. Any indication of dissatisfaction with the contracting officer's decision and an intention to appeal suffices; a letter to a government attorney which failed to even mention the issue in the contracting officer's decision over which the board had jurisdiction has been held to constitute adequate notice of appeal. A failure of the contracting officer to issue a decision within the required time periods will be deemed a decision denying the claim and will authorize the contractor to file an appeal or bring a suit on the claim. A contractor may hesitate to do so because the tribunal concerned is specifically authorized, at its option, to stay proceedings in order to obtain a decision on the claim by the contracting officer. An amount which is determined payable under the decision will normally be paid without awaiting contractor action concerning appeal, and such payment is without prejudice to the rights of either party. A letter from the contracting officer stating the agency's entitlement to liquidated damages and demanding their payment was ruled as a final decision from which the contractor could take an appeal to a board. A contracting officer may reconsider a decision even after an appeal has been taken and a board may assume jurisdiction over a timely appeal of the second decision. The appeal must be made by one who is a contractor; but if a novation has been executed, he may no longer be one. However, one board has held that a contractor may file an appeal after making an assignment.

Federal agencies are authorized to require a contractor to "proceed diligently with performance of the contract in accordance with the contracting officer's decision" pending final decision on appeal for final settlement. However, the prescribed clause limits the duty of the contractor to proceed with performance pending final restitution of any request for relief "*arising under* the contract." If a claim is for something not arising under some contract clause, an argument might be made that the contractor need not continue performance. Before passage of the Contract Disputes Act in 1978, the obligation to continue performance applied only to claims "arising under" a contract. The regulation suggests that if it is determined under agency procedures that continued performance is necessary "pending resolution of any claim *arising under or relating to* the contract," the clause should so state. However, it would appear to be difficult, if not impossible, to make this determination before the fact. Nevertheless, agency procedures now permit use of alternative language in contracts where it can be determined in advance that the "relating to" language will be needed; and in such a case the contractor would not be able to stop work for claim he might make.

To be covered by the Contract Disputes Act, a contract must exist. The Court of Appeals for the Federal Circuit has held that a board may not permit an agency to ratify a contract where the agency had no authority to make the contract in the first place; that is, when the contract is void. Boards of Contract Appeals lacked jurisdiction over a labor dispute under a contract's clause inasmuch as labor standards provisions deemed incorporated by operation of law into the contract vested exclusive jurisdiction over such disputes in the Secretary of Labor.

Boards consider cases de novo and are not bound by factual or legal findings made by contracting officers, provided that the facts and legal theories have been presented to the contracting officer for his decision. Boards may also decrease amounts awarded by the contracting officer.

Unlike other parts of an executive agency, boards of contract appeal may effectively inform the agency that their current or past actions are wrong and funds must be expended in order to correct them. Conceivably, the agency head could retaliate by reducing the funds budgeted for its board. Boards can issue subpoenas, but the Justice Department is needed to enforce them because boards are not in the judicial branch of the government. Since 1992, submission of defective certifications by contractors no longer deprives boards of contract appeals of jurisdiction to consider a claim. Certification defects need only be corrected by the contractor prior to entry of final judgment, provided the claim is not completely uncertified.

(b) The Disputes Clause and Contests Before Boards of Contract Appeals

The Contract Disputes Act of 1978 provides a comprehensive statutory system of legal and administrative remedies to resolve government contract claims. This statute codified much of the existing framework for resolution of contract disputes and provides alternate forums to handle the different types of disputes. The Act also provides for the payment of interest on contractor claims. It does not apply to any contract with a foreign government or agency of that government, or to an international organization, if the agency head determines that the application of the Act to the contract would not be in the public's interest. The Act applies to all other contracts with the executive branch of the government.

(c) Boards of Contract Appeal and Arbitration Distinguished

Proceedings before Boards of Contract Appeal may be compared with arbitration, but they are really quite different—they are much closer to bench trials in courts—i.e., courts without a jury. Thus, unlike the boards, with an arbitration there are no public records for use by the media or competitors. The parties can select their arbitrators. Normally, discovery in arbitration proceedings is severely limited. In California, discovery may be expanded by incorporating a provision of the Code of Civil Procedure into the arbitration agreement. Even when this is done, the taking of depositions is limited to perpetuation or preservation of testimony unless leave is granted by the arbitrator(s) to take depositions for discovery purposes. It has been held that the authority of Federal courts to issue subpoenas for use in proceeding in foreign or international tribunal does not apply to private commercial arbitration proceedings. Generally, an award will not be vacated even if an arbitrator misapplies legal principles unless a legal issue is submitted to the arbitrator and the error appears on the face of the award showing that he exceeded his powers. The award is usually not appealable. Some states authorize arbitration of public contracts. It has been held that a party may be bound by an arbitration clause which has never been read or discussed by the parties, in the absence of a defense of fraud or unconscionability. However, in 2003, the U.S. Court of Appeals for the Fifth Circuit held that a court, and not an arbitrator, must decide to challenge to the "very existence" of an underlying contract with an arbitration clause.

Where a provision in a subcontract between Ford and the Lawrence Livermore National Laboratory required Ford to arbitrate its claims against the Laboratory with American Arbitration Association and provided that the California Superior Court would be the exclusive forum for the confirmation, enforcement, vacation or correction of an award, a board of contract appeals had no jurisdiction to consider the subcontractor's appeal. The Energy Board of Contract Appeals stated, "The Board is not authorized by the Contract Disputes Act (CDA) or otherwise to hear an appeal from an arbitration award."

(d) Adjudication of "All Disputes" Following Final Decisions of Contracting Officer

The Contract Disputes Act of 1978 provided that agency boards have jurisdiction to decide any appeal from a decision of a contracting officer "relative to a contract" and that, in exercising such jurisdiction, the agency's board is authorized to "grant any relief that would be available to a litigant asserting a contract claim in the United States Court of Claims." Previously this obligation only applied to claims arising "under the contract." However, agencies may determine that continued performance is necessary pending resolution of a claim "relating" to it, such as breach of contract. Sanctions for failure to perform may include suspension and disbarment as well as damages.

(e) Accelerated Procedures for Claims Under $100,000

The Contract Disputes Act of 1978 requires each board to provide a procedure for accelerated disposition of any appeal from a decision by a contracting officer where the amount of the claim is $100,000 or less. However, a contractor's election to appeal that is processed under a board's accelerated procedure may be rejected where the total amount in dispute exceeds $100,000, even though each of his claims individually is under that amount. But, this procedure is only applicable if a contractor so elects, in which case the appeal must be resolved within 180 days from the date of such election "whenever possible." It is difficult to ascertain why a contractor with a claim for $100,000 or less would not normally elect to obtain its resolution within a six-month period. A contractor's request for the accelerated procedures has been viewed as an election to seek board review under the Contract Disputes Act. Where a contractor elects the preferential treatment of an accelerated appeal and later increases his claim to over $100,000, the appeal has not been entitled to be accelerated.

(f) Direct Appeals by Subcontractors

A lack of jurisdiction by a board of contract appeals over an appeal brought directly by a subcontractor under the Contract Disputes Act appeared clear from a 1983 decision

of the United States Court of Appeals for the Federal
Circuit. A board of contract appeals continued its attempts
to break down the wall of privity. It cited a 1949 decision of
the former Court of Claims, indicating that a finding of
privity between the subcontractor and the government was
not justified when certain factors were present, such as the
subcontract terms were subject to the contracting officer's
approval, and his written approval was required before the
subcontractor could begin performance, and the prime contract's terms and conditions were applicable to the subcontract. The Court of Appeals reversed the board's decision,
concluding that a subcontractor is not a "contractor" within the meaning of the Disputes Act of 1978, and there was
no contractual language providing that the government
would be directly liable to a subcontractor for goods or
services supplied to the prime. However, other boards of
contract appeal continued to entertain jurisdiction over
subcontract disputes. A board held that where a prime
contract included the duties of evaluating subcontractors'
claims, advising the government on the weaknesses and
aspects of the subcontractor's claims, and receiving the
government's approval before the subcontract could take
effect, the subcontractor had a contractual relationship
with the government for purposes of filing its own appeal
under the Contract Disputes Act. There was no clause in
both the prime and subcontract that specifically disclaimed
any direct contractual relationship between the government
and the subcontractor. Such a clause is sometimes called an
"ABC clause." The one in United States v. Johnson Controls, Inc. read as follows:

> Throughout the contract documents ... reference is
> made to (a) the government, Owner and/or Contracting
> Officer who for this project is the Department of Health
> Education and Welfare, (b) the Construction manager,

Turner, and/or Contractor, and (c) the Subcontractor, Bid Package Contractor, and/or Contractor.

A contractual relationship shall exist only between the parties of (a) and (b) and between the parties of (b) and (c). It is not intended to develop a relationship either contractually, administratively, operationally, or in any other manner between the parties of (a) and (c). However, it is the intent of the Construction Manager (b) without establishing a contractual relationship between (a) and (c) to pass on to the Subcontractor (c) as a tier contractor, the responsibilities the Construction Manager has assumed as defined within the Contract Documents unless specifically noted otherwise and toward this end the dual usage of Contractor is intended and shall be understood.

The court referred to this clause as "an important, if not determinative, factor in our analysis of the intent of the parties as seen through the contract documents. The 'ABC' clause unequivocally states that no contractual relationship shall exist between the government and the subcontractors."

A desire on the part of some boards to enhance their jurisdiction so as to include subcontract disputes may be avoided by including as standard language a provision disclaiming any direct contractual relationship between the government and a subcontractor, and requiring its inclusion in all subcontracts awarded by the prime contractor.

The case discussed above should be distinguished from those very limited types of prime contracts whose subcontracts formerly contained a "flow down" type of Disputes clause, approved by the government, granting the subcontractor direct access to a board. Indirect appeals by subcontractors, through their primes are covered in Chapter 44, infra. In Department of the Army v. Blue Fox, Inc., the

Supreme Court unanimously held that the Administrative Procedure Act does not waive sovereign immunity to permit an unpaid subcontractor to bring an action against the United States.

§ 33.29 Appeals to the Court of Federal Claims (COFC)

(a) In General—Evolution of the Court

The former Court of Claims was established in 1855. Until 1972, its jurisdiction was limited to money claims against the United States. The court was created as a "Court for the Investigation of Claims against the United States" to review claims and submit recommendations to Congress. In 1866, the Congress authorized suit against the government for money damages appealable to the United States Supreme Court. In 1887, the Tucker Act was passed, greatly expanding the jurisdiction of the court and authorizing the former Court of Claims, as well as United States district courts, to decide claims based on "express or implied contracts with the United States, or for liquidated damages in cases not sounding in tort." In this respect, the district courts' jurisdiction was concurrent with the Court of Claims except that the district courts were limited to claims not exceeding $10,000. Also, the Court of Claims had no equitable jurisdiction. In 1933, the United States Supreme Court ruled that the Court of Claims was a "legislative" court without a jury established under Article I, § 8 of the Constitution from Congressional power "to pay debts ... of the United States." But twenty years later, an act of Congress provided that it was "a court established under Article III of the Constitution of the United States." In 1972, the court was authorized to reinstate persons in office and correct employment records, as an incident to a money judgment.

In 1992, the name of the Claims Court was changed to the Court of Federal Claims (COFC) and its jurisdiction was extended to disputes "concerning termination of a contract, rights in tangible or intangible property, compliance with cost accounting standards, and other nonmonetary disputes on which a decision of the contracting officer has been issued under [the Contract Disputes Act]." This amendment effectively overturned a ruling that held that the court lacked jurisdiction to consider the propriety of the government's termination for default absent a specific claim for monetary relief. It did not change the requirement of the Contract Disputes Act that a final decision be made by the Contracting Officer. The Congress also made certification under the CDA nonjurisdictional.

In 1995, the U.S. Court of Appeals for the Federal Circuit sitting in banc ruled that except for demands like a voucher, invoice, or other "routine request for payment," the "plain meaning" of the definition of a "claim" under the Contract Disputes Act does not require that a payment demand be in dispute before being submitted to the contracting officer for decision. Past conflicting decisions were overruled. However, in 1998, the U.S. Court of Federal Claims (COFC) specifically rejected jurisdiction over a contractor's attachment to a Contract Disputes Act Claim of an Administrative Procedure Act (APA) claim for money damages stemming from an agency's failure to extend an 8(a) contract, because the APA does not provide for jurisdiction in the COFC over money claims. Later, the U.S. Court of Appeals for the Federal Circuit held that the APA does not waive sovereign immunity for a money claim presented as a claim for specific relief in a United States District Court.

Although a contractor has a choice of direct access appeal to the agency board of contract appeals or filing suit directly in the Court of Federal Claims (COFC), this choice (election) is binding. The COFC may lack jurisdiction to hear government set-offs asserted as counterclaims to contractor claims, under certain circumstances. Where the contracting officers of two agencies have concurrent, partial authority over an order under a Multiple Award Schedule (MAS) contract, a claim submitted to the ordering office's starts the 60 day statutory period for issuing a final decision.

As defendant in the Court of Federal Claims, the United States waived its sovereign immunity to an award of monetary sanctions for non-compliance with the court's orders. Further, a panel of the U.S. Court of Appeals for the Federal Circuit has held that the Claims Court lacked jurisdiction over the government's counterclaim for unliquidated progress payments. This was because the government's claim for the progress payments was not the subject of a contracting officer's final decision. The court stated, "I do not believe that a contracting officer can be divested of authority to issue a final decision on a government claim by the filing of a jurisdictionally defective suit on a separate contractor claim."

Although the U.S. Court of Federal Claims considers cases de novo, it is perfectly proper for it to use a contracting officer's decision as evidence for certain purposes. In one case an appellate court stated that a contracting officer's decision that established 260 days of delay, was favorable to the contractor and therefore constituted a strong evidentiary admission, subject to rebuttal, of the government's liability. A divided U.S. Court of Appeals for the Federal Circuit ruled that the former Claims Court failed to conduct a proper de novo review of a contracting officer's decision by treating the contracting officer's final decision on a contractor's delay claim as giving rise to a strong presumption, subject to rebuttal, of the extent of the government's liability. The majority opinion stated "De novo review precludes reliance upon the presumed correctness of the decision."

Judgments against the United States by the Court of Federal Claims are authorized to be paid and charged to a permanent judgment appropriation. The agency must then reimburse the permanent judgment appropriation "out of available funds" or by "obtaining an additional appropriation." But an Antideficiency Act violation does not occur when an agency has insufficient current appropriations to satisfy the award or judgment rendered against it pursuant to the Contract Disputes Act, because it does not involve a deficiency created by an administrative office.

In order to emphasize that it was not making any substantive attempt at a fresh start, the court ordered that "All published decisions of the [former] United States Court of Claims are accepted as binding precedent for the United States Claims Court, unless and until modified by decisions of the United States Court of Appeals for the Federal Circuit or the United States Supreme Court." Thus, the opportunity to encourage a new look at the law of government contracts was immediately squashed.

(b) Right of Direct Appeal to Court of Federal Claims

Under the Contract Disputes Act (CDA) of 1978, contractors can in effect "forum shop" by appealing a contracting officer's final decision to either the Court of Federal Claims or the board of contract appeals, but once a contractor first files a notice of appeal with the board of contract appeals, he loses his right of direct appeal to the Court of Federal Claims. A contractor has one year to file suit in the Court of Federal Claims which period does not begin running until a contractor has received the contracting officer's final decision. For example, the court has held that a default termination notice labeled as a final decision commences the 12–month period a contractor has in which to file suit challenging the termination. Although a contracting officer's decision may be final on one claim, that has been ruled not to preclude the contractor from asserting other claims arising out of the same circumstances.

Although the statute of limitations in the Court of Federal Claims for claims under the Tucker Act is six years from the time the claim arose, an appeal from an adverse decision by the contracting officer and commencement of the de novo proceeding must be within one year from the date of the contractor's receipt of that decision. This one-year limitation has also been held to apply to a claim deemed to have been denied due to a contracting officer's failure to issue a final decision in the same manner as if an express decision had been made.

The counterclaim jurisdiction of the Court of Federal Claims requires, as prerequisite, existence of a claim filed against the United States within Court's jurisdiction, and a dismissal of the complaint for lack of jurisdiction carries with it dismissal of any counterclaim filed in the matter by the United States. However, where the contractor filed a complaint setting forth a contract claim within jurisdiction of the former Claims Court, the fact that that court concluded a contractor's claim was not meritorious did not deprive that court of jurisdiction to hear a counterclaim filed by the United States.

§ 33.30 Court of Appeals for the Federal Circuit (CAFC)

In 1981, there were twelve Circuit Courts of Appeal. The Federal Courts Improvement Act (FCIA) of 1982 created a thirteenth court as of October 1, 1982, called the Court of Appeals for the Federal Circuit (CAFC) under Article III of the United States Constitution. This court is more specialized than the other twelve circuit courts.

The judges of the CAFC are circuit judges and are governed by the same tenure, residence, and salary provisions. The great difficulty in removing Federal judges could tend to promote some mediocrity. Unlike other appellate courts, it is authorized to sit en banc, or in panels of more than three judges. The opinion of a panel is binding and may be overruled only by the court acting en banc.

The Act requires the establishment of a rotation system for random assignment of cases to panels of judges in order to avoid over-specialization and, like the Court of Federal Claims, the CAFC is permitted to hold sessions elsewhere throughout the United States. In addition, the court is authorized to employ "technical assistants" with scientific or engineering expertise, as well as legal training. Although it is a court of limited jurisdiction, it has jurisdiction over all appeals from final decisions of the Court of Federal Claims (COFC) and agency boards of contract appeals pursuant to the Contract Disputes Act, whether initiated by the contractor or the government.

The decision of an agency board of contract appeals is final unless the contractor appeals "such a decision to the United States Court of Appeals for the Federal Circuit Court within 120 days from receipt of a copy thereof." Appeals go to the Court of Appeals for the Federal Circuit from the United States district courts (in patent cases), the United States Court of International Trade, the United States Court of Federal Claims, the Patent and Trademark Office, the United States International Trade Commission, and the agency boards of contract appeals. Although located in the District of Columbia, the CAFC is authorized to sit in any other of the twenty-six cities in which the twelve existing circuit courts are seated. The court has jurisdiction over interlocutory appeals from the allowance or denial by the CAFC of injunctive relief in pre-award contract disputes.

Although section 10(b) of the Contract Disputes Act continues the Wunderlich Act "substantial evidence" standard in appeals to the Court of Appeals for the Federal Circuit from decisions of boards of contract appeals, the silence of that Act on appeals from the Claims Court enabled the CAFC to decide that it would use the less stringent and more subjective "clearly erroneous" standard when entertaining such appeals. The United States Supreme Court has held that the requirement of Fed.R.Civ.P. Rule 52(a) that district court factual findings may not be set aside unless "clearly erroneous" applies to findings based on physical or documentary evidence, as well as to those based on witness credibility determinations, overruling some circuits that had held that an appellate court might exercise de novo review over findings not based on credibility determinations. Thus, the court has embraced a double standard for review of procurement cases. Because the current United States Supreme Court has generally refused to grant certiorari in procurement law cases—particularly where a change in contract clause or a regulation might ameliorate the problem—the CAFC effectively serves as the court of last resort in almost all procurement cases, as did the former Court of Claims, and it is reiterated that Congress may wish to consider this matter.

§ 33.32 Attorney's Fees and the Equal Access to Justice Act (EAJA)

A comprehensive treatment of the rights of attorneys to fees in government contracts is beyond the scope of this volume. However, certain aspects will receive some comment. In 1991, Texas became the first state to enact LLP laws was to prevent individual members of a firm being held personally liable for the negligence of other partners beyond the amount of their capital contributions to the firm. Thereafter, almost all of the other states enacted similar laws to allow professional firms to organize as limited liability partnerships.

(a) Fee Statutes and Attorney–Client Agreements

Attorneys deserve a reasonable fee for their services. Fees are normally the subject of a separate agreement between an attorney and the contractor. Under the "American Rule," and absent bad faith, attorney fees can only be awarded pursuant to a statute or agreement between the client and the attorney. Thus, the courts leave to the legislatures any change in this "American Rule," and no uniform or adequate approach is likely or possible without legislative guidelines. Although many statutes were enacted to provide for the award of "reasonable" attorneys fees, virtually none give any guidance concerning their computation. Several agencies (e.g., the Department of Energy) established regulations to control legal costs and to provide guidance regarding the reasonableness of outside legal costs (including the costs of litigation). The Supreme Court has upheld the forfeiture of a defendant's assets before he goes to trial when the forfeiture leaves him without funds to retain counsel of his choice.

In Buckhannon Board and Care Home, Inc. v. West Virginia Dep't of Health and Human Resources, the United States Supreme Court resolved a split among the Federal circuits about the meaning of the term "prevailing party." The Court expressly rejected the "catalyst theory" previously applied by some Federal courts, under which the plaintiff is considered a "prevailing party" if he or she achieves the desired result because the lawsuit brought about a voluntary change in the defendant's conduct. In order to be a "prevailing party," the Court held, the plaintiff must have been awarded some relief by the court. That relief may take the form of a judgment on the merits or a settlement agreement enforced through a consent decree. Applying *Buckhannon*, the Armed Services Board of Contract Appeals has held that a contractor that settled with the government and requested dismissal of its appeals without obtaining a consent decree is not a "prevailing party" and is therefore not entitled to attorneys' fees under the Equal Access to Justice Act. The ASBCA reached the same result in an appeal of a termination for default in which the contracting officer confirmed, on the first day of the hearing, that he was willing to convert the termination for default to one for convenience, after which the presiding judge dismissed the appeal as moot. Because the dismissal order was not a consent decree, the board held that the contractor was not a "prevailing party" and could not be awarded attorneys' fees. The General Accounting Office did not apply the same analysis in determining whether to recommend that an agency reimburse a protester's protest costs where an agency takes corrective action that results in dismissal of a protest. The Competition in Contracting Act (CICA) does not limit the GAO's authority to recommend reimbursement of protest costs to a "prevailing party;" it allows the GAO to recommend such reimbursement to an "appropriate interested party" whenever the GAO determines that any agency has violated a statute or regulation. The Court of Federal Claims, on the other hand, derives its authority to order reimbursement of protest costs from the EAJA, and is therefore bound by the Supreme Court's holding in *Buckhannon*.

Attorneys' fees have been charged to a contractor where he attempted to invoke a court's jurisdiction, duplicating a board of contract appeals proceeding in order to circumvent the Contract Disputes Act. The courts are split on whether attorney's fees may be recovered by an attorney whose only participation in a litigation was to refer the action to another attorney. However, the ABA Model Rules of Professional Conduct (2003 Edition) clearly states that:

A division of a fee between lawyers who are not in the same firm may be made only if:

(1) the division is in proportion to the services performed by each lawyer or each lawyer assumes joint responsibility for the representation;

(2) the client agrees to the arrangement, including the share each lawyer will receive, and the agreement is confirmed in writing; and

(3) the total fee is reasonable.

(b) Fee Amounts and Contingent Fees

In 1996, Chief Justice William H. Rehnquist stated:

Market capitalism has come to dominate the legal profession in the way it did not a generation ago. Law firms, whether in 1956 or 1996, have always had to run a profit. But today the profit motive seems to be written largely in a way that it was not in the past.

He pointed out that charging clients based on the hours spent working on his case "rewards inefficiency." Because such charges include profit, they actually constitute a cost-plus-percentage-of-cost (CPPC) system that is illegal under most circumstances.

The procurement regulation prescribes policies that restrict contingent fee arrangements for soliciting or obtaining government contracts. Like a lawyer's similar fee with a client, a contingent arrangement is defined as "any commission, percentage brokerage, or other fee that is contingent upon the success that a person or concern has in securing a government contract." This is similar to a lawyer's fee by an agreement, on a contingent fee basis, to represent his client on a case against the government. The procurement regulation notes that such fees "have been considered contrary to public policy because such arrangements may lead to attempted or actual exercise of improper influence."

The most controversial fee agreements are those directed to contingent fees. In a study the American Bar Foundation made on contingent fees, the practice was labeled "one of the most controversial features of the American Legal System." Yet, lawyers will also enter into such arrangements for (1) the client's liability for lawyer fees commences when the lawyer is able to settle the case favorably or obtain a judgment against the responsible person, and (2) the client will usually pay a 33–40% portion of the judgment or settlement to the lawyer. Although the percentage is sometimes negotiable, meaningful limitations on contingent fees are lacking in most cases. An attorney on a contingent fee contract may generally recover on the basis of quantum meruit following discharge of his client. California does not make any distinction as to the amount recoverable under a contingent fee contract by a discharged attorney on the basis of whether the discharge was "wrongful" or "for cause." In either case, at least a minority of courts will allow the attorney to recover on a quantum meruit basis; however, recovery may only be permitted if and when the client receives a favorable judgment on his claim. One board of contract appeals has barred recovery of contingent fees if based solely on a percentage of recovery but not if actual fees charged at an hourly rate were subject to payment contingent on the contractor's recovery. Common-law rules in most states prohibit compensating an expert witness on a contingency fee basis. In 1987, ABA Formal Opinion 87–354 relied on Model Rules of Professional Conduct Rule 3.4(b), which forbids offering an "inducement" to a witness that is "prohibited by law," and Rule 5.4(a), which forbids sharing fees with a nonlawyer. The Social Security Act limits contingent fees, providing that a court may allow "a reasonable fee . . . not in excess of 25 percent of the . . . past-due benefits" that are awarded to the claimant. The ABA Model Rules of Professional Conduct (2003 Edition) specifies that a fee may not be contingent in a matter prohibited by law.

Unlimited contingent fees are virtually unique to the United States. In England, France and Germany, such agreements are considered both unethical and unlawful, and are therefore void, and a lawyer entering into such an agreement would be subject to disciplinary sanctions. The same is true of American physicians. The system is so ingrained in this country that until recently little hope was seen for a change. Unlike the rule applicable to physicians, the ABA Model Rules of Professional Conduct state that "A fee may be contingent on the outcome of the matter for which the service is rendered." Perhaps it may occur in the early part of the 21st Century. Presently, the jury may be deceived by the attorney's arguments for the recovery of damages; arguments that convey the idea that since the plaintiff has suffered the injury, he will receive all of the damages. The fact that the lawyer is sharing these damages, and that the plaintiff only receives between 30–50% of an award made (less costs), is not mentioned to the jury; it has even been held that a jury verdict that includes attorney's fees is illegal. Every word in a trial is spoken by the lawyer "as if" it were only in his client's best interest, whereas such words are spoken in his own interest to the extent of the contingency. This interest is directly proportional to the award he extracts from the jury when the interest is significant, and often results in conflict as practiced in the United States.

In procurement by the Federal government, the cost-plus-percentage-of-cost (CPPC) system of contracting is outlawed by statute. Federal procurement regulations provide for procurement of services (or labor hours) on the basis of direct labor hours at specified fixed hourly rates (which rates include direct and indirect labor, overhead, general and administrative expenses, and profit.) However, before such an agreement can be awarded, a determination must be made that no other contract type is suitable, and the contract must include a ceiling price that the contractor exceeds at its own risk. Because of the necessity for cost control or labor efficiency, appropriate continued government surveillance of contractor performance is required to give reasonable assurance that efficient methods and effective cost controls are being used. The procurement of private attorneys fits the labor hours type of contract because the hourly rate always includes overhead and profit. However, seldom, if ever, are such controls maintained. Persons hiring attorneys either on a labor hours or a contingent fee basis normally give up effective control in order to make a determination of "reasonableness" of a fee.

(c) Fee Amounts Under the Equal Access to Justice Act (EAJA)

The Equal Access to Justice Act (EAJA) permits recovery of attorneys' fees by a successful litigant in suit against the government "to the same extent that any other party would be liable under the common law." It has been held that this provision does not permit recovery of fees from the government under either the common fund or common benefit exceptions to the American rule. The fact that his counsel was a "recognized specialist" in Federal procurement law did not entitle a contractor to a higher rate of reimbursement for attorney's fees under the Equal Access of Justice Act.

Statutes limiting maximum fees of attorneys for claimants are constitutional and the Equal Access to Justice Act (EAJA) placed a statutory cap on attorney's fees at $125 an hour; an increase in the cost of living or a special factor, such as the limited availability of qualified attorneys, may justify a higher fee.

The Supreme Court has stated that attorneys' fees may be awarded to a prevailing defendant when a district court finds "that the plaintiff's action was frivolous, unreasonable, or without foundation, even though not brought in subjective bad faith." The ABA Model Rules of Professional Conduct (2003 Edition) states that a lawyer shall not:

> in pretrial procedure, make a frivolous discovery request or fail to make reasonably diligent effort to comply with a legally proper discovery request by an opposing party.

An appellate court has held that those who qualify under statute because the "position of the United States ... was unreasonable" are per se entitled to award of fees for litigating the fee issue itself. The former Claims Court has held that the claims for purposes of ruling on fee applications is a matter of discretion. It ruled against the government where the contractor was only partially successful by obtaining bid preparation costs on an appeal (which made him "a prevailing party"); although he was still an unsuccessful bidder he was entitled to recover attorney fees under the Equal Access to Justice Act. Where the government was found to have acted in bad faith, a Circuit Court ruled that the fees were not recoverable under the statute.

As regards the costs of representing subcontractors, a board of contract appeals has held that a subcontractor who had prevailed in an appeal brought on his behalf in the name of his prime contractor (see Chapter 44, infra) was without standing to seek attorney fees. There was no waiver of the doctrine of sovereign immunity that would permit a subcontractor to prosecute a fee application in his name. The EAJA requires that an application for award of fees be submitted to the court within 30 days of "final judgment."

PART VI

SPECIAL CATEGORIES OF CONTRACTING

CHAPTER 35

RESEARCH AND DEVELOPMENT CONTRACTING

§ 35.1 Research and Development (R & D) and the Government

In the past, American predominance was recognized as a "brain drain" on much of the rest of the world's developed countries. This was partially illustrated by the fact that since the end of World War II, Americans have won an overwhelming majority of the Nobel prizes in science, although such prizes are often awarded for work done many years earlier. Helpful factors included financial support, informality, and decentralization of American science as compared to that in many other developed countries.

The American government has established 34 Federally Funded Research and Development Centers (FFRDCs) since 1972 which are sponsored by DoD, DOE, HHS, NASA, and the National Science Foundation (NSF). Forty-two years ago in his farewell address, President Eisenhower stated in 1961 that:

The prospect of domination of the nation's scholars by Federal employment, project allocations and the power of money is ever present, and is gravely to be regarded.

Yet, in holding scientific research and discovery in respect, as we should, we must also be alert to the equal and opposite danger that public policy could itself become the captive of a scientific-technological elite, a "technological race."

He added, "because of the huge costs involved, a government contract could become virtually a substitute for intellectual curiosity." In the second half of the 20th Century, the scientist-novelist C.P. Snow stated that the humanist who cannot describe the Second Law of Thermodynamics is "as illiterate as the scientist who has not read Shakespeare."

The agencies desire to obtain a broad base of the best contractor sources from the scientific and industrial community. These efforts include publicizing requirements through the Governmentwide Point of Entry (GPE), and seeking cooperation among government technical personnel to identify R & D needs. A work statement must be developed which allows contractors "freedom to exercise innovation and creativity" and be "individually tailored by technical and contracting personnel to attain the desired degree of flexibility for contractor creativity and the objectives of the R & D."

Lockheed Martin Corp. and the Boeing Co. were the largest Department of Defense research, development, test and evaluation (RDT & E) prime contractors, with $4.6 billion and $2.1 billion in awards, respectively, in fiscal year 1999. In 1995, the U.S. Court of Federal Claims ruled that Lockheed Martin did not retain substantial rights in its research under four of its contracts. The IRS had disallowed refund claims on the ground that the research expenses did not qualify for the tax credit because the research was "funded" by the government. The U.S. Court of Appeals for the Federal Circuit reversed, holding that the contracts permitted Lockheed Martin to use the research in its business, and therefore it retained "substantial rights" in its research.

§ 35.2 The Competitive Requirement

The use of negotiation in R & D contracting does not include the obligation to obtain competition beyond the solicitation of "other apparently qualified sources." Due to the importance of technical considerations in R & D, the choice of contract type will largely depend upon the recommendations of technical personnel. The difficulties in estimating costs with accuracy normally preclude using fixed-price contracting; cost-reimbursement contracting has become the usual way to proceed, together with a substantial administrative effort on the government's part. However, the regulation also provides that an agency may use solicitations which permit offerors to propose an alternative contract type.

The mere statement that an idea or product is new does not mean that this is true, even if the cognizant technical personnel think it is and have never heard of it before. In fact, direct negotiations without even soliciting other sources who might be cognizant of the same idea or product (or alternates which might accomplish the same objective at a similar or lesser price) violates the procurement laws respecting the necessity of competition.

Because the selection of an R & D contractor is substantially based on his scientific and technical abilities, it is important that such work not be subcontracted without protecting the government's interests by imposing prior approval requirements or otherwise.

§ 35.4   Government and Private Laboratories, FFRDC's "Skunk Works," Lead Users, and "Other Transactions"

A Federally Funded Research and Development Center (FFRDC) analyzes, performs or manages basic or applied research or R & D and receives 70% or more of its financial support from the government under a long-term agreement. It has access to government data, employees, and facilities beyond that found in a normal contractual relationship. It operates in the public interest with objectivity and independence, free of organizational conflict of interests. The agreement must prohibit competition with any non-FFRDC concern "in response to a Federal Agency request for proposal for other than the operation of an FFRDC;" all non-sponsor agency work must be within its mission and authorized by the sponsor agency administering the agreement.

Government agencies such as the National Science Foundation (NSF) have funded research largely through grants rather than contracts. Research contracts awarded to a large publicly financed research group such as the Los Alamos Laboratory in New Mexico and the Lawrence Livermore Laboratory in California have been run by the University of California which received a fee for doing so with little financial responsibility. Other research laboratories have been run privately with significant research capability such as General Electric, Dupont, Hughes, or Bell Laboratories (which was founded in 1925 and received its money from AT & T.) Public and private laboratories, as well as universities, generally retain a goal of keeping discoveries secret where they can be "publicized before being classified." The Patenting Process is a publication procedure.

Classification of information (largely confined to the Department of Defense and a few other agencies) is covered only to a limited extent by the Federal Acquisition Regulation.

Innovations may be irrational. One AT & T executive was reported to have said "I've been at the labs for a bit over 30 years, but I can't think of anything that ever came directly from the new product planning process;" much true development has been derived from lead users doing the development rather than by having it, hopefully, internally managed by and for a company.

CHAPTER 36

CONSTRUCTION AND ARCHITECT–ENGINEER CONTRACTS

A. TYPES OF CONSTRUCTION CONTRACTS

§ 36.1 In General

Generally, firm-fixed-price contracts are used in construction. They may be priced on a lump-sum basis (when a lump sum is paid for the total work or defined parts of the work), on a unit-price basis (when a unit price is paid for a specified quantity of work units), or on a combination of the two. However, lump-sum pricing must be used in preference to unit pricing except in certain circumstances, for example when large quantities of work such as grading, paving, building outside utilities, or site preparation are involved or where quantities of work, such as excavation, cannot be estimated with sufficient confidence to permit a lump-sum offer without a substantial contingency. Serious problems are likely to arise if cost-plus-fixed-fee, price-incentive or other types of contracts with cost variation or cost adjustment features are used concurrently at the same work site with a firm-fixed price, lump sum or unit price contract. In such cases, an incentive exists for a contractor to attempt to apply costs from the fixed or unit price work to that work being performed on cost-type or cost-variable contract in order to show increased profit. Hence, the award of such a mix of contracts can only be made with the prior approval of the head of the contracting activity. Such approval is also required prior to award of a contract for the construction of a project to the firm that designed the project or its subsidiaries or affiliates, because the lack of independence could tend to influence the way an architect-engineer may design the work or perform review work during the construction period.

§ 36.2   Statutory Cost Limitations

Appropriation acts frequently contain cost limitations on large construction contracts. Contracts for construction cannot be awarded at a cost to the government in excess of such limitations, unless they can be and are waived for the particular contract. It has been held that a bid need not be rejected if the contracting officer both determined that the price was reasonable and received a waiver of the cost limitation. Solicitations containing one or more items subject to statutory cost limitation must state the applicable cost limitation for each affected item in a separate schedule; an offer that does not contain separately-priced schedules will not be considered. Offers must contain the price on each schedule, including an approximate estimate of direct costs, allocable indirect costs, and profits. The government must reject an offer if its prices exceed applicable statutory limitations, unless laws or regulations provide exemptions. However, if it is in the government's interest, the contract may include a provision in the solicitation that permits the award of separate contracts for individual items whose prices are within or not subject to applicable statutory limitations.

§ 36.3   Evaluation Reports and the Determination of Responsibility

Unlike contracting for supplies or services (other than construction), there are typical requirements applicable to "construction contracts." Whenever a contractor's responsibility is being determined, the agency "may consider" performance reports which must be prepared on prior contracts above certain thresholds. If the evaluating official concludes that a contractor's overall performance was unsatisfactory, the contractor is so advised and, if he submits any written comments, they are included in the report along with appropriate changes in the report where necessary. The report is retained for at least six years by the contracting activity.

Other aspects of a construction contractor's responsibility have been considered above.

B. SPECIAL ASPECTS OF USE OF SEALED BIDDING PROCEDURES IN CONSTRUCTION CONTRACTS

§ 36.11 In General

As with supply contracts, sealed bid procedures must be used for construction contracts in all instances where time permits their being solicited and evaluated, the award will be based on price or price-related factors alone, and there is a reasonable expectation of receiving more than one sealed bid.

No discussions are necessary with individual potential offerors; however, prebid conferences with all or a group of potential offerors are something else. In supply contracts, individual discussions with responding offerors are not necessary for sealed bid procurements. But, in both supply and construction a prebid conference may be used to brief prospective bidders with respect to complicated specifications.

§ 36.12   Presolicitation Notices

For supplies or services contracts of $25,000 or more, contracting officers must disseminate information about the proposed contract action by publishing a synopsis through the Governmentwide Point of Entry (GPE). With construction contracts, contracting officers are required to send presolicitation notices to prospective bidders whenever the proposed contract is expected to equal or exceed $100,000, and must send the notices "sufficiently far in advance to stimulate the interest of the greatest number of prospective bidders." Such notices may also be sent to prospective bidders when the proposed contract is expected to be less than $100,000. In addition to describing the proposed work in some detail (including physical characteristics and estimated price range) such notice includes whether plans will be available for inspection and a date by which requests for the solicitation should be submitted. The notice also informs recipients that, if they do not submit a bid, they should advise the issuing office as to whether they want to receive further presolicitation notices. Although an independent government estimate of construction costs must be prepared for each proposed contract and for each contract modification anticipated to cost $100,000 or more, in no event can the statement of magnitude disclose the government's estimate, which is prepared "in as much detail as though the government were competing for award." However, an exception may be made during contract negotiation to allow identification of a specialized task and disclosure of the associated cost breakdown figures in the government estimate; but this can only be done to the extent deemed necessary to arrive at a fair and reasonable price. The "overall amount" of the government's estimate cannot be disclosed to a contractor.

Prospective offerors are notified regarding the time and place for inspection of the work site and the opportunity to examine data available to the government which may provide information concerning the performance of the work, such as boring samples, original boring logs, and records and plans of previous construction.

§ 36.13   Requests for Sealed Bids, Award Notices

All requests for sealed bids for construction are prepared in essentially the same manner as those for supply contracts. However, the regulation specifies that these requests must provide sufficient time for bids, giving due regard to the construction season and "the time necessary for bidders to inspect the site, obtain subcontract bids, examine data concerning the work, and prepare estimates based on plans and specifications."

When applicable, the solicitation must request the offeror to submit wage rates to be paid under the contract. The invitation should also include information concerning any facilities (such as utilities to be furnished during construction), information concerning the prebid conference, any special qualifications or experience requirements that will be considered in determining the responsibility of bidders and any special instructions concerning bids, alternate bids, and award, or concerning reporting requirements.

As with supply contracts, an award notice is issued which will identify the invitation and the contractor's bid, state the award price, advise the contractor that any required payment and performance bonds must be promptly executed and returned to the contracting officer, and specify the date of commencement of work, (or advise that a notice to proceed will be issued). A Preconstruction Conference may take place to inform the contractor concerning the labor standards clauses of the contract, when appropriate.

C. PRICE NEGOTIATION
OF CONSTRUCTION
CONTRACTS

§ 36.21 In General

The policies and procedures applicable to supply contracts are to be followed when negotiating prices for construction. The contracting office evaluates proposals and associated cost or pricing data and compares them to the government estimate; when any element of a proposal differs significantly from the government estimate, the offeror should be requested to submit cost or pricing data concerning that element (e.g., wage rates or fringe benefits, significant materials, equipment allowances, and subcontractor costs). In construction contracts, rough yardsticks may be developed and used (such as cost per cubic foot for structures, cost per linear foot and utilities, and cost per cubic yard for excavation or concrete) to compare proposed prices to current prices for similar types of work, adjusted for differences in the work site and the specifications.

D. CONSTRUCTION CONTRACT CLAUSES

§ 36.31 Substantial Performance and Economic Waste

Strict compliance with the contract and its specifications has been the general rule in government contracts with few exceptions by the Court of Claims or Boards of Contract Appeals. See Chapter 33, supra. However, state courts had been applying the economic waste rule, according to which the measure of damages for replacing material was found not in accordance with the specifications, beginning in 1921. This was the date of the decision, known to most law students, of Jacob & Youngs, Inc. v. Kent. The specification for plumbing stated that "[a]ll wrought-iron pipe must be well galvanized, lap welded pipe of the grade known as 'standard pipe' of Reading manufacture." When the builder installed Cohoes pipe, the owner instructed the builder to replace it with Reading pipe. The builder refused. In his opinion, Judge Cardozo founded the economic-waste doctrine because "the cost of completion is grossly and unfairly out of proportion to the good to be attained." In that case there was no difference in value between the two brands of pipe. However, the Restatement of Contracts later went beyond *Jacob & Youngs* by also providing for "unreasonable economic waste" where the owner's damages were limited to the difference between the value of the contract work and the value of the work actually performed. The Restatement (Second) provided that where the owner fails to establish lost value with sufficient certainty, he is entitled to recover cost-of-repair damages if these costs are not "clearly disproportionate to the probable loss in value." Where there is a clear disproportion, his recovery is limited to the diminished market price caused by the breach of contract. The courts were not uniform in applying the rule. Some examined the increase in the market value of the project because of the repairs whereas others looked at the cost of repairs relative to the contract price.

In 1992, the Court of Appeals for the Federal Circuit applied the economic-waste doctrine for the first time. Granite Construction Co. v. United States concerned a contract with the Army Corps of Engineers for the construction of a lock and dam in Mississippi that called for waterstop in the vertical joints between the walls to prevent leakage. The specification described performance characteristics of an off-the-shelf waterstop. General Provision ("GP") 10(b) of the contract, a clause that was in all construction contracts, required Granite to replace, without charge, any non-conforming material, "unless in the *public interest,* the government consents to accept such material or workmanship with an appropriate adjustment in the contract price." After about 10 percent of the "Saf–T–Grip" or "STG" brand was embedded in the walls, the Corps instructed Granite to remove and replace all the non-conforming STG waterstop. Granite performed the replacement and filed a claim for the cost of the repair work that was denied. Granite's expert witness testified that, although STG waterstop did not meet the contract specifications, it was adequate for the project's requirements.

The Federal Circuit Court held that the Board and the United States Claims Court erred in holding that the replacement of the STG waterstop did not constitute unreasonable economic waste. While the government usually has the right to require strict compliance with specifications, GP–10(b) of the contract included an obligation to consider the STG waterstop relative to the performance requirements. The Corps breached its duty when it failed to assess the STG waterstop and the Corps's rejection of the STG waterstop was "arbitrary and capricious." The court further found that Granite met the burden of proving that the existing work substantially complied with the contract specifications through its expert testimony and that replacement of the waterstop was "an economically wasteful course of performance." Hence, Granite, the contractor, could recover virtually all its costs for the replacement.

The potential extra costs to the government (taxpayer) of the use of this doctrine created the opportunity "for bidders on government contracts to underbid their competitors by calculating bids on less expensive materials and later support[ing] their bid by saying the materials used conform with the technical requirements of the contract specifications and are not of inferior quality." The government has a stronger incentive to incorporate more performance and fewer design specifications, in order to prevent unreasonable economic waste.

§ 36.32   Extension of Implied Warranty of Construction

Insertion of provisions in a government contract specifying dimensions imports a warranty that if the specifications are complied with the construction will be adequate. The key decision is United States v. Spearin. The contract was for the construction of a dry dock at a United States Navy shipyard in accordance with plans and specifications prepared by the government. The site selected was intersected by a six-foot brick sewer. Spearin had to relocate a section of this sewer before construction could begin on the dry dock. One year after its relocation, a heavy rain caused the relocated sewer to break. The government argued that Spearin had responsibility for remedying existing conditions and Spearin protested. Later the Navy annulled the contract and Spearin brought suit. The trial court found that if Spearin had been allowed to complete the contract he would have earned a profit of $60,000 and its judgment included that sum. The U.S. Supreme Court affirmed stating:

> But if the contractor is bound to build according to plans and specifications prepared by the owner, the contractor will not be responsible for the consequences of defects in plans and specifications ... The risk of the existing system proving adequate might have rested upon Spearin, if the contract for the dry dock had not contained the provision for the relocation of the 6–foot sewer. But the insertion of the articles prescribing the character, dimensions, and location of the sewer imported a warranty that if the specifications were complied with, the sewer would be adequate.

The court added "This implied warranty is not overcome by the general clauses requiring the contractor to examine the site, to check the plans, and to assume responsibility for the work until completion and acceptance." The breach of warranty, followed by the government's repudiation of all responsibility for the past and for making working conditions safe in the future, justified Spearin in refusing to resume the work.

This doctrine of implied warranty has been significantly extended by the Court of Claims, which held that communication by the government of knowledge of performance difficulties after award but prior to commencement of construction was a breach of implied warranty of the plans and specifications. In Poorvu v. United States, the government entered into a contract for architect-engineer (A–E) services for the design and supervision of construction of a Post Office. The A–E suggested to the agency that piling would be needed under the maneuvering and parking areas, but this advice was not taken and a contract was awarded to one Foreman to construct and lease to the government the building without the piling. Before beginning work, Foreman was made aware of the inadequacies of the plan. Less than three years after construction was completed, Foreman conveyed the property and assigned the lease to the plaintiffs. But within 18 months leaks and settlement of the building became extensive. Plaintiff made repairs and billed the government on the grounds of breach of warranty of the plans. The government pleaded that no representations were made to the plaintiffs. The Court of Claims, disagreeing with the Comptroller General, cited the decision of the Supreme Court in *Spearin* and permitted recovery for plaintiff on the theory of implied warranty that the plans would be sufficient whether the government was the owner or the lessee. The contractor, Foreman, was unaware of the problem until after bid opening. Certainly, at that point he could have refused to execute the contract awarded to him. His awareness prior to construction would also remove the case from the area of mutual mistake. It amounted to the reverse, namely, "mutual knowledge" of the condition. Although the information was made available after bid opening, the former Court of Claims ruled that that late date was not soon enough to free the government from the implied warranty. This was an extension of the *Spearin* Doctrine and one that has not yet been reviewed by the Supreme Court. Until the *Poorvu* decision, it was necessary for such recovery that the contractor discover the inadequacy of the plans after award and substantial work on the contract had been performed. In *Poorvu*, the contractor was aware of the inadequacy of the plans before the award and before he started work. The *Poorvu* decision allowed for the implied warranty to extend to successors in interest to the land and assignees of lessor under a lease, after several years had elapsed on the leaseback.

The former Court of Claims has, in effect, ruled that a long-term lessor may construct a building with full knowledge of defective plans, take a long-term lease, and then assign both the lease and a chose in action against the government to a future plaintiff who may have also accepted the assignment with knowledge of the defects. A better alternative might be to permit rescission if the contractor learned of materially defective plans or specifications prior to commencing work, which defect was known to the public body prior to award.

The articles used in construction contracts entitled "Suspension of Work" and "Government Delay in Work" are discussed in Chapter 42, infra.

§ 36.34   Certain Clauses in Construction Contracts: Differing Site Conditions

When a contractor during performance discovers subsurface conditions that delay or increase the cost of performance, he normally assumes this risk unless the government has agreed to assume the risk, misrepresented the conditions, or failed to disclose known difficulties. As a result, an incentive may exist to "pad" his bid price for such a contingency. In order to remove all or most of this contingency, a clause entitled "Differing Site Conditions" (formerly titled "Changed Conditions") is required in fixed price construction contracts. The condition must be in existence "at the time the contract was entered into and not one occurring thereafter." However, a contractor cannot recover for a condition he encountered during performance as a "differing site condition" on the grounds that neither the drawings nor specifications mentioned that condition.

Pursuant to this clause, the contractor is obliged to notify the government agency of "(1) subsurface or latent *physical* conditions at the *site* which differ *materially* from those indicated in this contract, or (2) unknown *physical* conditions at the *site,* of an *unusual* nature, which differ *materially* from those ordinarily encountered and generally recognized as inhering in work of the character provided for in this contract." The words italicized here have been the subject of some interpretation by the courts and boards. The agency then investigates the site conditions and if they "materially so differ and cause an increase or decrease in the contractor's cost of, or the time required for, performing any part of the work under the contract, whether or not changed as a result of such conditions, an equitable adjustment" is to be made.

Another mandatory clause in fixed price construction contracts is entitled "Site Investigation and Conditions Affecting the Work," according to which the contractor acknowledges that it has taken steps reasonably necessary to ascertain the nature and location of the work, and that it has investigated and satisfied itself as to the general and local conditions which can affect the work or its cost as well as "the character, quality, and quantity of surface and subsurface materials or obstacles to be encountered insofar as this information is reasonably ascertainable from an inspection of the site, including all exploratory work done by the government." In addition, a clause entitled "Physical Data" is used when a fixed-price construction contract is contemplated and physical data (e.g., test borings, hydrographic data, weather conditions data) will be furnished or made available.

The "changes" clause is treated in Chapter 43, infra.

E.   ARCHITECT–ENGINEER SERVICES

§ 36.51   In General

Although construction contracts are often awarded following the same sealed bidding procedures applicable to supply contracts, this has no longer been true with respect to the procurement of architect-engineer (A–E) services since the 1972 enactment of the so-called "Brooks Act." There, a political determination was made to prevent the Federal government from using sealed bid procedures (and forcing negotiation of all such contracts) and contractor selection without initial consideration of price.

Architect engineering firms have been held to lack standing to challenge an agency's procurement action because they are not in the position of the disappointed bidder who is protected by the *Scanwell* decision. The stated purpose of the Brooks Acts is "to establish a Federal policy concerning the selection of firms and qualified architects and engineers to design and provide consultant services in carrying out Federal construction and related programs." The rationale for its policy is that the quality of these services is basic and essential to the quality of construction; their cost generally represents but a smaller part of the total cost of construction. It was thought important to be less cost conscious in the selection, of an A–E and that price competition could be detrimental to selection, although no empirical data specifically supported this. The Act requires negotiation on the basis of qualification for the type of professional services required, without any price competition.

Transportation officials from two states have reported that price competition for architect-engineer services has not adversely affected the design quality of highway projects. This report reviewed the merits of requiring states to use a qualifications-based method—rather than a determination based on price—to select architect-engineer services for federally assisted highway and transit projects. It was noted that, unlike the Federal government, many states use methods that consider price as a factor in the selection process. For example, the Maryland official stated price did not affect design quality in Maryland. Under the price factor system in the state, price could not be given more than 50 percent consideration in the A–E selection process, and in most cases was given less than 50 percent. The Pennsylvania official also disagreed that price competition led to less qualified firms receiving contracts; he stated that he did not believe that quality is lowered under the price factor method and noted that most of the firms that ranked first technically also submitted the lowest price. The Pennsylvania official rejected the contention that price competition led to awards to less qualified firms. Congress may consider revision of the Brooks Act. Such considerations also apply to other professions. For example, the Florida Supreme Court has held unconstitutional a regulation prohibiting certified public accountants from making competitive bids.

A–E services are defined "by applicable state law." It is not required that contracts be awarded to A–E firms merely because architects or engineers might do part of the contract work. The GAO has recognized that such determinations are the responsibility of the contracting agency and, therefore, has recognized broad discretion on the part of the agency in making such determinations. The GAO has stated that its "proper role ... is to defer to the judgment of the agency unless the agency's conclusions are so egregious as to demonstrate a clear intent either to circumvent the Act or to employ the noncompetitive procedures enunciated by the Act to secure services that should properly be solicited by competitive means." Competition was upheld in a solicitation for drilling soil samples, analysis of the soil samples, and submitting a report on the results of the testing together with recommendations on construction methods and design. The preponderance of the work did not constitute professional A–E services under the Brooks Act—although, professional A–E firms often perform these services. The Brooks Act is not applicable in procuring a research contract of a contractor expected to use engineers, where it is unnecessary for the contractor to be a professional engineering firm in order to successfully perform the contract. In 1991, the regulation was revised to include services "incidental thereto" such as "surveying and mapping," "soils engineering" and "preparation of operating and maintenance manuals ... that logically or justifiably require performance by registered architects or engineers or

their employees." When the work includes both A–E and
other services, the procedures for A–E's is to be used if the
statement of work "substantially or to a dominant extent
specifies performance or approval by a registered or licensed architect or engineer." Services that do not require
a licensed A–E should be acquired by sealed bid or negotiation "notwithstanding the fact that architect-engineers also
may perform these services." However, A–E contracts can
no longer be offered under GSA multiple-award schedule, or
task and delivery order contracts, unless such services are
performed under the direct supervision of a licensed architect or engineer.

Prior to announcing a requirement for architect-engi-
neering services for the design of a facility, the contracting
officer must ask the technical official responsible for the
facility being designed to specifically identify any areas
where recovered materials cannot be used in the facility
construction. Agencies are to evaluate each potential contractor in terms of its demonstrated success in prescribing
the use of recovered materials and achieving waste reduction and energy efficiency in facility design.

The selection procedure thus requires the government to
publicly announce all requirements for architect-engineer
services, and negotiate contracts for these services. Selection criteria peculiar to A–E's includes professional qualifications, specialized experience and technical competence in
the type of work required, location in the general geograph-
ical area of the project and knowledge of the locality of the
project, provided that "an appropriate number of qualified
firms" are left, given the nature and size of the project.
This is accomplished by one or more permanent or ad hoc
architect-engineer evaluation boards composed of members
who, collectively, have experience in architecture, engineering, construction, and government and related acquisition

matters. Members are to be appointed from among highly qualified professional employees of the agency or other agencies, and "if authorized by agency procedure, private practitioners of architecture, engineering, or related professions." No firm is eligible for award of an architect-engineer contract during the period in which any of its principals or associates are participating as members of the awarding agency's evaluation board. The board is to hold discussions with at least three of the most highly qualified firms regarding concepts and the relative utility of alternative methods of furnishing the required services. At least three firms are recommended for the services in order of preference. A "designated selection authority" then makes the final selection and if the particular firm listed as the most preferred is not the firm recommended as the most highly qualified by the evaluation board, the selection authority must provide "for the contract file" a written explanation of the reason for the preference. No other firms may be added to the selection report. However, if the firms recommended in the report are not deemed to be qualified, the selection authority records the reasons and then returns the report to the evaluation board for appropriate revision.

There is also a short selection process for contracts not exceeding the simplified acquisition threshold (normally $100,000). There, the selection report serves as the final selection list and is provided directly to the contracting officer to serve as an authorization to commence negotiations. The board may then decide that formal action by the board is not necessary in connection with a particular selection. The chairperson of the board then furnishes the contracting officer with a copy of the report that serves as authorization for him to commence negotiations.

An architect-engineer evaluation board must review the information in the qualifications statements and performance data required to be submitted by A–E firms in determining the firms with which discussions will be held. It has been held that such a board may be convened even though none of its members is an architect or an engineer. The board must hold discussions with at least three of the most highly qualified firms regarding concepts, the relative utility of alternative methods and feasible ways to prescribe the use of recovered materials and achieve waste reduction and energy-efficiency in facility design.

§ 36.52   Performance Evaluation

In the case of architect-engineer contractors, a performance evaluation report must be prepared. The threshold is a contract of more than $25,000. Although a report may also be prepared for contracts less than that amount, this is unlikely to be done. This threshold may appear low, but it is necessary in order to adequately protect the taxpayer in view of the fact that the resulting construction may cost hundreds of thousands of dollars. The report is made after final acceptance of the work or after contract termination, as appropriate. If the evaluating official concludes that a contractor's overall performance was unsatisfactory, the contractor is so advised in writing and if the contractor submits any written comments, they are included in the report along with any appropriate changes. Such reports are reviewed by an official who is normally at an organizational level above that of the evaluating official in order to ensure that it is accurate and fair. These reports are to be retained in the office file for six years after the date of the report. An evaluation board is required to consider these reports prior to making a recommendation to the contract selection officer. The Regulation states that a performance evaluation of the A & E design "may" also be prepared after actual construction of the project. Traditionally, A–E's would perform work during construction.

§ 36.53   Negotiations for A–E Services

The requirements for preparation of an independent government estimate of the cost of architect-engineer services are identical to those pertaining to estimates for construction contracts except, of course, that threshold is much lower for A–E contracts; the estimate must only be prepared before commencing negotiations for each proposed contract or contract modification expected to exceed $100,000. Access to the information concerning the government estimate is limited and its overall amount cannot be disclosed except as permitted by agency regulations. It is not to be disclosed during negotiations except "to identify a specialized task and disclose associated cost breakdown figures in the government estimate, but only to the extent deemed necessary to arrive at a fair and reasonable price."

Negotiation is required with the selected firm first and a proposal is requested from that firm. Only if a mutually satisfactory contract cannot be negotiated is that firm notified that negotiations have been terminated (following its submission of a best and final offer). Then negotiations are initiated with the next firm on the final selection list. This procedure is to be continued until a mutually satisfactory contract has been negotiated. If the government cannot negotiate a reasonable contract with any of the three or more firms selected, the selection process is then to be repeated for a new slate of firms.

The reasonableness of the price factor is to be considered in the selection process, only after relative competence has been determined. In competitive contracts, competence (responsibility) is a prerequisite to a contract award.

The National Society of Professional Engineers' ban on competitive bidding by its members has been held to constitute per se unlawful price fixing violative of Section I of the Sherman Act. In December, 1975, a Federal district court ruled that provisions of a code of ethics prohibiting members of the National Society of Professional Engineers from submitting competitive bids for their engineering services were per se violations of the Sherman Act's Section I prohibition against price fixing. A direct appeal of that decision was made to the U.S. Supreme Court, which rejected the argument that public safety and health risks inherent in competition justify a professional engineering society's ethical ban on competitive bidding by its members. This decision could be helpful in connection with private procurement of A–E's and their procurement by most state and local governments; however, it would not effect A–E procurement by the Federal government, unless and until the "Brooks Architect–Engineers Act" were amended.

§ 36.54 Liability for Government Costs Resulting From Design Errors or Deficiencies

Architect-engineer contractors are responsible for the professional quality, technical accuracy, and coordination of all services required under their contracts. A firm may be liable for such costs to the government as those resulting from a modification to a construction contract which is required because of an error or deficiency in the services provided under an architect-engineer contract. In such instance, technical personnel and legal counsel must consider the extent to which the architect-engineer contractor may be reasonably liable, and the government must enforce the liability and collect the amount due, "if the recoverable cost will exceed the administrative cost involved or is otherwise in the government's interest." In this connection, it should be noted that a contract provision that releases an architectural firm from all liability, including design errors, before construction of the project is begun has been held to be unenforceable. This is because such provisions are inconsistent with duties of inspection and "there is no point in calling upon the architect ... to inspect the progress ... if the architect may, without incurring any liability, do that work incompetently or not at all."

An appellate decision in New York recognized a contractor's right to sue an architect/engineer for negligent design and administration of a construction project. Although previous decisions in that state had held that a contractor had no cause of action against a design professional because of lack of privity, that court held that the contractor's reliance on the architect/engineer's work product created a relationship equivalent to privity.

§ 36.55   Design Within Funding Limitations and Re-design Responsibility for Design Errors or Deficiencies

The government may require the architect-engineer contractor to design the project so that construction costs will not exceed a contractually specified dollar limit (funding limitation). This amount is established during negotiations between the contractor and the government. This estimated construction contract price takes into account any statutory or other limitations and excludes any allowances for government supervision and overhead and any amounts set aside by the government for contingencies. In negotiating the amount, the agency makes available to the contractor the information upon which the government has based its initial construction estimate and any subsequently acquired information that may affect the construction costs. If the price of construction proposed in response to a government solicitation exceeds the construction funding limitation in the architect-engineer contract, the firm becomes solely responsible for redesigning the project within the funding limitation without any increase in the price of the contract. If the cost of proposed construction, however, is affected by events beyond the firm's reasonable control (e.g., if there is an increase in material costs which could not have been anticipated, or an undue delay by the government in issuing a construction solicitation), then the firm is not obligated to redesign at no cost to the government. However, if a firm's design fails to meet the contractual limitation on construction cost, the government may well determine that that firm should not redesign the project.

Architect-engineers must stand by their own work and they are required to make necessary corrections at no cost to the government when the designs, drawings, specifications, or other items or services furnished contain any errors, deficiencies, or inadequacies. If, in a given situation, the government does not require a firm to correct such errors, the contracting officer must include a written statement of the reasons for that decision in the contract file.

PART VII

CONTRACT MANAGEMENT

CHAPTER 42

CONTRACT ADMINISTRATION

§ 42.1 In General

General policies and procedures of the government for performing contract administration functions and related audit services, for the most part, are outside the scope of a volume on the contract law. These include procedures for obtaining and providing interagency contract administration and audit services in order to provide specialized assistance through field offices located at or near contractors' establishments, to avoid or eliminate overlapping and duplication of government effort, and to provide more consistent treatment of contractors. These also include procedures for assigning, retaining, or reassigning contract administration responsibility, withholding normal functions or delegating additional functions when assigning contracts for administration, and when requesting and performing supporting contract administration. Assignment of a contract to a contract administration office (CAO) for administration automatically carries with it the authority to perform the normal functions applicable to the contract, to the extent specified by the contracting office. A contractor can expect to be notified concerning the extent of the authority assigned or retained. For example, a prime contractor is responsible for managing its subcontracts and the CAO's concern with subcontracts is normally limited to evaluating the prime contractor's management thereof. Supporting contract administration is not to be used for subcontracts unless the government would otherwise incur undue cost, or successful completion of the prime contract is threatened.

§ 42.3　Corporate Administrative Contracting Officer

Since the turn of the 3rd Millennium, many corporate boards have courted huge scandals by meeting only a few times each year and ceding too much power to management. For example, in 2002, two former WorldCom, Inc. employees plead guilty of conspiring to prop up the foundering telecommunications company by hiding more than $3.8 billion in debt from shareholders and creditors. As a result of similar scandal at the Enron Corporation (the world's largest energy-trading firm), "the defunct Arthur Andersen LLP" accounting firm was sentenced to a $500,000 fine after a jury in 2002 convicted Andersen of destroying Enron documents to thwart a Securities and Exchange Commission inquiry into Enron's activities.

The Sarbanes–Oxley Act of 2002 was enacted to improve corporate governance, public auditing, and Securities and Exchange Commission oversight. It imposes burdens on, and poses risks to, government contractors. There is also a provision requiring lawyers for publicly traded companies to report material violations of securities laws up the chain of command, all the way to the board, if necessary. The Act was implemented in January 2003 by the Securities Exchange Commission (SEC) to ban personal loans to directors and executives, to forbid auditors auditing their own work, and require that lawyers report securities law violations. Auditors who assist executives who lie on financial statements by shredding documents face 10 years in prison; however, it does not require those who suspect fraud to quit, because that would appear to violate the attorney-client privilege. More independent, outside, nonexecutive directors have been elected to boards of publicly owned corporations to provide accountability, diverse experience and credibility. However, a 2003 survey of the 200 largest U.S. law firms showed that only two of 49 responding law firms included nonpartner, nonemployees on their governing boards; they claimed this was due to rule 5.4 (d) of the ABA Model Rules which prohibit outside directors who are nonlawyers.

However, in that year a revision to Model Rule 1.6 (Confidentiality of Information) permits a lawyer to reveal information relating to the representation of a client to the extent the lawyer believes necessary to prevent the client from committing a crime or fraud that would lead to "substantial injury to the financial interests or property of another and in furtherance of which the client has used or is using the lawyer's services." Furthermore, Model Rule 1.13 (Organization as Client) was then revised to allow a lawyer who knows that actions by officers or employees will likely harm the company to refer the matter to "higher-ups" unless the lawyer reasonably believes that it is not necessary in the best interest of the organization to do so, otherwise, he may reveal information "if and to the extent the lawyer reasonably believes necessary to prevent substantial injury to the organization."

§ 42.4   Indirect Cost Rates

(a) In General

"Indirect cost rate" means "the percentage or dollar factor that expresses the ratio of indirect expenses incurred in a given period to direct labor cost, manufacturing cost, or another appropriate base for the same period." One method has been to provide for reimbursement of a proportion of the total overhead applicable to the total direct labor hours, or direct machine dollars, spent under the contract. When the total allowable overhead costs are divided by the total dollars (or hours), the result is a per-dollar (or per-hour) rate for overhead allocation. This rate can be stated as a percentage of direct labor dollars, or as a dollar rate per hour.

A contractor cannot allocate as indirect costs those that do not benefit the contractor generally. It has been held that he cannot charge, as indirect costs allocable to all its government contracts, litigation expenses incurred in connection with a particular contract.

In government contracting, a single agency is responsible for establishing indirect cost rates for each business unit that are binding on all agencies and their contracting offices, unless otherwise specifically prohibited by statute. The interim billing rate for interim reimbursement of incurred indirect costs is established unilaterally, by the contracting officer or the auditor, on the basis of information resulting from recent review, previous rate audits or experience, similar reliable data or experience, or other contracting activities. The regulation only permits billing rates to be prospectively or retroactively revised bilaterally—"by mutual agreement of the contracting officer" or auditor and the contractor at either party's request. However, an agency has been held to have breached its agreement by failing to make provisional payments for overhead costs pending completion of an audit that had not yet been started.

Until 1956, many agencies and departments utilized final predetermined negotiated fixed overhead rates for reimbursement of overhead costs under cost-type contracts. This was changed when the Comptroller General held that use of the predetermined fixed percentage rate makes the contract one for payment on a cost-plus-percentage-of-cost (CPPC) basis, which is illegal.

Effective October 1, 1995, a rule prohibited contracting officers from accepting billing rates or final indirect cost rate proposals, or agreeing to billing or final indirect cost rates, until the contractor certifies that the proposed costs are allowable and allocable. Agency heads or designers can waive the certification requirement if doing so is in the interest of the United States and if the reasons for the waiver is set forth in writing and made available to the public. If the contractor refuses to certify the indirect cost proposal, and a waiver is not granted, then the contracting officer unilaterally establishes the indirect rates. These rates are based on audited historical data or other available data as long as unallowable costs are excluded; and "set low enough to ensure that potentially unallowable costs will not be reimbursed."

Except for certain educational institutions, the current procedure for establishing final indirect cost rates calls for "negotiation" with the contractor on these costs. The contractor submits to the agency (or to the cognizant auditor) a final indirect cost rate proposal reflecting actual cost experience during the covered period, together with supporting cost or pricing data. The auditor then submits to the contracting officer an advisory audit report identifying any relevant advance agreements or restrictive terms of specific contracts and other information. Next, the parties "negotiate" final indirect rates and execute a "written indirect cost rate agreement." In addition, the government's negotiating team must prepare and place in the contractor general file a "negotiation memorandum" covering, inter alia, a reconciliation of all costs questioned, with "identification of items and amounts allowed or disallowed in the final settlement" as well as the disposition of period costing or allocability issues, the "reasons why any recommendations of the auditor or other government advisors were not followed," and "identification of cost or pricing data submitted during the negotiations and relied upon in reaching a settlement."

If the regulation were revised to state that there would be "discussions" with the contractor concerning overhead, the contracting officer, as the representative of the government agency, could make decisions which vary from the advice of auditors or other advisors only after making a "finding of fact"; no compromise of a significant indirect cost would be permitted simply to reach an agreement. If this were the intent, contracting officers would no longer be "judged" by their alleged ability to reach agreement by compromising the government's right to a more accurate determination of costs. A "quick-closeout procedure" is required to be negotiated to settle indirect costs when a cost-type contract of less than $1,000,000 is "physically complete" and does not exceed 15% of their estimated cost; otherwise, it may not exceed 10%. The alternative "Auditor determination procedure" states, "If agreement with the contractor is not reached, [the auditor shall] forward the audit report to the contracting officer (or cognizant Federal agency official) identified in the Directory of Contract Administration Services Components ... , who will then resolve the disagreement." His final decision not settled by mutual agreement may require a notification of a potential dispute by the contractor. Effective February 20, 2002, the process of final settlement of contractor indirect cost rates under cost-reimbursement contracts (1) extends the time period within which a contractor must submit an indirect cost rate proposal (from 90 days) to 6 months after the end of the contractor's fiscal year, (2) permits extensions of the six-month time period for exceptional circumstances only, and (3) provides a specific reference to the Defense Contract Audit Agency pamphlet that contains guidance on what generally constitutes an adequate final indirect cost rate proposal and supporting data.

A partial solution was in the Department of Defense (DoD) FY 1986 Authorization Act, which contained a provision that, in proceeding before courts or boards, defense *contractors* have a burden of proof for the reasonableness of claims for indirect costs. This provision was adopted to modify the unfortunate rule adopted by the Court of Claims forty years ago (and followed by succeeding board decisions) that the contractor's indirect costs were "presumed" to be reasonable. This new standard effective February 20, 2002, requires the contractor to submit to the agency "a final indirect cost rate proposal" after using a "negotiation process as efficient as possible."

The Federal Acquisition Regulation states that a cost is reasonable if it "would be incurred by a prudent person in the conduct of competitive business," but notes the need for "particular care in connection with firms or their separate divisions that may not be subject to effective competitive restraints." Further, "the burden of proof" is now upon all Federal contractors to establish the reasonableness of costs incurred.

Effective October 1, 1994, sections of the regulation provide that penalties may be assessed if unallowable costs are included in final indirect cost rate proposals, or in final statements of costs incurred or estimated to be incurred under fixed-price incentive contracts and cost reimbursement contracts. The government's rights under the penalty provisions are ensured by incorporation of the new "Penalties for Unallowable Costs" clause. The provisions will apply to all contracts in excess of $500,000 except fixed-price contracts without cost incentives and firm fixed-price contracts for the purchase of commercial items. The contracting officer unilaterally determines and assesses the penalty, with the advice and recommendation of the contract auditor.

When the submitted cost is expressly unallowable under the FAR cost principles or agency supplements, the penalty is equal to the amount of the disallowed cost, plus interest on any portion of the cost that has been paid. When the submitted cost was previously determined to be unallowable, then the penalty is equal to two times the amount of the disallowed cost, plus interest on any portion of the cost that has been paid.

The penalty is equal to the amount of the disallowed costs allocated to contracts for which an indirect cost proposal has been submitted, plus interest on the paid portion, if any, of the disallowance. If the indirect cost was determined to be unallowable for that contractor before proposal submission, the penalty is two times the amount of the disallowed costs allocable to the contracts for which an indirect cost proposal has been submitted.

(b) Educational Institutions

Although so called "postdetermined" final indirect cost rates are used in the settlement of indirect costs for all cost-reimbursement contracts with educational institutions, "predetermined" final indirect cost rates have also been authorized. This was made possible by a special statute applicable to indirect costs in connection with cost-type research and development contracts with educational institutions. The use of predetermined rates is permissible in grants to nonprofit institutions other than educational institutions. However, unless their use is approved at a level in the agency higher than the contracting officer, predetermined rates cannot be used when there has been no recent audit of the indirect costs, there has been frequent or wide fluctuations in the indirect cost rates and the bases over a period of years, or the estimated reimbursable costs for any individual contract are expected to exceed $1 million annually.

(c) Cost–Sharing Rates and Limitations on Indirect Cost Rates

Cost-sharing agreements may call for the contractor to participate in the costs of the contract by accepting indirect rates lower than the anticipated actual rates. In such cases, a "predetermined" indirect cost rate ceiling may be incorporated into the contract for prospective application. Such a rate may also be included in a contract when the proposed contractor is a new or recently reorganized company and there is no past or recent record of incurred indirect costs, he has a recent record of a rapidly increasing indirect cost rate due to a declining volume of sales without a commensurate decline in indirect expenses, or he seeks to enhance his competitive position in a particular circumstance by basing the proposal on indirect cost rates lower than those that may reasonably be expected to occur during contract performance (thereby causing a cost overrun).

When ceiling provisions are utilized, the contract provides that the government will not be obligated to pay any additional amount should the final indirect cost rate exceed the negotiated ceiling rates. Also, in the event the final indirect cost rates are less than the negotiated ceiling rates, the negotiated rates will be reduced to conform to the lower rates.

§ 42.5 Disallowance of Costs; Bankruptcy

A cost-reimbursement contract, a fixed-price incentive contract, or a contract providing for price redetermination contains a clause entitled "Notice of Intent to Disallow Costs." At any time during the performance, the cognizant contracting officer may issue the contractor a written notice of intent to disallow specified costs incurred or planned for incurrence. Its purpose is to notify the contractor as early as practicable during contract performance that the cost is considered unallowable under the contract terms and to provide for timely resolution of any resulting disagreement. In the event of disagreement, the contractor may submit to the contracting officer a written response. If the notice is not withdrawn, then the contracting officer must make a written decision within 60 days that may be a subject for dispute. The regulation refers to "discussions" with the contractor rather than to "negotiations" (the term used in connection with indirect costs, described in § 42.4 above).

Costs may also be disallowed after incurrence in connection with cost-reimbursement contracts, the cost-reimbursement portion of fixed-price contracts, letter contracts that provide for reimbursement of costs, and time-and-material and labor-hour contracts. Whenever such contractors submit a voucher that raises a question regarding the allowability of a cost under the contract terms, the auditor, after informal "discussion" (not negotiation), may issue a notice

of contract costs suspended and/or disapproved for deduction from current payments with respect to costs claimed.
In such an event, the contractor may agree or, alternatively, either submit a written request to the cognizant contracting officer to "discuss" the findings or file a claim
under the Disputes clause, or both. Presumably, he would
do both whenever he felt that either the discussion would
be fruitless or, by resorting to the disputes procedure, he
might attempt to negotiate (i.e., compromise) the matter.

A section and clause were added to the regulation to
provide guidance concerning the treatment of contractors
who enter into bankruptcy. The regulation enables the
government to deal with potentially significant events in a
contractor's operation that could impact on the government's ability to obtain the requisite contract performance
and provides procedural guidance for addressing such situations. A Federal district court held that a contractor's
discharge in bankruptcy did not prevent the Navy from
recovering $2 million in overpayments from the company
that acquired the contractor.

§ 42.6   Novation and Change-of-Name Agreements

When a contractor wishes the government to recognize a
successor in interest to these contracts, or a name change,
he submits a written request to the responsible contracting
officer. Each contract administration office (and contracting
office affected by a proposed agreement for recognizing a
successor in interest) is notified and requested to submit
their comments within 30 days. The responsible contracting
officer then determines whether or not it is in the government's interest to recognize the proposed successor in interest. This is essential because the proposed successor must
be determined to be "responsible." Although the law prohibits transfer of government contracts by a contractor, the

government may, in its interest, recognize a third party as the successor in interest when the third party's interest in the contract arises out of the transfer of all the contractor's assets or the entire portion of the assets involved in performing the contract. When the government does not concur in the transfer of a contract from one company to another company, the original contractor remains under contractual obligation to the government, and the contract may be terminated for default, should the original contractor not perform. Where the government concurs, a novation (or tripartite) agreement is executed by the contractor (transferor), the successor in interest (transferee), and the government. According to this agreement, the transferor guarantees performance of the contract, the transferee assumes all obligations under the contract, and the government recognizes the transfer of the contract and related assets. The novation ordinarily provides, inter alia, that the transferee assumes all the transferor's obligations under the contract, the transferor waives all rights under the contract against the government, the transferor guarantees performance of the contract by the transferee, and that nothing in the agreement shall relieve the transferee from compliance with any Federal law.

The right of the government to demand that a contractor, in which a third party acquires a controlling interest, negotiate a novation agreement has not been litigated; however, its authority to do so may also be derived from other Federal statutes; the assignment of government claims or contracts is prohibited by two statutes.

In one case, a contractor argued that the transfer of right and duties under the contracts had taken place by operation of law and there was no requirement for a novation agreement; the novation lacked consideration and was a nullity. The argument was later rejected on the grounds that the government's good faith forbearance in not asserting a bar against the "transfer" of this contract under the anti-assignment statutes was sufficient consideration for the novation agreement. The agreement to recognize a successor in interest in the FAR specifies that the government is not obligated to pay any costs arising out of the novation "other than those that the government in the absence of this transfer or agreement would have been obligated to pay."

§ 42.7   Suspension of Work

Under a clause for use in fixed price construction contracts, the parties agree that the contracting officer may order the contractor in writing to suspend, delay or interrupt all or any part of the work for such period of time as he determines is appropriate for the convenience of the government. If the suspension is for "an unreasonable period of time," an adjustment is to be made for all increases in the cost of performance (excluding profit). No adjustment is made to the extent that performance would have been delayed, or interrupted by any other cause, including the fault or negligence of the contractor. In addition, if an equitable adjustment is provided for (or excluded) under any other provision of the contract, it is not covered by this clause; where a claim for delay expenses might be made under the changes clause, the adjustment must be made thereunder. But, the granting of an extension of time under the "Delays–Damages" clause does not preclude a price adjustment under the Suspension of Work clause. The contractor must notify the contracting officer within 20 days of incurring the costs.

Boards of contract appeals had expanded their jurisdiction over the "changes" article where the contracting officer did not issue any written change order under that article, through the doctrine of "constructive changes." In like manner, they extended their jurisdiction with the "Suspension Article" through a doctrine of "constructive suspension." However, this "hoisting" was actually initiated by the former Court of Claims. The Suspension clause only applied where, in its absence, the government would have breached the contract. In T.C. Bateson Constr. Co. a board of contract appeals held that a strike caused by the government's action in taking possession of a plant prior to its completion was not a suspension of the work under the clause, stating:

> In the absence of a contract giving the government the right to suspend the contractor's work or otherwise delay the contractor's performance, a work stoppage caused by the government would ordinarily be a breach of contract giving rise to an action at law for damages, but a suspension of work caused by the government is not a breach of contract when done pursuant to a right granted to the government by the terms of the contract itself. The "Suspension of Work" clause gives the government the right under the contract to suspend the contractor's work, in exchange for which it gives the contractor the right under the contract to an equitable adjustment in price for the loss or additional expense incurred by the contractor as a result of the government's exercise of its right of suspension.

However, the former Court of Claims disagreed and found that a suspension of work had been ordered "constructively," and held that the contracting officer should have suspended the work and an equitable adjustment should have been made under Article GC–11 (Suspension of Work). The former Court of Claims decided to substitute its determination for that of the contracting officer even though only the latter's determination had been agreed to by the parties to the contract in the event of a suspension of work.

A claim for "unreasonable delays" must originate from government action, not action on the part of third parties. A threat by two Navajo Indian women to blow up construction equipment with dynamite (because they objected to the contractor's use of a burial pit which they claimed to be of ceremonial significance) did not authorize the granting of a suspension of work, and the government's counterclaim for the costs of a temporary two-day suspension was sustained.

§ 42.8   Delays in Construction Projects

(a) Reasonable and Unreasonable Delays

A contractor who suffered an unreasonable delay as a result of the inefficiency of another contractor has been held to be entitled to an equitable adjustment in the contract price to cover added costs attributable to the delay, even if the government was neither negligent nor at fault in any way. Where the government chose to award several prime contracts rather than a single contract to a general contractor with subsequent subcontracts, the government was held *not* to be the guarantor of the various contractors' performances; however, the government was obligated to use reasonable efforts to obtain cooperation, non-influence, and compliance with established schedules for completion. A more recent board held that a contractor need not prove that it notified the government of its intent to complete a contract early in order to recover on its claims for government-caused delay.

A clause entitled "Schedules for Construction Contracts" is prescribed in fixed-price construction contracts which are expected to exceed the small purchase limitation and performance is expected to exceed 60 days. It authorizes an acceleration by stating that "if, in the opinion of the contracting officer, the contractor falls behind the approved schedule, the contractor shall take steps necessary to improve its progress." These steps may be required by the contracting officer "without additional cost to the government" and include an "increase in the number of shifts, overtime operations, days of work, and/or the amount of construction plant." A failure to comply with the requirements constitutes grounds for a determination that "the contractor is not prosecuting the work with sufficient diligence" and the contracting officer may terminate the contractor's right to proceed with the work, in accordance with the default article.

Some acts or omissions of the government can fall under either the changes clause or the suspension clause; the suspension clause expressly excludes its application, permitting recovery delays under the changes clause. The Suspension of Work clause specifically states, "No adjustment shall be made under this clause for any suspension, delay, or interruption ... for which an equitable adjustment is provided for or excluded under any other term or condition of this contract." A board has permitted recovery under the suspension clause where recovery could not be had under the changes clause because the contractor had failed to give notice under that clause. Another Board decision apportioned a claim between the changes and suspension of work clauses.

(b) *Unabsorbed Overhead—Eichleay Formula*

In 1960, the Eichleay Corporation appealed decisions of the contracting officer determining the amount of equitable adjustments due to the contractor under the suspension of work provisions of the certain contracts. Eichleay based its claim on an allocation of the total recorded main office expense to the contract in the ratio of contract billings to total billings for the period of performance. The resulting determination of a contract allocation was divided into a daily rate, which was multiplied by the number of days of delay to arrive at the amount of the claim. The Armed Services Board of Contract Appeals accepted the method of computing overhead expenses of the contractor during delays in work ordered by the government and permitted the contractor to compute its claimed amount by determining a daily overhead dollar amount and multiplying it by the agreed number of days' delay. This ruling was affirmed on reconsideration in spite of the Board's finding that:

> There appears in the record no showing of any actual increase in the overhead rate and no showing that the appellant took any action to mitigate its loss on overhead facilities made idle by government delays, by either laying off personnel or taking on new business for the period of such delays.

The method became known as the *"Eichleay* Formula." Because there are generally no direct costs that result from the impact of delays when the government suspends contract performance and home office overhead is seldom affected, the automatic use of the formula has became subject to question and the boards split concerning its validity and use. Underabsorbed overhead (often also applicable to manufacturing accounting) results from an increase in the rate of allocation of indirect costs to work other than that work which has been delayed. In 1983, the Claims Court decided that a contractor who was delayed by government-ordered changes had "simply failed to carry its burden ... by a preponderance of evidence, that the existence of an additional performance period required an additional increase in the contract price to offset the greater proportion of (his) continuing home office costs." The following year, in an appeal before the Court of Appeals for the Federal Circuit, the government argued that an automatic application of the *Eichleay* formula allowed a contractor (Capital Electric Co.) to escape the burden of proof of establishing the fact of injury faced by all claimants. The Court pointed to Capital's evidence to show that it could not have taken on any large construction jobs during the various delay periods due to the uncertainty of the delays and reversed both the Board and Claims Court, quoting from the *Eichleay* opinion: "The mere showing of these facts is sufficient to transfer to the government the burden of going forward with proof that [the Contractor] suffered no loss or should have suffered no loss." The Appellate Court applied the formula with very limited analysis stating that such a precedent "can only be overruled by the Federal Circuit sitting en banc" or by Congress. Although a subsequent Board decision initially appeared to refuse to use the formula, it fell in line.

In C.B.C. Enterprises Inc. v. United States, the Court of Appeals for the Federal Circuit held the *raison d'etre* of *Eichleay* requires at least some element of uncertainty arising from suspension, disruption, or delay of contract performance. Such delays are sudden, sporadic and of uncertain duration. As a result, it is impractical for the contractor to take on other work during these delays. There, the contractor was unable to show government-caused delay, suspension, disruption, or "standby" sufficient to support recovery.

Under *Eichleay*, a contractor must attempt to mitigate its damages. Some boards have applied the *Eichleay* formula to nonconstruction contracts. In 1998, the U.S. Court of Appeals for the Federal Circuit held that a contractor need not show it was impossible to take on any additional work while it was on standby as a result of the suspension. The contractor may indicate that it was "impractical" for it to take on "replacement work." At the same time, a board held that, although the government had acknowledged causing delays in the work, the contractor had failed to prove it was "on standby" for a period of uncertain duration. In similar fashion, another board held that where a contract is substantially completed, the contractor might not recover unabsorbed overhead costs under the *Eichleay* formula for the length of time required to negotiate modifications for additional work. In 1999, the Federal Circuit held that the government could be liable for a subcontractor's unabsorbed overhead costs resulting from government-caused delay even though the prime contractor completed its contract on time. In 2001, the ASBCA held that the government owed a construction contractor *Eichleay* damages for unabsorbed home office overhead even though its workforce was not completely idle during the government-caused delay period. The U.S. Court of Appeals for the Federal Circuit remanded a decision of that board because it "did not adequately explain" why it rejected a contractor's claim for *Eichleay* damages; the board reaffirmed its decision in 2002 and denied the contractor's appeal. However, in 2003, the Federal Circuit Court held that the Eichleay formula can only be used in a complete suspension of activity, the delay was both substantial and of uncertain duration, and that during the delay, the contractor had been ready to resume the work.

(c) *The Total Cost Basis and Jury Verdict Method, Government–Caused Delays*

Using a contractor's historical costs, some courts have permitted recovery of alleged total costs without giving much consideration to possible inefficiencies. Other tribunals facing positions taken by the parties during litigation have used a "jury verdict" method—a figure which "in the view of the trier of the facts is fair in the light of all of the facts of the case."

In J.D. Hedin Constr. Co. v. United States, the former Court of Claims stated that it disliked the total cost method, and limited its use to situations "where there is no other alternative." In one case in which an equitable adjustment was allowed on the basis of a "jury verdict" approach, a board apportioned the fault for delay 60% to contractor and 40% to the government.

However, a board rejected the total cost method for government-caused delays which would have the effect of shifting the costs for certain factors that did cause a delay, such as rain or failure of ironworkers to appear on a particular day. The record contained nothing from which it could be determined which costs should properly be borne by the government and the board remarked that the total cost method depends on proof that (1) the nature of the particular losses made it impossible or highly impracticable to determine them with reasonable accuracy, (2) the contractor's bid was realistic, (3) actual costs were reasonable, and (4) the contractor was not responsible for the added costs. Such proof was absent there.

The total cost approach may fail to account for problems caused by the contractor and modifications of that approach have been undertaken. For example, it has been modified to avoid the government having to pay for the responsibilities or for mistaken estimates.

Nevertheless, some boards continued to use this approach. In one case after entitlement had been decided, a board found that a jury verdict was appropriate even though the contractor had an information system capable of tracking costs associated with changes.

However, in 2001, the U.S. Court of Federal Claims was requested to make an award on the total cost method, so that a contractor could recover the difference between its costs of performance and its bid price. The contractor had abandoned its records documenting its cost under the contract modifications for its $3.2 million adjustment claim. The court stated that it was "disinclined to allow a plaintiff to rely on that method based on a bed of its own making," and added:

> Such a holding would also, as a practical matter, abrogate various clauses, all visible in this Contract, designed to forestall exactly the scenario that occurred here—a failure to document costs; a failure to preserve necessary records; a failure to notify timely the government, in writing, that a modification is having a cost impact; and, ultimately, the belated assertion of a claim which, not surprisingly, and perhaps inevitably, lacks adequate documentation.

(1) it is impossible or impracticable to prove actual losses directly,

(2) its bid or estimate was realistic,

(3) its actual costs are reasonable, and

(4) it was not responsible for the added expenses.

§ 42.9　Contractor Past Performance Information

Beginning January 1, 1998, agencies have been required to prepare an evaluation of contractor performance for most contracts in excess of $100,000. This is because of its likely use as "past performance" information in connection with future contractor selections. Although it became controversial, it has been regarded as a generally needed procedure in view of the use of information from the government's prior contract dealings.

An agency's evaluation must be provided to the contractor "as soon as practicable" and the contractor is given a minimum of 30 days to submit his comments. The ultimate conclusion is a decision of the contracting agency and is marked "Source Selection Information." It is not to be released to anyone other than government personnel (including those from other departments and agencies) and the contractor. Nevertheless, it has been argued by the private bar that "the collection and evaluation of contractor past performance data discourages contractors from pressing legitimate contract disputes" (citing only cases on abuse of the process).

The agency's procedures must generally provide for input from the technical office, contracting office, and end users where appropriate. There are a number of due process protections for contractors. Perhaps most importantly, the contractor must be provided a copy of the evaluation as soon as practicable after completion, and must be given at least 30 days to respond. Disagreements about the evaluation must be resolved at a level above the contracting officer. Although past performance information is shared with other agencies, it is considered "source selection information" and must be protected from unauthorized disclosure. "The past performance information may not be retained to provide source selection information for longer than three years after completion of contract performance."

On April 1, 2002, the OFPP Administrator indicated to Federal agencies that a contractor's filing of protests or claims, or the use of alternative dispute resolution "must not be considered in either past performance evaluations or source selection decisions." Nevertheless, the importance cannot be overemphasized.

By statute, past performance evaluations are a mandatory evaluation factor for all source selections for negotiated competitive acquisitions expected to exceed $100,000, unless the contracting officer makes a written determination that its use is "not an appropriate evaluation factor for the acquisition."

CHAPTER 43

CONTRACT MODIFICATIONS

A. AUTHORITY TO MODIFY CONTRACTS

§ 43.1   In General

The authority to issue a direction or order on behalf of the government has been discussed above. In addition to an authority to contract, as a general rule, an agreement to pay a higher price for performance of an obligation to which the seller is already bound lacks consideration at common law. Even though the buyer (the government) approves the higher price verbally, or in writing, there is no legal "change of position" on the part of the contractor. A contracting officer is without authority to modify an agreement in certain instances to the pecuniary detriment of the United States. To modify the performance normally requires a price adjustment; however, this may not be necessary if the modification is the result of the settlement of a claim. In one case, a contract provided for delivery of air conditioners at a price of $612,904. A modification purported to change the specifications to include a high pressure cut out switch. The modification stated that "this supplemental agreement ... shall be a full, complete and final settlement of any claims" which the parties may have had. Later the contracting officer claimed the right to reduce the contract price by $20,568, because the original contract required the contractor to furnish the switch. The contractor appealed the reduction in price because the original contract requirement for the switch was doubtful and the

474

modification was stated to be a "final settlement of any claims" as a result of the modification. The appeal was sustained. A contractor's agreement to waive his claim for the cost of a change given in exchange for the government's making it permanent (and thus applicable to future procurements) has been held not supported by valid consideration because this was beyond his authority; only contracting officers acting within the scope of their authority are empowered to execute contract modifications on behalf of the government.

§ 43.2   "Changed" Contracts

After award, the contractor may offer to change the way he is to perform and an unsuccessful proposer will protest the acceptance of this offer on the grounds that the change was being made without competition; such a modification could be viewed as an attempt to circumvent the competitive procurement statutes. A modification may be equivalent to a sole source award under a new procurement. However, if it is found that the changes made are small and the item being procured was not substantially different, new competition will not be required. The GAO has also looked to decisions of the former Court of Claims involving the "cardinal changes" doctrine discussed below. This concept was developed in order to deal with contractors' claims that the government had breached by ordering changes that were outside the general scope of the contract pursuant to the changes clause; the doctrine is utilized as a standard whether or not the modified job is essentially the same work for which the parties contracted. The GAO has applied this standard to situations where a firm that is not a party to the contract complains that a modification is not within the scope of the competition that initially was conducted. In one case, a protest was sustained against a modification to a contract for gas powered and fired heaters that permitted diesel powered and fired heaters. The modification necessitated numerous other changes in the contract, including the substitution of a diesel engine for a gasoline engine, a 29 percent increase in the unit price, and doubling of the delivery time. The modified contract was so different from the completed contract that the government should have solicited new proposals for its modified requirement. This criteria for competition may not apply in instances where the agency should have known of the need for the change in specifications before award and the protest, if sustained, can result in a new solicitation without significant cost to the government. Otherwise, it would appear that the overriding goal of fair competition might have been compromised.

A bilateral agreement (i.e. a supplemental agreement) is used for agreements of the parties modifying the contract, such as a quantity increase or change not covered by any other contract clause. On the other hand, a unilateral modification (signed only by the contracting officer) is used to make changes that are authorized by clauses within the contract.

§ 43.3   Modification Resulting From Economic Duress—Aggressiveness Distinguished

Where two contractors, faced with a choice of either agreeing to a contract modification proposed by the government or becoming bankrupt, so agreed, the modifications were held by a board to be invalid because the contractors had consented under economic duress. The former Court of Claims had occasion to consider the government's bargaining power and also refused to grant relief on that account. The case concerned a corporation that had been in default on several contracts for aircraft parts. A procurement office, obtained an agreement on new delivery dates after remarking that he may have to place the contractor on a list (called a "Contractor Experience List") of companies whose capability must be evaluated prior to the award of any contract. In commenting on the possible factor of duress, the court stated, "Mere aggressiveness of a government representative in pursuing his duties can hardly rise to the status of coercion." Similarly, a demand of $120,000 in extra costs of completion by a subcontractor in a dire financial condition, was countered by a general contractor's offer of $67,000. The latter offer that was accepted by the subcontractor, and was held under Wisconsin law to be not such "threat" as would render contract settlement unenforceable. According to the court, the argument of the subcontractor that the prime contractor said, "give up $53,000 of your claim for extras, or you will get nothing" was recast as "I promise to pay you $67,000 for a release of your claim."

The reservations of the Claims Court respecting unconscionability as a defense in government contracts have been expressed as follows: the more modern concept of unconscionability, which stresses inequality of bargaining power, particularly in consumer transactions, is quite dissimilar to the realities of dealing with the Federal government as one's contracting partner. It should come as no surprise to find that there is no case in either this court or our predecessor court, where a plaintiff has prevailed by invoking the theory of unconscionability to void a perceived unfavorable contract or contract provision.

B.   CHANGE ORDERS—MODIFICATIONS WHICH ARE ORDERED PURSUANT TO A CLAUSE IN THE ORIGINAL AGREEMENT OF THE PARTIES

§ 43.11   Supply Contracts—In General

A method, peculiar to government contracting, is the inclusion of an authorization for one party to make changes within the general scope of the original contract. The consideration and mutual consent for such subsequent changes are derived from those needed to make the original contract binding on the parties. The document that accomplishes such a change is called a "change order" and it is issued by the government. The "Changes" clause used in fixed-price supply contracts provides that the Contracting Officer may at any time, by written order, "make changes within the general scope" of the contract. These changes may be in the "drawings, designs, or specifications when the supplies to be furnished are to be specially manufactured for the Government" in accordance therewith or in the "[m]ethod of shipment or packing," and "place of delivery." The clause applicable to fixed-price construction contracts is similar, except that in addition to ordering changes in the specifications, it also provides the right to direct changes in "the method or manner of performance of the work ... [i]n the Government-furnished facilities, equipment, materials, service, or site; or ... [d]irecting acceleration in the performance of the work."

The Changes clause has been one of the most litigated clauses in government contracts. Where a contractor makes changes without any reliance on a statement by a contracting officer, there has been no change under the Changes article; and if an after-the-fact agreement is made, any payment may be subject to the argument that past consideration is no consideration. Where a contractor voluntarily accelerates performance for its own purposes, it may not recover the costs of acceleration. The regulation lists the issuance of an order under the changes clause as a "unilateral modification" and the negotiation of an equitable adjustment resulting from the issuance as a supplemental agreement or "bilateral" change order. Where the contractor either does not agree to that adjustment, or delays in doing so issuance may be required of a unilateral notice that is signed only by the contracting officer.

§ 43.12   Negotiation of Equitable Adjustment

In case of change, the agency is directed to negotiate the equitable adjustment in "the shortest practicable time;" The contractor must normally continue performance of the successful contract as changed. Negotiation requires agreement on both sides. If this is accomplished, then in order to avoid subsequent controversies that may result from a supplemental agreement containing an equitable adjustment as the result of a change order, a clause is included in the Supplemental Agreement releasing the government from liability for further equitable adjustments attributable to such facts or circumstances giving rise to the "proposal(s) for adjustment."

Where agreement cannot be reached within a reasonable time, it is proper for the Contracting officer to make a unilateral determination of the adjustment. This is transmitted to the contractor with a notification that it constitutes his final decision and advising him of his right to appeal under the Disputes clause. The contractor may either appeal, or his claim will be dismissed for failure to bring a timely appeal.

§ 43.14   The Concept of Equitable Adjustment

The term "equitable adjustment" was first used in the standard Changes and Changed Conditions articles and was later taken over for other clauses, such as the "suspension of work" and "government-furnished property" provisions. It has been used to permit recovery of the reasonable value for the work under which no agreement was reached on price (called quantum meruit (for services) or quantum valebat (for supplies) at common law). It would not include anticipatory profit.

§ 43.15   Cardinal Changes

The Changes article permits the government to make changes within the general scope of the contract. It has been ruled that the Changes article does not authorize a "cardinal" change, a modification "beyond the general scope" of the contract. The basic standard is whether the modified job was essentially the same work as the parties bargained for when the contract was awarded.

Because the boards may take jurisdiction of any claim "relating to" a contract, their jurisdiction in this area is the same as that of the Court of Federal Claims. The former Court of Claims ruled that a cardinal change is a contract breach, entitling the contractor to damages, and even lost profits in some cases. Although the Cardinal Change Doctrine was developed to deal with contractors' claims that the government ordered changes outside the scope of the Changes clause, it has been converted into use for a completely different purpose by the continued characterization of the Court of Claims that such an order is a "breach of contract." That ruling resulted in confusion because, without the existence of a contractual duty, the issuance of a cardinal change cannot result in a breach of contract. Where one party to a contract orders something that the other party has no duty to perform, the order may be insignificant except to the extent that the government may possibly become unjustly enriched. A breach of contract requires the existence of a duty without which there simply cannot be breach. Although there is no express duty not to issue a change order beyond the general scope of the contract, one could argue that such a duty could be implied. However, implied terms are considered supplementary rather than mandatory. Something "beyond the general scope of the contract" is a matter for future agreement and normally not binding on the parties. Relief for cardinal changes which are performed by a contractor lies in unjust enrichment.

The factors in deciding whether a change or a series of changes is "beyond the general scope of the contract" include not only the number of changes, but also their character, timing, and the amount of development work needed to be done by the contractor and the cost of the changed work as compared with the original scope. If work was done beyond the general scope, neither the number of changes nor the character of the work performed is necessarily conclusive on whether or not a change is cardinal; it is the magnitude and quality of the change, in light of the circumstances. Where the finished product is substantially the same as the one originally contracted for, there has been no cardinal change.

§ 43.16 "Constructive Changes" Doctrine and Its Elimination in Certain Current Clauses

An express change takes place when a contracting officer purposely utilizes a Changes article in the contract and issues a written order that is covered by it. A constructive change is a change that a contractor argues that he has to make even though he has not been issued a written order under a Changes article. For example, in Southwest Welding & Mfg. Co. v. United States, a Federal contracting officer ordered a contractor to remove and replace welds, even though these welds had been examined radiographically and passed by government inspectors. He complied but protested that this constituted extra work. When a board of contract appeals denied the claim under the Disputes article of the contract, the contractor appealed to the former Court of Claims, which adopted an opinion of a commissioner. "The government clearly ordered extra work above and beyond the requirements of the contract which it had drafted and it should reimburse the contractor therefor pursuant to the standard 'Changes' clause contained in this contract"—even though the order was not issued pursuant to that clause.

The principal problems with the constructive change doctrine are three-fold. The first is concerned with the authority of the person who would order the work. If he lacked authority, no recovery can be allowed for such work that was done, absent unjust enrichment. This has not always been examined by the tribunals. Secondly, the doctrine may conflict with the contract made by the parties. If work is requested by the government without the issuance of a written order pursuant to the Changes article, the contractor becomes a volunteer. Normally, he can claim damages outside of the express contract; that is, in an implied contract to the extent that the government becomes unjustly enriched.

Absent a statute, no court or board appears to have the express authority to bring into the Changes clauses of the contract that which the parties did not expressly include in the contract or include by reasonable implication either at the time it was executed or subsequent thereto pursuant to the method set forth in a clause of that contract, namely, a written change order under the Changes article or another clause. Hence, the doctrine has been regarded as a device whereby Boards of Contract Appeals have asserted jurisdiction over situations in which normally they would have none. This practice was contained due to its sanction by the former Court of Claims.

§ 43.18 The Changes Clause in Construction Contracts

The changes clause of the standard construction contract is similar to the changes clause in supply contracts in that it authorizes the agency to unilaterally order the contractor to perform changes in the contract—work including the design, specifications, method of performance, or equipment or facilities furnished by the government—"within the general scope of the contract." There may be a possible increase or decrease in the contract price in the form of an "equitable adjustment" where the contractor submits a proposal within 30 days of receipt of the order. This is discussed above in connection with contract modification of supply contracts.

Herein are discussed provisions of the article peculiar to constructive changes arising out of a contractor's requests for compensation which are not expressly covered in formal change orders. The applicable clause also specifies that the term change order includes "any written or oral ... direction, instruction, interpretation or determination ... from the Contracting Officer" which causes any such change. With the respect to these directions, the contractor is required to give the agency written notice of the circumstances, and source of order and state that he "regards the order as a change order." Further, except for claims based on defective specifications, or where a waiver is made, no claim is allowed for any costs incurred more than 20 days before the contractor gives written notice as therein required. The 20–day cut off period is an attempt to control claims for constructive changes and it was intended not to be subject to waiver by the contracting officer or boards of contract appeal.

Although the clause excludes costs incurred in attempting to comply with defective specifications, this may not permit recovery of costs incurred after the contractor knew or should have known of such defect. A few boards have interpreted the language according to the requirement for a written notice under this clause; others appear to have disregarded that 20–day notice requirement. Thirty years ago, a board imputed knowledge of a government inspection and a base civil engineer to the contracting officer and stated that where the government "knew or should have known" this substitutes for the written notice required by the contract language, in refusing to follow the contract language:

> Rather, we favor the approach of permitting an appellant to "have his day in court" if there is any reasonable basis to do so. In short we believe that the ends of justice are best served by strictly constructing contract provisions authored by the government which, whether intentionally or not, appear to be designed to limit the remedies which otherwise would be available to an aggrieved contractor to redress injuries suffered at the hands of the government. We are aware of no reason which would justify our treating the aforesaid 20–day notice requirement of the "Changes" clause any differently, nor has any been pointed out to us.

It substituted its favor and its philosophy of justice for that set forth in the agreement of the parties; there was no duress, the contract had not been determined to be unconscionable and no statutory or constitutional issues were involved.

During World War II, Rice contracted to install plumbing, heating and electrical equipment in a veterans' home while another contractor was to construct the building. Rice agreed to complete his work by the time the other contract was completed. Construction was delayed because a site change was required due to unsuitable soil conditions. As a result, overhead expenses accumulated for Rice during the period of the delay. Rice received an extension of time and liquidated damages were waived. He nevertheless sued in the Court of Claims for damages suffered by the delay, a portion of which arose from overhead costs. The government contended that the change in specifications precipitating the delay was not a breach because a contract provision merely required the government to grant an extension of time. The Supreme Court concurred with the government's position stating:

> It seems wholly reasonable that "an increase or decrease in the amount due" should be met with an alteration of price, and that an "increase or decrease ... in the time required" should be met with alteration of the time allowed; for "increase or decrease of cost" plainly applies to the changes in cost due to the structural changes required by the altered specification and not to consequential damages which might flow from delay taken care of in the "difference in time" provision.

Nowhere did the clauses expressly limit or apply increases in costs solely to changes in cost due to "structural changes required by the altered specification." A quarter century was to elapse before the government was to achieve

this result by the promulgation of new and expanded clauses for construction contracts in November 1967, following
an interdepartmental study. The revised language of this
portion of the Changes article reads as follows:

If any such change causes an increase or decrease in the
cost of, or the time required for performance of any part
of the work under this contract, whether or not changed
by any such order, the contracting officer shall make an
equitable adjustment and modify the contract in writing.

The amount of equitable adjustment under the Changes
article is measured by the reasonable value of the work
done pursuant to a change order that was issued within the
general scope of the contract. The question then arises
whether this value is determined by the market value of the
cost of the change order or the actual (or historical) cost to
the contractor—which could be quite different and possibly
significantly higher depending upon the contractor's efficiency and the circumstances existing at the time the work
was performed. The latter point of view (which is generally
favorable to the contractor) was adopted by the former
Court of Claims as a presumptive criterion for such
changes. There, Bruce Construction Corporation contracted
to construct building blocks of a certain texture. Subsequently, Bruce was required to change from concrete to
sand blocks. The price paid was the same for either but the
contractor argued that it was entitled to an adjustment
because "the fair market value" was greater for the sand
block. The court ruling that price adjustments are based on
reasonable costs went on to hold that the actual costs to
Bruce constituted the proper measure in the absence of
evidence that such costs were unreasonable. The court
made a statement that "where there is an alleged disparity

between 'historical' and 'reasonable' costs, the historical costs are presumed reasonable."

The court held that evidence of the fair market value of the blocks 18 months after the transaction did "not rebut the presumption that the cost [to plaintiff] of the item was reasonable at the time of the transaction." The reasonable costs were presumptively held to be the same as actual costs, which was a departure from a standard of quantum valebant—the test generally used to determine reasonable costs in private contracts. The concurring opinion stated, "The only evidence of value at the time was the invoice showing the price plaintiff paid for the blocks. In the absence of any other evidence of value at the time of the purchase, I would adopt the invoice price as the proper measure of value."

Any approved changes initiated by the contractor may or may not be entitled to an equitable adjustment of the contract price depending on the terms of that approval. For example, the request in one case was for a revised schedule reducing the 350–day contract schedule to 225–day schedule, in order to complete the work before winter, thus avoiding the costs of a shut-down until spring. The government approved the revised schedule, but specifically stated that the approval was neither a directive to complete the work within the new schedule or a guarantee that the schedule could be met. When unexpected problems arose, the contractor went into overtime to complete within the revised schedule. He then sought additional funds to offset these increased costs, claiming that the government had accelerated the performance. The board held that the decision to incur extra costs to complete the work before winter was an exercise of the contractor's own business judgment for which it was entitled to no additional compensation from the government.

§ 43.19 Constructive Changes Doctrine and Its Partial Elimination by Being Incorporated Into Current Contract Clauses

The Doctrine of Constructive Changes has been discussed above, largely in connection with the Changes article in supply contracts. A constructive change clause has been implied into a contract; anytime an express clause completely covers a matter, no constructive clause is possible. An example in a construction context using a former version of the Changes clause concerned Norair Eng'g. Corporation's contract to complete the building of Smithsonian Institution's Museum of History and Technology (now the National Museum of American History) within 900 calendar days. When it was noticed that certain columns were misaligned, a change order was issued. The museum was substantially completed 524 days after the original contract date. The contracting officer granted an extension as excusable delay for all of those days because of several strikes, bad weather, and a total of 158 change orders. Norair sought $1.65 million in damages for consequential changes in its planned sequence of production and alleged orders to accelerate. A board of contract appeals ruled that certain letters from the government could not constitute acceleration orders because the contract that was 524 days late and the letters were not acceleration orders in the sense of being mandatory.

Nonetheless, the former Court of Claims reversed, holding "there is nothing 'incongruous' about an acceleration order on a contract that is 524 days late, as long as those additional days were excusable" and added "we may not assume that the post hoc extension was some sort of gratuity." Possibly the contracting officer thought that he could excuse the delay (and thus not charge the contractor) but also thought that the government would not be charged for letters urging early completion. The Court added "even an expression of concern about lagging process may have the same effect as an order." This was an approach not following the former contract language regarding change orders; the standard language has been modified and the following paragraph added to that clause.

(b) Any other written or oral order (which, as used in this Paragraph (b), includes direction, instruction, interpretation, or determination) from the contracting officer that causes a change shall be treated as a change order under this clause; provided, that the contractor gives the contracting officer written notice stating (1) the date, circumstances, and source of the order and (2) that the contractor regards the order as a change order.

(c) Except as provided in this clause, no order, statement, or conduct of the contracting officer shall be treated as a change under this clause or entitle the contractor to an equitable adjustment.

In construction contracts there are no longer "constructive" changes because virtually all changes are contained in the contract clause itself. Construction contract change orders have cost the government approximately $3 billion a year and provided a significant potential for waste, fraud, and abuse, according to an audit report presented to the President's Council on Integrity and Efficiency.

CHAPTER 44

SUBCONTRACTING

§ 44.1 Subcontractors

(a) Who Are Subcontractors

While the term "subcontractor" has no single specific meaning, the regulation defines him as any supplier, distributor, vendor, or firm that furnishes supplies or services to or for a prime contractor or another subcontractor (at another tier downward). However, it may have a more restrictive meaning in certain instances. Under the Miller Act, for example, the above definition is too general.

In one case, the MacEvoy Co. agreed to construct dwelling units under a CPFF contract and executed a payment bond for $1 million conditioned on prompt payment to all persons supplying labor and material. MacEvoy purchased certain building materials under subcontract with the J. H. Miller Company. Miller in turn purchased these materials from the Tomphins Co., who sued MacEvoy and the surety for nonpayment. Under the Miller Act, when a person supplies materials to a materialman of a government contractor and that person has an unpaid balance due him, the materialman cannot recover on the payment bond executed by the contractor. The right to bring suit on a payment is limited to those materialmen, laborers and subcontractors who deal directly with the prime contractor (MacEvoy) or who, lacking express or implied contractual relationship with the prime contractor, have direct contractual relationship with a subcontractor (Miller) and give the statutory notice of their claims to the prime contractor. The Supreme Court recognized that:

> In a broad, generic sense a subcontractor includes anyone who has a contract to furnish labor or material to the prime contractor. In that sense, Miller was a subcontractor. But under the more technical meaning, as established by usage in the building trades, a subcontractor is one who performs for and takes from the prime contractor a specific part of the labor or material requirements of the original contract, thus excluding ordinary laborers and materialmen.

A subcontractor must look exclusively to the general contractor or his surety for payment; he cannot obtain liens on the Federal projects and buildings, and cannot collect directly from the treasury due to sovereign immunity.

(b) Subcontractor Tiers

A subcontractor may either be one tier below the prime contractor, or several tiers down; as noted above, all tiers are generally assumed to be subcontractors unless the contrary is shown to be intended. This may be the case with certain standard contract clauses. Some prime contractors are small business enterprises, and some subcontractors are large enterprises; there is no necessary relation between size and tier.

A board of contract appeals has held that second-tier subcontractors lack standing to pursue contract appeals in their own name.

§ 44.2 Consent to Subcontracts

(a) In General

Agencies exercise primary oversight of competition in procurement by contractors through requirements for con-

sent (or approval) of individual procurements and review
and approval of a contractor's purchasing system. An agency's consent to subcontracts is not normally required under
prime contracts that are firm-fixed-price. It is required
when the subcontract work is under a cost-type contract,
above a certain dollar value, or the government's interest is
not adequately protected by competition. Such consent is
required with respect to subcontracts under firm fixed price
prime contracts or other fixed price prime contracts where
the contractor has an approved purchasing system. If he
does not have an approved purchasing system, consent is
required for certain types of subcontracts and then only if
they are above certain dollar thresholds (normally
$100,000).

Consent is required under cost-type and letter contracts
for subcontracts for special test equipments and a number
of other cases which largely depend upon whether the
contractor has an approved purchasing system. With an
approved system, most consent requirements disappear except for those identified with subcontract clauses of the
contract. An agency may also consent by authorizing a
contractor to purchase from government sources under a
special contract clause.

Such consent entails considerable review by agency personnel of a number of considerations. However, the regulation excludes from the review of the contractor's purchasing
system subcontracts awarded exclusively in support of government contracts that are competitively-awarded firm-
fixed-price, competitively-awarded fixed price with economic
price adjustment, or awarded for the acquisition of commercial items (See Chapter 12, supra).

There are also agreements with respect to which the
agency cannot consent, such as cost-reimbursement con-

tracts where the fee exceeds the statutory fee limitations, cost-plus-percentage of cost subcontracts, or agreements that bind the government to the result of arbitration, judicial determination, or settlements between the prime and the subcontractor.

(b) Subcontracting and Collective Bargaining Agreements

Under the National Labor Relations Act (NLRA), a company may not refuse to bargain collectively with the union in its plants on conditions of employment; hence, to the extent that a change in such conditions is effected by contracting out work without bargaining thereon, such subcontracting may constitute a violation of the Act.

Construction work under government contracts which is in excess of $2,000 is done under the Davis–Bacon Act, the provisions of which were enacted during the depression of the 1930s and require payment of wages prevailing in the region for such work. Such wages are generally higher than those being paid to maintenance employees who are currently performing similar work in an employer's plant. Government contracts in excess of $500,000 ($1,000,000 for construction) contain provisions requiring the contractor to establish and conduct a small business subcontracting program which will enable small businesses to be considered fairly as subcontractors and suppliers. Absent proof of antiunion motivation, the subcontracting of work during a lockout has been held not inherently destructive of employee rights and not in violation of Section 8(a)(3) of the NLRA. However, where an employer is motivated primarily by desire to improve profitability, he may refuse to bargain over subcontracting that is not a "term or condition" of employment.

Suits by and against labor unions may be brought in the United States District Court having jurisdiction of the parties under § 301 of the Taft–Hartley Act, but state courts may also entertain suits arising under § 301 provided they apply Federal law. Section 301 not only grants a forum for disputes but also expresses a Federal policy in favor of enforcing collective bargaining agreements—including specific performance of arbitration provisions contained therein. In 1960, in the so-called "steelworkers trilogy," the Supreme Court indicated that unless the parties expressly provide otherwise, the determination of arbitrability rests with the courts to ascertain whether the party seeking arbitration is making a claim that appears to be governed by the contract. Later, the Supreme Court reiterated that "whether or not the company was bound to arbitrate, as well as what issues it must arbitrate, is a matter to be determined by the Court on the basis of the contract entered into by the parties." In Independent Petroleum Workers of America, Inc. v. American Oil Company, the Court of Appeals, refusing to compel arbitration of contracting out, stated:

Plaintiff's claim for relief is based entirely upon "alleged violations of the terms of this agreement." The question immediately arises—What terms? The recognition clause makes no reference either to arbitration or to the contracting out of work.

The proposition has been reiterated by subsequent decisions. An appellate court stated:

[O]ne who has not agreed to arbitrate will not be forced to arbitrate. The Steelworkers trilogy did not change the long-established principle of law that compulsory arbitration cannot be properly awarded absent a contract between the parties agreeing thereto.

Where the arbitration clause is specifically limited to the collective bargaining agreement, and that agreement nowhere discusses subcontracting, the issue of whether a grievance is subject to arbitration is not an arbitrable issue. Although a company must bargain with the union on the subject of contracting out work, the obligation to bargain is not necessarily the obligation to agree. An employer who is a government contractor must consider the clauses of his contract and absent an agreement to the contrary, there is no general duty to go beyond discussions with the union on a subcontract's basis or at the time that classes of subcontracts are let. If a union threatens to strike at the time of the letting of a subcontract, or classes of subcontracts, there is no duty to arbitrate the contracting out issue if the collective bargaining agreement contains clauses that pertain to questions that may be referred to arbitration and which relate to the specific terms of that agreement. (See § 15, Make or Buy Programs of Prime Contractors, supra.)

For his part, the contracting officer may become obliged—both at the time of negotiation of a collective bargaining agreement and during the period it is being administered—(1) to attempt to persuade a contractor not to accept a union's position respecting the subcontracting of certain items which should be subcontracted in accordance with the government's policies and regulations and (2) to attempt to persuade a union to modify or withdraw its position thereon. In addition, (3) if these attempts were to prove unsuccessful, he may find it necessary to request the contractor to litigate the issue of arbitrability of subcontracting under the terms of the collective bargaining agreement where the issue does not appear to be arbitrable or seek injunctive relief against a threatened strike; and (4) where these actions were to prove abortive, the government, in order to carry out its policies, would have to consider deleting work it had previously determined should be subcontracted from the existing contract, and letting another prime contract for this work.

In one case a union of government employees proposed a collective bargaining provision that would require the agency to make contracting-out decisions in accordance with Circular A–76 in deciding whether to contract work out to the private sector. See Chapter 7, Title VII of the Civil Service Reform Act, which requires that the agencies and employee unions bargain in good faith over "conditions of employment." However, a "management rights clause" of the statute contains provisions stating that: "nothing in this chapter shall affect the authority of any management official of any agency . . . in accordance with applicable laws . . . to make determinations with respect to contracting out." It also bars negotiation over contract proposals that are "inconsisten[t] with any Federal law or government-wide rule or regulation." A Federal Circuit Court held that a union's proposal violated both of these statutes and was not the subject of bargaining.

(c) Extension of Delivery Dates on Subcontracts Under Cost–Type Prime Contracts

Sometimes, cost-type contractors automatically grant delivery date extensions to suppliers who are unable to meet original delivery dates and the agency administering the prime contract may or may not be consulted thereon. Where the agency must approve the prime contractor's procurement procedures, it is normal to protect the government's interest by requiring that the contractor obtain a concession before agreeing to an extended delivery date. The buyer may consider such factors as whether delivery can be made within an acceptable period, the additional costs that may be incurred by the contractor or the government as a result of the late delivery, and the length of the delivery date extension. In some cases, the vendor may be entitled to a time extension as a matter of law, and the subcontract may be amended to provide for a later delivery date. The prime contractor's procedures may provide that if it is determined that the vendor will not meet the delivery date, either a new delivery date should be set or the subcontract should be terminated at the appropriate time.

Certain consequences flow from a grant of a time extension or from a termination for default: if an extension is granted at too early a date, the need for the item being procured may cease to exist between the date the time extension is granted and the date the item was to be delivered. In this event, the contractor might have the right to terminate only for convenience where, but for the time extension, he might have been able to terminate for default. Another example is that, in a particular given case, the vendor may be justified in failing to make delivery on time.

§ 44.3   Subcontract Clauses

Many standard clauses in prime contracts contain provisions making them applicable to subcontracts and these must be carefully drafted by the prime contractor or his attorneys. It is not practicable to always refer to the prime contract and state generally that to the extent they apply to the prime contract, they apply to the subcontracts. For this reason, a Subcontracting Committee of the American Bar Association Section of Public Contract Law has prepared some helpful models. In 2001, the ABA published the 222–page "Guide to Fixed–Price Supply Subcontract Terms and Conditions" and the Model to assist both prime contractors and subcontractors in drafting and negotiating subcontracts under Federal supply contracts. One law requires that all contractors, with the exception of small businesses, who receive a Federal prime contract or subcontract over

$500,000 ($1 million for construction) that has subcontracting opportunities, include a plan for subcontracting with small and small disadvantaged businesses.

There are some 36 or more contract clauses in the regulation containing mandatory requirements which "flow down" to subcontractors should the clause appear in the prime contract. These are of varying degrees of importance to the parties; for example, one large aerospace contractor considers the more important clauses to be the pricing and CAS provisions. (See Chapter 15, supra). There are some clauses containing optional requirements that do not specifically "flow down" to subcontracts.

§ 44.6   Subcontractor Claims

(a) *Privity of Contract*

The fact that the entire cost of the project is paid by the government does not create a contractual obligation between the government and subcontractors under contracts to which the government was not a party. Also, the fact that the government approves a subcontract does not break down the bar of lack of privity. Subcontractors cannot sue the government directly unless there exists an implied or express contract between them as well as with the prime contractor.

In an early case, the government entered into a cost-plus-fixed-fee (CPFF) contract with Nickel requiring the disassembly and removal of 900 housing units from one place and their subsequent reconstruction elsewhere. The contract also provided that the contractor could employ subcontractors to do part of the work. Nickel entered into a subcontract with Pollia for the removal and reinstallation of the plumbing and heating fixtures on 402 of the units. Later, it was discovered that Pollia had not done items for which it had been paid. After Pollia stopped work, his subcontract was terminated. When Pollia brought suit against the government to recover for work performed and materials delivered under his subcontract, the court held that there was no privity of contract between Pollia and the United States:

> His contract was with Nickel alone, and it was to Nickel alone that he must look for payment under his subcontract. [T]he fact that the entire cost of the project came from the government, did not create a contractual obligation between the government and the subcontractors under contracts to which the government was not a party.

In general, "subcontractors and suppliers, claiming amounts due for labor and materials furnished to a defaulted prime contractor, may not bring a claim directly against the government when, under any common law theory, they lack privity of contract with the government." The Comptroller General held that under the Contract Disputes Act of 1978, "a contracting officer does not have authority to settle claims of subcontractors who were not parties to the prime contract, even when such firms agree to accept pro rata settlement from remaining contract funds." The Supreme Court has held that a subcontractor that was not paid by the prime contractor for work performed on a Federal contract cannot sue the government directly by asserting an equitable lien on funds held by the government.

Other methods have been developed by subcontractors to obtain a direct remedy against the government: a subcontractor has been considered a creditor-beneficiary of the agreement between the government and prime contractor, a novation has resulted in the subcontractor replacing the

prime contractor, the government representative's actions
have resulted in an implied in fact contract with the government, or the contractor has become an agent of the
government. These theories ran into difficulty in that facts
were generally lacking for their support.

(b) Prosecution by Prime Contractor of a Claim by Subcontractor (Indirect Appeals)

Although subcontractors cannot sue the government directly unless there exists an implied or express contract
between them (as well as with the prime contractor), during
World War II a prime contractor sued the government for
work to be performed by the prime contractor which had
been subcontracted. In United States v. Blair, the U.S.
Supreme Court permitted a prime contractor to recover
against the government, on behalf of a subcontractor, for
costs of extras wrongly required by the United States.
Recovery could be barred if the subcontract contains a
disclaimer of liability by the prime contractor to the subcontractor. In Severin v. United States, a contract was entered
into with the United States to furnish labor and materials
and perform all work required for the construction of a post
office. A subcontractor was to cut marble caps and do
ornamental work. Because of the failure of the United
States to furnish the models for the exterior marble column
caps for the porticos, a change order was issued extending
the time for completion of the contract for 21 days. No
allowance was made in this change order for the actual loss
sustained by the prime contractor and its subcontractor by
reason of the fact that the delay caused the contractor
(plaintiffs) to stop work. The subcontractor had its force
ready to go to work carving the column caps, and it was
impossible for plaintiffs to complete the roofs of the porticos
because the columns were to serve as supports for the roofs.

The prime contractor brought suit for damages it sustained as a result of the government's breach of contract and also for damages sustained by the subcontractor. The court ruled that if the prime contractor had proved that "in the performance of its contract with the government (it) became liable to (its) subcontractor for the damages which the latter suffered, that liability might well constitute actual damages" to the prime contractor. However, the proof showed the opposite since the subcontract contained a clause stating that "the Contractor or Subcontractor shall not in any event be held responsible for any loss, damate (sic), detention or delay caused by the Owner or any other Subcontractor upon the building." The prime contractor effectively protected itself from any damage by way of shifting liability over to the subcontractor for breach of contract by the government. Without such a disclaimer, a prime contractor can recover on behalf of its subcontractor only if the contractor has suffered actual damages, and this is established "only when the prime contractor has reimbursed its subcontractor for the latter's damages or remains liable for such reimbursement in the future."

In order to push the remedy to its maximum, the former Court of Claims ruled that the burden of establishing that the prime contractor has no liability to its subcontractor for the latter's damages is on the government. At the trial of one case, the prime contractor failed to introduce any evidence of its liability to the subcontractor and the court went so far as to rule against the government because it did not offer proof of an exculpatory provision in the subcontract. The normal contract rule requires a contractor to prove his damages, and any release must expressly negate any liability of the prime contractor to the subcontractor. The Court read releases so as to interpret them as not expressly negating such liability. In J. L. Simmons Co. v.

United States, the former Court of Claims rejected the government's argument that a consolidation agreement served as an absolute release because the prime contractor's liability would be negated regardless of the success of its claims on the merits. The court stated that the agreement did not expressly negate the prime contractor's liability, but "simply purport[ed] to set forth the manner in which the [prime's] liability [was] *to be extinguished.*" The courts reasoning in these decisions has been said to be "based on nothing but a legal fiction."

In one case, the former Court of Claims allowed a subcontractor to avoid the court's lack of jurisdiction over his claim by permitting the substitution of the prime contractor. Even though the substitution was after the time for filing the claim had expired, the claim, with the prime substituted as the claimant, related back to the date it was originally filed by the subcontractor. The government objected to this and to the fact that the prime (Folk) was not liable to the subcontractor (Cross) "because Cross first sued Folk on the same claim, and then dismissed the suit because, Cross says, it found Folk not at fault, only the defendant. This must mean, according to the government, that Cross is not entirely barred from suing Folk." The court stated that it "has refined the *Severin* doctrine so that it requires an iron-bound release or contract provision immunizing the contractor completely from any liability to the sub [citations]. If the contract is silent as to the prime's ultimate liability to the sub, suit by the former will generally be permitted." At this stage the court authorized any suit against the government by a subcontractor, provided it was sponsored by the prime contractor.

Two cases involving the same over-all contract illustrate the central issues involved in a subcontractor's appeal of an adverse decision of a contracting officer by having its appeal made directly to the government. These cases further illustrate the extent to which subcontractors were permitted to appeal adverse decisions of the contracting officer to administrative boards under the sponsorship of the prime contractor in spite of the certification requirement and a lack of privity. Turner Controls, the prime contractor, entered into a construction management contract with the Department of Health, Education, and Welfare. Turner entered into approximately 74 construction subcontracts, one of which was with Johnson Controls. That subcontract included provisions that the government retained the right to approve all subcontracts, and that the terms of the prime contract were incorporated by reference into the subcontract.

In spite of an unusual amount of control exercised by the government in the performance of the subcontract, the court held that it was not enough to establish privity of contract between Johnson and the government: Johnson was identified as a "subcontractor" (not as a contractor); the subcontract expressly stated that it was not intended to create a contractual relationship between Johnson and the government; Turner furnished the required Miller Act bonds to which Johnson could look, instead of to the government, for relief in the absence of payment; and there was no express contract provision authorizing a direct right of appeal by subcontractors. The court held that, in the absence of privity of contract, the subcontractor could not maintain an appeal against the government.

In another case involving the same over-all construction project, Turner sponsored a claim for and on behalf of Industrotech Contractors, Inc. and because the prime contract obligated Turner to assist the government in analyzing and defending claims of subcontractors, Turner was in rather a precarious position. On one hand, he could refuse to certify subcontractor claims and expose himself to possible litigation by the subcontractor (even though the party at interest was the government). On the other hand, Turner could sponsor and certify subcontractor claims against the government and then be required to assist the government in refuting these same claims. When Turner chose the latter course, the government argued that Turner's act of identifying deficiencies in the very claim which it had certified rendered Turner's certification ineffective. After suggesting that the subcontractor's remedy would be a suit in a state court, the board without analysis answered that such multiple litigation was wasteful and unnecessary.

The government also argued that the indemnification exacted by Turner from the subcontractor violated the spirit of the certification requirement and "literally slap[ped] at any good faith presentation." The Board, again without analysis, found that Turner's action was "sound business practice." The holding removed responsibility for certification from the prime contractor. The Board stated the prime's duty is limited to ascertaining whether the subcontractor's claim "is made in good faith and is not frivolous or a sham."

The Procurement Commission approved of the indirect appeal procedure because: (1) it provided a means for administering procurement through a single focal point; (2) it might eliminate frivolous claims; and (3) it permitted the prime contractor and subcontractor to work out their differences in a commercial setting. Some of the boards noted that these reasons do not justify the approach of the former Court of Claims and boards which permitted the subcontractor to ignore the prime contractor in connection with the subcontractor's claims. One board held that it is not necessary that the prime contractor and the government "disagree" on the claim for the board to obtain jurisdiction.

In 1984, the Court of Appeals for the Federal Circuit finally placed a some outer limitations on the expanding sponsorship process. After noting that in the former Court of Claims, "it was quite usual for prime contractors to step aside and allow counsel retained by subcontractors to prosecute claims, though always in the name and right of the prime," the court stated it had directed the clerk in this case to accept briefs on behalf of subcontractors in their own names. But it remarked that:

[B]y hindsight, this was probably a mistake . . .

[The] unfortunate consequence of our decision was that the brief writers, giving lip service to the rule that the subcontractors had no privity of contract with the government, in practice seemed to assume that the contrary was the law.

It then notified the bar: [It stated "Notice is hereby given"] that, in the future, only the prime contractor may be the appellant. The court officially recognized that it had been ignoring the law of privity for many years.

Parties make contracts and courts should not abolish the no privity rule for subcontractors in the absence of consent of the parties or legislation to that effect and the Commission on Government Procurement recommended against such legislation. In enacting the Contract Disputes Act of 1978, Congress reasoned, inter alia, that prime contractor personnel, being more familiar with commercial practices than most bureaucrats, would be better able to administer subcontracts. The Equal Access to Justice Act (EAJA) authorizes award of attorneys' fees and expenses incurred by that party to a party that prevails against the government. However, this statute does not allow a prime contractor to recover attorneys' fees and costs incurred by a subcontractor in litigating a so-called "pass-through" claim for costs.

(c) Subcontract Clause on Sponsorship by the Prime Contractor With a Belief

Although the regulation is silent on the sponsorship discussed above, it does give specific recognition to the possible use of a non-standard clause giving the subcontractor the right of "indirect appeal to an agency board of contract appeals if the subcontractor is affected by a dispute between the government and the prime contractor." Such a clause may permit prosecution of an appeal by the prime contractor on the subcontractor's behalf and provide that "the prime and subcontractor shall be equally bound by the contracting officer's or board's decision." But it prohibits any "attempt to obligate the contracting officer or the appeals board to decide questions that do not arise between the Government and the prime contractor." Where the subcontractor desires a remedy for questions that do not arise between the government and the prime contractor, he must exclude them from the subcontract clause prepared pursuant to this regulation and provide for them separately.

The prime contractor must independently certify the claim of its subcontractor. The Contract Dispute Act (CDA) requires the certification to be unequivocal. That is, it requires the prime contractor to certify that "[t]he amount requested accurately reflects the contract adjustment for which the contractor believes the government is liable." The Court of Appeals for the Federal Circuit reduced this burden to one where the prime contractor must merely certify to a belief that there is "good ground" for the claim.

One category of "subcontracts" created under the Department of Energy (DOE) and created under the former Atomic Energy Commission (AEC) was unique: the management contract or "operating" contract. A board of contract appeals found that an agency relationship existed between the government and DOE management; a party ("subcontractor") who enters into a contract with an agent of the government can be deemed "a party to a Government contract" for purposes of direct appeal rights under the Contract Disputes Act of 1978. The AEC (the predecessor of the DOE) had established a long-standing practice of allowing subcontractors under the AEC to include a "Disputes" clause allowing resolution by its board.

§ 44.7   The Law Governing Subcontracts; Federal Law or State Law

In 1925, the Supreme Court held that a subcontractor could not recover against the United States under the Tucker Act because there was no "contract, express or implied in fact, by the government with the plaintiff." There appeared to be no reason for applying Federal law to an agreement that was not made by the government. State law would be applied as determined by the conflict of laws principles where the law, regulation, and agreement were silent thereon. Nevertheless, like prime contracts, some subcontract disputes were also tried in Federal court. This is normally done on grounds of diversity of citizenship jurisdiction and then, ordinarily, state law is applicable. However, in the case of certain subcontracts, one appellate court has applied Federal law on the grounds that the subcontract involved "an area 'in which the policy of the law is so dominated by the sweep of Federal statutes' that legal relations within that area must be regulated by Federal law," and that the construction of subcontracts, let under prime contracts connected with the national security, should be regulated by a uniform Federal law. The Supreme Court has held that Federal law applied where "the scope of the remedy as well as the substance of the rights created [in that case by the Miller Act] is a matter of Federal, not state law." The Court stressed the importance of finding a need for uniformity and the lack of governing state law on the subject matter. That case did not resolve the question of which law to apply to ordinary subcontract cases. On the contrary, a number of courts have used state law in the interpretation of subcontracts. State law has been applied in interpreting a subcontract that requires no construction of a Federal statute and "Federal law does not provide sufficient guidance in deciding the contract law issues presented."

Many states share a general statute of limitations period of six years for breach of contract. However, they frequently exempt claims arising under the Uniform Commercial Code. UCC § 2–275(a) provides that "[a]n action for breach of any contract of sale must be commenced within four years after the cause of action has accrued." However, UCC § 2–275 permits the parties to a contract to reduce the limitations period down to one year.

In addition to direct government procurement, a large volume of procurement financed with government funds is affected by cost-type contractors of the various departments and agencies. Procurement expenses are an allowable cost under such a contract, and the contractor is not bound by the statutes imposing advertising and bid procedures which would control a government agency carrying on a similar function. Payments made to the subcontractor are part of the direct cost to contractors who are reimbursed in full from the United States Treasury. Many are called "Operating Contracts." Procurement by the contractor is closely policed and his whole program is generally administered by a government agency or department. The application of Federal law has not generally been extended to these subcontracts.

Even if the government, in a similar case, would award to a bidder who claims to have withdrawn, a prime contractor cannot do likewise unless the law gives him the power to hold the bidder to his bid. While this is true of fixed price contractors, because of the rights and interests of the Federal government noted above, it is particularly important in the case of cost-type prime contractors who are operating on the basis of advances of public funds and who seldom dip into their own funds to finance contract work. Some contractors are hired by the government for the purpose of building or managing and operating a government-owned site as well as for other purposes, such as research and development. The procurement function in such cases may be accomplished in two ways: (1) the government can purchase the equipment and furnish the item to the contractor; or (2) the contractor can make the purchases directly, using advances of public funds to pay for them, with the government exercising some control over these expenditures. Both methods are used in practice. Although the Federal law governing interpretation of government contracts would clearly be applicable to the first method, state law would normally apply to the second method where the government decided to have the prime contractor perform the procurement function in the interest of economy or efficiency or some other reason.

Northrop Corp. v. AIL Systems, Inc., Eaton Corp. involved a contract dispute concerning a teaming arrangement to obtain a contract for the electronic countermeasures system for the B–1B bomber. The agreement required AIL, as the prime contractor, to award subcontracts to Northrop. Northrop alleged breach when AIL did not award Northrop a particular subcontract. The complaint was dismissed for lack of Federal common law jurisdiction. In affirming the dismissal, Seventh Circuit U.S. Court of Appeals stated that a significant conflict must exist "between an identifiable Federal policy or interest and the application of state law to the dispute, or the application of state law would frustrate specific objectives of Federal interest sufficient to support Federal legislation." It held that the teaming arrangement did not rise to the level of a unique Federal interest, and the existence of Federal regulations governing the teaming of contractors on Federal procurements did not create a unique Federal interest so as to give Federal courts jurisdiction. There was no need for a uniform body of Federal "common law" to interpret teaming agreements for Federal contracts and state law did not conflict with any government interest.

Similarly, the U.S. Court of Appeals for the Second Circuit held that a second-tier subcontractor on a contract involving the F–22 fighter plane might not invoke Federal common law in its contract breach action against a first-tier subcontractor.

§ 44.8   Subcontractor's Oral Bids and Modification of Subcontracts

Modifications of written subcontracts for goods, which exclude modification except by a signed writing, must be in writing, if the UCC rule currently applicable to parties of private contracts is followed. That rule would appear appropriate for subcontracts using public funds. It has been held that a subcontractor is not estopped to assert a state statute of frauds despite a general contractor's reliance on an oral bid by a subcontractor in connection with calculation of the bid of the prime contractor. Borg–Warner, a subcontractor, submitted to C. R. Fedrick, the prime contractor, an oral sub-bid for pumps for use in Fedrick's bid on a construction project. After the general contract was awarded to Fedrick, Borg–Warner revoked its bid and refused to sell the pumps at the original price. Fedrick subsequently purchased the pumps from another supplier, incurring alleged damages of $95,903. Fedrick asserted that its reliance on Borg–Warner's oral sub-bid in calculating its prime bid made it irrevocable despite statute of frauds problems. The suit, brought in a California court by Fedrick, was removed to the United States District Court for the Northern District of California under diversity jurisdiction. The Federal court was required to apply the substantive law of California. The court granted a summary judgment in favor of Borg–Warner, on the grounds that the state's statute of frauds barred the plaintiff's action and a promissory estoppel argument was not warranted. In affirming this judgment, the United States Court of Appeals for the Ninth Circuit based its decision on the ground that a dispute over the actual terms of the subcontractor's bid constituted a revocation of the oral bid prior to receipt of any confirmatory writing from Fedrick, and none of Fedrick's subsequent writings to Borg–Warner were sufficient to confirm the contract.

Although the UCC does not directly address the issue of whether the doctrine of promissory estoppel is available to preclude assertion of the statute of frauds, a California court has applied the doctrine of promissory estoppel to promises and to subcontractors' bids. An Arizona Appellate Court held that when a case is clearly within the statute of frauds, a writing is required to enforce an oral contract, and the promise is not enforceable through promissory estoppel.

Unless one accepts the concept that a court may overrule the legislature on the basis that they somehow have greater experience and knowledge, estoppel of the statute of frauds is objectionable on constitutional grounds; namely, it operates as a violation of the separation of powers.

§ 44.9   Subcontracts for Commercial Items and Components

Implementing a statute, the regulations require contractors and subcontractors at all tiers to incorporate commercial items or nondevelopmental items to the maximum extent practicable as components or items delivered to the government. A new contract clause limits the contract clauses a prime contractor may be required to apply to any subcontractors that are furnishing commercial items or commercial components in accordance with that law.

CHAPTER 49

TERMINATION OF GOVERNMENT CONTRACTS

A. INTRODUCTION

§ 49.1 Authority to Terminate Contracts and Types of Terminations

Most government contracts contain prescribed termination clauses. These clauses authorize contracting officers to enter into settlement agreements, to terminate contracts for convenience, or for default—although as at common law, no clause is necessary to terminate for default. Only a termination for convenience is dependent on a contract clause. However, when the price of the undelivered balance of a contract is less than $5000, the contract is not normally terminated for convenience; rather it is permitted to run to completion. Contracts are terminated for convenience or default only by a written notice to the contractor. Upon receipt of the notice the contractor is, of course, bound to comply with the termination clause in his contract. An improper termination can result in high expenditures of taxpayer funds.

There are three types of termination: two are initiated by a notice of termination (default and convenience termination), and one by agreement of the parties. The latter, called a no-cost settlement, is to be used in lieu of issuing a termination notice when it is known that the contractor will accept one; government property was not furnished;

513

and there are no outstanding payments, debts due the government, or other contractor obligations.

In 1996, the U.S. Supreme Court extended the protection of the First Amendment to government contracts terminated for reasons of speech. The contractor brought an action against two members of a county's board who voted to terminate his contract, alleging that the termination of his contract was in retaliation for his public criticisms of the county and board. The U.S. Court of Appeals for the Tenth Circuit held that "an independent contractor is protected under the First Amendment from retaliatory governmental action, just as an employee would be." The Supreme Court affirmed, and as a matter of first impression applied the "existing framework for government employee cases to independent contractors." The Court explained that the "unconstitutional conditions" doctrine holds that the government "may not deny a benefit to a person on a basis that infringes his constitutionally protected freedom of speech" even if he has no entitlement to that benefit.

B. TERMINATION FOR DEFAULT

§ 49.11   In General

Termination for default is generally "the exercise of the government's contractual right to completely or partially terminate a contract because of the contractor's actual or anticipated failure to perform its contractual obligation." For example, under the default clause for fixed-price contracts, the government has the right to terminate the contract completely, or partially, for default if (1) the contractor fails to make delivery of the supplies, perform the services within the time specified in the contract, perform any other provision of the contract, or make progress and (2) that failure endangers performance of the contract.

A failure by the contractor to furnish required performance and payment bonds may properly result in a default termination. As one board noted, "This failure alone is enough to justify the termination." However, a contractor's notice to the government that it could not begin contract performance on the date specified in the contract to commence work was held to be neither abandonment nor even a default six days later.

In one case a contractor sent the government a copy of a draft letter notifying the contractor's employees that it planned to discontinue performance at the contract site within 60 to 90 days and that the employees would be terminated under the Worker Adjustment and Retraining Notification (WARN) Act. The letter indicated that the contractor would soon request a "no cost" termination; but it also stated that the contractor would not leave the government agency without services or supplies. These actions were held by a board of contract appeals as "ambiguous, uncertain, and doubtful" intentions and insufficient to justify a termination for default.

In Danzig v. AEC Corporation, the United States Court of Appeals for the Federal Circuit extended the concept of anticipatory repudiation beyond the unequivocal repudiation standard to include the failure to provide adequate assurance of further performance. The boards of contract appeals have differed in their application of this new concept.

The government is not liable for the contractor's costs on undelivered work, and is entitled to the repayment of advance and progress payments, if any, applicable to that work. The government may also elect to require the contractor to transfer title and deliver to the government completed supplies and manufacturing materials. However, the Default clause is not to be used by the government as authority to acquire any completed supplies or manufacturing materials unless it has been ascertained that the government does not already have title under some other provision of the contract. The contractor is liable for any excess costs incurred by the government in reprocuring supplies or services similar to those in the contract terminated for default and regardless of whether a repurchase was effected for other damages (such as liquidated damages).

The former Court of Claims on occasion observed that a default termination is a drastic sanction even though the default clause has been part of the agreement. The courts and boards have held a termination to be unconscionable; in connection with the Sale of Goods under the Uniform Commercial Code, a termination of a contract by one party without the happening of an agreed event, and upon an agreement dispensing with notification, is only invalid "if its operation would be unconscionable;" otherwise, it is valid.

Having concurrent jurisdiction, a board and the Court of Federal Claims (COFC) disagreed with respect to their jurisdiction and the reasons therefor. The COFC has suggested that it is insufficient to hold a separate trial on the question of whether a default termination was improperly granted from the claim for convenience cost in the event the answer was in the affirmative. No convenience termination claim is possible until the default termination is overturned. A board ruled to the contrary.

Where a contractor was clearly in default, it has been wrong to set aside that termination because it was also found that the government no longer wanted to deal with the contractor. But, in other cases, the Government mostly seeks to collect on a default termination. For example, in 2002, the Navy demanded that General Dynamics Corp. and The Boeing Co. Pay approximately $2.3 billion that the companies owed in litigation concerning the default termination of the development contract for the A–12 aircraft; this figure represented $1.3 billion in progress payments made by the Navy in 1991, plus $1.0 billion in interest.

A board held that where the contracting officer gave mistaken advice regarding the contractor's appeal right, jurisdiction existed over a contractor's appeal of a default termination that was filed more than 90 days after the contractor received the decision. Further, the government may not terminate for default if government-caused delays also caused the contractor's loss of an established vendor for critical long-lead time components. On the other hand, a default has been sustained in the face of the argument by the contractor that escalating material costs since the time of offer would put a contractor in a loss position.

§ 49.13   Duty to Terminate for Default

The government should not terminate for convenience, or effect a no-cost settlement when a contractor is in default, and the government needs the supplies or services; if a contractor is in default, the government is entitled to issue a termination for default notice, under the default clause. A question can arise whether the contracting officer can issue a termination for convenience notice to a contractor who is in fact in default.

For example, the Court of Claims has held that the Navy breached its equitable duty to a surety by failing to terminate a contractor whose performance was over two years behind schedule and had incurred overruns. The Court stated:

An admittedly irresponsible, dishonest, incompetent, and abusive contractor was allowed almost three years and [$2.68 million] to only partially complete a job that should have, by the Navy's own estimates, been fully completed in nine months at a total cost of [$2.59 million]. While it is not this court's function to say whether the fault lies with individual Navy officials or with an overloaded and overly bureaucratic system, it would be manifestly unjust to make the surety pay for the Navy's mistake.

If the agency refuses to terminate for default in order to maintain "good relations" with the contractor, the system fails and taxpayers may suffer an economic loss; nevertheless, in many instances, a cure notice is preferable to a termination, where the items are still needed. It may be possible to arrive at a no-cost settlement if they are no longer needed. However, if such an agreement cannot be reached and in other instances a default notice may be necessary to protect taxpayer interests. A contract terminated for default may be reinstated by mutual agreement where the contracting officer determines that such reinstatement is "advantageous to the government." It has been held that a contracting officer's reconsideration of a decision to terminate a contract for default suspends the finality of the decision.

§ 49.21   Default of Subcontractors

Can a prime contractor be excused from default upon alleging and proving that his failure to perform was due to the default of a subcontractor? In Whitlock Corp. v. United States, a wholesale hardware jobber contracted to supply the Philadelphia Quartermaster Depot with brass buckles at a unit price of $0.064. The jobber planned to subcontract the entire order, basing its bid on a commitment obtained from the Hatheway Manufacturing Company. When the jobber learned of Hatheway's insolvency and inability to perform the subcontract, he solicited bids from other manufacturers and then asked for an increase in the contract price to $0.08 per unit. The contracting officer terminated the jobber's contract for default. The Court of Claims held that the default clause excused the jobber from performance for the default of its subcontractor only if the subcontractor's failure to perform was attributable to certain enumerated causes beyond its control and without its fault or negligence. Because insolvency of the subcontractor was not included in the enumeration of excuses, the contracting officer's finding that the jobber's failure to perform was not beyond its control was upheld. The default clause now specifies that in order for such delays to be excusable to prime contractors, they must be beyond the control and without the fault or negligence of both the prime contractor and the subcontractor. Also, the prime contractor has the burden of establishing that these criteria are met.

In Schweigert, Inc. v. United States, the Court of Claims held that a contractor was excused for a delay caused by a second-tier subcontractor on the ground that the clause did not specifically exclude a lower tier subcontractor who was not in privity of contract with the prime contractor and that the court always applies the doctrine of contra proferentem against the government. Where the prime contractor cannot complete work involving equipment which was delayed due to fault of the government or another prime contractor, that delay is excused. This excuse is illustrated by a case where Morris Mechanical Enterprises was awarded a prime construction contract with GSA, providing that Morris purchase and deliver an air chiller that was to be installed by another prime contractor. The Morris contract also provided for assessment of liquidated damages at $100 per day's unexcused delay. The subcontractor delayed delivery for 231 days and Morris asked that the balance of its price ($23,100 withheld) be paid to it. Because Morris could not complete his job until after the installation of the chiller, he was held to be entitled to an extension to permit such completion, and the GSA could not withhold the liquidated damages. The government has been held entitled to terminate a contract because of the contractor's failure to make progress, even though the delays were caused by subcontractors who were government-approved sole sources. A contractor is not excused for failure to deliver where the contractor instructed its supplier to put its order on hold pending resolution of an agency-level protest and the government did not order suspension of the contractor's work.

§ 49.22   Excusable Causes

Applicable clauses in both construction contracts and contracts for supplies and services excuse a termination for default for "causes beyond the control and without the fault or negligence of the Contractor." Each clause includes identical lists of examples of such causes; except that only the construction clause contains the excuse relating to "acts of another Contractor in the performance of a contract with the government." Both types of contracts excuse delays of a subcontractor at any tier if the cause of default is beyond the control and without the fault or negligence of both the contractor and the subcontractor.

There are many types of excusable delays, or arguments that they should exist. Some of those that are more frequently litigated are discussed herein. The duration of time that may constitute an excusable delay depends upon its foreseeability. Unless inclement weather is "unusually severe," it does not constitute an excusable delay. Financial incapacity to perform a contract is not ordinarily regarded as "beyond the control of the contractor" because submission of a bid or proposal and a determination of responsibility and a resulting award means that the contractor is deemed to have financial capacity to perform. Thin capitalization that "made it impossible for (a contractor) to absorb even routine and foreseeable problems" is not excusable. Strikes may also become factors beyond the control of the contractor.

A party's agreement to attempt to perform the impossible is not against public policy. There is no "law of impossibility;" however, the "so-called law of impossibility" derives from an interpretation of the parties' intent as express or implied in a contract. It is sometimes found that the parties did not intend to perform something that cannot be accomplished at any cost by anyone, or that it can only be done with extreme and unreasonable difficulty or expense. Where another contractor had successfully performed the contract, it was neither impossible to perform nor commercially impracticable. To prevail, the event that causes the inability to perform must have been unforeseeable and cannot be due to the fault or negligence of the contractor. Mere suggestions by the government as to suppliers or modes of performance are not warranties. On the other hand, one board held a contract interpretation by the government unreasonable because it made it impossible to perform the contract within the specified time. Although an unforeseeable market shortage may excuse performance, a contractor may not be excused for the inability of its supplier to supply needed materials where the contractor's decision to use and stay with a particular supplier was a business decision.

Similarly, a contractor assumes the risk of loss in shipping goods by a method other than that specified in the contract unless the parties' course of conduct has modified the contract.

The former Court of Claims has taken the view that the government's wrongful refusal to make progress payments called for by the contract constitutes an inability to continue performance. This decision was made without ascertaining whether the contractor could borrow these funds (by assigning portions of his contract receipts) and requesting interest thereon as his claim for damages. In some instances, however, a construction contract may call for the performing of labor and furnishing of materials covering "a long period of time and involving large expenditures," and "a stipulation for payments on account to be made from time to time during the progress of the work must be deemed so material that a substantial failure to pay would justify the contractor in declining to proceed." The Supreme Court stated it may have been "in the contemplation of the parties that the contractor could not be expected to finance the operation to completion without receiving the stipulated payments on account as the work progressed. In such cases a substantial compliance as to advance payments is a condition precedent to the contractor's obligation to proceed." However, in general, a court may find that "nonpayment of installment obligations is not in and of itself such prevention of performance as will make possible suit for loss of profits even though the party entitled to payment may lack working capital." Normally, the Progress clause represents a promise by the government the breach of which would give rise to a duty to pay damages (interest); it would not be a material condition which must occur before the contractor needs to continue his performance.

As regards the standard of commercial impracticability, the former Court of Claims has remarked that it "can be easily abused; thus this court has not applied it with frequency or enthusiasm. It is not invoked merely because costs have become more expensive than originally contemplated."

§ 49.23   Conversion of Erroneous Default Into a Termination for Convenience—Funds Remain Obligated

If a contracting officer believes that a contractor is in default, he may issue a notice of default under the standard clause. If it is later determined that no default occurred, the former Court of Claims took the position that this notice resulted in a breach of contract. In Klein v. United States, the Beam Radionics Corporation negotiated a contract with the Army Corps of Engineers for the furnishing of 1,000 electric lighting sets at prescribed prices and delivery dates. A sample submitted by the contractor did not pass a rigorous test required under the contract. The contracting officer notified Beam of the termination of contract for default and he appealed. The Board of Contract Appeals held that the government had, by its conduct, waived compliance with the delivery dates prescribed in the contract. Thereafter the contracting officer wrote Beam: "In view of said decision the government deems the above notice of default to have been issued pursuant to Clause 21 of the contract entitled, 'Termination for the Convenience of the Government.'" The Court of Claims held that the contractor, Beam, was entitled to recover damages caused to him by the wrongful termination of the contract, that is, for the breach of its contract. The dissent in this opinion stated that if the government had a right to terminate, there was no breach at all. Possibly, there was a procedural error, but such error does not have the effect of a breach of contract. He cited Professor Williston, who stated that, "To hold, as a broad proposition, that stating one reason for refusing to accept tendered performance precludes a promisor from later stating another reason ... seems almost grotesque."

Thereafter, the default clause was revised so as to make the matter moot. Both of the current default clauses for fixed-price supply and service contracts and fixed price construction contracts contain the following paragraph:

> If, after termination, it is determined that the Contractor was not in default, or that the default was excusable, the rights and obligations of the parties shall be the same as if the termination had been issued for the convenience of the government.

Where a termination for default is being appealed, funds obligated for a defaulted contract are not deobligated. Thus, if the contractor is successful on his appeal in the following fiscal year, the termination (converted to convenience) would result in the funds remaining obligated, where a replacement contract had been made. However, the original obligation would no longer be available if the replacement contract had not yet been awarded and the cost of the replacement contract would then be charged to the appropriation current at the time the need arose. In the past it has been held that a default termination may be converted into a termination for convenience but not vice versa. Where a contractor attempts to convert a default termination to a termination for the convenience of the government and in fact does not seek any monetary damages, his claim is not subject to the certification requirements of the Contract Disputes Act.

C. THE POWER TO SETTLE CONTRACTS AND TO TERMINATE THEM FOR THE CONVENIENCE OF THE GOVERNMENT

§ 49.31   The Power to Settle

The power to contract carries with it the power to settle with the contractor for partial performance when the purchaser finds that the goods are no longer needed. In 1875, the U.S. Supreme Court held that a government department as purchaser had the power to settle a contract, the performance of which it had suspended. Thereafter, the Navy Department suspended work. The contractor offered to take all the machinery involved and receive $150,000, or to deliver it to a Navy yard for $259,068. The department accepted the latter in settlement. It stated that the completion of the contract had become unnecessary from the termination of the civil war. The secretary, "in the exercise of his judgment ... suspended the work. He was authorized to agree with the claimant upon the compensation for the partial performance, and that settlement thus made it binding upon the government." The decision was expressly limited to a settlement "made with full knowledge of all the facts, without concealment, misrepresentation, or fraud." We have seen that a different result is reached where the latter criteria are involved. Also, as is the case today, that decision did not involve any statutory authority to settle.

During World War I, Congress enacted a statute concerning the settlement of contracts terminated for the convenience of the government. The President was authorized "to modify, suspend, cancel, or requisition any existing or future contract for the building, production or purchase of ships or material." This statute also excluded an award of "anticipated" profits. Such an exclusion is also set forth in all subsequent termination for convenience clauses.

A termination for convenience article for lump sum supply contracts was published in War Department Procurement Regulation 324 in 1942, but the best-known World War II statute was the Contract Settlement Act of 1944 which established the Office of Contract Settlement for "war" contracts and subcontracts.

At this date, the subject of termination of contracts for the convenience of the Government is essentially confined to contract clauses and regulations concerning their administration. The definition of termination for convenience is: "the exercise of the government's right to completely or partially terminate performance of work under a contract when it is in the government's interest."

§ 49.32   The Bases for a Termination for Convenience

Under a Termination for Convenience clause, performance of work under a contract may be terminated by the government in whole or in part whenever the contracting officer determines such termination to be "in the government's interest." The termination is accomplished by delivery to the contractor of a written notice of termination. Upon receipt of the notice, the contractor must stop work, terminate all subcontracts, notify the government of any legal proceedings growing out of any subcontract, settle such liabilities, and submit to the contracting officer his termination claim. Upon a termination for the convenience of the government, a contractor is required to submit termination inventory schedules within 120 days from the date of termination, unless this period is extended by the contracting officer. The contractor must submit a final termination settlement proposal within one year of the effective date of termination. A failure to timely submit this settlement proposal precludes a contractor from asserting all claims arising prior to the termination. Thereafter, the contractor and Terminating Contracting Officer (TCO) may agree upon the whole or any part of the amount to be paid to the contractor, or they may execute a no-cost settlement where the contractor has not incurred costs or he is willing to waive them and no amounts are due the government. However, in the absence of an agreement, the TCO must determine the amount he determines to be due in accordance with criteria set forth in the termination clause, including any cost principles incorporated by reference. A contractor has an incentive not to agree to a no-cost settlement; unlike many commercial contractors, making a claim against the government will not normally jeopardize his future bids on proposals for government business.

A contractor's protection on a convenience-termination is that he normally becomes entitled to the cost of the work performed plus a profit thereon and the cost of settling his proposal and subcontract claims. The principal difference between the sum calculated under this standard and the amount recoverable in a common law action for breach of contract is the omission in the former of anticipated but unearned profits. This is true even where the government breaches the contract. However, as pointed out in Section 43.15, supra, a so-called "cardinal change" (a change ordered by the government which is beyond the general scope of the contract) should not result in a breach of contract. It is one that a contractor can elect to perform or not. If the contractor chooses to perform, he may recover for unjust enrichment at the request of the government. See Section 33.22, supra. The U.S. Court of Appeals for the Federal Circuit in 1999 held that where the government had increased the estimates under a requirements contract, it neither constituted a cardinal change under the circumstances, nor was the government liable for breach when it terminated the contract for convenience and recompeted for the items.

In another case, a board held that the General Services Administration (GSA) breached its duty to deal with the contractor fairly and in good faith by misleading the contractor as to the amount of work under the contract. The majority found that GSA's estimate under an indefinite quantity contract for travel services were "vastly overstated." However, the U.S. Court of Appeals for the Federal Circuit reversed, holding that when a "contract between a contracting party and the government clearly indicates that the contracting party is guaranteed no more than a nonnominal minimum amount of sales, purchases exceeding that minimum amount satisfy the government's legal obligation under the contract." Because GSA met the requirements of the contract, its failure to disclose a change in the estimated orders under the contract before award, which the court deemed "less than ideal contracting tactics," failed to constitute a breach. By agreeing to the termination clause, a contractor relinquishes the common law damage formula and acquiesces in the substitution of a rule under which profit is allowed only on the work actually performed. This situation is changed in a "loss" contract because an injured party should not be put in a better position than if the contract had been performed. It has been held that "the burden is on defendant to prove that full performance would have resulted in a net loss."

However, some courts have been more generous to the contractor and have measured the benefit conferred on the party in breach by the injured party's part performance under a losing contract and then allowed the injured party restitution of that sum. This requires the court to measure the benefit. A contractor whose work has been terminated for convenience may also submit a breach of contract claim independent of its termination settlement with the government.

The government may assert its right to apply the contract price as a ceiling on recovery by the contractor where a fixed-price construction contract is terminated for the convenience of the government. Because the contract cost principles in FAR 31 apply to contracts terminated for convenience, it is often argued that the decisions in cases upholding a waiver of the limitation of Costs article in cost-type contracts (many of which decisions are highly questionable, see § 32.28, supra), should also apply as a waiver of the price in a fixed price contract. This was addressed in a recent case as follows:

> While the cost principles applicable to cost reimbursable contracts do come into play in a termination for convenience, the principles that the contract price serves as a ceiling on recovery, that a profit allowance is partially or totally eliminated on a loss contract, and the recovery of actual costs may be reduced by a loss factor, also come into play. These principles are not consistent with treating the fixed price contract as actually converted to a cost reimbursable contract.

A terminated fixed-price contract is not converted to a true cost reimbursable contract, and there was no reasonable basis to extend the waiver concept to this case.

§ 49.33 Allowability of Costs Claimed Following Termination

Except with respect to commercial items, termination settlements even for fixed price contracts are governed by cost principles that on occasion disallow costs. That is, the termination clauses make the cost principles applicable which contain a number of express disallowances that are discussed elsewhere in this treatise. The termination may essentially convert what was a fixed price contract prior to termination into a cost type contract for part of the work after termination, when the cost provisions come into play, and the costs may be staggering. (See exception as noted in § 49.32, supra.)

Settlement expenses are allowed in connection with a termination for convenience, including accounting and legal expenses "reasonably necessary for the preparation of the termination settlement." In Kalvar Corp. v. United States, the former Court of Claims noted that § 2412 of title 28 of the U.S. Code prohibits the court from awarding attorneys' fees in "any civil action brought by or against the United States." However, it viewed the statute to be "inapplicable to costs which, had proper procedures been followed, would naturally have arisen in the process of settlement rather than in a court action brought against the United States." Where a termination settlement proposal is not disputed, there is no claim against which interest accrues under the Contract Disputes Act.

The regulations provide for the determination of profit on terminated work (but not on settlement expense) and no anticipated profits or consequential damages are allowed. Further, profit is not allowed the contractor for undelivered material or services that as of the effective date of termination have been incurred by a subcontractor, "regardless of the percentage of completion." "Cost of materials cancelled due to termination of a contract for the convenience of the government may not be charged against the government for any purpose, including calculation and assessment of burden and profits. However, to the extend that costs associated with canceling those materials can be established, they would be recoverable under 'other costs' under provision in the Federal procurement regulations." Under the Termination for Convenience clause, where a contractor would have sustained a loss on the entire contract had it been completed, the contracting officer must reduce the settlement to reflect the indicated rate of loss.

A board held that a termination notice must always be equivalent to an order issued under the Changes article and the notice waives a ceiling price in the contract. The termination notice added new work described in the Termination for Convenience clause; and if the notice did not serve to waive the contract ceiling price, under the contract's Limitation of Cost clause, a contractor could refuse to perform the tasks described in the Termination clause. Where a contract was terminated for convenience, a board has ruled that a contractor can recover the costs of settling subcontractor claims even though they had neither been included in pricing the prime contract nor charged directly to the contract prior to termination.

PART VIII

CLAUSES AND FORMS

CHAPTER 52

SOLICITATION PROVISIONS AND CONTRACT CLAUSES

§ 52.1 Subcontract Clauses

This volume is subject to a number of limitations. One is the length of discussion devoted to many of the standard clauses set forth in the Regulation. FAR Part 52, "Solicitation Provisions and Contract Clauses," and Part 53, "Forms," contain the bulk of that discussion. FAR Subpart 52.1, "Instructions for Using Provisions and Clauses," organizes the contract clauses and solicitation provisions that it discusses by numbering them according to the FAR part in which they are prescribed. FAR Subpart 52.2, "Text of Provisions and Clauses," lists the particular provisions and assigns a six-digit number to each one. The first three digits, 52.2, remain constant throughout as they refer to that Subpart of Chapter 52. The next two digits refer to the FAR part that prescribes the clause; for example, FAR 52.215–1 lists a provision "Instructions to Offerors–Competitive Acquisition" which pertains to Part 15, "Contracting by Negotiation." The last digit, preceded by a hyphen, denotes each section within Subpart 52.2. The clauses are grouped by contract type (rather than by subject) and although many of them are mentioned or discussed in this volume, no single volume could treat them all adequately.

While the FAR does not attempt to do so, some of the clauses may be generally classified according to the subject category to which they relate. For example,

1.	*Performance of Scope of Work & Specifications*	(Approximately 80% of standard clauses)
	Definitions	FAR 52.202–1 (and other provisions)
	Changes	FAR 52.243–1 through 52.243–7
	Inspection	FAR 52.246–1 through 52.246–15
	Disputes	FAR 52.233–1
	Protests	FAR 52.233–2 through 52.233–3
	Payment, Interest, Funds	FAR 52.232–1 through 52.232–19
	Delivery Terms	FAR 52.247–29 through 52.247–49
2.	*Political Objectives*	
	Small Business	FAR 52.219–1 through 52.219–12
3.	*Economic, Labor*	
	Walsh–Healy Public Contracts Act	FAR 52.222–20
	Buy American Act	FAR 52.225–1–4, 9, 11
4.	*Social*	
	Equal Opportunity	FAR 52.222–26
	Convict Labor	FAR 52.222–3
	Covenant Against Contingent Fees	FAR 52.203–5

But virtually all of these categories except the first overlap; that is, they are socioeconomic and political, and they essentially boil down to two categories: (1) those clauses needed by the government primarily because it is a public buyer and hence sometimes more restricted in its policies than most commercial buyers, and (2) those clauses imposed upon government contracts by mostly political factors. The author of this volume would place about 80 clauses in category (2) out of the more than 570 clauses listed on the FAR Index; if so about 7 out of 8 of the standard clauses would belong in category (1). This may come as a surprise to many people in the field.

Nevertheless, a serious question arises concerning the effect and value of the many socioeconomic and political clauses in category 2 (and applicable regulations concerning their use) on the Federal procurement market. A study of the procurement system was based on a nationwide survey of small businesses that received Federal government contracts. "Seven hundred twenty six contractors responded to a survey mailed to approximately 2,530 Federal contractors under a grant from the Small Business Administration. The contractors included in the survey were drawn from all sectors of the Federal procurement market, including service, production and research contractors." Many groups said the procurement system was unnecessarily laden with numerous regulations to achieve nonprocurement goals. These "socioeconomic laws," as they were called, overburdened small business Federal contractors, created inefficiencies in procurement process, and discouraged many private sector firms from attempting to sell to the Federal government. The major finding was that, although Federal contract requirements were apparently having "little direct impact on modifying firm behavior, the cost of the regulatory process to contracting firms, and to society, was found to be quite large."

It must have been discouraging to find that such a broad study not only showed that the government's attempt to use the procurement system to achieve the social goals of society was costly, but also that "[t]axpayers, workers, and businesses are losers in the process, (and) the biggest losers are those individuals and groups who are the intended beneficiaries of socioeconomic regulations." Although reform was needed, it could not be accomplished until Congress would consider a different and more effective means of accomplishing its socioeconomic goals.

The American Bar Association's (ABA) Public Contract Section prepared Model Subcontract terms and conditions compatible with the FAR at that time, including Fixed Price Subcontracts, Cost-plus-fixed-fee Research and Development Subcontracts, and others.

Currently, there are four mandatory "flow-down" clauses for contracts for commercial items: (1) FAR 52.219–8, Utilization of Small Business Concerns; (2) FAR 52.222–26, Equal Opportunity; (3) FAR 52.222–35, Equal Opportunity for Special Disabled Veterans, Veterans of the Vietnam Era, and Other Eligible Veterans; and (4) FAR 52.222–36, Affirmative Action for Workers with Disabilities.

§ 52.2   The Use and Abuse of the Doctrine of Contra Proferentem in Negotiated Procurements

As discussed in Chapter 33, supra, except where specifically covered by statute or valid implementing regulations, Federal contract law is the "general law of contracts." Where a party assents to a standardized agreement that is a writing he has reason to believe is regularly used in similar agreements to embody terms of the same type (as is the case with respect to all the standard clauses on the Federal Acquisition Regulation), he adopts that writing as an integrated agreement with respect to all its terms. Further, such a writing is interpreted wherever reasonable as treating alike all those similarly situated, without regard to their knowledge or understanding of the standard terms of the writing. With few exceptions all prior inconsistent agreements are discharged. The Restatement (Second) would incorporate the UCC's language respecting usage and course of dealing in interpreting all contracts. Evidence thereof would be admissible to determine the meaning of a writing, whether or not integrated. A court's mere characterization of a term as ambiguous permits the introduction of evidence to clarify its meaning.

The doctrine of contra proferentem is derived from the maxim "Omnia praesumuntur contra proferentum," which expresses the principle that if a written contract contains a word or phrase capable of two reasonable meanings, the preferred interpretation will be that which is less favorable to the party who drafted the contract and had control over choice of words. It is most strongly used in so-called "adhesion contracts." Such contracts have "been called a standardized form for mass use. It is imposed upon the ... consumer. He takes it or leaves it. No bargaining is engaged in respect to it." It has been used to characterize insurance contracts; however, even there the Supreme Court has stated that "it furnishes no warrant for avoiding hard consequences by importing into a contract an ambiguity which otherwise would not exist, or, under the guise of construction, by forcing from plain words unusual and unnatural meanings." But a student of insurance law has stated, "The conclusion is inescapable that courts have sometimes invented ambiguity where none existed, then resolving the invented ambiguity contrary to the plainly expressed terms of the contract document." The same comment may be made with respect to many, if not most, decisions on government contracts whether or not the clause may be the subject of bargaining (e.g., negotiated procurements, see Chapter 15, supra). Application of the doctrine would appear particularly inappropriate in the context of contracts for commercial items because the contractor is free to propose use of its own standard clauses, and, to the maximum extent practicable, "the contracting officer is supposed to include in the contract" only those clauses required by law or executive order or determined to be applicable to commercial items "or" to be consistent with customary commercial practice.

Standard contract clauses are prescribed by regulation giving an organization which plans to compete for a contract only the choice of accepting terms or not. Contra proferentem was held inapplicable to a regulation incorporated as a contract term, when the term was fully bargained for by the parties to the contract, or where the drafting party cannot be ascertained. But these contracts are not necessarily contracts of adhesion in the same sense as are commercial contracts. First, unlike clauses used in commercial contracting, all the FAR regulations, including the clauses, were published as proposals and the views of private, nongovernmental organizations were and must continue to be considered in their formulation. This includes giving notice in the Federal Register and normally allowing at least 60 days for receipt of comments. Consideration must also be given to unsolicited recommendations for revisions of the FAR "that have been submitted in writing with sufficient data and rationale to permit their evaluation." Further, public meetings are held intermittently "when a decision to adopt, amend, or delete coverage is likely to benefit from significant additional views and discussion." If any agency were to suggest different, more restrictive clauses, it would have to go through the deviation procedure. Unlike clauses in commercial contracts, historically more of these clauses have included a high degree of fairness to both parties to the contract. Yet, the court decisions almost uniformly fail to discuss this matter. Sir Ernest Gowers' book, The Complete Plain Words, contains a chapter entitled "A Digression on Legal English." His arguments have been summarized as follows:

> The most commonly seen forms of legal writing occur in documents that concern the rights and obligations of individuals, organizations, and governments. But the purpose of these documents is not to describe those rights and obligations; it is to define them. It follows that the paramount goal of such legal writing is not to be readily intelligible; it is to be *unambiguous*. In writing a legal document, therefore, one must guard against every conceivable interpretation that conflicts with the intended rights and obligations. In part this is achieved by the seemingly endless enumeration and delimitation of possibilities. In part it is achieved by *the stilted avoidance of pronouns*, so that questions of antecedents never arise. And in part it is achieved by relying on those hackneyed phrases and constructions that make legal language such an easy target for satire.

A comparison has been made with computer terminology.

Like trouble with legal documents, trouble with computer documentation arises from the prevalence of technical terminology and slang. But trouble also arises from another similarity between legal writing and computer documentation—the *importance of being unambiguous*.

> Being readily intelligible is less important for specifications than being complete and unambiguous, which further illustrates the analogy with legal English.

Most standard clauses are, nevertheless, in fact intelligible to the intelligent or experienced reader on either side of a Federal contract, even though sometimes they can be less "user-friendly" than one of the parties may desire.

An attorney representing a major government contractor, almost all of whose business is with the Federal government, has referred to the "monopsony of the U.S. Government." However, although a monopsony in economic theory has been defined as "a market situation in which there is only one buyer," a large encyclopedia gives the example of "a firm that is the only buyer of labor in an isolated town. Such a firm is able to pay lower wages than it would under competition." The U.S. government appears to fall outside of that category not only because it purchases everywhere, but also because of extensive legislation regarding wages and other matters. As noted elsewhere the overwhelming majority of Federal procurements are negotiated. In addition, we have seen that most of the clauses may be subject to some modification during negotiation of the contract. Although attempts have been and continue to be made so as to make complex contract clauses more readable, perfection here may be elusive for both contractual parties. No system will produce clauses devoid of all ambiguity real or imagined.

The basic rules of interpretation attempt to ascertain the true intent of the parties to a contract. But a virtually permanent rule of contra proferentem is particularly harsh against the taxpayer because its application ignores any attempt to seek the true intent of the parties. Its application makes that intent less relevant. In commercial contracts it is to be applied only after the rules of interpretation have been exhausted. However, as one board pointed out, "In their fascination with contra proferentem, which had generated enough decisional law in the field of government contracts alone to support at least three law review articles, the Court of Claims and the Boards have lost sight of its subordinate position in the contract interpretation scheme." The former Court of Claims even used the doctrine where there was no ambiguity. In one case, Instruments for Industry (IFI) was awarded a contract for electronic equipment. After delivery and acceptance, the Navy notified IFI that the equipment was defective and claimed $340,000 under the guarantee (warranty) clause requiring the contractor to correct or replace the defective supplies within a year after delivery or to "repay such portion of the contract price of the supplies as is equitable in the circumstances." The government's claim was made within one year. The contractor argued that this clause did not survive final acceptance in spite of the fact that the "Inspection" clause specifically stated that the acceptance was "Except as otherwise provided in this contract," thus making the two clauses compatible. Yet the court not only agreed with the contractor but did so on the principle of contra proferentem:

> Contractors could not be expected to anticipate that this camouflaged and unusual reversal of the normal role of subpart (d) of the "Inspection" clause would follow from the bland generality of "[e]xcept as otherwise provided in this contract," especially since there is no reference to any particular clause which "provides otherwise" and no indication in the "Guaranty" article that it has any impact on the "Inspection" provision.

The court's reasoning was highly questionable. As noted elsewhere herein, all guarantees (warranties) begin only after acceptance, and there is no reason to require more direct language than that in the contract. As a result of this decision, the standard clause language was eventually modified to contain a specific reference to the inspection clause; however, the question arises why unambiguous language of a contract should not be honored by the courts unless it is against some unambiguous public policy.

Some decisions of the court would preclude application of contra proferentem to an ambiguity if it is "obvious," the contractor's construction is "twisted or strained into an ambiguity," or where the contractor is aware of an ambiguity and ought to seek its clarification. But the rule has also been used against the government with respect to a contractor's ambiguous letter that was incorporated into the contract. The proponent must also show that he relied on his interpretation. This is the so-called "zone of reasonableness" and it constitutes the only restriction on the proponent's (contractor's) reading or argument. Once he has acted within this zone, then he automatically wins. The fact that another and equally reasonable reading existed was simply irrelevant to the Court of Claims. In WPC Enterprises, Inc. v. United States, the court applied contra proferentem after finding,

> Both [the contractor's] and [the government's] interpretations lie within the zone of reasonableness; neither appears to rest on an obvious error in drafting, a gross discrepancy, or an inadvertent but glaring gap; the arguments, rather, are quite closely in balance.

The court followed the contractor's interpretation even though the government's reading was actually found to be "more reasonable."

One board has followed the former Court of Claims application of the rule but felt it necessary to actually state, "In truth we believe that [the government's] interpretation is the best and preferred one but that is not the test." This application indicates that the new courts, the Court of Federal Claims and Court of Appeals for the Federal Circuit, should seek to do a more balanced job than they are now doing.

Whatever value may be put on the use of contra proferentem in procurement by sealed bidding, a new look must be taken with respect to negotiated agreements, which constitute the overwhelming majority of the awards made by Federal agencies. The Competition in Contracting Act deleted the requirement that a special determination be made in order to justify negotiating a contract. Although the former Court of Claims had refused to apply contra proferentem against the government in a contract that "*was not a standard-form agreement* but an ad hoc arrangement negotiated by the parties for a special situation" (emphasis added), it applied the rule to standard clauses in a negotiated agreement when the parties were well aware that the majority of those clauses were negotiable.

Problems embraced by contracts of adhesion concern the "consumer class" of "buyers" who are individuals—a group to which bidders and public contractors generally do not belong. The doctrine may not be generally applicable against either party to a private or commercial agreement arrived at by negotiation; contra proferentem has been severely criticized. "The rule of interpreting against the drafter, if not discarded entirely, should be relegated to a rule of last resort in contract interpretation."

The doctrine is compounded in the case of many subcontracts, if all the government clauses contained in them (many of which are mandatory when applicable) are similarly interpreted against the prime contractor. In the case of cost-type contractors, the government funds many of the extra costs the prime incurs. The doctrine becomes an unwritten flexible punitive damage clause that the courts incorporate into the contract or subcontract. For the most part, the prime contractor is not the drafter; that distinction belongs in part to the government and those in industry who commented on the clause (when it was being proposed) and the American Bar Association (which adopted most of these clauses for use in subcontracts). Most prime contractors and subcontractors are equally familiar with the clauses. Virtually all subcontracts are negotiated because few, if any, prime contractors use sealed bidding. Thus, the situation is about the same as with contracts awarded by the government by other than sealed bids: the prime contractor is normally as aware of the meaning of standard clauses as the government agency making the award.

*

INDEX

MARKET RESEARCH
Acquisition planning, § 10.1

MATERIAL OR MATERIALS
Describing agency needs, other than new material acquired, § 11.3
Federal Acquisition Regulation, time and materials (T & M) contracts, § 1.24(c)
Qualifications of contractors, use of materials related to projections, § 9.5(d)
Time and materials (T & M) contracts, §§ 1.24(c), 16.51

MERGER GUIDELINES
Competition, § 6.1

METHODS
Accounting, qualifications of contractors, § 9.5(b)
Contracting, § 13.1

MICRO–PURCHASES
Simplified acquisition procedures, § 13.6

MINOR INFORMALITIES THAT MAY BE WAIVED BY GOVERNMENT
Sealed bidding, § 14.36(b)

MISTAKES OR ERRORS
Architect-engineer services, design errors, §§ 36.54, 36.55
Conversion of erroneous default into termination for convenience of government, § 49.23
Negotiation, disclosure before award, § 15.32
Sealed bidding, mistakes in bids, §§ 14.39–14.41

MODEL RULES OF PROFESSIONAL CONDUCT OF AMERICAN BAR ASSOCIATION
Negotiation as legal speciality, § 15.73(c)

MODIFICATION
Administration of contracts, change of name agreements, § 42.6
Bids, sealed bidding, § 14.34
Federal Acquisition Regulation, changes based on National Performance Report (NPRT), § 1.7
Negotiation or Negotiations, this index

MODIFICATIONS OF CONTRACTS
Aggressiveness and economic duress distinguished, § 43.3
Authority to modify contracts, §§ 43.1–43.3
Cardinal changes, modifications ordered pursuant to clause in original agreement of parties, § 43.15
'Changed' contracts, § 43.2
Clause in original agreement of parties, modifications ordered pursuant to, §§ 43.11–43.19
Concept of equitable adjustment, modifications ordered pursuant to clause in original agreement of parties, § 43.14

†